Microsoft **Windows** 2000 **Administrator's Pocket Consultant**

William R. Stanek

PUBLISHED BY
Microsoft Press
A Division of Microsoft Corporation
One Microsoft Way
Redmond, Washington 98052-6399

Library of Congress Cataloging-in-Publication Data

Stanek, William R.
 Microsoft Windows 2000 Administrator's Pocket Consultant / William R. Stanek.
   p. cm.
 ISBN 0-7356-0831-8
 1. Microsoft Windows (Computer file) 2. Operating systems (Computers)

 QA76.76.063 S73447 1999
 005.4'4769--dc21   99-059355

Printed and bound in the United States of America.

   6 7 8 9   MLML   5 4 3 2 1 0

Distributed in Canada by Penguin Books Canada Limited.

A CIP catalogue record for this book is available from the British Library.

Microsoft Press books are available through booksellers and distributors worldwide. For further information about international editions, contact your local Microsoft Corporation office or contact Microsoft Press International directly at fax (425) 936-7329. Visit our Web site at mspress.microsoft.com.

Macintosh is a registered trademark of Apple Computer, Inc. Intel is a registered trademark of Intel Corporation. JScript, Microsoft, Microsoft Press, MS-DOS, Win32, Windows, and Windows NT are either registered trademarks or trademarks of Microsoft Corporation in the United States and/or other countries. Other product and company names mentioned herein may be the trademarks of their respective owners.

The example companies, organizations, products, people, and events depicted herein are fictitious. No association with any real company, organization, product, person, or event is intended or should be inferred.

Acquisitions Editor: Juliana Aldous
Project Editor: Julie Miller

Contents at a Glance

Part IV
Microsoft Windows 2000 Network Administration

Table of Contents

Part III
Microsoft Windows 2000 Data Administration

10   Managing File Systems and Drives   213

14 Data Backup and Recovery 307

Part IV
Microsoft Windows 2000 Network Administration

Tables

Acknowledgments

Writing *Microsoft Windows 2000 Administrator's Pocket Consultant* was a lot of fun—and a lot of work. It is gratifying to see techniques I've used time and again to solve problems put into a printed book so that others may benefit from them. But no man is an island and this book couldn't have been written without help from some very special people.

As I've stated in *Microsoft Windows NT Server 4.0 Administrator's Pocket Consultant* and in *Microsoft SQL Server 7.0 Administrator's Pocket Consultant*, the team at Microsoft Press is top-notch. I owe many thank yous to Anne Hamilton as publisher and Stuart Stuple as managing editor both for recognizing the potential of my practical and useful approach to the Pocket Consultant series and for their willingness to run with the approach. Juliana Aldous handled acquisitions and helped make sure I had the tools I needed to write this book. Julie Miller, Maureen Zimmerman, and Tracy Thomsic managed the editorial process from the Microsoft Press side. Lisa Wehrle headed up the editorial process for nSight, Inc. Their professionalism, thoroughness, and attention to every detail is much appreciated!

Unfortunately for the writer (but fortunately for readers), writing is only one part of the publishing process. Next came editing and author review. I must say, Microsoft Press has the most thorough editorial and technical review process I've seen anywhere—and I've written a lot of books for many different publishers. Special thanks to both Julie and Lisa for helping me to meet review deadlines. Eben Werber, Richard Taha, and Darian Taha were the technical editors for the book. Special thanks to Richard for suggestions made in Chapters 14, 15, and 19 and for his work during crunch time. I'd also like to thank Joseph Gustaitis for his careful copy editing of this book.

Thanks also to Studio B literary agency and my agents, David Rogelberg and Neil Salkind. David and Neil are great to work with.

Hopefully, I haven't forgotten anyone but if I have, it was an oversight. *Honest.* ;-)

Introduction

Microsoft Windows 2000 Administrator's Pocket Consultant is designed to be a concise and compulsively usable resource for Microsoft Windows 2000 administrators. This is the readable resource guide that you'll want on your desk at all times. The book covers everything you need to perform the core administrative tasks for Windows 2000 server and workstation systems. Because the focus is on giving you maximum value in a pocket-sized guide, you don't have to wade through hundreds of pages of extraneous information to find what you're looking for. Instead, you'll find exactly what you need to get the job done.

In short, the book is designed to be the one resource you turn to whenever you have questions regarding Windows 2000 administration. To this end, the book zeroes in on daily administration procedures, frequently used tasks, documented examples, and options that are representative while not necessarily inclusive. One of the goals is to keep the content so concise that the book remains compact and easy to navigate while at the same time ensuring that the book is packed with as much information as possible—making it a valuable resource. Thus, instead of a hefty 1,000-page tome or a lightweight 100-page quick reference, you get a valuable resource guide that can help you quickly and easily perform common tasks, solve problems, and implement advanced Windows 2000 technologies like Active Directory, Dynamic Host Configuration Protocol (DHCP), Windows Internet Naming Service (WINS), and Domain Name Service (DNS).

Who Is This Book For?

Microsoft Windows 2000 Administrator's Pocket Consultant covers the workstation and server versions of Windows 2000. The book is designed for

- Current Windows 2000 system administrators
- Accomplished users who have some administrator responsibilities
- Administrators upgrading to Windows 2000 from Windows NT
- Administrators transferring from other platforms

To pack in as much information as possible, I had to assume that you have basic networking skills and a basic understanding of Windows 2000 and that Windows 2000 is already installed on your systems. With this in mind, I don't devote entire chapters to understanding Windows 2000 architecture, installing Windows 2000, or Windows 2000 startup and shutdown. I do, however, cover Windows 2000 workstation and server configuration, Group Policy, security, auditing, data backup, system recovery, and much more.

I also assume that you are fairly familiar with Windows 2000 commands and procedures as well as the Windows 2000 user interface. If you need help learning Windows 2000 basics, you should read the Windows 2000 documentation.

How Is This Book Organized?

Microsoft Windows 2000 Administrator's Pocket Consultant is designed to be used in the daily administration of Windows 2000 networks, and, as such, the book is organized by job-related tasks rather than by Windows 2000 features. If you are reading this book, you should be aware of the relationship between Pocket Consultants and Administrator's Companions. Both types of books are designed to be a part of an administrator's library. While Pocket Consultants are the down-and-dirty, in-the-trenches books, Administrator's Companions are the comprehensive tutorials and references that cover every aspect of deploying a product or technology in the enterprise.

Speed and ease of reference is an essential part of this hands-on guide. The book has an expanded table of contents and an extensive index for finding answers to problems quickly. Many other quick reference features have been added as well. These features include quick step-by-step instructions, lists, tables with fast facts, and extensive cross-references. The book is broken down into both parts and chapters. Each part contains an opening paragraph or two about the chapters contained in that part.

Part I, "Microsoft Windows 2000 Administration Fundamentals," covers the fundamental tasks you need for Windows 2000 administration. Chapter 1 provides an overview of Windows 2000 administration tools, techniques, and concepts. Chapter 2 explores the tasks you'll need to manage Windows 2000 systems. Chapter 3 covers monitoring processes, services, and events. The final chapter in this part covers automating administrative tasks, policies, and procedures.

In Part II, "Microsoft Windows 2000 Directory Services Administration," you'll find the essential tasks for administering user, computer, and group accounts. Chapter 5 introduces Active Directory Service structures and details how to work with Active Directory domains. Chapter 6 explores core Active Directory Service administration. You'll learn how to manage computer accounts, domain controllers, and organizational units. Chapter 7 explains how to use system accounts, built-in groups, user rights, built-in capabilities, and implicit groups. You'll find extensive tables that tell you exactly when you should use certain types of accounts, rights, and capabilities. The core administration tasks for creating user and group accounts are covered in Chapter 8, with a logical follow-up for managing existing user and group accounts covered in Chapter 9.

The book continues with Part III, "Microsoft Windows 2000 Data Administration." Chapter 10 starts by explaining how to add hard drives to a system and how to partition drives. Then the chapter dives into common tasks for managing file systems and drives, such as defragmenting disks, compression, encryption, and more. In Chapter 11, you'll find tasks for managing volume sets and RAID arrays, as well as detailed advice on repairing damaged arrays. Chapter 12 focuses on managing files and directories and all the tasks that go along with it. You'll even find tips for customizing folder views with folder templates. Chapter 13 details how to enable file, drive, and directory sharing for remote network and Internet users; it then goes on to cover Active Directory Service object security and auditing. Chapter 14 examines data backup and recovery and includes a section on managing media pools.

Part IV, "Microsoft Windows 2000 Network Administration," covers advanced administration tasks. Chapter 15 provides the essentials for installing, configuring, and testing Transmission Control Protocol/Internet Protocol (TCP/IP) networking on Windows 2000 systems—covering everything from installing network adapter cards to actually connecting a computer to a Windows 2000 domain. Chapter 16 begins with a troubleshooting guide for common printer problems and then goes on to cover tasks for installing and configuring local printers and network print servers. The final three chapters in this section focus on the key Windows 2000 services: DHCP, WINS, and DNS. DHCP is used to assign dynamic IP addresses to network clients. WINS is used to resolve computer names to IP addresses. DNS is used to resolve host names to IP addresses.

Conventions Used in This Book

I've used a variety of elements to help keep the text clear and easy to follow. You'll find code terms and listings in monospace type, except when I tell you to actually type a command. In that case, the command appears in **bold** type. When I introduce and define a new term, I put it in *italics*.

Other conventions include

Note To provide details on a point that needs emphasis.

Tip To offer helpful hints or additional information.

Caution To warn you when there are potential problems you should look out for.

More Info To provide more information on the subject.

Real World To provide real-world advice when discussing advanced topics.

Best Practice To examine the best technique to use when working with advanced configuration and administration concepts.

I truly hope you find that *Microsoft Windows 2000 Administrator's Pocket Consultant* provides everything you need to perform essential administrative tasks on Windows 2000 systems as quickly and efficiently as possible. You are welcome to send your thoughts to me at win2000-consulting@tvpress.com. Thank you.

Support

Every effort has been made to ensure the accuracy of this book. Microsoft Press provides corrections for books through the World Wide Web at *http://mspress. microsoft.com/support.*

If you have comments, questions, or ideas about this book, please send them to Microsoft Press using either of the following methods:

Postal Mail:

Microsoft Press
Attn: *Microsoft Windows 2000*
Administrator's Pocket Consultant Editor
One Microsoft Way
Redmond, WA 98052-6399

E-mail:

MSPINPUT@MICROSOFT.COM

Please note that product support is not offered through the mail addresses. For support information, visit Microsoft's web site at *http://www.microsoft.com/support.*

Part I

Microsoft Windows 2000 Administration Fundamentals

The fundamental tasks you need for Microsoft Windows 2000 administration are covered in Part I. Chapter 1 provides an overview of Windows 2000 administration concepts, tools, and techniques. Chapter 2 explores the tools you'll need to manage Windows 2000 workstations and servers. Chapter 3 covers monitoring events and performance. Chapter 4 explains how to automate common administrative tasks.

Chapter 1

Overview of Microsoft Windows 2000 System Administration

Microsoft Windows 2000 is the most powerful PC operating system on the market. It offers a whole new window to workstation and server environments and introduces revolutionary system management and administration concepts. Some of these are

- **Active Directory** An extensible and scalable directory service that uses a namespace based on the Internet standard Domain Name System (DNS).

- **IntelliMirror** Change and configuration management features that support mirroring of user data and environment settings as well as central management of software installation and maintenance.

- **Terminal Services** Services that allow you to remotely log on to and manage other Windows 2000 systems.

- **Windows Scrip Host** A scripting environment for automating common administration tasks, such as creating user accounts or generating reports from event logs.

Although Windows 2000 has dozens of other new features, each of the four features just listed has far-reaching effects on how you perform administrative tasks. None has more effect than Active Directory technology, which represents a fundamental shift in the way you manage users, groups, and systems. So much so that a sound understanding of Active Directory structures and procedures is essential to your success as a Windows 2000 systems administrator.

Microsoft Windows 2000 Professional and Server

The Windows 2000 family of operating systems consists of the Professional, Server, Advanced Server, and Datacenter Server versions. Each edition has a specific purpose:

- **Windows 2000 Professional** Windows 2000 Professional is designed primarily for workstations and network clients. It's a direct replacement for

Windows 4.0 Workstation and has a representative set of features for end users. The focus on end users sets Windows 2000 Professional apart from the server versions and, accordingly, this edition supports a limited set of services.

- **Windows 2000 Server** Windows 2000 Server is designed to provide services and resources to other systems on the network. It's a direct replacement for Windows NT 4.0 Server and has a rich set of features and configuration options. Windows 2000 Server supports up to two CPUs.

- **Windows 2000 Advanced Server** Windows 2000 Advanced Server extends the features provided in Windows 2000 Server to include support for load balancing and clustering. It also supports very large memory configurations of up to 64 GB and can handle up to four CPUs.

- **Windows 2000 Datacenter Server** Windows 2000 Datacenter Server is the most robust Windows server. It supports more advanced clustering than the Advanced Server and can handle up to 16 CPUs.

 Note The various server editions support the same core features and administration tools. This means you can use the techniques discussed in this book regardless of which Windows 2000 edition you're using. On the other hand, if you're using the Windows 2000 Professional edition, you'll need to install the Windows 2000 administration tools before you can perform administration tasks.

When you install a Windows 2000 system, you configure the system according to its role on the network.

- Workstations and servers are generally assigned to be part of a workgroup or a domain.

- Workgroups are loose associations of computers in which each individual computer is managed separately.

- Domains are collections of computers that can be managed collectively by means of domain controllers, which are Windows 2000 servers that manage access to the network, to the directory database, and to shared resources.

Domain Controllers and Member Servers

When you install Windows 2000 Server on a new system, you can configure the server to be a member server, a domain controller, or a stand-alone server. The difference between these types of servers is extremely important. Member servers are a part of a domain but do not store directory information. Domain controllers are distinguished from member servers because they store directory information and provide authentication and directory services for the domain. Stand-alone servers are not a part of a domain and have their own user database. Because of this, a stand-alone server also authenticates logon requests themselves.

Windows 2000 doesn't designate primary or backup domain controllers. Instead, Windows 2000 supports a multimaster replication model. In this model any domain controller can process directory changes and then replicate those changes to other domain controllers automatically. This differs from the Windows NT singlemaster replication model in which the primary domain controller stores a master copy and backup controllers store backup copies of the master. Additionally, Windows NT distributed only the SAM (security access manager) database, but Windows 2000 distributes an entire directory of information called a *data store*. Inside the data store are sets of objects representing user, group, and computer accounts as well as shared resources, such as servers, files, and printers.

Domains that use Active Directory services are referred to as Active Directory (or Windows 2000) domains. This distinguishes them from Windows NT domains. While Active Directory domains can function with only one domain controller, multiple domain controllers can and should be configured on the domain. This way, if one domain controller fails, you can rely on the other domain controllers to handle authentication and other critical tasks.

In an Active Directory domain, any member server can be promoted to a domain controller, and you don't need to reinstall the operating system as you had to in Windows NT. To promote a member server, all you need to do is install the Active Directory component on the server. You can also demote domain controllers to be member servers, provided that the server isn't the last domain controller on the network. You promote and demote domain controllers by using the Active Directory Installation Wizard and following these steps:

1. Click Start.
2. Click Run.
3. Type **dcpromo** in the Open field, and then click OK.

Add-On Components and Services

In Windows 2000 most of the Windows NT Option Pack components are now integrated with the operating system and provided on the distribution CD-ROM as add-on components. For example, if you add the indexing component to a server, you can index drives, folders, and files so they can be quickly searched. If you add transaction services, the server can use the Microsoft Distributed Transaction Coordinator to handle distributed transactions.

In Windows 2000 servers are configured based on the services they offer. You can add or remove services at any time by using the Configure Your Server utility and following these steps:

1. Click Start.
2. Click Programs.
3. Click Administrative Tools, and then select Configure Your Server.

Any server can support one or more of the following services:

- **Active Directory**   A server that provides directory services for the domain (a domain controller).
- **File Server**   A server that serves files to other systems on the network.
- **Print Server**   A server that manages printers and print queues.

- **Web/Media Server** A server that provides Internet or streaming media services, or both. Internet services include Web, File Transfer Protocol (FTP), and Simple Mail Transfer Protocol (SMTP).

- **Networking Server** A server that provides essential network services (Dynamic Host Configuration Protocol (DHCP), Domain Name System (DNS), remote access, or routing).

- **Application Server** A server that provides messaging, database, and other types of business client/server applications. Application servers can also handle group policies, IntelliMirror, and Terminal Services.

- **Advanced Server** A server that is configured to use advanced components, such as message queuing, certificate authority, or remote installation.

Other Windows 2000 Resources

Before we examine administration tools, let's look at other resources that you can use to make Windows 2000 administration easier. One of the system administrator's greatest resources is the Windows 2000 distribution disks. They contain all the system information you'll need whenever you make changes to a Windows 2000 system. Keep the disks handy whenever you modify a system's configuration. You'll probably need them.

To avoid having to access the Windows 2000 distribution disk whenever you make system changes, you may want to copy the system resource directory to a network drive. For example, on an Intel system you would copy the \I386 directory to a network drive. When you're prompted to insert the CD-ROM and specify the source directory, you simply point to the directory on the network drive. This technique is convenient and saves time. Other resources you may want to use are examined in the sections that follow.

Windows 2000 Support Tools

While you're working with the distribution CD-ROM, you may want to install the Windows 2000 Resource Kit Support Tools. The support tools are a collection of utilities for handling everything from system diagnostics to network monitoring.

Installing the support tools You can install the support tools by completing the following steps:

1. Insert the Windows 2000 CD-ROM into the CD-ROM drive.

2. When the Autorun screen appears, click Browse This CD. This starts Microsoft Windows Explorer.

3. In Windows Explorer, double-click Support and then click Tools.

4. Double-click Setup. This starts the Windows 2000 Support Tools Setup Wizard. Read the Welcome dialog box and then click Next.

5. Enter your user information and then click Next.

6. Select the installation type: Typical or Custom. If this is the first time you're using the support tools, you may want to install all of the tools. Later, you

can remove the tools you don't want to use by rerunning the installation process and selecting Add/Remove.

Note Throughout this book, I refer to double-clicking, which is the most common technique used for accessing folders and running programs. With a double-click, the first click selects the item and the second click opens/runs the item. In Windows 2000 you can also configure single-click open/run. Here, moving the mouse over the item selects it and a click opens/runs the item. You can change the mouse click options with the Folder Options utility in the Control Panel. To do this, select the General Tab, and then choose Single-Click To Open Item or Double-Click To Open Item, as appropriate.

7. If you've selected a typical or complete install, click Next twice to start the installation. If you've selected a custom install, you'll need to select the utilities to add and then complete the installation.

8. Click Finish. When prompted, select Yes to restart the system or No if you want to restart the system later.

Using the support tools After installation you can access the support tools through the Windows 2000 Support Tools Console shown in Figure 1-1. To start the console, click Start, click Programs, click Windows 2000 Support Tools, and then select Tools Management Console.

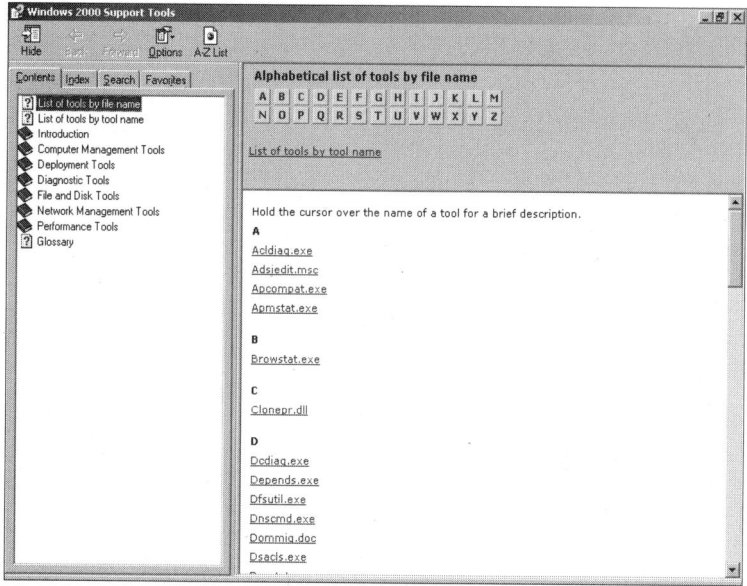

Figure 1-1. *Use support tools to perform such tasks as system diagnostics and network monitoring.*

As the figure shows, the tools are organized into folders by category and can also be accessed through the list of tools. If you double-click List of Tools By File Name, you'll see an alphabetical list of all the support tools you installed.

Service Packs and Hot Fixes

As in other Windows operating systems, service packs are used to distribute updates that should be applied to the operating system. When you install a Windows 2000 operating system, you should also install the latest service pack—provided it's proven to be stable. Service packs are numbered sequentially, with the latest service pack having the highest number. By installing a service pack, you can ensure that your workstations and servers operate smoothly.

In addition to service packs, you can also find hot fixes for Windows 2000. Hot fixes are used to patch specific problems you're encountering with the operating system. Because most hot fixes haven't been regression tested, if you're not encountering the referenced problem, you shouldn't install the hot fix.

You can find current service packs and hot fixes for Windows 2000 at the Microsoft FTP site *(ftp://ftp.microsoft.com/bussys/)* or the Microsoft Web site *(http://www.microsoft.com/support/)*. When you access this directory, you'll need to navigate country, language, and product subdirectories. Most hot fixes are provided as self-installing executable files. Before you install a hot fix, you should read the README.TXT file located in the hot fix directory. This file explains what the hot fix is used for and contains instructions for applying it. If you want to extract the hot fix and examine the files it contains before installation, follow the executable file name with the /x option. You can then apply the hot fix using the enclosed HotFix utility.

Frequently Used Tools

Many utilities are available for administrating Windows 2000 workstations and servers. The tools you'll use the most include

- **Control Panel** A collection of tools for managing Windows 2000 workstation and server configuration. You can access these tools by selecting Start, then choosing Settings, and then selecting Control Panel.

- **Graphical administrative tools** The key tools for managing network computers and their resources. You can access these tools by selecting them individually on the Administrative Tools submenu or by double-clicking Administrative Tools in the Control Panel.

- **Administrative wizards** Tools designed to automate key administrative tasks. Unlike in Windows NT, there is no central place for accessing wizards. Instead, you access wizards by selecting the appropriate menu options in other administrative tools.

- **Command-line utilities** You can launch most administrative utilities from the command line. In addition to these utilities, Windows 2000 provides others that are useful for working with Windows 2000 systems.

The following sections provide brief introductions to these administrative utilities. Additional details for key tools are provided throughout this book. Keep in mind that to use these utilities you may need an account with administrator privileges.

Using Control Panel Utilities

Control Panel contains utilities for working with a system's setup and configuration. Figure 1-2 shows the Control Panel.

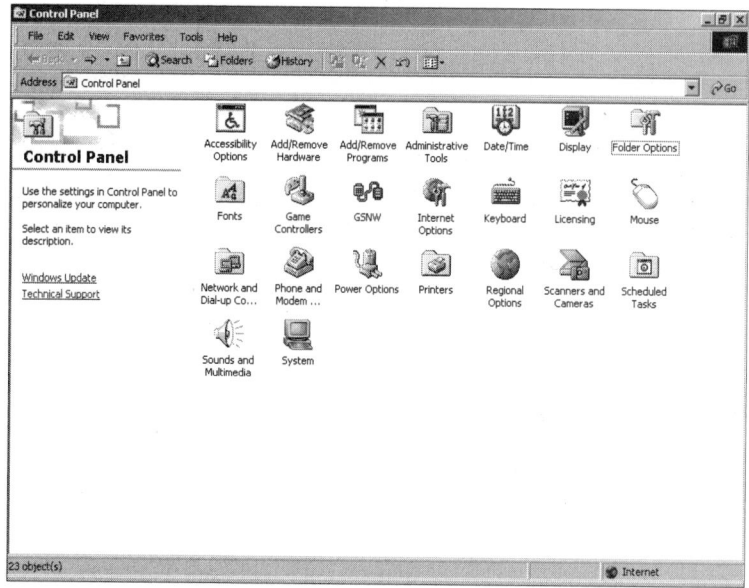

Figure 1-2. *Use Control Panel utilities to manage a system's setup and configuration.*

The key utilities you'll use in system administration are listed below. To run any one of them, simply double-click its icon in Control Panel.

- **Add/Remove Hardware**   Starts the Add/Remove Hardware Wizard, which can be used to add hardware, troubleshoot hardware problems, and uninstall hardware. You make updates to hardware and their associated drivers through this wizard.

- **Add/Remove Programs**   Used to install programs and automatically remove all components of software that support this utility. Also used to modify Windows 2000 setup components. For example, if you didn't install an add-on component, such as Certificate Services, during installation of the operating system, you can use this utility to add it later.

- **Date/Time** Used to view or set a system's date, time, and time zone. Rather than manually setting the time on individual computers in the domain, you can use the NET TIME command to automatically synchronize time. You can use NET TIME in the user logon script for the domain. In the logon script, insert the command NET TIME*servername*/set where *servername* is the computer name of the server with which you want to synchronize time. Logon scripts are discussed in Chapter 6.

- **Display** Used to configure backgrounds, screen savers, video display mode, and video settings. You can also use this utility to specify desktop icons and to control visual effects, such as the menu fade effect. To make changes, select the Effects tab and then use its options. For example, to turn off the menu fade effect, you would clear the Use Transition Effects For Menus And Tooltips check box.

- **Folder Options** Used to set a wide variety of folder and file options, including the type of desktop used, the folder views used, whether offline files are used, and whether you need to single-click or double-click to open items. On a laptop, you may want to configure offline files to allow users to access key files while disconnected from the network.

- **Licensing** On a workstation, you use this utility to manage licenses on a local system. On a server, it also allows you to change the client-licensing mode of installed products, such as Windows 2000 Server or Microsoft SQL Server.

- **Network And Dial-Up Connections** Used to view network identity information, to add network components, and to establish network connections. You can also use this utility to change a system's computer name and domain. See Chapters 6 and 15 for details.

- **Printers** Provides quick access to the Printers folder, which you can use to manage printers on a system. See Chapter 16 for more information on managing network printers.

- **Scheduled Tasks** Allows you to view and add scheduled tasks. You can schedule tasks on a one-time or recurring basis to handle common administrative jobs. To learn more about scheduled tasks, see Chapter 4.

- **System** Used to display and manage system properties, including properties for startup/shutdown, environment, hardware profiles, and user profiles. This utility is explored in Chapter 2.

Using Graphical Administrative Tools

Windows 2000 provides several types of tools for system administration. The GUI-based tools are the ones you'll use the most. Usually, you can use graphical administrative tools to manage the system to which you're currently logged on, as well as systems throughout Windows 2000 domains. For example, in the Component Services console you specify the computer you want to work with by right-clicking the Event Viewer entry in the left panel and then choosing Connect To Another Computer. This opens the Select Computer dialog box shown in Figure 1-3. You can then choose Another Computer and enter the name of the computer, as shown.

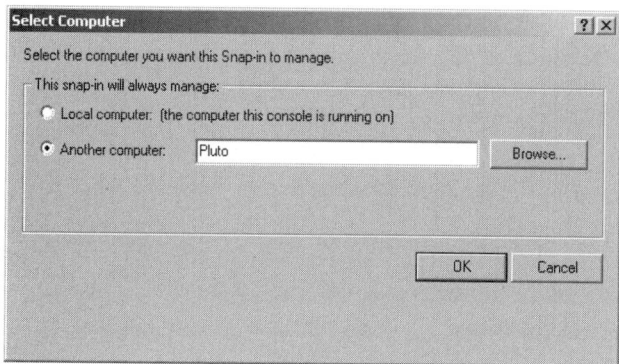

Figure 1-3.   *Connecting to another computer allows you to manage remote resources.*

Key Graphical Administrative Tools

Table 1-1 lists the key graphical administrative tools and their uses. You can access these tools by selecting them on the Administrative Tools submenu (click Start, click Programs, click Administrative Tools, and then select the tool you want to work with) or by double-clicking Administrative Tools in the Control Panel.

Table 1-1.   Quick Reference for Key Windows 2000 Administrative Tools

Administrative Tool	Purpose
Active Directory Domains and Trusts	Manage the trust relationships between domains
Active Directory Sites and Services	Create sites to manage the replication of information used for Active Directory
Active Directory Users and Computers	Manage users, groups, computers, and other objects in Active Directory
Component Services	Configure and manage COM+ applications; manage events and services
Computer Management	Start and stop services, manage disks, and access other system management tools
Configure Your Server	Add, remove, and configure Windows services for the network
Data Sources (ODBC)	Add, remove, and configure Open Database Connectivity (ODBC) data sources and drivers

(continued)

Table 1-1. *(continued)*

Administrative Tool	Purpose
DHCP	Configure and manage the Dynamic Host Configuration Protocol (DHCP) service
Distributed File System	Create and manage distributed file systems that connect shared folders from different computers
DNS	Manage the Domain Name System (DNS) service
Domain Controller Security Policy	Create and manage security policies on the current domain controller
Domain Security Policy	Create and manage security policies in the domain
Event Viewer	Manage events and logs
Internet Authentication Service	Manage authentication, authorization, and accounting of remote Internet users
Internet Services Manager	Manage Web, FTP, and SMTP servers
Licensing	Manage client access licensing for server products
Local Security Policy	Manage security policies on the local computer
Microsoft Network Monitor	Monitor network traffic and troubleshoot networking problems
Performance	Display graphs of system performance and configure data logs and alerts
QoS Admission Control	Manage the Quality of Service (QoS) Admissions Control service, which provides resource and bandwidth management for network traffic
Remote Storage	Manage the Remote Storage service, which automatically transfers data from infrequently used files on the hard disk to tape libraries
Routing and Remote Access	Configure and manage the Routing and Remote Access service, which controls routing interfaces, dynamic IP routing, and remote access
Server Extensions Administrator	Manage server extensions, such as the FrontPage Server extensions for Internet Information Server (IIS)
Telephony	Integrate the IP protocol suite over Public Switched Telephone Network (PSTN)
Terminal Services Licensing	Manage client access licensing for Terminal Services
WINS	Manage the Windows Internet Name Service, which resolves NetBIOS names to IP addresses and is needed for backward compatibility with Windows NT

Tools and Configuration

Which administrative tools are available on your system depends on its configuration. When you add services, the tools needed to manage those services are installed on the server. These same tools may not be available in Windows 2000 Professional. In this case, you may want to install the administration tools on the workstation you're using. To install Windows 2000 Administration Tools, complete the following steps:

1. Log on to the workstation using an account with administrator privileges.

2. Click Start, point to Setting, and then click Control Panel.

3. Double-click Add/Remove Programs.

4. To add or modify current administrative tools configuration, click Change or Remove Programs, and then click Windows 2000 Administration Tools. This expands the entry in the right pane. Click Change.

5. To install administrative tools for the first time, click Add New Programs and then click CD or Floppy. Click Next. Then in the Run Installation Program dialog box, click Browse. In the Browse dialog box, double-click I386 and then select AdminPak.MSI. Click Finish.

6. You should now see the Windows 2000 Administrative Tools Setup Wizard. Click Next. Select Install All Of The Administrative Tools and then click Next again.

7. The administrative tools are installed on your system. Click Finish to complete the process.

Note You can use the same procedure to add all the administrative tools to a server.

Using Command-Line Utilities

Many command-line utilities are included with Windows 2000. Most of the utilities you'll work with as an administrator rely on the TCP/IP protocol. Because of this, you should install TCP/IP networking before you experiment with these tools.

Utilities to Know

As an administrator, you should familiarize yourself with the following command-line utilities:

- **ARP** Displays and manages software-to-hardware address mappings used by Windows 2000 to send data on the local network.
- **AT** Schedules programs to run automatically.
- **FTP** Starts the built-in FTP client.
- **HOSTNAME** Displays the computer name of the local system.

- **IPCONFIG** Displays the TCP/IP properties for network adapters installed on the system. You can also use it to renew and release DHCP information.
- **NBTSTAT** Displays statistics and current connections for NetBIOS over TCP/IP.
- **NET** Displays a family of useful networking commands.
- **NETSTAT** Displays current TCP/IP connections and protocol statistics.
- **NSLOOKUP** Checks the status of a host or IP address when used with DNS.
- **PING** Tests the connection to a remote host.
- **ROUTE** Manages the routing tables on the system.
- **TRACERT** During testing, determines the network path taken to a remote host.

To learn how to use these command-line tools, type the command name at the prompt without any flags. Windows 2000 will then provide an overview of how the command is used (in most cases).

Using NET Tools

You can more easily manage most of the tasks performed with the NET commands by using graphical administrative tools and Control Panel utilities. However, some of the NET tools are very useful for performing tasks quickly or for obtaining information, especially during telnet sessions to remote systems. These commands include

- **NET SEND** Sends messages to users logged in to a particular system.
- **NET START** Starts a service on the system.
- **NET STOP** Stops a service on the system.
- **NET TIME** Displays the current system time or synchronizes the system time with another computer.
- **NET USE** Connects and disconnects from a shared resource.
- **NET VIEW** Displays a list of network resources available to the system.

To learn how to use any of the NET command-line tools, type **NET HELP** followed by the command name, such as **NET HELP SEND**. Windows 2000 will then provide an overview of how the command is used.

Chapter 2

Managing Microsoft Windows 2000 Workstations and Servers

Workstations and servers are the heart of any Microsoft Windows 2000 network. As an administrator, one of your primary responsibilities is to manage these resources. Your key tool is the Computer Management console, which provides a single integrated interface for handling such core system administration tasks as

- Obtaining summary information on system hardware, components, and software
- Managing user sessions and connections
- Managing file, directory, and share usage
- Setting administrative alerts
- Managing applications and network services
- Configuring hardware devices
- Viewing and configuring disk drives and removable storage devices

While the Computer Management console is great for remote management of network resources, you also need a tool that gives you fine control over system environment settings and properties. This is where the System utility comes into the picture. You'll use this utility to

- Configure application performance, virtual memory, and registry settings
- Manage system and user environment variables
- Set system startup and recovery options
- Manage hardware and user profiles

Managing Network Systems

The Computer Management console is designed to handle core system administration tasks on local and remote systems. You'll spend a lot of time working with this tool, and you should get to know every nook and cranny. Access the Computer Management console with either of the following techniques:

- Choose Start, then Programs, then Administrative Tools, and finally Computer Management.
- Select Computer Management from the Administrative Tools folder.

As Figure 2-1 shows, the main window has a two-pane view that's similar to Windows Explorer. You use the console tree in the left pane for navigation and tool selection. Tools are divided into three broad categories:

- **System Tools**   General purpose tools for managing systems and viewing system information.
- **Storage**   Displays information on removable and logical drives and provides access to drive management tools.
- **Services And Applications**   View and manage the properties of services and applications installed on the server.

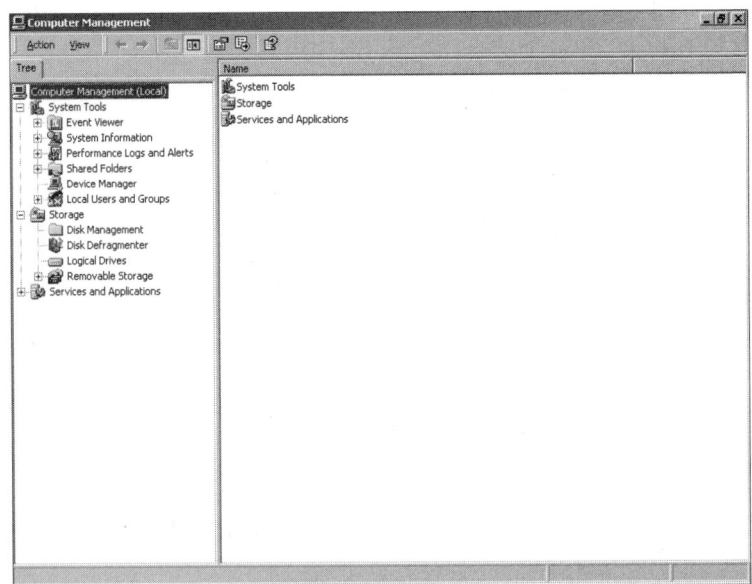

Figure 2-1. *Use the Computer Management console to manage network computers and resources.*

The tools available through the console tree provide the core functionality for the Computer Management console. When Computer Management is selected in the console tree, three important tasks can be easily accessed:

- Connecting to other computers
- Sending console messages
- Exporting information lists

The following sections examine these tasks, and then we'll take a detailed look at working with tools in the Computer Management console.

Connecting to Other Computers

The Computer Management console is designed to be used with local and remote systems. You can select a computer to manage by right-clicking the Computer Management entry in the console tree and then selecting Connect To Another Computer on the shortcut menu. This opens the Select Object dialog box, and you can now choose the system you want to work with by completing the following steps:

1. Use the Look In selection list to choose the domain you want to work with. By default, the current domain will be selected.

2. In the object list, choose a computer or simply type the computer name in the Name field.

3. Click OK.

Sending Console Messages

You can use the Computer Management console to send messages to users logged on to remote systems. These messages appear in a dialog box that the user must click to close.

You send messages to remote users by completing the following steps:

1. In the Computer Management console, right-click the Computer Management entry in the console tree. Then, on the shortcut menu select All Tasks and then choose Send Console Message. This opens the dialog box shown in Figure 2-2.

2. Type the text of the message in the Message area. In the Recipients area, you should see the name of the computer you're currently connected to.

3. If you want to send a message to users of this system, click Send. Otherwise, use the Add button to add recipients or the Remove button to delete a selected recipient. Then, when you're ready to send the message, click Send.

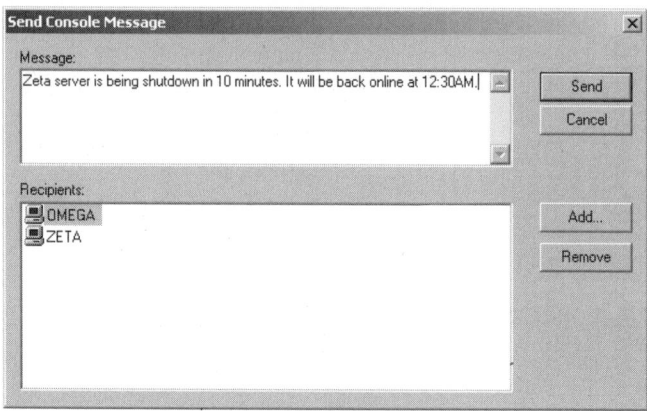

Figure 2-2. *Use this dialog box to send console messages to other systems.*

 Note Only users logged on to the selected system will receive the message. Other users do not. Additionally, Windows NT and Windows 2000 systems must be running the Messenger service to send and receive console messages. Windows 95 and Windows 98 systems running the WinPopup utility can also send and receive console messages.

Exporting Information Lists

The ability to export information lists is one of my favorite features of the Computer Management console, and if you maintain system information records or regularly work with Windows scripting it'll probably be one of yours. The Export List feature allows you to save textual information displayed in the right pane to a tab or comma-delimited text file. You could, for example, use this feature to save detailed information on all the services running on the system by completing the following steps:

1. In the Computer Management console, click the plus sign (+) next to the Services And Applications node. This expands the node to display its tools.

2. Right-click Services, and then from the shortcut menu select Export List. This opens the Save As dialog box.

3. Use the Save In selection list to choose the save location and then enter a name for the export file.

4. Use the Save As Type selection list to set the formatting of the export file. You can separate columns of information with tabs or commas and save as ASCII text or Unicode text. In most cases, you'll want to use ASCII text.

5. Click Save to complete the export process.

You can use a similar procedure to export lists of other information displayed in the Computer Management console.

Using Computer Management System Tools

The Computer Management system tools are designed to manage systems and view system information. The available system tools are

- **Performance Logs And Alerts** Monitor system performance and create logs based on performance parameters. You can also use this tool to notify or alert users of performance conditions. For more information on alerts and monitoring systems, see Chapter 3.

- **Local Users And Groups** Manage local users and local user groups on the currently selected computer. Working with users and groups is covered in Part II along with other types of accounts that you can manage in the Active Directory service.

Note Local users and local user groups aren't a part of the Active Directory and are managed instead through the Local Users And Groups view. Domain controllers don't have entries in the Local Users And Groups view.

- **System Information** Display system configuration information for hardware resources, components, and software environment. If you want to write the configuration information to a file, use the Export List feature described previously in the section of this chapter entitled "Exporting Information Lists."

- **Services** Manage services and service properties. As you'll learn in Chapter 3, Windows 2000 has powerful features that help you efficiently manage services.

- **Shared Folders** Manage the properties of shared folders, user sessions, and open files. Managing user sessions, open files, and network shares is covered in Chapter 12.

- **Event Viewer** View the event logs on the selected computer. Event logs are covered in Chapter 3.

- **Device Manager** Use as a central location for checking the status of any device installed on a computer and for updating the associated device drivers. You can also use it to troubleshoot device problems. Managing devices is covered later in the chapter.

Using Computer Management Storage Tools

The Computer Management storage tools display drive information and provide access to drive management tools. The available storage tools are

- **Removable Storage** Manages removable media devices and tape libraries. Tracks work queues and operator requests related to removable media devices.

- **Disk Defragmenter** Corrects drive fragmentation problems by locating and combining fragmented files.

- **Logical Drives**   Display and manage logical drives on the system.
- **Disk Management**   Manages hard disks, disk partitions, volume sets, and RAID arrays. Replaces the Disk Administrator utility in Windows NT 4.0.

Working with files, drives, and storage devices is the subject of Part III.

Working with Services and Applications

The Computer Management services and applications tools are used to manage services and applications installed on the server. Any application or service-related task that can be performed in a separate tool can be performed through the Services And Applications node as well. For example, if the currently selected system has Dynamic Host Configuration Protocol (DHCP) installed, you can manage DHCP through the Server Applications And Services node. You could also use the DHCP tool in the Administrative Tools folder. You can perform the same tasks either way.

This technology is possible because the DHCP tool is a Microsoft Management Console snap-in. When you access the DHCP tool in the Administrative Tools folder, the snap-in is displayed in a separate console. When you access the DHCP tool through the Server Applications And Services node, the snap-in is displayed within the Computer Management console. Working with services and applications is discussed in Chapter 3 and elsewhere in the book.

Managing System Environments, Profiles, and Properties

You use the System utility to manage system environments, profiles, and properties. Start it by double-clicking the System icon in the Control Panel. This opens the dialog box shown in Figure 2-3. As you see, the dialog box is divided into five tabs. Each of these tabs is discussed in the sections that follow.

The General Tab

General system information is available for any Windows 2000 workstation or server through the System utility's General tab, which is shown in Figure 2-3. To access the General tab, start the System utility by double-clicking the System icon in the Control Panel. Then click the General tab.

The information provided on the General tab includes

- Operating system version
- Registered owner
- Windows 2000 serial number
- Computer type
- Amount of RAM installed on the computer

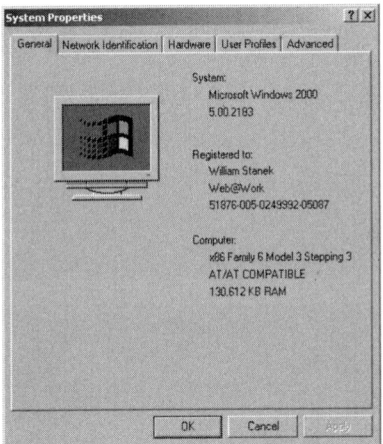

Figure 2-3.   *Use the System utility to manage system environment variables, profiles, and properties.*

A more detailed listing of system information can be obtained in the Computer Management console. Work your way down to the System Information folder, which is found in the System Tools node, and then select System Summary. The information provided by the System Summary helps you determine the following:

- Operating system name, such as Microsoft Windows 2000 Advanced Server
- Operating system version, such as 5.0.2381, where 5 is the major version, 0 is the revision number, and 2381 is the build
- OS manufacturer
- System name and type
- Processor and basic input/output system (BIOS) version
- Windows installation directory
- Country code and time zone
- Total physical and virtual memory available
- Page file space

The Network Identification Tab

The computer's network identification can be displayed and modified with the System utility's Network Identification tab, shown in Figure 2-4. As the figure shows, the tab displays the fully qualified domain name of the system and the domain membership. The fully qualified domain name is essentially the Domain Name System (DNS) name of the computer, which also identifies the computer's place within the Active Directory hierarchy.

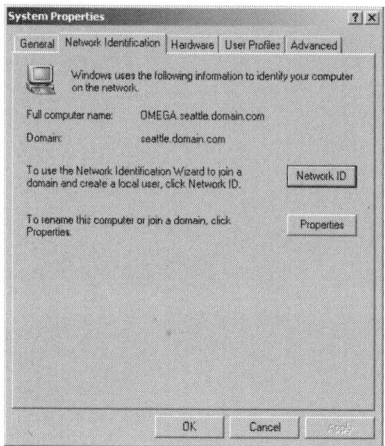

Figure 2-4. *Use the Network Identification tab to display and configure system identification. Notice that you can't change the identification or access information for domain controllers.*

To access the Network Identification tab, start the System utility by double-clicking the System icon in the Control Panel; then click the Network Identification tab. You can now

- Click Network ID to start the Network Identification Wizard, which guides you through modifying network access information for the computer.

- Click Properties to change the system name and domain associated with the .computer.

   Real World   You cannot change the network information for a domain controller. Because of this, the Network ID and Properties buttons will not be available. One way to change the network information on a domain controller would be to demote the domain controller to a member server, change the necessary information, and then promote the server back to a domain controller. For more information on promoting and demoting a domain controller, see the section of Chapter 6 entitled, "Installing and Demoting Domain Controllers."

The Hardware Tab

Windows 2000 workstations and servers can use multiple hardware profiles. Hardware profiles are most useful for mobile computers, such as laptops. Using hardware profiles, you can configure one profile for when the computer is connected to the network (*docked*) and one profile for when the computer is mobile (*undocked*).

Configuring the Way Hardware Profiles Are Used

To configure hardware profiles, access the System utility's Hardware tab and then click the Hardware Profiles button. This opens the dialog box shown in Figure 2-5. As with systems with multiple operating systems, Windows 2000 allows you to configure the way hardware profiles are used as follows:

- Set a default profile by changing the profile's position in the Available Hardware Profiles list. The top profile is the default profile.

- Determine how long the system displays the startup hardware profile menu by setting a value using the field Select The First Profile Listed If I Don't Select A Profile. The default value is 30 seconds.

- Have the system wait indefinitely for user input by selecting Wait Until I Select A Hardware Profile.

Configuring for Docked and Undocked Profiles

To configure a computer for docked and undocked profiles, complete the following steps:

1. In the Available Hardware Profiles list, select Original Profile, and then click Copy.

2. In the Copy Profile dialog box, type a name for the Docked profile in the To field.

3. Select the new profile, and then click on the Properties button.

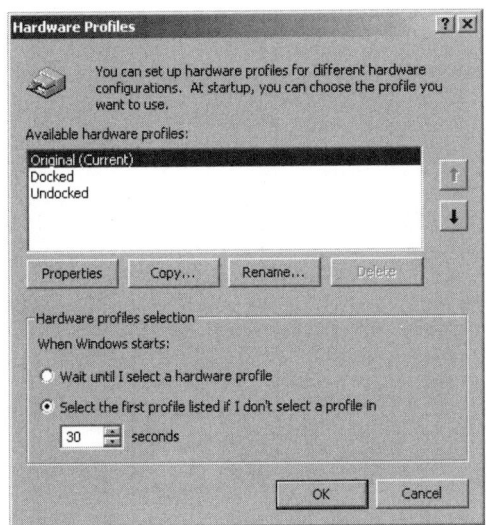

Figure 2-5. *Multiple hardware profiles can be configured for any Windows 2000 system.*

4. Select the This Is A Portable Computer check box, and then choose The Computer Is Docked.

5. Select Include This Profile As An Option When Windows Starts, and then click OK.

6. Select Original Profile in the Available Hardware Profiles list, and then click Copy.

7. In the Copy Profile dialog box, type a name for the Undocked profile in the To field.

8. Select the new profile, and then click on the Properties button.

9. Select the This Is A Portable Computer check box, and then choose The Computer Is Undocked.

10. Select Include This Profile As An Option When Windows Starts and then click OK.

11. Now set the default hardware profile as appropriate for the computer's current state as either docked or undocked.

12. You're done. Click OK.

When the system is booted, the hardware profiles are displayed and the user can select the appropriate profile.

The User Profiles Tab

User profiles are configured with the System utility's User Profiles tab. Managing user profiles in the System utility is covered in the section of Chapter 9 entitled "Managing User Profiles."

The Advanced Tab

Application performance and virtual memory are configured with the System utility's Advanced tab, shown in Figure 2-6. To access the Advanced tab, start the System utility by double-clicking the System icon in the Control Panel; then click the Advanced tab.

Setting Application Performance

Application performance determines the responsiveness of the current active application (as opposed to background applications that may be running on the system). You control application performance by completing the following steps:

1. Access the Advanced tab in the System utility and then display the Performance Options dialog box by clicking the Performance Options button.

2. To give the active application the best response time and the greatest share of available resources, select Applications.

3. To give background applications a better response time than the active application, select Background Services.

4. Click OK.

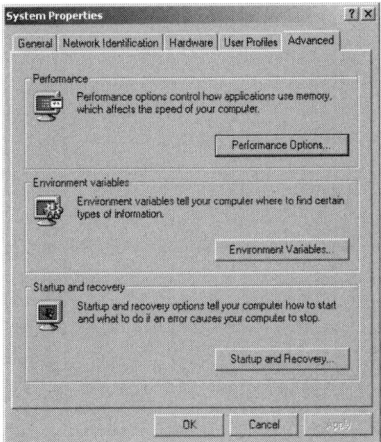

Figure 2-6. *The Advanced tab lets you configure advanced options, including performance options, environment variables, and startup and recovery.*

Setting Virtual Memory

Virtual memory allows you to use disk space to extend the amount of available RAM on a system. This feature of Intel 386 and later processors writes RAM to disks using a process called *paging*. With paging, a set amount of RAM, such as 32 MB, is written to the disk as a paging file, where it can be accessed from the disk when needed.

An initial paging file is created automatically for the drive containing the operating system. By default, other drives don't have paging files, and you must create these paging files manually if you want them. When you create a paging file, you set an initial size and a maximum size. Paging files are written to the volume as a file called PAGEFILE.SYS.

Best Practice   Microsoft recommends that you create a paging file for each physical volume on the system. On most systems, multiple paging files can improve the performance of virtual memory. Thus, instead of a single large paging file, it's better to have many small ones. Keep in mind that removable drives don't need paging files.

Configuring Virtual Memory

You can configure virtual memory by completing the following steps:

1. Start the System utility by double-clicking the System icon in the Control Panel; then click the Advanced tab.

2. Choose Performance Options to display the Performance Options dialog box. Then click Change to display the Virtual Memory dialog box shown in Figure 2-7.

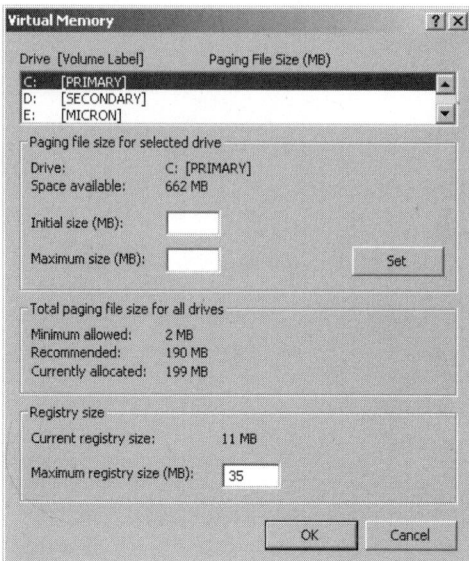

Figure 2-7. *Virtual memory extends the amount of RAM on a system.*

* The Drive header shows how virtual memory is configured currently on the system. Each volume is listed with its associated paging file (if any). The paging file range shows the initial and maximum size values set for the paging file.

* Paging File Size For Selected Drive provides information on the currently selected drive and allows you to set its paging file size. Space Available tells you how much space is available on the drive.

* Total Paging File Size For All Drives provides a recommended size for virtual RAM on the system and tells you the amount currently allocated. If this is the first time you're configuring virtual RAM, you'll note that the recommended amount has already been given to the system drive (in most instances).

Tip Although Windows 2000 can expand paging files incrementally as needed, this can result in fragmented files, which slow system performance. For optimal system performance, set the initial size and maximum size to the same value. This ensures that the paging file is consistent and can be written to a single contiguous file (if possible, given the amount of space on the volume).

3. In the Drive list box, select the volume you want to work with.

4. Use the Paging File Size For Selected Drive area to configure the paging file for the drive. Enter an initial size and a maximum size, and then click Set to save the changes.

5. Repeat steps 3 and 4 for each volume you want to configure.

Note   The paging file is also used for debugging purposes when a STOP error occurs on the system. If the paging file on the system drive is smaller than the minimum amount required to write the debugging information to the paging file, this feature will be disabled. If you want to use debugging, the minimum size should be set to the same figure as the amount of RAM on the system. For example, a system with 128 MB of RAM would need a paging file of 128 MB on the system drive.

6. Click OK, and if prompted to overwrite an existing PAGEFILE.SYS file, click Yes.

7. Close the System utility and choose Yes to restart the system when prompted.

Setting Registry Size

Windows 2000 allows you to control the maximum amount of memory and disk space used by the registry. Setting a size limit on the registry doesn't allocate space or guarantee that space is available if needed. Instead, space is used only as required up to the maximum allowable value. You set a limit on the registry by completing the following steps:

1. Log on to the system using an account with administrator privileges.

2. Start the System utility by double-clicking the System icon in the Control Panel; then click the Advanced tab.

3. Choose Performance Options to display the Performance Options dialog box. Then click Change to display the Virtual Memory dialog box.

4. In the Virtual Memory dialog box, enter a new maximum registry size using the Maximum Registry Size field.

Configuring System and User Environment Variables

System and user environment variables are configured by means of the Environment Variables dialog box, shown in Figure 2-8. To access this dialog box, start the System utility by double-clicking the System icon in the Control Panel; then click the Advanced tab and choose Environment Variables.

Creating an Environment Variable

You can create environment variables by completing the following steps:

1. Click the New button under System Variables or User Variables, whichever is appropriate for the type of environment variable you want to create. This opens the New System Variable dialog box or the New User Variable dialog box, respectively.

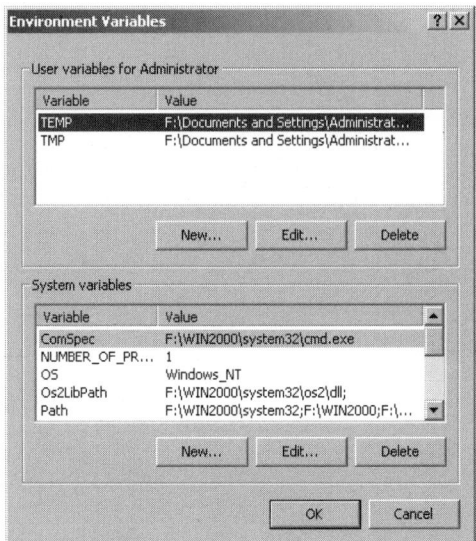

Figure 2-8. *The Environment Variables dialog box lets you configure system and user environment variables.*

2. In the Variable Name field, type the variable name. Then in the Variable Value field type the variable value.

3. Choose OK.

Editing an Environment Variable

You can edit an existing environment variable by completing the following steps:

1. Select the variable in the System Variables or User Variables list box.

2. Click the Edit button under System Variables or User Variables, whichever is appropriate for the type of environment variable you're modifying. This opens the Edit System Variable dialog box or the Edit User Variable dialog box, respectively.

3. Enter a new value in the Variable Value field.

4. Choose OK.

Deleting an Environment Variable

You can delete an environment variable by selecting the variable and then clicking the Delete button.

 Note When you create or modify system environment variables, the changes take effect when you restart the computer. When you create or modify user environment variables, the changes take effect the next time the user logs on to the system.

Configuring System Startup and Recovery

System startup and recovery properties are configured by means of the Startup And Recovery dialog box, shown in Figure 2-9. To access this dialog box, start the System utility by double-clicking the System icon in the Control Panel. Then click the Advanced tab and click the Startup And Recovery button.

Setting Startup Options

The System Startup area of the Startup And Recovery dialog box controls system startup. To set the default operating system, select one of the operating systems listed in the Default Operating System field. These options are obtained from the operating system section of the system's BOOT.INI file.

At startup, Windows 2000 displays the startup configuration menu for 30 seconds by default. You can

- Boot immediately to the default operating system by clearing the Display List Of Operating Systems For check box.

- Display the available options for a specific amount of time by selecting the Display List Of Operating Systems For check box and then setting a time delay in seconds.

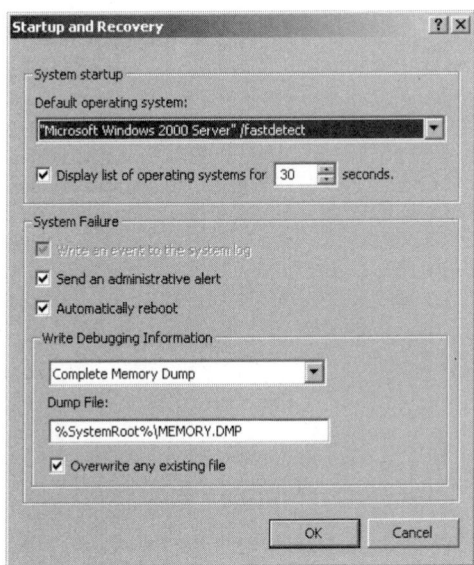

Figure 2-9. *The Startup And Recovery dialog box lets you configure system startup and recovery procedures.*

Generally, on most systems you'll want to use a value of 3–5 seconds. This is long enough to be able to make a selection, yet short enough to expedite the system startup process.

Setting Recovery Options

Recovery options allow administrators to control precisely what happens when the system encounters a fatal system error (also known as a STOP error). You can set these options using the System utility's Startup/Shutdown tab. The available options include

- **Write an event to the system log**   Logs the error in the system log, which allows administrators to review the error later using the Event Viewer.

- **Send an administrative alert**   Sends an alert to the recipients specified in the Alert dialog box.

- **Write debugging information**   Select a dump option other than (none) to instruct the system to write debugging information to a dump file, which can be used to diagnose the problem. If you set this option, you must specify a file name.

- **Overwrite any existing file**   Ensures that any existing dump files are overwritten if a new STOP error occurs. Generally, it's a good idea to select this option, especially if you have limited drive space.

 Best Practice   A complete memory dump can only be created if the system is properly configured. The system drive must have a sufficiently large memory paging file (as set for virtual memory with the Advanced tab), and the drive where the dump file is written must have free space of equal size. For example, my server has 128 MB of RAM and requires a paging file on the system drive of the same size—128 MB. Since the same drive is used for the dump file, the drive must have at least 256 MB of free space to create the debugging information correctly (that's 128 MB for the paging file and 128 MB for the dump file).

- **Automatically reboot**   Check this option to have the system attempt to reboot when a fatal system error occurs.

 Note   Configuring automatic reboots isn't always a good thing. Sometimes you may want the system to halt rather than reboot, which should ensure that the system gets proper attention. Otherwise, you can only know that the system rebooted when you view the System logs or if you happen to be in front of the system's monitor when it reboots.

Managing Hardware Devices and Drivers

Windows 2000 provides three key tools for managing hardware devices and drivers. These tools are

- Device Manager
- Add/Remove Hardware Wizard
- Hardware Troubleshooter

You'll use these tools whenever you install, uninstall, or troubleshoot hardware devices and drivers.

Viewing and Managing Hardware Devices

You can view a detailed list of all the hardware devices installed on a system by completing the following steps:

1. Choose Start, Programs, then Administrative Tools, and then Computer Management.
2. In the Computer Management console, click the plus sign (+) next to the System Tools node. This expands the node to display its tools.
3. Select Device Manager. You should now see a complete list of devices installed on the system. By default, this list is organized by device type.
4. Click the plus sign (+) next to a device type to see a list of the specific instances of that device type.
5. If you right-click the device entry, you can manage the device using the shortcut menu. Which options are available depends on the type of device, but they include

   - **Properties**   Displays the Properties dialog box for the device.
   - **Uninstall**   Uninstalls the device and its drivers.
   - **Disable**   Disables the device but doesn't uninstall it.
   - **Enable**   Enables a device if it's disabled.

Tip The device list shows warning symbols if there are problems with a device. A yellow warning symbol with an exclamation point indicates a problem with a device. A red X indicates a device that's improperly installed or has been disabled by the user or administrator for some reason.

You can use the options on the View menu in the Computer Management console to change the defaults for what types of devices are displayed and how the devices are listed. The options are

- **Devices by type**   Displays devices by the type of device installed, such as Disk Drive or Printer. The connection name is listed below the type. This is the default view.

- **Devices by connection** Displays devices by connection type, such as System Board or Logical Disk Manager.

- **Resources by type** Displays the status of allocated resources by type of device using the resource. Resource types are direct memory access (DMA) channels, input/output (I/O) ports, interrupt request (IRQ), and memory addresses.

- **Resources by connection** Displays the status of all allocated resources by connection type rather than device type.

- **Show hidden devices** Displays non-Plug and Play devices as well as devices that have been physically removed from the computer but haven't had their drivers uninstalled.

Installing and Uninstalling Device Drivers

To keep devices operating smoothly, it's essential that you keep the device drivers current. You can install device drivers by completing the following steps:

1. In the Computer Management console, access Device Manager.

2. Devices may be listed by type, resource, or connection. Right-click the connection for the device you want to manage and then choose Properties from the shortcut menu. This opens the Properties dialog box for the device.

3. To uninstall a device driver (and the related device), select the Driver tab and then click the Uninstall button. When prompted to confirm the deletion, choose OK.

4. To install or reinstall device drivers, choose the Driver tab and click Update Driver to start the Upgrade Device Driver Wizard. Read the Welcome dialog box and then click Next to continue.

Best Practice Updated drivers can add functionality to a device, improve performance, and resolve device problems. However, you should rarely install the latest drivers on a deployment server without first testing the drivers in a test environment. Test first, then install.

5. As shown in Figure 2-10, you can determine whether you want to search for the drivers or select drivers from a list of known drivers.

6. If you choose to select drivers, you'll need to specify the device type, such as Modem or Network Adapter. Then the wizard displays a selection dialog box similar to the one shown in Figure 2-11. Scroll through the list of manufacturers to find the manufacturer of the device, then choose the appropriate device in the Models panel.

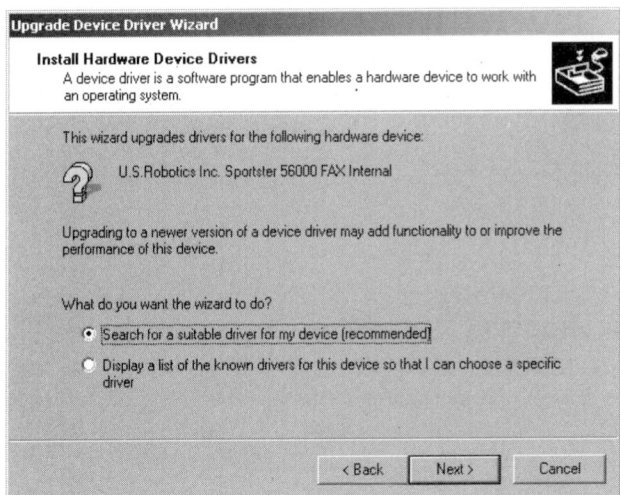

Figure 2-10. *Specify whether to search for the necessary drivers or select the drivers from a list of known drivers.*

If you search for drivers, the wizard checks the driver database on the system for drivers and any of the optional locations you specify, such as a floppy disk or CD-ROM. Any matching drivers found are displayed, and you can select a driver.

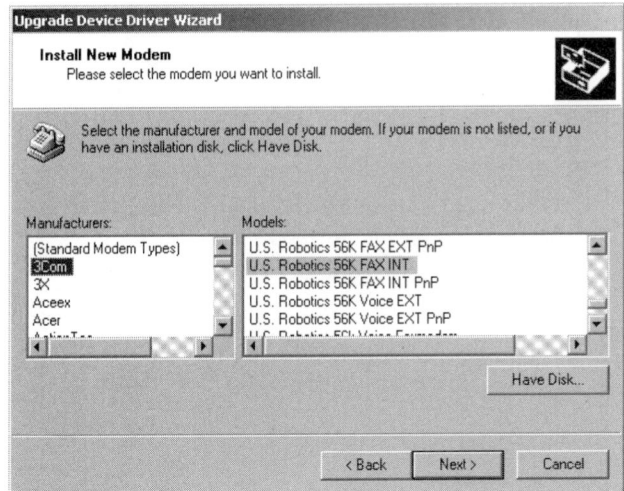

Figure 2-11. *Select the device driver by manufacturer and type.*

Note If the manufacturer or device you want to use isn't listed, insert your device driver disk into the floppy drive and then click on the Have Disk button. Follow the prompts. Afterward, select the appropriate device.

After selecting a device driver through a search or a manual selection, continue through the installation process by clicking Next. Click Finish when the driver installation is completed.

Installing, Uninstalling, and Troubleshooting Hardware

You can install or uninstall hardware devices on a system through the Add/Remove Hardware Wizard. You can also use this wizard to troubleshoot problems with existing hardware. To start and use the wizard, complete the following steps:

1. Start the System utility by double-clicking the System icon in the Control Panel. Click the Hardware tab, and then choose Hardware Wizard.

2. To add new hardware or troubleshoot existing hardware, select Add/Troubleshoot A Device. See Figure 2-12.

3. To uninstall hardware, select Uninstall/Unplug A Device.

4. Installing, uninstalling, and troubleshooting procedures are examined in the sections that follow.

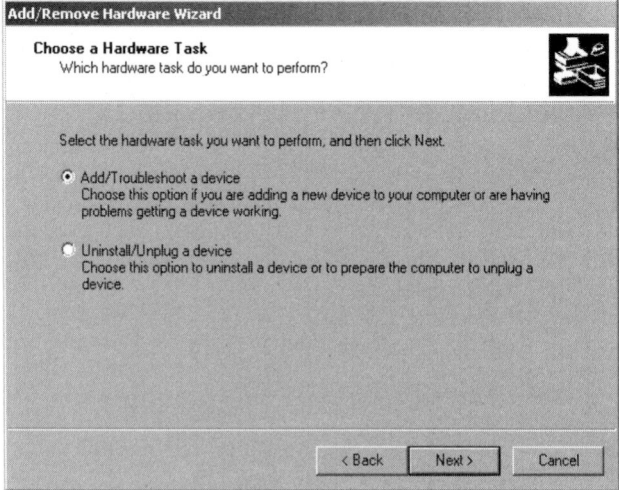

Figure 2-12. *Use the Add/Remove Hardware Wizard to install, uninstall, or troubleshoot hardware devices.*

Installing Hardware

The Windows 2000 Plug and Play technology does a good job of detecting and automatically configuring new hardware. However, if the hardware doesn't support Plug and Play or isn't automatically detected, you'll need to tell Windows 2000 about the new hardware. You do this by installing the hardware device and its related drivers on the system using the Add/Remove Hardware Wizard. You use the wizard to install hardware by completing the following steps:

1. Start the Add/Remove Hardware Wizard as explained previously, and then select Add/Troubleshoot A Device.

2. Click Next. Windows 2000 searches for new hardware to install as well as currently installed hardware. If new hardware isn't detected automatically, select Add A New Device and click Next.

3. In the Find New Hardware dialog box determine whether the wizard should search for new hardware or whether you want to select the hardware from a list.

4. If you choose Yes, the wizard will perform a thorough device search and automatically detect new hardware. The process takes a few minutes to go through all the device types and options. When the search is completed, any new devices found are displayed, and you can select a device.

5. If you choose No, or if no new devices are found in the automatic search, you'll have to select the hardware type yourself. Select the type of hardware, such as Modem or Network Adapter, and then click Next. Scroll through the list of manufacturers to find the manufacturer of the device, and then choose the appropriate device in the Models panel.

6. The remaining steps of the installation process depend on the type of device you're installing. Follow the prompts and then complete the installation by clicking Finish.

Uninstalling Hardware

You can use the Add/Remove Hardware Wizard to uninstall or unplug hardware devices by completing the following steps:

1. Start the Add/Remove Hardware Wizard as explained previously and then select Uninstall/Unplug A Device.

2. In the Choose A Removal Task dialog box, specify whether you're uninstalling or unplugging a device. When you uninstall a device, you permanently remove a device and its drivers. When you unplug a device, you temporarily disable or eject it.

3. Select the device you want to uninstall or unplug.

4. Confirm that you want to uninstall or unplug the device by choosing Yes, I Want To Uninstall This Device or Yes, I Want To Unplug This Device.

5. When you click Next, the device is uninstalled or unplugged, as appropriate. Click Finish to complete the process.

Troubleshooting Hardware and Device Problems

You can also use the Add/Remove Hardware Wizard to troubleshoot hardware problems. To do this, complete the following steps:

1. Start the Add/Remove Hardware Wizard as explained previously, and then select Add/Troubleshoot A Device.

2. In the Choose A Hardware Device dialog box, select the device you want to troubleshoot. Click Next to continue.

3. The final wizard dialog box provides a device status. When you click Finish, the wizard does one of two things. If an error code is shown with the device status, the wizard accesses the error code in the online help documentation—if it's available and installed. Otherwise, the wizard starts the Hardware Troubleshooter, which attempts to solve the hardware problem using your responses to the questions that it asks.

You can also access the Hardware Troubleshooter directly. To do that, complete the following steps:

1. In the Computer Management console, access Device Manager.

2. Devices may be listed by type, resource, or connection. Right-click the connection for the device you want to troubleshoot and then choose Properties on the shortcut menu. This opens the Properties dialog box for the device.

3. In the General tab, start the Hardware Troubleshooter by clicking on the Troubleshooter button.

Chapter 3

Monitoring Processes, Services, and Events

As an administrator, it's your job to keep an eye on the network systems. The status of system resources and usage can change dramatically over time. Services may stop running. File systems may run out of space. Applications may throw exceptions, which in turn can cause system problems. Unauthorized users may try to break into the system. The techniques discussed in this chapter will help you find and resolve these and other system problems.

Managing Applications, Processes, and Performance

Anytime you start an application or type a command on the command line, Microsoft Windows 2000 starts one or more processes to handle the related program. Generally, processes that you start in this manner are called *interactive* processes. That is, the processes are started *interactively* with the keyboard or mouse. If the application or program is active and selected, the related interactive process has control over the keyboard and mouse until you switch control by terminating the program or selecting a different one. When a process has control, it's said to be running *in the foreground*.

Processes can also run *in the background*. With processes started by users, this means that programs that aren't currently active can continue to operate—only they generally aren't given the same priority as the active process. You can also configure background processes to run independently of the user logon session; such processes are usually started by the operating system. An example of this type of background process is a batch file started with an AT command. The AT command tells the system to run the file at a specified time, and (if permissions are configured correctly) the AT command can do so regardless of whether a user is logged on to the system.

Task Manager

The key tool you'll use to manage system processes and applications is Task Manager. You can access Task Manager using any of the following techniques:

- Press CTRL+SHIFT+ESC.
- Press CTRL+ALT+DEL, and then select the Task Manager button.
- Type **taskmgr** into the Run utility or a command prompt.
- Right-click the taskbar and select Task Manager from the pop-up menu.

Techniques you'll use to work with Task Manager are covered in the following sections.

Administering Applications

Task Manager's Applications tab is shown in Figure 3-1. This tab shows the status of the programs that are currently running on the system. You can use the buttons on the bottom of this tab as follows:

- Stop an application by selecting the application and then clicking End Task.
- Switch to an application and make it active by selecting the application and then clicking Switch To.

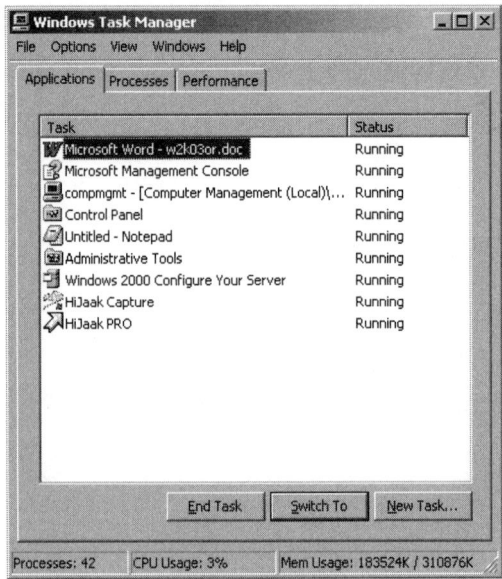

Figure 3-1. *The Applications tab of the Windows Task Manager shows the status of programs currently running on the system.*

- Start a new program by selecting New Task and then enter a command to run the application. New Task functions like the Start menu's Run utility.

Tip   The Status column tells you if the application is running normally or if the application has gone off into the ozone. A status of Not Responding is an indicator that an application may be frozen, and you may want to end its related task. However, some applications may not respond to the operating system during certain process-intensive tasks. Because of this, you should be certain the application is really frozen before you end its related task.

Right-Clicking a Listing

Right-clicking an application's listing displays a pop-up menu that allows you to

- Switch to the application and make it active
- Bring the application to the front of the display
- Minimize and maximize the application
- Tile or end the application
- Go to the related process in the Processes tab

Note   The Go To Process is very helpful when you're trying to find the primary process for a particular application. Selecting this option highlights the related process in the Processes tab.

Administering Processes

The Task Manager Process tab is shown in Figure 3-2 . This tab provides detailed information on the processes that are running. As you examine processes, note that although applications have a main process, a single application may start multiple processes. Generally, these processes are dependent on the main application process and are stopped when you terminate the main application process or use End Task. Because of this, you'll usually want to terminate the main application process or the application itself rather than dependent processes.

The fields of the Processes tab provide lots of information about running processes. You can use this information to determine which processes are hogging system resources, such as CPU time and memory. Additional uses for the tab include

- Stopping a process by selecting it and then choosing End Process
- Stopping a process and its subprocesses by right-clicking it and then choosing End Process Tree
- Setting a process's priority by right-clicking it and then choosing Set Priority from the pop-up menu

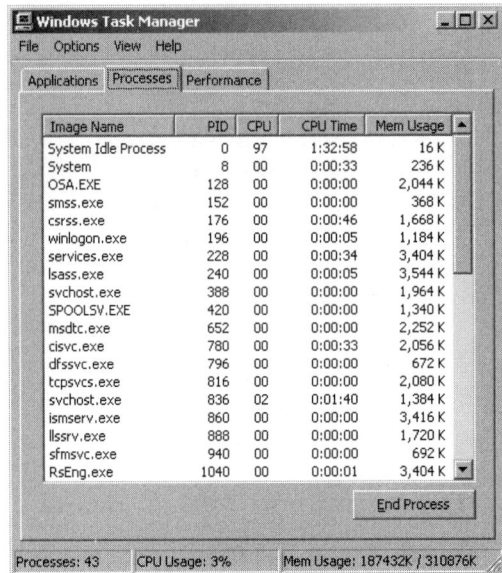

Figure 3-2. *The Processes tab provides detailed information on running processes.*

 Note If you examine processes running in Task Manager, you'll note a process called System Idle Process. You can't set the priority of this process. Unlike other processes that track resource usage, System Idle Process tracks the amount of system resources that aren't used. Thus, a 99 in the CPU column for the process means 99 percent of the system resources currently aren't being used.

Priority determines how much of the system resources are allocated to a process. Most processes have a normal priority by default. To increase priority, set the priority to high. To decrease priority, set the priority to low. The highest priority is given to real-time processes.

Viewing System Performance

The Task Manager Performance tab provides an overview of CPU and memory usage. As shown in Figure 3-3, the tab displays graphs as well as statistics. This information gives you a quick check on system resource usage. For more detailed information, use Performance Monitor, as explained later in this chapter.

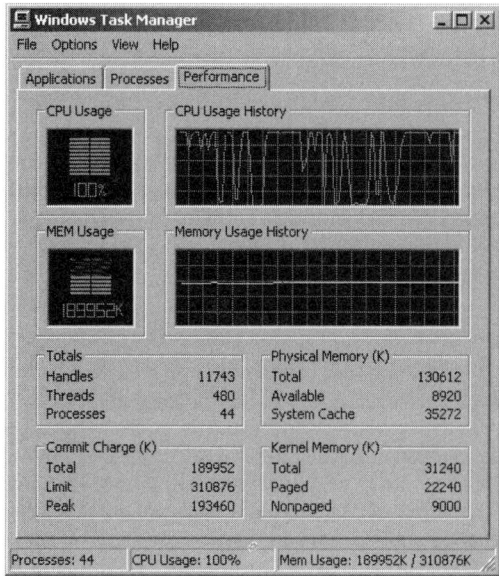

Figure 3-3. *The Performance tab provides a quick check on system resource usage.*

Graphs on the Performance Tab

The graphs on the Performance tab provide the following information:

- **CPU Usage**   The percentage of processor resources being used
- **CPU Usage History**   A history graph of CPU usage plotted over time
- **MEM Usage**   The amount of memory currently being used on the system
- **Memory Usage History**   A history graph of memory usage plotted over time

Tip   To view a close-up of the CPU graphs, double-click within the Performance tab. Double-clicking again returns you to normal viewing mode.

Customizing and Updating the Graph Display

To customize or update the graph display, use the following options on the View menu:

- **Update Speed**   Allows you to change the speed of graph updating as well as to pause the graph.
- **CPU History**   On multiprocessor systems, allows you to specify how CPU graphs are displayed.

- **Show Kernel Times** Allows you to display the amount of CPU time used by the operating system kernel.

Beneath the graphs you'll find several lists of statistics. These statistics provide the following information:

- **Commit Charge** Provides information on the total memory used by the operating system. *Total* lists all physical and virtual memory currently in use. *Limit* lists the total physical and virtual memory available. *Peak* lists the maximum memory used by the system since bootup.

- **Kernel Memory** Provides information on the memory used by the operating system kernel. Critical portions of kernel memory must operate in RAM and can't be paged to virtual memory. This type of kernel memory is listed as *Nonpaged.* The rest of kernel memory can be paged to virtual memory and is listed as *Paged.* The total amount of memory used by the kernel is listed under *Total.*

- **Physical Memory** Provides information on the total RAM on the system. *Total* shows the amount of physical RAM. *Available* shows the RAM not currently being used and available for use. *System Cache* shows the amount of memory used for system caching.

- **Totals** Provides information on CPU usage. *Handles* shows the number of I/O handles in use. *Threads* shows the number of threads in use. *Processes* shows the number of processes in use.

Managing System Services

Services provide key functions to Windows 2000 workstations and servers. To manage system services, you'll use the Services entry in the Computer Management console, which you start by completing the following steps:

1. Choose Start, Programs, then Administrative Tools, and finally Computer Management. Or select Computer Management in the Administrative Tools folder.

2. Right-click the Computer Management entry in the console tree and select Connect To Another Computer on the shortcut menu. You can now choose the system whose services you want to manage.

3. Expand the Services And Applications node by clicking the plus sign (+) next to it, and then choose Services.

 Note Windows 2000 provides several other ways to access services. For example, you can also use the Services entry in the Component Services utility.

Figure 3-4 shows the Services view in the Computer Management console. The key fields of this dialog box are used as follows:

- **Name**   The name of the service. Only services installed on the system are listed here. Double-click an entry to configure its startup options. If a service you need isn't listed, you can install it by using the Network Connection Properties dialog box or the Windows Optional Networking Components Wizard. See Chapter 15 for details.

- **Description**   A short description of the service and its purpose.

- **Status**   Whether the status of the service is started, paused, or stopped. (Stopped is indicated by a blank entry.)

- **Startup Type**   The startup setting for the service. Automatic services are started at bootup. Manual services are started by users or other services. Disabled services are turned off and can't be started while they remain disabled.

- **Log On As**   The account the service logs on as. The default in most cases is the local system account.

Note   Both the operating system and users can disable Services. Generally, Windows 2000 disables services if there is a possible conflict with another service.

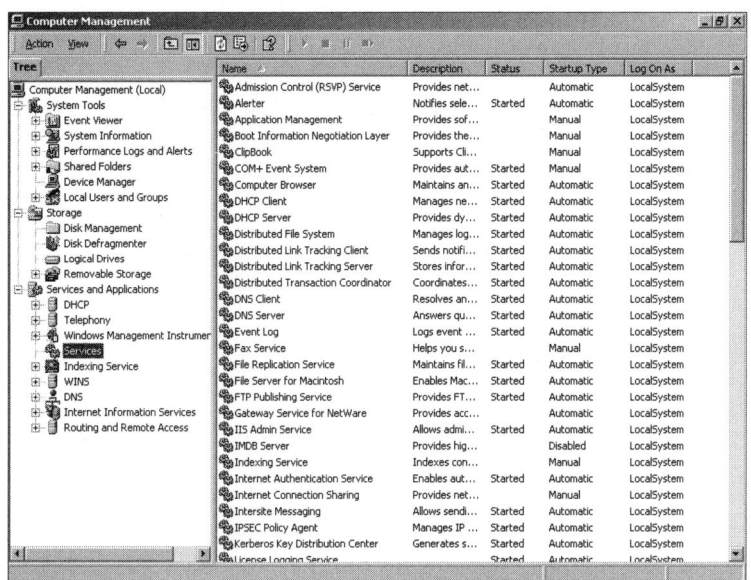

Figure 3-4.   *Use the Services view to manage services on Windows 2000 workstations and servers.*

Common Windows 2000 Services

Table 3-1 provides a summary of common services that you'll see on Windows 2000 systems. Keep in mind that the type and number of services running on a Windows 2000 system depend on its configuration. To install or remove services, you use the Configure Your Server administration tool.

Table 3-1. Common Services That May Be Installed on Windows 2000 Systems

Service Name	Description
Alerter	Sends administrative alert messages
Application Management	Provides software installation services
ClipBook	Enables remote viewers to see local pages with ClipBook Viewer
COM+ Event System	Provides automatic distribution of events to subscribing COM components
Computer Browser	Enables computer browsing; maintains a list of resources used for network browsing
Dynamic Host Configuration Protocol (DHCP) Client	Manages network configuration by registering and updating Internet Protocol (IP) addresses and Domain Name System (DNS) names
DHCP Server	Provides dynamic IP address assignment and network configuration for DHCP clients
Distributed Transaction Coordinator	Coordinates distributed transactions for resource managers
DNS Client	Resolves and caches DNS names
DNS Server	Manages DNS names and queries
Event Log	Logs event messages issued by applications and the operating system
File Server for Macintosh	Enables Macintosh users to store and access files on the server system
Gateway Service for NetWare	Provides access to file and print resources on NetWare networks
Intersite Messaging	Allows sending and receiving of messages between Active Directory sites
License Logging Service	Tracks license usage and compliance
Messenger	Sends and receives messages transmitted by administrators or by the Alerter service
Net Logon	Authenticates user logons
Network dynamic data exchange (DDE)	Supports DDE between applications

(continued)

Table 3-1. *(continued)*

Service Name	Description
Network DDE DSDM	Manages shared dynamic data exchange and is used by Network DDE
NT LM Security Support Provider	Provides security to Remote Procedure Call (RPC) programs that don't use named pipes
Performance Logs and Alerts	Configures performance logs and alerts
Plug and Play	Manages device installation and configuration and notifies programs of device changes
Print Server for Macintosh	Enables Macintosh users to send print jobs to Windows
Print Spooler	Spools printer files
Protected Storage	Provides protected storage for sensitive data, such as private keys
RPC	Provides RPC services for distributed applications
RPC Locator	Manages the RPC name service database
Routing and Remote Access	Provides routing and remote access services
Secondary Logon Service	Enables Run As, where you can run processes as another user
Security Accounts Manager	Stores security information for local user accounts
Server	Provides RPC server services, including file sharing, printer spooling, and named pipes
Simple Transmission Control Protocol/Internet Protocol (TCP/IP) Services	Supports the TCP/IP services Character Generator, Daytime, Discard, Echo, and Quote of the Day
System Event Notification	Tracks system events and notifies COM+ Event System subscribers of these events
Task Scheduler	Enables job scheduling
TCP/IP NetBIOS Helper Service	Enables support for NetBIOS over TCP/IP and NetBIOS name resolution
Telnet	Allows a remote user to log on to the system and run console programs using the command line
Windows Internet Name Service (WINS)	Provides a NetBIOS name service for TCP/IP clients
Workstation	Provides services for network connections and communications

Starting, Stopping, and Pausing Services

As an administrator, you'll often have to start, stop, or pause Windows 2000 services. To start, stop, or pause, complete the following steps:

1. Start the Computer Management console.

2. Right-click the Computer Management entry in the console tree and select Connect To Another Computer on the shortcut menu. You can now choose the system whose services you want to manage.

3. Expand the Services And Applications node by clicking the plus sign (+) next to it, and then choose Services.

4. Right-click the service you want to manipulate, and then select Start, Stop, or Pause, as appropriate. You can also choose Restart to have Windows stop and then start the service after a brief pause. Additionally, if you pause a service, you can use the Resume option to resume normal operation.

 Note When services that are set to start automatically fail, the status is listed as blank and you'll usually receive notification in a pop-up dialog box. Service failures can also be logged to the system's event logs. In Windows 2000, you can configure actions to handle service failure automatically. For example, you could have Windows 2000 attempt to restart the service for you. See the section of this chapter entitled "Configuring Service Recovery" for details.

Configuring Service Startup

You can set Windows 2000 services to start manually or automatically. You can also turn them off permanently by disabling them. You configure service startup by completing the following steps:

1. In the Computer Management console, connect to the computer whose services you want to manage.

2. Expand the Services And Applications node by clicking the plus sign (+) next to it, and then choose Services.

3. Right-click the service you want to configure and then choose Properties.

4. In the General tab, use the Startup Type drop-down list box to choose a startup option, as shown in Figure 3-5. Select Automatic to start services at bootup. Select Manual to allow the services to be started manually. Select Disabled to turn off the service.

5. Click OK.

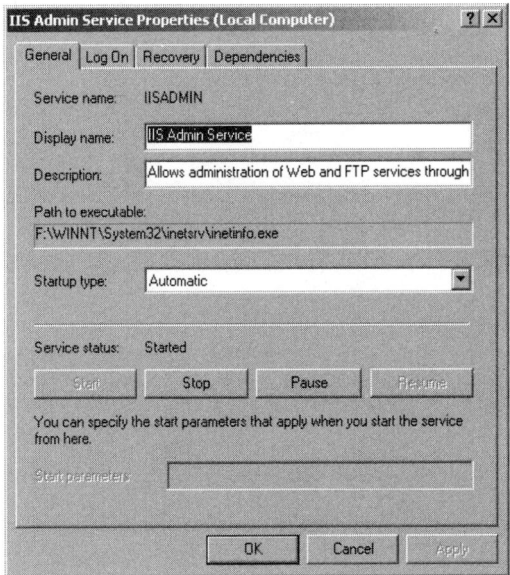

Figure 3-5. *Use the General tab's Startup drop-down list box to configure service startup options.*

Configuring Service Logon

You can configure Windows 2000 services to log on as a system account or as a specific user. To do either of these, complete the following steps:

1. In the Computer Management console, connect to the computer whose services you want to manage.

2. Expand the Services And Applications node by clicking the plus sign (+) next to it, and then choose Services.

3. Right-click the service you want to configure and then choose Properties.

4. Select the Log On tab, shown in Figure 3-6.

5. Select Local System Account if the service should log on using the system account (which is the default for most services).

6. Select This Account if the service should log on using a specific user account. Be sure to type an account name and password in the fields provided. Use the Browse button to search for a user account, if necessary.

7. Click OK.

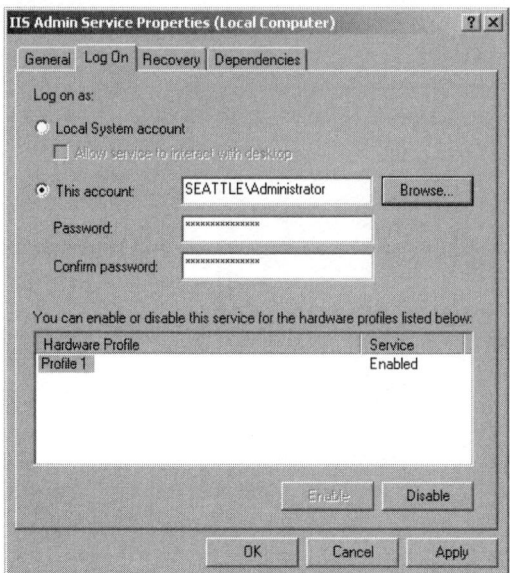

Figure 3-6. *Use the Log On tab to configure the service logon account.*

Configuring Service Recovery

You can configure Windows 2000 services to take specific actions when a service fails. For example, you could attempt to restart the service or run an application. To configure recovery options for a service, complete the following steps:

1. In the Computer Management console, connect to the computer whose services you want to manage.

2. Expand the Services And Applications node by clicking the plus sign (+) next to it, and then choose Services.

3. Right-click the service you want to configure and then choose Properties.

4. Select the Recovery tab, shown in Figure 3-7.

 Note Windows 2000 automatically configures recovery for some critical system services during installation. In Figure 3-7, you see that the IIS (Internet Information Server) Admin Service is set to run a file if the service fails. This file is an application that corrects service problems and safely manages dependent IIS services while working to restart the service.

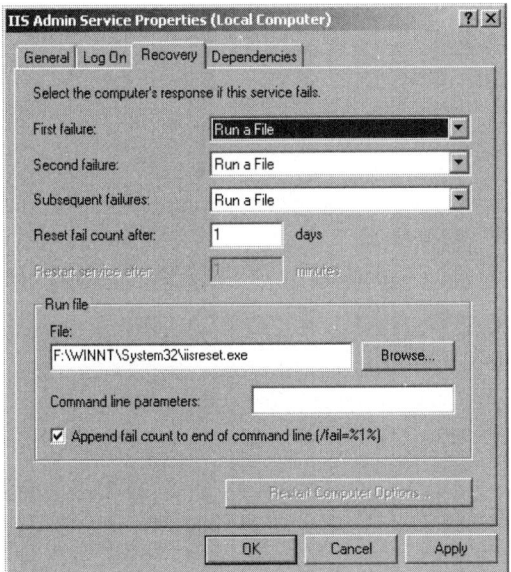

Figure 3-7. *Use the Recovery tab to specify actions that should be taken in case of service failure.*

5. You can now configure recovery options for the first, second, and subsequent recovery failures. The available options are

   - Take No Action
   - Restart the Service
   - Run a File
   - Reboot the Computer

Best Practice When you configure recovery options for critical services, you may want to try to restart the service on the first and second attempts and then reboot the server on the third attempt.

6. Configure other options based on your previously selected recovery options. If you elected to run a file as a recovery option, you'll need to set options in the Run File panel. If you elected to restart the service, you'll need to specify the restart delay. After stopping the service, Windows 2000 waits for the specified delay before trying to start the service. In most cases a delay of 1–2 minutes should be sufficient.

7. Click OK.

Event Logging and Viewing

Event logs provide historical information that can help you track down system and security problems. The event-logging service controls whether events are tracked on Windows 2000 systems. When this service is started, you can track user actions and system resource usage events with the following event logs:

- **Application Log**   Records events logged by applications, such as the failure of MS SQL to access a database.

- **Directory Service**   Records events logged by Active Directory and its related services.

- **DNS Server**   Records DNS queries, responses, and other DNS activities.

- **File Replication Service**   Records file replication activities on the system.

- **Security Log**   Records events you've set for auditing with local or global group policies.

 Note   Any user who needs access to the security log must be granted the user right to Manage Auditing and the Security Log. By default, members of the Administrators group have this user right. To learn how to assign user rights, see Chapter 7.

- **System Log**   Records events logged by the operating system or its components, such as the failure of a service to start at bootup.

Accessing and Using the Event Logs

You access the event logs by completing the following steps:

1. In the Computer Management console, connect to the computer whose event logs you want to view or manage.

2. Expand the System Tools node by clicking the plus sign (+) next to it and then double-click Event Viewer. You should now see a list of logs, as shown in Figure 3-8.

3. Select the log you want to view.

Entries in the main panel of Event Viewer provide a quick overview of when, where, and how an event occurred. To obtain detailed information on an event, double-click its entry. The event type precedes the date and time of the event. Event types include

- **Information**   An informational event which is generally related to a successful action.

- **Success Audit**   An event related to the successful execution of an action.

- **Failure Audit**   An event related to the failed execution of an action.

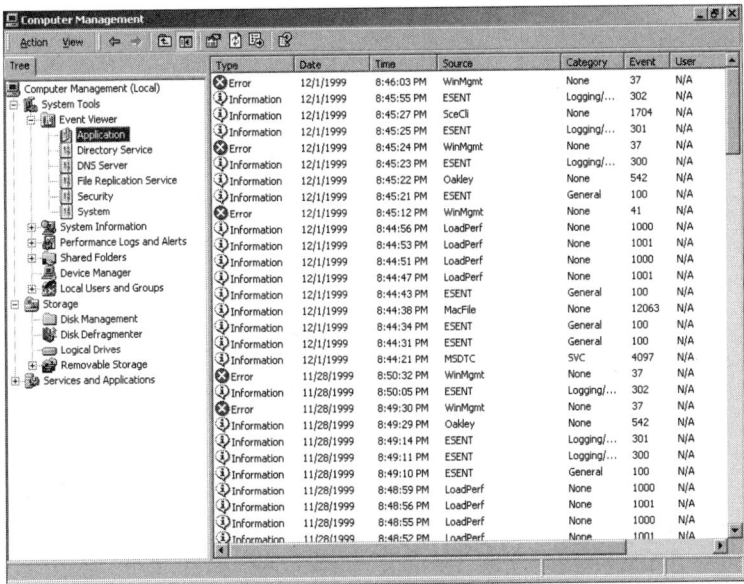

Figure 3-8. *Event Viewer displays events for the selected log.*

- **Warning** A warning. Details for warnings are often useful in preventing future system problems.

- **Error** An error, such as the failure of a service to start.

Note Warnings and errors are the two types of events that you'll want to examine closely. Whenever these types of events occur and you're unsure of the cause, double-click the entry to view the detailed event description.

In addition to type, date, and time, the summary and detailed event entries provide the following information:

- **Source** The application, service, or component that logged the event.

- **Category** The category of the event, which is sometimes used to further describe the related action.

- **Event** An identifier for the specific event.

- **User** The user account that was logged on when the event occurred.

- **Computer** The name of the computer where the event occurred.

- **Description** In the detailed entries, a text description of the event.

- **Data** In the detailed entries, any data or error code output by the event.

Setting Event Log Options

Log options allow you to control the size of the event logs as well as how logging is handled. By default, event logs are set with a maximum file size of 512 KB. Then, when a log reaches this limit, events older than seven days are overwritten to prevent the log from exceeding the maximum file size.

To set the log options, complete the following steps:

1. In the Computer Management console, double-click the Event Viewer entry. You should now see a list of event logs.

2. Right-click the event log whose properties you want to set and select Properties from the shortcut menu. This opens the dialog box shown in Figure 3-9.

3. Enter a maximum size in the Maximum Log Size field. Make sure that the drive containing the operating system has enough free space for the maximum log size you select. Log files are stored in the *%SystemRoot%*\system32\config directory by default.

 Note Throughout this book you'll see references to *%SystemRoot%*. This is an environment variable used by Windows 2000 to designate the base directory for the Windows 2000 operating system, such as C:\WIN2000. For more information on environment variables, see Chapter 9.

4. Determine what happens when the maximum log size is reached. The options available are

   • **Overwrite Events As Needed** Events in the log are overwritten when the maximum file size is reached. Generally, this is the best option on a low priority system.

   • **Overwrite Events Older Than . . . Days** When the maximum file size is reached, events in the log are overwritten only if they are older than the setting you select. If the maximum size is reached and the events can't be overwritten, the system generates error messages telling you the event log is full.

   • **Do Not Overwrite Events (Clear Log Manually)** When the maximum file size is reached, the system generates error messages telling you the event log is full.

5. Click OK when you're finished.

 Note On critical systems where security and event logging is very important, you may want to use Overwrite Events Older Than . . . Days or Do Not Overwrite Events (Clear Log Manually). When you use these methods, you may want to archive and clear the log file periodically to prevent the system from generating error messages.

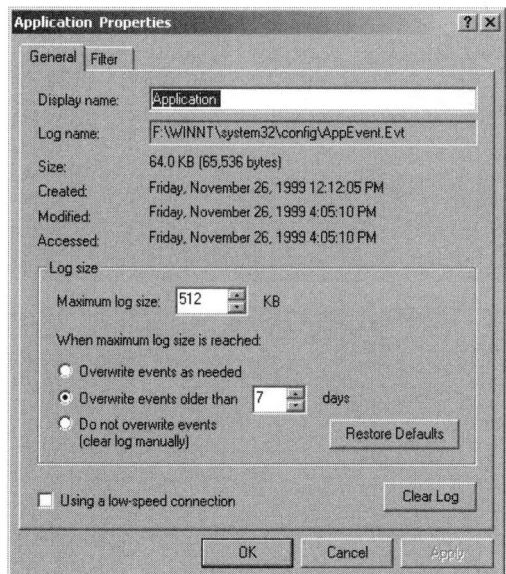

Figure 3-9. *You should configure log settings according to the level of auditing on the system.*

Clearing the Event Logs

When an event log is full, you need to clear it. To do that, complete the following steps:

1. In the Computer Management console, double-click the Event Viewer entry. You should now see a list of event logs.

2. Right-click the event log whose properties you want to set and select Clear All Events from the shortcut menu.

3. Choose Yes to save the log before clearing it. Choose No to continue without saving the log file.

Archiving the Event Logs

On key systems such as domain controllers and application servers, you'll want to keep several months worth of logs. However, it usually isn't practical to set the maximum log size to accommodate this. Instead, you should periodically archive the event logs.

Archive Log Formats

Logs can be archived in three formats:

- Event log format for access in Event Viewer
- Tab-delimited text format, for access in text editors or word processors or import into spreadsheets and databases
- Comma-delimited text format, for import into spreadsheets or databases

When you export log files to a comma-delimited file, each field in the event entry is separated by a comma. The event entries look like this:

```
9/7/99,9:43:24 PM,DNS,Information,None,2,N/A,ZETA,The DNS Server
has started.
```

```
9/7/99,9:40:04 PM,DNS,Error,None,4015,N/A,ZETA,The DNS server has
encountered a critical error from the Directory Service (DS). The
data is the error code.
```

The format for the entries is as follows:

```
Date, Time, Source, Type, Category, Event, User, Computer,
Description.
```

Creating Log Archives in the Event Viewer Format

To create a log archive in the Event Viewer file format, complete the following steps:

1. In the Computer Management console, double-click the Event Viewer entry. You should now see a list of event logs.
2. Right-click the event log you want to archive and select Save Log File As from the shortcut menu.
3. In the Save As dialog box, select a directory and a log filename.
4. In the Save As Type dialog box, Event Log (*.evt) will be the default file type.
5. Choose Save.

 Note If you plan to archive logs regularly, you may want to create an archive directory. This way you can easily locate the log archives. You should also name the log file so that you can easily determine the log file type and the period of the archive. For example, if you're archiving the system log file for January 2000, you may want to use the filename System Log Jan. 2000.

Creating Log Archives in Other Formats

To create a tab- or comma-delimited log archive, follow these steps:

1. In the Computer Management console, double-click on the Event Viewer entry. You should now see a list of event logs.
2. Right-click on the event log you want to archive and select Save Log File As from the shortcut menu.
3. In the Save As dialog box, select a directory and a log filename.

4. Using the Save As Type drop-down list box select the Text or CSV log file format.

5. Choose Save.

Viewing Log Archives

You can view log archives in text format in any text editor or word processor. You should view log archives in the event log format in Event Viewer. You can view log archives in Event Viewer by completing the following steps:

1. In the Computer Management console, right-click the Event Viewer entry. On the shortcut menu, select Open Log File. You should now see the Open dialog box shown in Figure 3-10.

2. Select a directory and a log filename.

3. Choose the log file type and then enter a display name for the log.

4. Enter a display name for the log file.

5. Click Open. The archived log is displayed as a separate view in Event Viewer. Select this view to display the saved events in the log.

Monitoring Server Performance and Activity

Monitoring a server isn't something you should do haphazardly. You need to have a clear plan—a set of goals that you hope to achieve. Let's take a look at the reasons you may want to monitor a server and at the tools you can use to do this.

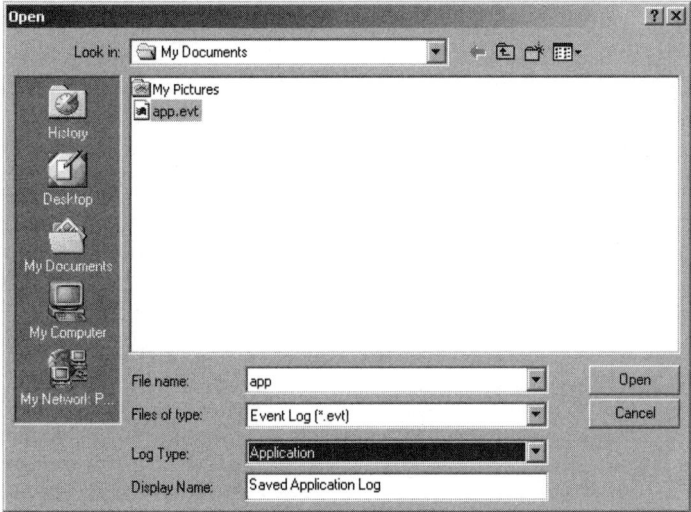

Figure 3-10. *Use the Open dialog box to open the saved event log in a new view.*

Why Monitor Your Server?

Troubleshooting server performance problems is a key reason for monitoring. For example, users may be having problems connecting to the server and you may want to monitor the server to troubleshoot these problems. Here, your goal would be to track down the problem using the available monitoring resources and then to resolve it.

Another common reason for wanting to monitor a server is to improve server performance. You do this by improving disk I/O, reducing CPU usage, and cutting down on the network traffic load on the server. Unfortunately, there are often trade-offs to be made when it comes to resource usage. For example, as the number of users accessing a server grows, you may not be able to reduce the network traffic load, but you may be able to improve server performance through load balancing or by distributing key data files on separate drives.

Getting Ready to Monitor

Before you start monitoring a server, you may want to establish baseline performance metrics for your server. To do this, you measure server performance at various times and under different load conditions. You can then compare the baseline performance with subsequent performance to determine how the server is performing. Performance metrics that are well above the baseline measurements may indicate areas where the server needs to be optimized or reconfigured.

After you establish the baseline metrics, you should formulate a monitoring plan. A comprehensive monitoring plan includes the following steps:

1. Determining which server events should be monitored in order to help you accomplish your goal.
2. Setting filters to reduce the amount of information collected.
3. Configuring monitors and alerts to watch the events.
4. Logging the event data so that it can be analyzed.
5. Analyzing the event data in Performance Monitor.

These procedures are examined later in the chapter. While you should develop a monitoring plan in most cases, there are times when you may not want to go through all these steps to monitor your server. For example, you may want to monitor and analyze activity as it happens rather than logging and analyzing the data later.

Using Performance Monitor

Performance Monitor graphically displays statistics for the set of performance parameters you've selected for display. These performance parameters are referred to as *counters*. You can also update the available counters when you install services and add-ons on the server. For example, when you configure DNS on a server, Performance Monitor is updated with a set of objects and counters for tracking DNS performance.

Performance Monitor creates a graph depicting the various counters you're track-ing. The update interval for this graph is completely configurable but by default is set to one second. As you'll see when you work with Performance Monitor, the tracking information is most valuable when you record the information in a log file and when you configure alerts to send messages when certain events occur or when certain thresholds are reached, such as when a the CPU processor time reaches 99 percent. The sections that follow examine key techniques you'll use to work with performance monitor.

Choosing Counters to Monitor

The Performance Monitor only displays information for counters you're tracking. Dozens of counters are available—and as you add services, you'll find there are even more. These counters are organized into groupings called *performance objects*. For example, all CPU-related counters are associated with the Processor object.

To select which counters you want to monitor, complete the following steps:

1. Select the Performance option on the Administrative Tools menu. This dis-plays the Performance console.

2. Select the System Monitor entry in the left pane, shown in Figure 3-11.

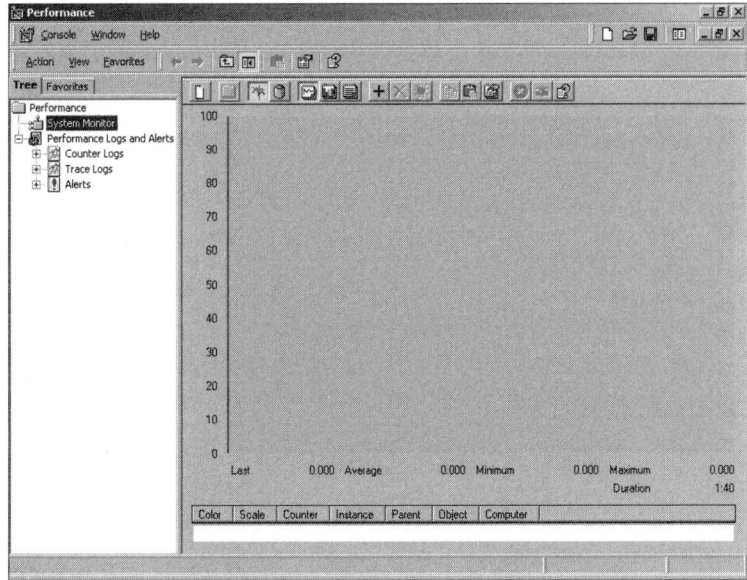

Figure 3-11. *Counters are listed in the lower portion of the Performance Monitor window.*

3. Performance Monitor has several different viewing modes. Make sure you're in View Chart display mode by selecting the View Chart button on the Performance Monitor toolbar.

4. To add counters, select the Add button on the Performance Monitor toolbar. This displays the Add Counters dialog box shown in Figure 3-12. The key fields are

- **Use Local Computer Counters**   Configure performance options for the local computer.

- **Select Counters From Computer**   Enter the Universal Naming Convention (UNC) name of the server you want to work with, such as \\ZETA. Or use the selection list to select the server from a list of computers you have access to over the network.

- **Performance Object**   Select the type of object you want to work with, such as Processor.

 Note   The easiest way to learn what you can track is to explore the objects and counters available in the Add Counters dialog box. Select an object in the Performance Object field, click the Explain button, and then scroll through the list of counters for this object.

- **All Counters**   Select all counters for the current object.

- **Select Counters From List**   Select one or more counters for the current object. For example, you could select % Processor Time and % User Time.

- **All Instances**   Select all counter instances for monitoring.

- **Select Instances From List**   Select one or more counter instances to monitor.

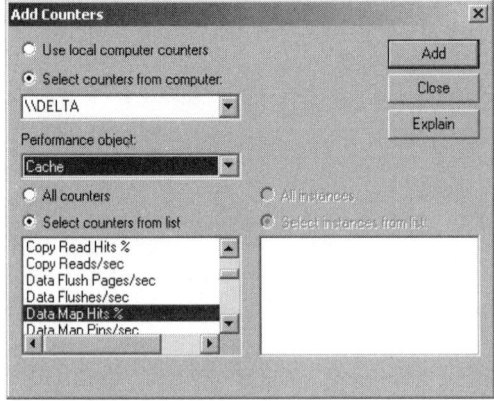

Figure 3-12. *Select counters you want to monitor.*

Tip   Don't try to chart too many counters or counter instances at once. You'll make the display difficult to read and you'll use system resources—namely CPU time and memory—that may affect server responsiveness.

5. When you've selected all the necessary options, click Add to add the counters to the chart. Then repeat this process, as necessary, to add other performance parameters.

6. Click Done when you're finished adding counters.

7. You can delete counters later by clicking on their entry in the lower portion of the Performance window and then clicking Delete.

Using Performance Logs

You can use performance logs to track the performance of a server and you can replay them later. As you set out to work with logs, keep in mind that parameters that you track in log files are recorded separately from parameters that you chart in the Performance window. You can configure log files to update counter data automatically or manually. With automatic logging, a snapshot of key parameters is recorded at specific time intervals, such as every 10 seconds. With manual logging, you determine when snapshots are made. Two types of performance logs are available:

- **Counter Logs**   These logs record performance data on the selected counters when a predetermined update interval has elapsed.

- **Trace Logs**   These logs record performance data whenever their related events occur.

Creating and Managing Performance Logging

To create and manage performance logging, complete the following steps:

1. Access the Performance console by selecting the Performance option on the Administrative Tools menu.

2. Expand the Performance Logs And Alerts node by clicking the plus sign (+) next to it. If you want to configure a counter log, select Counter Logs. Otherwise, select Trace Logs.

3. As shown in Figure 3-13, you should see a list of current logs in the right pane (if any). A green log symbol next to the log name indicates logging is active. A red log symbol indicates logging is stopped.

4. You can create a new log by right-clicking in the right pane and selecting New Log Settings from the shortcut menu. A New Log Settings box appears, asking you to give a name to the new log settings. Type a descriptive name here before continuing.

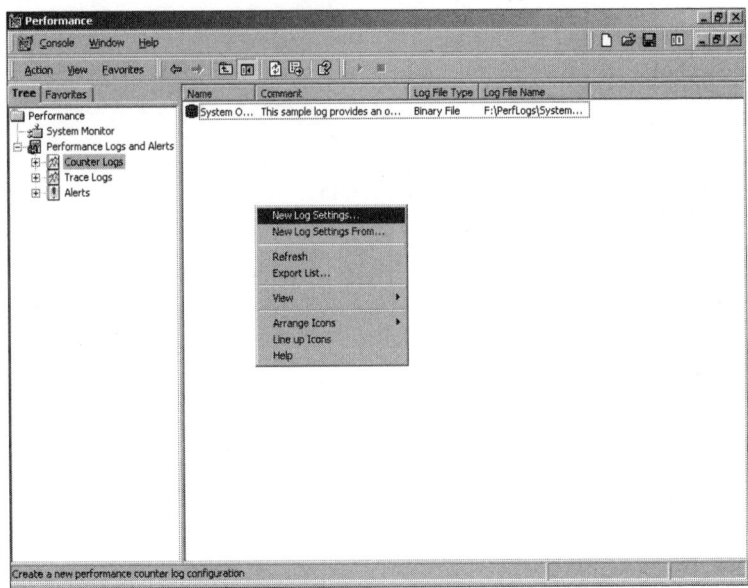

Figure 3-13. *Current performance logs are listed with summary information.*

5. To manage an existing log, right-click its entry in the right pane and then select one of the following options:

- **Start** To activate logging.
- **Stop** To halt logging.
- **Delete** To delete the log.
- **Properties** To display the log properties dialog box.

Creating Counter Logs

Counter logs record performance data on the selected counters at a specific sample interval. For example, you could sample performance data for the CPU every 15 minutes. To create a counter log, complete the following steps:

1. Select Counter Logs in the left pane of the Performance console and then right-click in the right pane to display the shortcut menu. Choose New Log Settings.

2. In the New Log Settings dialog box, type a name for the log, such as System Performance Monitor or Processor Status Monitor. Then click OK.

3. In the General tab, click Add to display the Select Counters dialog box. This dialog box is identical to the Add Counters dialog box shown previously in Figure 3-12.

4. Use the Select Counters dialog box to add counters for logging. Click Close when you're finished.

5. In the Sample Data Every ... field, type in a sample interval and select a time unit in seconds, minutes, hours, or days. The sample interval specifies when new data is collected. For example, if you sample every 15 minutes, the log is updated every 15 minutes.

6. Click the Log Files tab, shown in Figure 3-14, and then specify how the log file should be created using the following fields:

   - **Location** Sets the folder location for the log file.
   - **File Name** Sets the name of the log file.
   - **End File Names With** Sets an automatic suffix for each new file created when you run the counter log. Logs can have a numeric suffix or a suffix in a specific date format.
   - **Start Numbering At** Sets the first serial number for a log that uses an automatic numeric suffix.
   - **Log File Type** Sets the type of log file to create. Use Text File – CSV for a log file with comma-separated entries. Use Text File – TSV for a log file with tab-separated entries. Use Binary File to create a binary file that can be read by Performance Monitor. Use Binary Circular File to create a binary file that overwrites old data with new data when the file reaches a specified size limit.

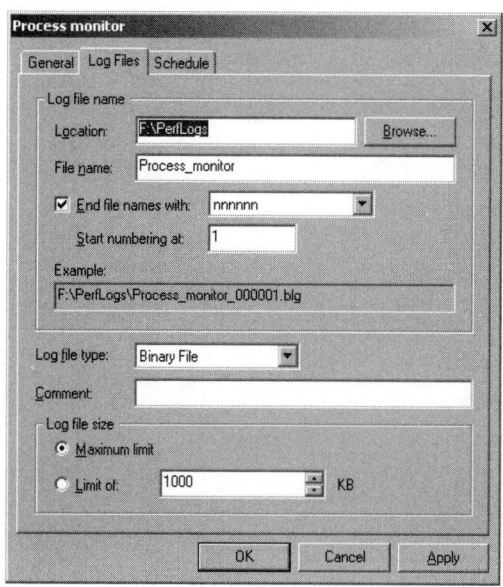

Figure 3-14. *Configure the log file format and usage.*

Tip If you plan to use Performance Monitor to analyze or view the log, use one of the binary file formats.

- **Comment** Sets an optional description of the log, which is displayed in the Comment column.
- **Maximum Limit** Sets no predefined limit on the size of the log file.
- **Limit Of** Sets a specific limit in KB on the size of the log file.

7. Click the Schedule tab, shown in Figure 3-15, and then specify when logging should start and stop.

8. You can configure the logging to start manually or automatically at a specific date. Select the appropriate option and then specify a start date if necessary.

 Tip Log files can grow in size very quickly. If you plan to log data for an extended period, be sure to place the log file on a drive with lots of free space. Remember, the more frequently you update the log file, the higher the drive space and CPU resource usage on the system.

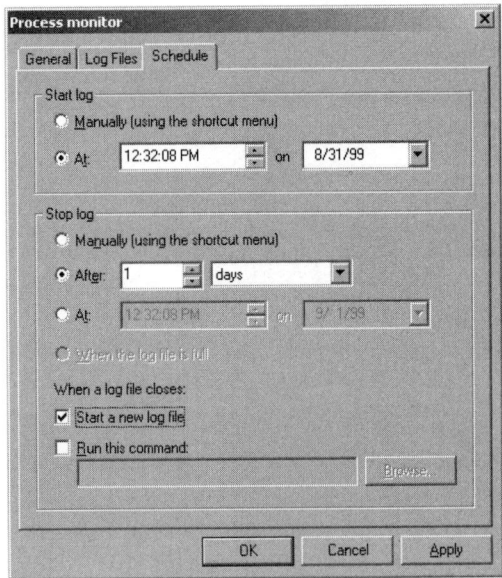

Figure 3-15. *Specify when logging starts and stops.*

9. The log file can be configured to stop

   - Manually
   - After a specified period of time, such as seven days
   - At a specific date and time
   - When the log file is full (if you've set a specific file size limit)

10. Click OK when you've finished setting the logging schedule. The log is then created, and you can manage it as explained in the "Creating and Managing Performance Logging" section of this chapter.

Creating Trace Logs

Trace logs record performance data whenever events for their source providers occur. A source provider is an application or operating system service that has traceable events. On domain controllers you'll find two source providers: the operating system itself and Active Directory:NetLogon. On other servers, the operating system will probably be the only provider available.

To create a trace log, complete the following steps:

1. Select Trace Logs in the left pane of the Performance console and then right-click in the right pane to display the shortcut menu. Choose New, and then select New Log Settings.

2. In the New Log Settings dialog box, type a name for the log, such as Logon Trace or Disk I/O Trace. Then click OK. This opens the dialog box shown in Figure 3-16.

3. If you want to trace operating system events, select the Events Logged By System Provider option button. As shown in Figure 3-16, you can now select system events to trace.

Caution Collecting page faults and file detail events puts a heavy load on the server and causes the log file to grow rapidly. Because of this, you should collect page faults and file details only for a limited amount of time.

4. If you want to trace another provider, select the Nonsystem Providers option button and then click Add. This displays the Add Nonsystem Providers dialog box, which you'll use to select the provider to trace.

5. When you're finished selecting providers and events to trace, click the Log Files tab. You can now configure the trace file as detailed in step 6 of the section of this chapter entitled "Creating Counter Logs." The only change is that the log file types are different. With trace logs, you have two log types:

   - **Sequential Trace File** Writes events to the trace log sequentially up to the maximum file size (if any).
   - **Circular Trace File** Overwrites old data with new data when the file reaches a specified size limit.

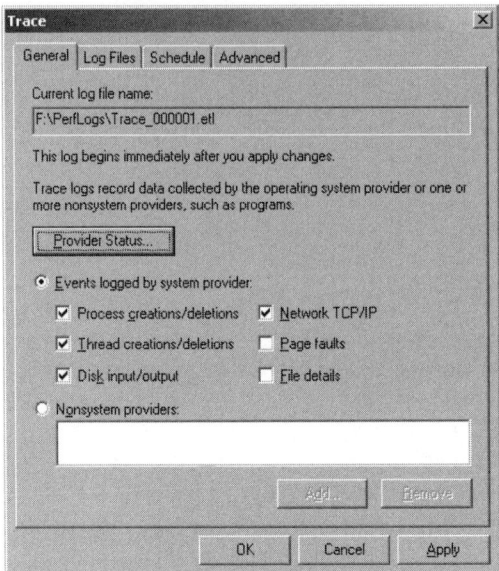

Figure 3-16. *Use the General tab to select the provider to use in the trace.*

6. Choose the Schedule tab and then specify when tracing starts and stops.

7. You can configure the logging to start manually or automatically at a specific date. Select the appropriate option and then specify a start date, if necessary.

8. You can configure the log file to stop manually, after a specified period of time (such as seven days), at a specific date and time, or when the log file is full (if you've set a specific file size limit).

9. When you've finished setting the logging schedule, click OK. The log is then created and can be managed as explained in the section of this chapter entitled "Creating and Managing Performance Logging."

Replaying Performance Logs

When you're troubleshooting problems, you'll often want to log performance data over an extended period of time and analyze the data later. To do this, complete the following steps:

1. Configure automatic logging as described in the "Using Performance Logs" section of this chapter.

2. Load the log file in Performance Monitor when you're ready to analyze the data. To do this, select the View Log File Data button on the Performance Monitor toolbar. This displays the Select Log File dialog box.

3. Use the Look In selection list to access the log directory, and then select the log you want to view. Click Open.

4. Counters you've logged are available for charting. Click the Add button on the toolbar and then select the counters you want to display.

Configuring Alerts for Performance Counters

You can configure alerts to notify you when certain events occur or when certain performance thresholds are reached. You can send these alerts as network messages and as events that are logged in the application event log. You can also configure alerts to start applications and performance logs.

To add alerts in Performance Monitor, complete the following steps:

1. Select Alerts in the left pane of the Performance console, and then right-click in the right pane to display the shortcut menu. Choose New Alert Settings.

2. In the New Alert Settings dialog box, type a name for the alert, such as Processor Alert or Disk I/O Alert. Then click OK. This opens the dialog box shown in Figure 3-17.

3. In the General tab, type an optional description of the alert. Then click Add to display the Select Counters To Log dialog box. This dialog box is identical to the Add Counters dialog box shown previously in Figure 3-12.

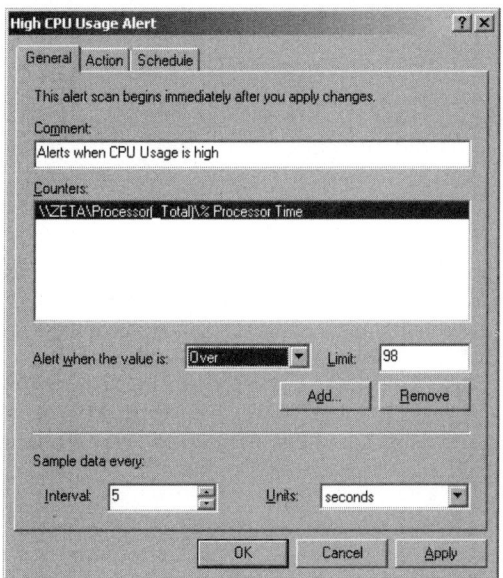

Figure 3-17.   *Use the Alert dialog box to configure counters that trigger alerts.*

4. Use the Select Counters To Log dialog box to add counters that trigger the alert. Click Close when you're finished.

5. In the Counters panel, select the first counter and then use the Alert When The Value Is ... field to set the occasion when an alert for this counter is triggered. Alerts can be triggered when the counter is over or under a specific value. Select Over or Under, and then set the trigger value. The unit of measurement is whatever makes sense for the currently selected counter(s). For example, to alert if processor time is over 98 percent, you would select Over and then type **98** as the limit. Repeat this process to configure other counters you've selected.

6. In the Sample Data Every ... field, type in a sample interval and select a time unit in seconds, minutes, hours, or days. The sample interval specifies when new data is collected. For example, if you sample every 10 minutes, the log is updated every 10 minutes.

 Caution Don't sample too frequently. You'll use system resources and may cause the server to seem unresponsive to user requests.

7. Select the Action tab, shown in Figure 3-18. You can now specify any of the following actions to happen when an alert is triggered:

   • **Log An Entry In The Application Event Log** Creates log entries for alerts.

   • **Send A Network Message To** Sends a network message to the computer specified.

   • **Run This Program** Sets the complete file path of a program or script to run when the alert occurs.

   • **Start Performance Data Log** Sets a counter log to start when an alert occurs.

 Tip You can run any type of executable file, including batch scripts with the .BAT or .CMD extension and Windows scripts with the .VB, .JS, .PL, or .WSC extension. To pass arguments to a script or application, use the options of the Command Line Arguments panel. Normally, arguments are passed as individual strings. However, if you select Single Argument String, the arguments are passed in a comma-separated list within a single string. The Example Command Line Arguments list at the bottom of the tab shows how the arguments would be passed.

8. Choose the Schedule tab and then specify when alerting starts and stops. For example, you could configure the alerts to start on a Friday evening and stop on Monday morning. Then each time an alert occurs during this period, the specified action(s) are executed.

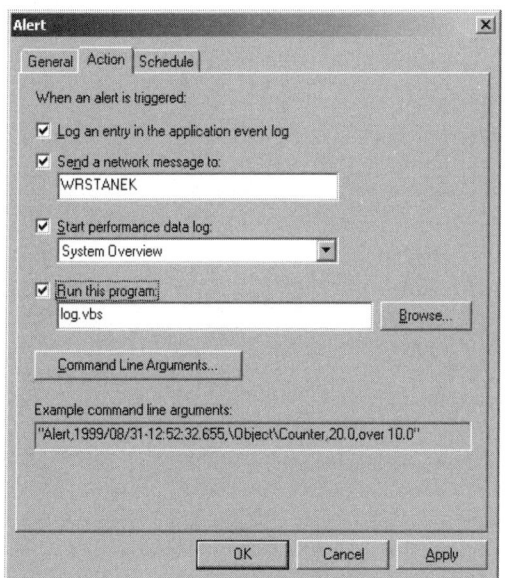

Figure 3-18.   *Set actions that are executed when the alert occurs.*

9. You can configure alerts to start manually or automatically at a specific date. Select the appropriate option and then specify a start date, if necessary.

10. You can configure alerts to stop manually, after a specified period of time, such as seven days, or at a specific date and time.

11. When you've finished setting the alert schedule, click OK. The alert is then created, and you can manage it in much the same way that you manage counter and trace logs.

Chapter 4

Automating Administrative Tasks, Policies, and Procedures

Performing routine tasks day after day, running around policing systems, and walking users through the basics aren't efficient uses of your time. You'd be much more effective if you could automate these chores and focus on more important issues. Well, increasing productivity and allowing you to focus less on mundane matters and more on important ones is what automation is all about.

Microsoft Windows 2000 provides many resources that help you automate administrative tasks, policies, and procedures. This chapter concentrates on three areas:

- Group policy management
- User and computer script management
- Scheduling Tasks

Group Policy Management

Group policies simplify administration by giving administrators central control over privileges, permissions, and capabilities of both users and computers. Through group policies you can

- Create centrally managed directories for special folders, such as Desktop. This is covered in this chapter in the section entitled "Centrally Managing Special Folders."
- Control access to Windows components, system resources, network resources, control panel utilities, the desktop, and the Start menu. This is covered in this chapter in the section entitled "Using Administrative Templates to Set Policies."
- Define user and computer scripts to run at specified times. This is covered in this chapter in the section entitled "User and Computer Script Management."

- Configure policies for account lockout and passwords, auditing, user rights assignment, and security. This is covered in Part II of this book, "Microsoft Windows 2000 Directory Services Administration."

The sections that follow explain how you can work with group policies. The focus is on understanding and applying group policies.

Understanding Group Policies

You can think of a group policy as a set of rules that helps you manage users and computers. Group policies can be applied to multiple domains, to individual domains, to subgroups within a domain, or to individual systems. Policies that apply to individual systems are referred to as *local group policies* and are stored on the local system only. Other group policies are linked as objects in the Active Directory service.

To understand group policies, you need to know a bit about the structure of Active Directory directory service. In Active Directory, logical groupings of domains are called *sites* and subgroups within a domain are called *organizational units*. Thus, your network could have sites called NewYorkMain, CaliforniaMain, and WashingtonMain. Within the WashingtonMain site, you could have domains called SeattleEast, SeattleWest, SeattleNorth, and SeattleSouth. Within the SeattleEast domain, you could have organizational units called Information Services (IS), Engineering, and Sales.

Group policies only apply to systems running Windows 2000. You set policies for Microsoft Windows NT 4.0 systems with the System Policy Editor (poledit.exe). For Microsoft Windows 95 and Microsoft Windows 98, you need to use the System Policy Editor provided with Windows 95 or Windows 98, respectively, and then copy the policy file to the SYSVOL share on a domain controller.

In What Order Are Multiple Policies Applied?

When multiple policies are in place, policies are applied in the following order:

1. Windows NT 4.0 policies (NTConfig.pol)
2. Local group policies
3. Site group policies
4. Domain group policies
5. Organizational unit group policies
6. Child organizational unit group policies

If there are conflicts among the policy settings, the policy settings applied later have precedence and overwrite previously set policy settings. For example, organizational unit policies have precedence over domain group policies. As you might expect, there are exceptions to the precedence rule. These exceptions are discussed later in the section of this chapter entitled "Blocking, Overriding, and Disabling Policies."

When Are Group Policies Applied?

As you'll discover when you start working with group policies, policy settings are divided into two broad categories:

- Those that apply to computers
- Those that apply to users

While computer policies are normally applied during system startup, user policies are normally applied during logon.

The exact sequence of events is often important in troubleshooting system behavior. The events that take place during startup and logon are as follows:

1. The network starts and then Windows 2000 applies computer policies. By default, the computer policies are applied one at a time in the previously specified order. No user interface is displayed while computer policies are being processed.

2. Windows 2000 runs startup scripts. By default, startup scripts are executed one at a time, with each completing or timing out before the next starts. Script execution isn't displayed to the user unless specified.

3. A user presses CTRL+ALT+DEL to log on. After the user is validated, Windows 2000 loads the user profile.

4. Windows 2000 applies user policies. By default, the policies are applied one at a time in the previously specified order. The user interface is displayed while user policies are being processed.

5. Windows 2000 runs logon scripts. Group policy logon scripts are executed simultaneously by default. Script execution isn't displayed to the user unless specified. Scripts in the Netlogon share are run last in a normal command-shell window as in Windows NT 4.0.

6. Windows 2000 displays the start shell interface configured in Group Policy.

Managing Local Group Policies

Each computer running Windows 2000 has one local group policy. You manage local policies on a computer by completing the following steps:

1. Open the Run dialog box by clicking Start and then clicking Run.

2. Type **mmc** in the Open field and then click OK. This opens the Microsoft Management Console (MMC).

3. In MMC, click Console, then click Add/Remove Snap-In. This opens the Add/Remove Snap-In dialog box.

4. On the Standalone tab, click Add.

5. In the Add Snap-In dialog box, click Group Policy, and then click Add. This opens the Select Group Policy Object dialog box.

6. Click Local Computer to edit the local policy on your computer or browse to find the local policy on another computer.

7. Click Finish, and then click Close.

8. Click OK. You can now manage the local policy on the selected computer. For details, see the section of this chapter entitled "Working with Group Policies."

Local group policies are stored in the %SystemRoot%\system32\GroupPolicy folder on each Windows 2000 computer. In this folder you'll find the following subfolders:

• **Adm** Stores administrative template files currently being used. These files end with the .adm file extension. The Adm folder is only on domain controllers.

• **Machine** Stores computer scripts in the Script folder and registry-based policy information for HKEY_LOCAL_MACHINE (HKLM) in the Registry.pol file.

• **User** Stores user scripts in the Script folder and registry-based policy information for HKEY_CURRENT_USER (HKCU) in the Registry.pol file.

 Caution You shouldn't edit these folders and files directly. Instead, you should use the appropriate features of the Group Policy console.

Managing Site, Domain, and Unit Policies

Each site, domain, and organization unit can have one or more group policies. Group policies listed higher in the Group Policy list have a higher precedence than policies listed lower in the list. As stated earlier, group policies set at this level are associated with Active Directory. This ensures that site policies get applied appropriately throughout the related domains and organizational units.

Creating and Editing Site, Domain, and Unit Policies

You create and edit site, domain, and unit policies by completing the following steps:

1. For sites, you start the Group Policy snap-in from the Active Directory Sites And Services console. Open the Active Directory Sites And Services console.

2. For domains and organizational units, you start the Group Policy snap-in from the Active Directory Users And Computers console. Open the Active Directory Users And Computers console.

3. In the console root, right-click the site, domain, or unit on which you want to create or manage a group policy. Then select Properties on the shortcut menu. This opens a properties dialog box.

4. In the properties dialog box, select the Group Policy tab. As Figure 4-1 shows, existing policies are listed in the Group Policy Object Links list.

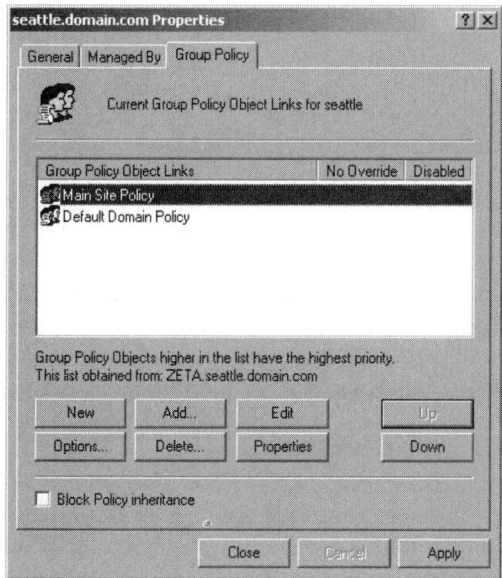

Figure 4-1. *Use the Group Policy tab to create and edit policies.*

5. To create a new policy or edit an existing policy, click New. You can now configure the policy as explained in the section of this chapter entitled "Working with Group Policies."

6. To edit an existing policy, select the policy and then click Edit. You can now edit the policy as explained in the section of this chapter entitled "Working with Group Policies."

7. To change the priority of a policy, use the Up or Down buttons to change its position in the Group Policy Object Links list.

Site, domain, and unit group policies are stored in the %SystemRoot%\SYSVOL\domain\policies folder on domain controllers. In this folder you'll find one subfolder for each policy you've defined on the domain controller. Within these individual policy folders, you'll find

- **Adm** Stores administrative template files currently being used. These files end with the .adm file extension. The Adm folder is only on domain controllers.

- **Machine** Stores computer scripts in the Script folder and registry-based policy information for HKEY_LOCAL_MACHINE (HKLM) in the Registry.pol file.

- **User** Stores user scripts in the Script folder and registry-based policy information for HKEY_CURRENT_USER (HKCU) in the Registry.pol file.

Caution You shouldn't edit these folders and files directly. Instead, you should use the appropriate features of the Group Policy console.

Blocking, Overriding, and Disabling Policies

You can block policy inheritance at the site, domain, and organizational unit level. This means that you could block policies that would otherwise be applied. At the site and domain level, you can also enforce policies that would otherwise be contradicted or blocked. This gives top-level administrators the ability to enforce policies and prevent them from being blocked. Another available option is to disable policies. You can disable a policy partially or entirely without deleting its definition.

You configure these policy options by completing the following steps:

1. Access the Group Policy tab for the site, domain, or organizational unit you want to work with as specified in steps 1–4 of the "Creating and Editing Site, Domain, and Unit Policies" section of this chapter.

2. Select Block Policy Inheritance to prevent the inheritance of higher-level policies (unless those policies have the No Override option set).

3. Use the No Override option to prevent lower-level policies from blocking the policy settings. Set or clear the No Override option by double-clicking in the appropriate column to the right of the group policy entry. A check mark indicates the option is selected.

4. Use the Disabled option to prevent the policy from being used. Set or clear the Disabled option by double-clicking in the appropriate column to the right of the group policy entry. A check mark indicates the option is selected.

 Tip Another way to disable a policy is to block Computer Configuration or User Configuration settings, or both. To do this, click Properties in the Global Policy tab, then set or clear Disable Computer Configuration Settings and Disable User Configuration Settings.

Applying an Existing Policy to a New Location

Any group policy that you've created can be associated with another computer, unit, domain, or site. By associating the policy with another object, you can use the policy settings without having to recreate them.

You apply an existing policy to a new location by completing the following steps:

1. Access the Group Policy tab for the site, domain, or organizational unit you want to work.

2. In the Group Policy tab, click Add. As shown in Figure 4-2, this opens the Add A Group Policy Object Link dialog box.

3. Use the tabs and fields provided to find the group policy you want to apply to the current location. When you find the policy, click OK.

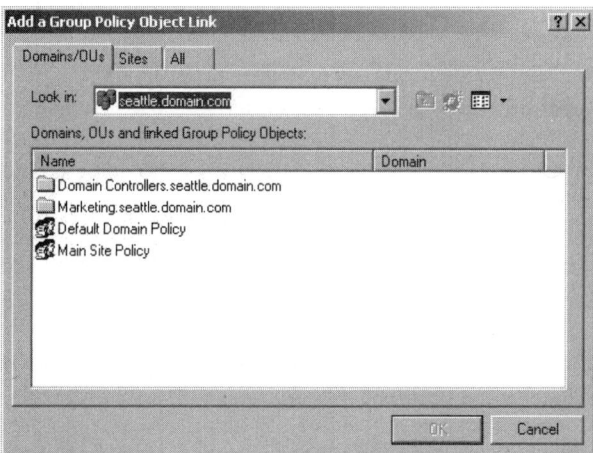

Figure 4-2. *Use the Add A Group Policy Object Link dialog box to link existing policies to new locations without having to recreate the policy definition.*

4. Active Directory creates a link between the group policy object and the site, domain, or unit container you're working with. Now when you edit the policy in any location, you edit the master copy of the object and the changes are reflected globally.

Deleting a Group Policy

You can disable or delete group policies that you don't use. To disable a policy, see the section of this chapter entitled "Blocking, Overriding, and Disabling Policies." To delete a policy, follow these steps:

1. Access the Group Policy tab for the site, domain, or organizational unit you want to work with as specified in steps 1–4 of the section of this chapter entitled "Creating and Editing Site, Domain, and Unit Policies."

2. Select the policy you want to delete and then click Delete.

3. If the policy is linked, you have the option of deleting the link without affecting other containers that use the policy. To do this, in the Delete dialog box select Remove The Link From The List.

4. If the policy is linked, you can also delete the link and the related policy object, which permanently deletes the policy. To do this, select Remove The Link And Delete The Group Policy Object Permanently.

Working with Group Policies

Once you've selected a policy for editing or created a new policy, you use the Group Policy console to work with group policies. Techniques for working with this console are examined in this section.

Getting to Know the Group Policy Console

As Figure 4-3 shows, the Group Policy console has two main nodes:

- **Computer Configuration** Allows you to set policies that should be applied to computers, regardless of who logs on.

- **User Configuration** Allows you to set policies that should be applied to users, regardless of which computer they log on to.

The exact configuration of Computer Configuration and User Configuration depends on the add-ons installed and which type of policy you're creating. Still, you'll usually find that both Computer Configuration and User Configuration have subnodes for

- **Software Settings** Sets policies for software settings and software installation. When you install software, subnodes may be added to Software Settings.

- **Windows Settings** Sets policies for folder redirection, scripts, and security.

- **Administrative Templates** Sets policies for the operating system, Windows components, and programs. Administrative templates are configured through template files. You can add or remove template files whenever you need to.

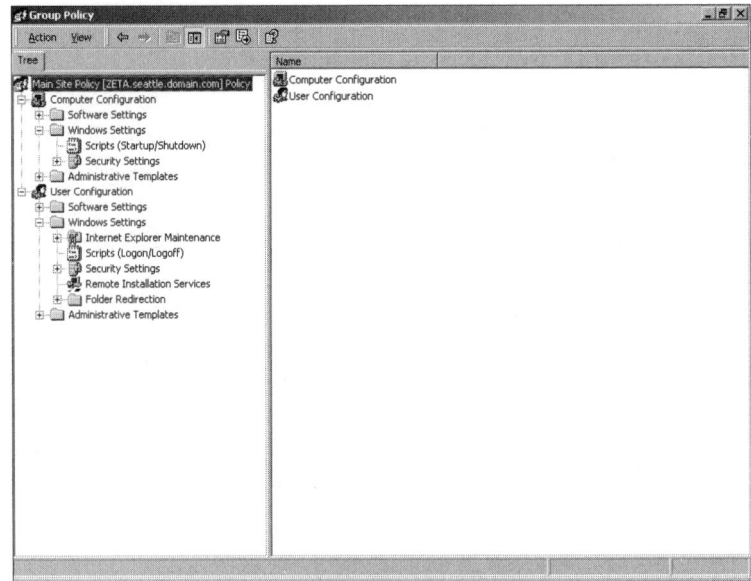

Figure 4-3. *The configuration of the Group Policy console depends on the type of policy you're creating and the add-ons installed.*

Note   A complete discussion of all the available options is beyond the scope of this book. The sections that follow focus on using folder redirection and administrative templates. Scripts are discussed in the section entitled "User and Computer Script Management." Security is covered in Part II of this book, "Microsoft Windows 2000 Directory Services Administration."

Centrally Managing Special Folders

You can centrally manage special folders used by Windows 2000 through folder redirection. You do this by redirecting special folders to a central network location instead of using multiple default locations on each computer. The special folders you can centrally manage are

- Application Data
- Desktop
- Start Menu
- My Documents
- My Pictures

You have two options for redirection. You can redirect a special folder to the same network location for all users or you can designate locations based on user membership in security groups. In either case, you should make sure that the network location you plan to use is available as a network share. See Chapter 13 for details on sharing data on the network.

Redirecting a Special Folder to a Single Location

You redirect a special folder to a single location by completing the following steps:

1. Access the Group Policy console for the site, domain, or organizational unit you want to work with as specified in the section of this chapter entitled "Creating and Editing Site, Domain, and Unit Policies."

2. In the User Configuration node, you'll find Windows Settings. Expand this entry by double-clicking it, and then select Folder Redirection.

3. Right-click the special folder you want to work with, such as Application Data, and then select Properties on the shortcut menu. This opens a properties dialog box similar to the one shown in Figure 4-4.

4. In the Target tab, use the Setting selection list to choose Basic - Redirect Everyone's Folder To The Same Location.

5. Enter the folder path to use in the Target Folder Location field. The folder you select is where all data for the special folder is stored. The folder path should be set to a shared folder that is available on the network through a Universal Naming Convention (UNC) path, such as \\Zeta\UserData. Click Browse to search for the folder in the Browse For Folder dialog box.

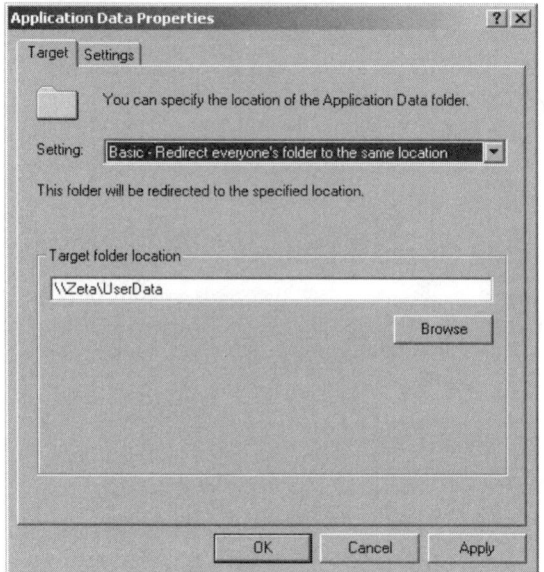

Figure 4-4. *Set options for the redirection using the Application Data Properties dialog box.*

 Tip Normally, user data isn't stored separately. To specify that user data should be placed in subfolders that are specific to the user, add %UserName% to the path. For example, instead of setting the folder path to \\Zeta\UserData, you would use \\Zeta\UserData\ %UserName%.

6. Click the Settings tab, and then configure additional options using the following fields:

  • **Grant The User Exclusive Rights To ...**   Gives users full rights to access their data in the special folder.

  • **Move The Contents Of ... To The New Location**   Moves the data in the special folders from the individual systems on the network to the central folder(s).

7. Click OK to complete the process.

Redirecting a Special Folder Based on Group Membership

You redirect a special folder to a single location by completing the following steps:

1. Access the Group Policy console for the site, domain, or organizational unit you want to work with.

2. In the User Configuration node, you'll find Windows Settings. Expand this entry by double-clicking it, and then select Folder Redirection.

3. Right-click the special folder you want to work with, such as Application Data, and then select Properties on the shortcut menu.

4. In the Target tab, use the Setting selection list to choose Advanced - Specify Locations For Various User Groups. As shown in Figure 4-5, a Security Group Membership panel is added to the properties dialog box.

5. Click Add to display the Specify Group And Location dialog box. Or select an existing group entry and click Edit to modify its settings.

6. In the Security Group Membership field, type the name of the security group for which you want to configure redirection. Click Browse to find a security group to add.

7. In the Target Folder Location field, type the folder path to use. The folder you select is where the related data for the selected group is stored. The folder path should be set to a shared folder that is available on the network through a UNC path, such as \\Zeta\UserData. Click Browse to search for the folder in the Browse For Folder dialog box.

Tip Normally, user data isn't stored separately. To specify that user data should be placed in subfolders that are specific to the user, add %UserName% to the path. For example, instead of setting the folder path to \\Zeta\UserData, you would use \\Zeta\UserData\%UserName%.

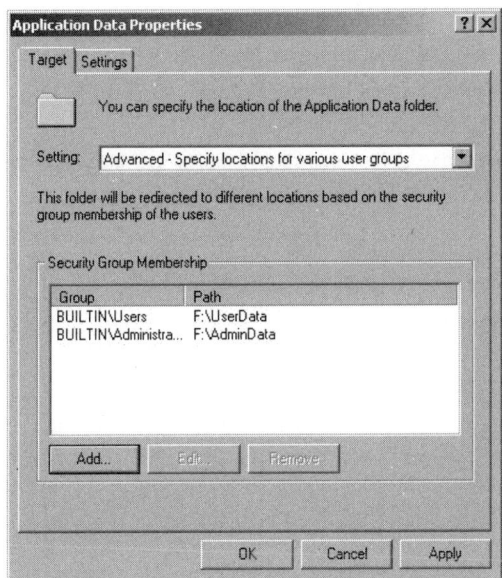

Figure 4-5. *Configure advanced redirection using the Security Group Membership panel.*

8. Click OK. Then repeat steps 5–7 for other groups that you want to configure.

9. When you're done creating group entries, click the Settings tab and then configure additional options using the following fields:

- **Grant The User Exclusive Rights To ...** Gives users full rights to access their data in the special folder.

- **Move The Contents Of ... To The New Location** Moves the data in the special folders from the individual systems on the network to the central folder(s).

Removing Redirection

Sometimes you may want to remove redirection from a particular special folder. You remove redirection by completing the following steps:

1. Access the Folder Redirection subnode in the Group Policy console.

2. Right-click the special folder you want to work with, and then select Properties on the shortcut menu.

3. Select the Settings tab, and then make sure that an appropriate Policy Removal option is selected. Two options are available: Leave The Folder In The New Location When Policy Is Removed or Redirect The Folder Back To The Local Userprofile Location When Policy Is Removed. If you select the first option, files and folders remain in the redirected location even when redirection is removed. If you select the second option, files and folder are moved back to their local userprofile location.

4. If you changed the Policy Removal option, click Apply. Then select the Target tab. Otherwise just select the Target tab.

5. To remove all redirection definitions for the special folder, use the Setting selection list to choose No Administrative Policy Specified.

6. To remove redirection for a particular security group, select the security group in the Security Group Membership panel and then click Remove.

7. Click OK.

Using Administrative Templates to Set Policies

Administrative templates provide easy access to registry-based policy settings that you may want to configure.

Viewing Administrative Templates and Policies

As Figure 4-6 shows, a default set of administrative templates is configured for users and computers in the Group Policy console. You can add or remove administrative templates as well. Any changes you make to policies available through the administrative templates are saved in the registry. Computer configurations are saved in HKEY_LOCAL_MACHINE (HKLM) and user configurations are saved in HKEY_CURRENT_USER (HKCU).

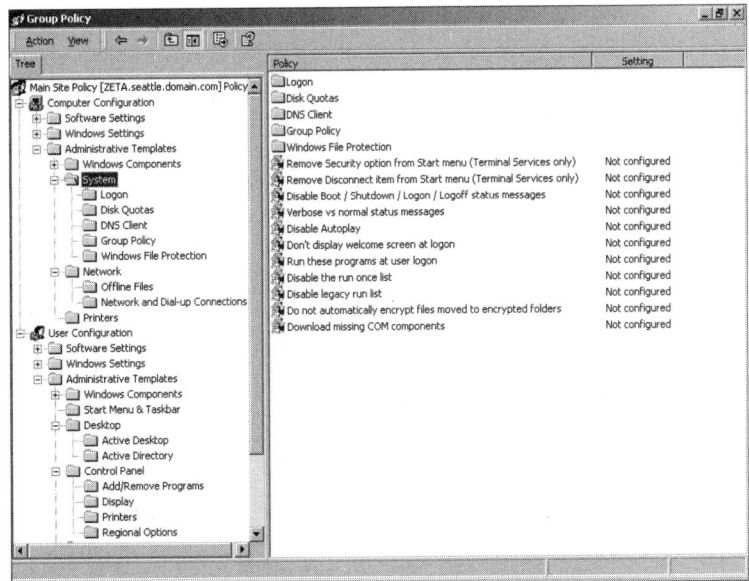

Figure 4-6. *Policies are set through administrative templates.*

You can view the currently configured templates in the Group Policy console's Administrative Templates node. This node contains policies that can be configured for local systems, organizational units, domains, and sites. Different sets of templates are found under Computer Configuration and User Configuration. You can manually add additional templates containing new policies in the Group Policy console and when you install new Windows components.

You set the user interface for the Administrative Templates node in .adm files. These files are formatted as ASCII text and can be edited or created using a standard text editor. When you set policies through the Administrative Templates node, the policy settings are saved in Registry.pol files. Separate Registry.pol files are used for HKEY_LOCAL_MACHINE (HKLM) and HKEY_CURRENT_USER (HKCU).

The best way to get to know what administrative template policies are available is to browse the Administrative Templates nodes in the Group Policy console. As you browse the templates, you'll find that policies are in one of three states:

- **Not Configured**   The policy isn't used and no settings for it are saved in the registry.

- **Enabled**   The policy is actively being enforced and its settings are saved in the registry.

- **Disabled**   The policy is turned off and isn't enforced unless overridden. This setting is saved in the registry.

Enabling, Disabling, and Configuring Policies

You can enable, disable, and configure policies by completing the following steps:

1. Access the Group Policy console for the site, domain, or organizational unit you want to work with.

2. Access the Administrative Templates folder in the Computer Configuration or User Configuration node, whichever is appropriate for the type of policy you want to set.

3. In the left pane, click the subfolder containing the policies you want to work with. The related policies are then displayed in the right pane.

4. Double-click or right-click a policy and choose Properties to display its related properties dialog box.

5. Click the Explain tab to see a description of the policy. The description is only available if one is defined in the related .adm file.

6. To set the policy's state, click the Policy tab and then use the radio buttons provided to change the state of the policy:

   - **Not Configured**   The policy is not configured.
   - **Enabled**   The policy is enabled.
   - **Disabled**   The policy is disabled.

 Note   Computer policies have precedence in Windows 2000. So, if there is a conflict between a computer policy setting and a user policy setting, the computer policy is the one that is enforced.

7. If you enabled the policy, set any additional parameters specified on the Policy tab, and then click Apply.

8. Use the Previous Policy and Next Policy buttons to manage other policies in the current folder. Then configure them in the same way.

9. Click OK when you're finished managing policies.

Adding or Removing Templates

You can add or remove template folders in the Group Policy console. To do this, complete the following steps:

1. Access the Group Policy console for the site, domain, or organizational unit you want to work with.

2. Right-click the Administrative Templates folder in the Computer Configuration or User Configuration node, whichever is appropriate for the type of template you want to add or remove. This displays the Add/Remove Templates dialog box shown in Figure 4-7.

3. To add new templates, click Add. Then, in the Policy Templates dialog box, click the template you want to add and click Open.

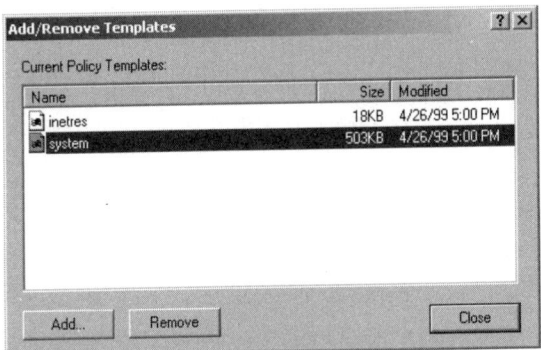

Figure 4-7. *You can use the Add/Remove Templates dialog box to add more templates or remove existing ones.*

4. To remove an existing template, select the template to remove, and then click Remove.

5. When you're finished adding and removing templates, click Close.

User and Computer Script Management

With Windows 2000 you can configure four types of scripts:

- **Computer Startup** Executed during startup.
- **Computer Shutdown** Executed prior to shutdown.
- **User Logon** Executed when a user logs on.
- **User Logoff** Executed when a user logs off.

You can write scripts as command-shell batch scripts ending with the .BAT or .CMD extension or as scripts that use the Windows Script Host (WSH). WSH is a new feature of Windows 2000 that lets you use scripts written in a scripting language, such as VBScript, without the need to insert the script into a Web page. To provide a multipurpose scripting environment, WSH relies on scripting engines. A scripting engine is the component that defines the core syntax and structure of a particular scripting language. Windows 2000 ships with scripting engines for VBScript and JScript. Other scripting engines are also available.

Assigning Computer Startup and Shutdown Scripts

Computer startup and shutdown scripts are assigned as part of a group policy. In this way, all computers that are members of the site, domain, and/or organizational unit execute scripts automatically when they're booted or shut down.

Note You can also assign computer startup scripts as scheduled tasks. You schedule tasks using the Task Scheduler Wizard. See the "Scheduling Tasks" section of this chapter for details.

To assign a computer startup or shutdown script, follow these steps:

1. For easy management, copy the scripts you want to use to the Computer\ Scripts\Startup or Computer\Scripts\Shutdown folder for the related policy. Policies are stored in the %SystemRoot%\SYSVOL\domain\policies folder on domain controllers.

2. Access the Group Policy console for the site, domain, or organizational unit you want to work with.

3. In the Computer Configuration node, double-click the Windows Settings folder. Then click Scripts.

4. To work with startup scripts, right-click Startup and then select Properties. Or right-click Shutdown and then select Properties to work with Shutdown scripts. This opens a dialog box similar to the one shown in Figure 4-8.

5. Click Show Files. If you copied the computer script to the correct location in the policies folder, you should see the script.

6. Click Add to assign a script. This opens the Add A Script dialog box. In the Script Name field, type the name of the script you copied to the Computer\ Scripts\Startup or the Computer\Scripts\Shutdown folder for the related policy. In the Script Parameter field, enter any command-line arguments to pass to the command-line script or parameters to pass to the scripting host for a WSH script. Repeat this step to add other scripts.

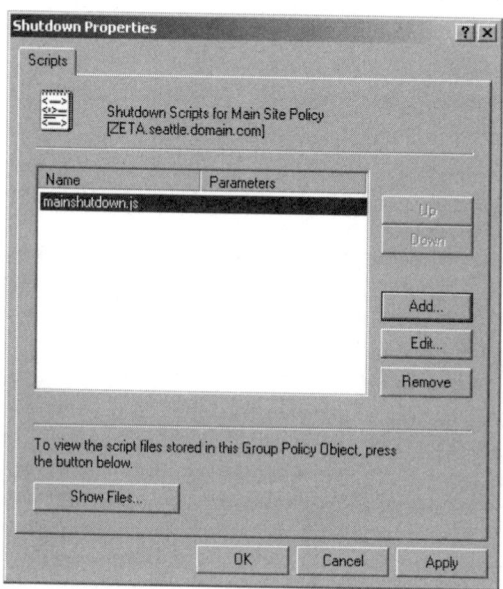

Figure 4-8. *Add, edit, and remove computer scripts using the Shutdown Properties dialog box.*

7. During startup or shutdown, scripts are executed in the order in which they're listed in the properties dialog box. Use the Up or Down buttons to reposition scripts as necessary.

8. If you want to edit the script name or parameters later, select the script in the Script For list and then click Edit.

9. To delete a script, select the script in the Script For list, and then click Remove.

Assigning User Logon and Logoff Scripts

User scripts can be assigned in one of three ways:

- You can assign logon and logoff scripts as part of a group policy. In this way, all users that are members of the site, domain, and/or organizational unit execute scripts automatically when they log on or log off.

- You can also assign logon scripts individually through Active Directory Users And Computers console. In this way, you can assign each user or group a separate logon script. See Chapter 9 for details.

- You can also assign individual logon scripts as scheduled tasks. You schedule tasks using the Task Scheduler Wizard. See the "Scheduling Tasks" section of this chapter for details.

To assign a group policy user script, complete the following steps:

1. For easy management, copy the scripts you want to use to the User\Scripts\Logon or the User\Scripts\Logoff folder for the related policy. Policies are stored in the %SystemRoot%\SYSVOL\domain\policies folder on domain controllers.

2. Access the Group Policy console for the site, domain, or organizational unit you want to work with.

3. Double-click the Windows Settings folder in the User Configuration node. Then click Scripts.

4. To work with logon scripts, right-click Logon and then select Properties. Or right-click Logoff and then select Properties to work with Logoff scripts. This opens a dialog box similar to the one shown in Figure 4-9.

5. Click Show Files. If you copied the user script to the correct location in the policies folder, you should see the script.

6. Click Add to assign a script. This opens the Add A Script dialog box. In the Script Name field, type the name of the script you copied to the User\Scripts\Logon or the User\Scripts\Logoff folder for the related policy. In the Script Parameter field, enter any command-line arguments to pass to the command-line script or parameters to pass to the scripting host for a WSH script. Repeat this step to add other scripts.

7. During logon or logoff, scripts are executed in the order in which they're listed in the properties dialog box. Use the Up or Down buttons to reposition scripts as necessary.

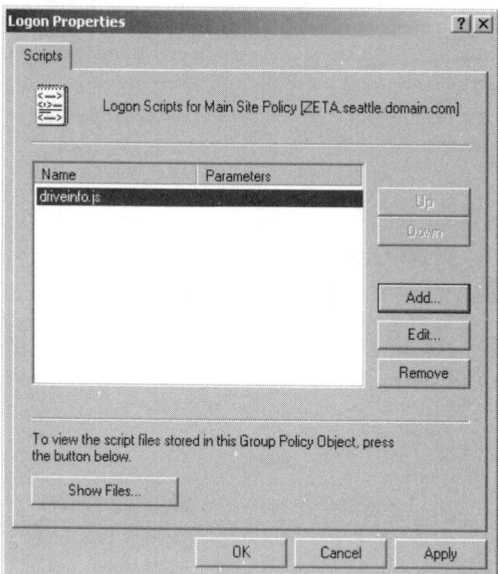

Figure 4-9. *Add, edit, and remove user scripts using the Logon Properties dialog box.*

8. If you want to edit the script name or parameters later, select the script in the Script For list and then click Edit.

9. To delete a script, select the script in the Script For list, and then click Remove.

Scheduling Tasks

When you manage systems, you'll often want to perform tasks like updates or maintenance during nonbusiness hours. This way, you don't affect productivity and workflow. But who wants to come in at 3 A.M. on a Monday morning? Fortunately, using the Task Scheduler service you can schedule one-time or recurring tasks to run automatically at any hour of the day or night.

You automate tasks by running command-shell scripts, Windows Script Host scripts, or applications that execute the necessary commands for you. For example, if you wanted to back up the system drive every weekday at midnight, you could create a script that runs backups for you and records progress and success/failure in a log file.

Utilities for Scheduling Tasks

In Windows 2000, you can schedule tasks on local and remote systems using the Task Scheduler Wizard or the command-line AT scheduler. Each utility has its advantages and disadvantages.

Task Scheduler Wizard provides a point-and-click interface to task assignment. This makes it easy to quickly configure tasks without having to worry about syntax issues. The disadvantage is that you don't have a central location that you can use to check for scheduled tasks throughout the enterprise, and you have to access the wizard separately on each individual system that you want to configure.

The command-line AT scheduler, on the other hand, doesn't have a friendly point-and-click interface. This means you'll have to learn the necessary command syntax and type in commands. The advantage to AT is that you can designate a single server as a task scheduler and you can view and set tasks throughout the enterprise on this single server.

Preparing to Schedule Tasks

Task Scheduler logs on as the LocalSystem account by default. This account usually doesn't have adequate permissions to perform administrative tasks. Because of this, you should configure Task Scheduler to use a specific user account that has adequate user privileges and access rights to run the tasks you want to schedule. You should also make sure that the Task Scheduler service is configured to start automatically on all the systems on which you want to schedule tasks. Set the Task Scheduler startup and logon account as specified in the sections of Chapter 3 entitled "Configuring Service Startup" and "Configuring Service Logon."

A script should configure whatever user settings are necessary. This ensures that everything the script does is under its control and that domain user settings, such as drive mappings, are available as necessary.

Scheduling Tasks with Task Scheduler

You can use Task Scheduler to schedule tasks on the local or remote system to which you're currently connected. You access the Task Scheduler Wizard and currently scheduled tasks through the Scheduled Tasks folder.

Accessing the Scheduled Tasks Folder

You can access the Scheduled Tasks folder on a local system with either of the following techniques:

- Start Microsoft Explorer, double-click Control Panel, and then click Scheduled Tasks.
- Click Start, click Settings, click Control Panel, and then double-click Scheduled Tasks.

You can access the Scheduled Tasks folder on a remote system by completing the following tasks:

1. Start Explorer and then use the My Network Places node to navigate to the computer you want to work with.
2. Double-click the computer's icon and then double-click Scheduled Tasks.

Viewing and Managing Existing Tasks

As Figure 4-10 shows, entries in the Scheduled Tasks folder show currently scheduled tasks. You can work with entries in the Scheduled Tasks folder by completing the following steps:

1. Double-click Add Scheduled Task to start the Task Scheduler Wizard.

2. Double-click an existing task entry to view or change its properties. You can set advanced options through the Settings tab.

3. Select a task entry and press Delete to delete the task.

Creating Tasks with the Task Scheduler Wizard

To schedule a task with the Task Scheduler Wizard, follow these steps:

1. Start the Task Scheduler Wizard by double-clicking Add Scheduled Task in the Scheduled Tasks folder. Read the welcome dialog box and then click Next.

2. Using the dialog box shown in Figure 4-11, select a program to schedule. The dialog box shows key applications registered on the system, such as Disk Cleanup and Synchronize. The dialog box doesn't show available scripts, however. Click Browse to open the Select Program To Schedule dialog box. Use the dialog box to find a command-shell or WSH script you want to run.

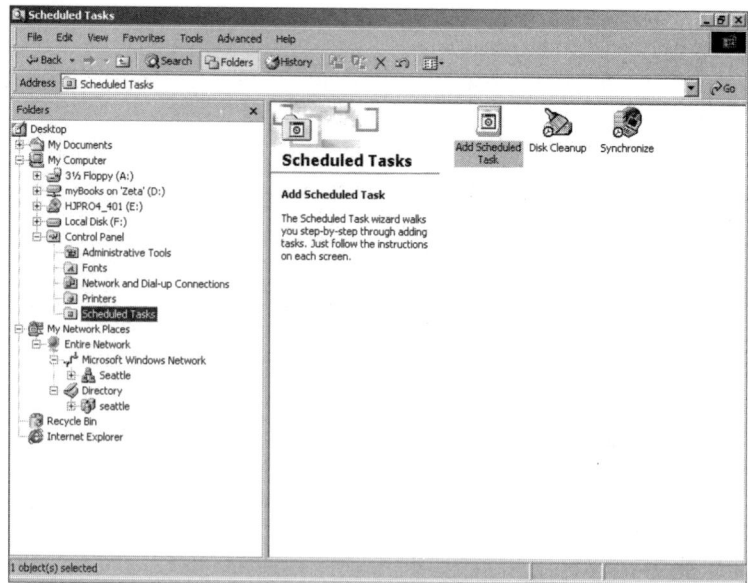

Figure 4-10. *Existing tasks are available in the Scheduled Tasks folder. Click Add Scheduled Task to start the Task Scheduler Wizard.*

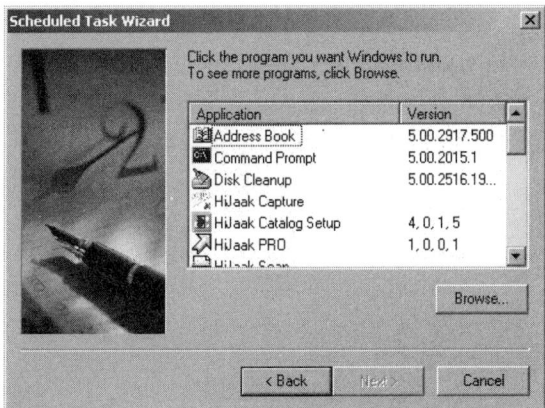

Figure 4-11. *Select a program to run. Click Browse to find scripts and other applications.*

3. Type a name for the task, as shown in Figure 4-12. The name should be short but descriptive so you can quickly determine what the task does.

4. Select a run schedule for the task. Tasks can be scheduled to run periodically (daily, weekly, or monthly), or when a specific event occurs, such as when the computer starts or when the task's user logs on.

5. Click Next and then select a date and time to run the scheduled task. The next dialog box you see depends on when the task is scheduled to run.

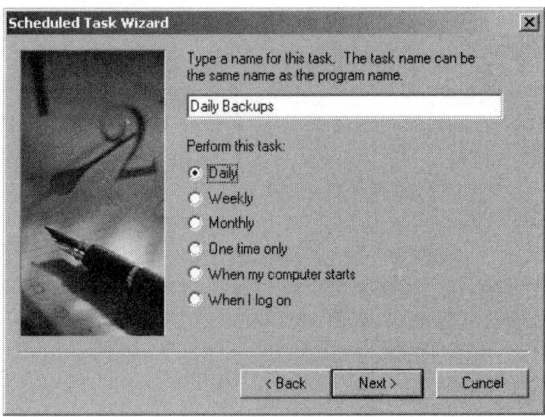

Figure 4-12. *Type a name for the task, and then select a run schedule.*

Figure 4-13. *Configuring a daily scheduled task.*

6. If you've selected a daily running task, the date and time dialog box appears as shown in Figure 4-13. Set a start time and date. Daily scheduled tasks can be configured to run

- **Every Day**   Seven days a week.
- **Weekdays**   Monday through Friday only.
- **Every ... Days**   Every 2, 3, ... N days.

7. If you've selected a weekly running task, the date and time dialog box appears as shown in Figure 4-14. Configure the task using these fields:

- **Start Time**   Sets the start time of the task.
- **Every ... Weeks**   Allows you to run the task every week, every 2 weeks, or every N weeks.

Figure 4-14. *Configuring a weekly scheduled task.*

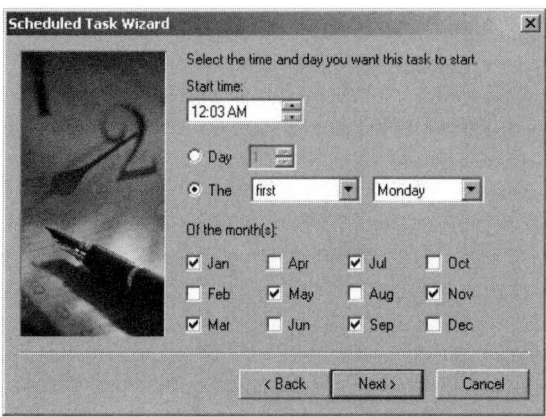

Figure 4-15. *Configuring a monthly scheduled task.*

- **Select The Day(s) Of The Week Below**   Sets the day(s) of the week when the task runs, such as on Monday or on Monday and Friday.

8. If you've selected a monthly running task, the date and time dialog box appears as shown in Figure 4-15. Configure the task using these fields:

   - **Start Time**   Sets the start time of the task.

   - **Day**   Sets the day of the month the task runs. For example, if you select 5, the task runs on the fifth day of the month.

   - **The ... Day**   Sets task to run on the Nth occurrence of a day in a month, such as the second Monday or the third Tuesday of every month.

   - **Of The Month(s)**   These check boxes let you select which months the task runs on.

9. If you've selected One Time Only for running the task, the date and time dialog box appears as shown in Figure 4-16. Set the start time and start date.

10. With tasks that run when the computer starts or when the task's user logs on, you don't have to set the start date and time. The task runs automatically when the startup or logon event occurs.

Tip   If you want to configure a startup task for a specific user through the wizard, you'll need to log on as that user and then run the wizard.

11. After you've configured a start date and time, click Next to continue. Then type a username and password that can be used when running the scheduled task. This username must have appropriate permissions and privileges to run the scheduled task.

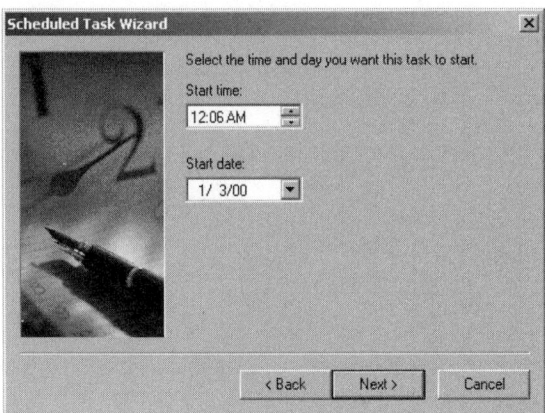

Figure 4-16. *Configuring a one time only scheduled task.*

12. The final wizard dialog box provides a summary of the task you're scheduling. Click Finish to complete the scheduling process. If an error occurs when you create the task, you'll see an error prompt. Click OK. The task should still be created. Afterward, in Explorer double-click the task to correct the problem in the related properties dialog box.

Scheduling Tasks with the At Utility

You can also control the Windows 2000 Task Scheduler service with the At utility. With At you can schedule tasks anywhere on the network and you don't have to log on to remote systems. You can set tasks to run once or periodically at a specific time.

Using the At Utility

To schedule tasks with At, you should be a member of the local Administrators group. Tasks are scheduled using a 24-hour clock where 12:00 is noon and 00:00 is midnight. The At utility doesn't automatically load the command interpreter before running built-in command-line utilities, such as DEL, COPY, or MOVE. You'll need to explicitly load cmd.exe at the beginning of a command. For example, if you wanted to copy *c:\mydata*.** to *e:\backups\mydata*, you would need to enter the following command:

```
AT 00:00 /every:M,T,W,Th,F   cmd /c copy /Q c:\mydata\*.*
e:\backups\mydata
```

When you work with programs and utilities that have separate executables, you don't have to start an instance of the command interpreter. You can work with the executable directly. Still, the executable must be in a directory accessible along the command path (the %PATH% environment variable). Here's how you could schedule a backup script to run every other day at 1 A.M.:

```
AT 01:00 /every:1,3,5,7,9,11,13,15,17,19,21,23,25,27,29,31
backup.js
```

As you can see, when you use numeric dates you can use any value in the range 1–31. You schedule tasks to run relative to the current date as well. To do this, specify only a start time and not a run date. For example, to start a cleanup script at 3 A.M., you could use the following command:

```
AT 03:00 cleanup.js
```

You can also schedule tasks to run on the next occurrence of a day. For example, if today is Tuesday and you want the task to run on Friday, you could use the following command:

```
AT 08:10 /next:F update.vbs
```

Normally, scheduled tasks run as background processes. You can, however, set tasks to run interactively. To do this, use the /interactive switch, such as:

```
AT 03:00 /interactive /every:T,Th backup.vbs
```

Scheduling Tasks on Remote Systems

The AT command makes it easy to schedule tasks to run on remote systems. Simply type the UNC name of the computer before you specify other parameters. For example, if you wanted to schedule a task to run on a computer called PLUTO, you could type the following command at the command line on your system:

```
AT \\PLUTO 08:10 /next:F update.vbs
```

You could also use the Internet Protocol (IP) address of the computer, such as:

```
AT \\192.51.62.8 09:30 /every:M,W,F cleanup.js
```

Only use this option if the IP address is static.

Scheduling tasks on remote systems assumes that

1. You've configured the Task Scheduler service on PLUTO to use a logon with appropriate permissions.
2. The Task Scheduler service is running.
3. The scripts are located in directories that can be found along the path set for the service logon account.

Viewing Scheduled Tasks

You can view scheduled tasks on local and remote systems. On a local system, type **AT** on a line by itself and press Enter.

On a remote system, type **AT** followed by the UNC name of the system you want to examine:

```
AT \\PLUTO
```

When you view tasks, the output you get is similar to the following:

```
Status    ID      Day                Time           Command Line

          1       Each M W F         3:00 AM        backup.vbs

          2       Each T Th          5:00 AM        cleanup.js

          3       Each Su            8:00 AM        update.js
```

The output tells you a lot about the scheduled tasks. You can determine

- **Status** Shows the status of each task. A blank entry indicates a status of OK. Otherwise, you'll see an error message, such as ERROR.

- **ID** Shows the unique identifier for each task.

- **Day** Shows when the task is scheduled to run. Recurring tasks begin with the keyword Each, such as Each M for every Monday. One-time tasks begin with the keyword Next, such as Next 3 for the next time it's the third day of the month.

- **Time** Shows the time the command is scheduled to run. Note that the time is displayed with an A.M. or P.M. indicator rather than the 24-hour clock used for scheduling tasks.

- **Command Line** Shows the command or executable run at the scheduled time.

You can use the status ID to display individual tasks, such as:

```
AT 2
```

Or

```
AT \\zeta 2
```

Deleting Tasks

You can use the ID number to delete tasks as well, or you can cancel all scheduled tasks. You delete a specific task as follows:

```
AT 2 /delete
```

Or

```
AT \\zeta 2 /delete
```

You cancel all tasks by typing the */delete* switch without a task ID, such as:

```
AT /delete
```

Or

```
AT \\zeta /delete
```

Part II
Microsoft Windows 2000 Directory Services Administration

In this part you'll find essential tasks for managing Microsoft Windows 2000 Directory services. Chapter 5 introduces Active Directory directory service. Chapter 6 explores core Active Directory administration tasks. Chapter 7 provides insight into using system accounts, built-in groups, user rights, built-in capabilities, and implicit groups. Creating user and group accounts is covered in Chapter 8. A logical follow-up for managing existing user and group accounts is covered in Chapter 9.

Chapter 5

Using Active
Directory Service

Active Directory is an extensible and scalable directory service that enables you
to efficiently manage network resources. As an administrator, you'll need to be
very familiar with how Active Directory technology works, and that's exactly what
this chapter is about. If you haven't worked with Active Directory technology
before, one thing you'll note immediately is that the technology is fairly advanced
and has many features. To help manage this complex technology, I'll start with
an overview of Active Directory and then explore its components.

Introducing Active Directory Service

Active Directory directory service is the heart of Microsoft Windows 2000. Just
about every administrative task you'll perform will affect Active Directory in some
way. Active Directory technology is based on standard Internet protocols and has
a design that helps you clearly define the structure of your network.

Active Directory and DNS

Active Directory uses the Domain Name System (DNS). DNS is a standard Internet
service that organizes groups of computers into domains. Unlike Windows NT
4.0 domains that have a flat structure, DNS domains are organized into a hierarchical structure. The DNS domain hierarchy is defined on an Internet-wide basis
and the different levels within the hierarchy identify computers, organizational
domains, and top-level domains. DNS is also used to map host names, such as
microsoft.com, to numeric Transmission Control Protocol/Internet Protocol (TCP/
IP) addresses, such as 192.168.19.2. Through DNS an Active Directory domain
hierarchy can also be defined on an Internet-wide basis, or the domain hierarchy can be separate and private.

When you refer to computer resources in this type of domain, you use the fully
qualified host name, such as zeta.microsoft.com. Here, zeta represents the name of
an individual computer, webatwork represents the organizational domain and com
is the top-level domain. Top-level domains are at the root of the DNS hierarchy and
are therefore also called *root domains.* These domains are organized geographically,
by using two-letter country codes, such as CA for Canada; by organization type, such
as *com* for commercial organizations; and by function, such as *shop* for online stores.

Normal domains, such as microsoft.com, are also referred to as *parent domains*. They have this name because they're the parents of an organizational structure. Parent domains can be divided into subdomains, which can be used for different offices, divisions, or geographic locations. For example, the fully qualified host name for a computer at Microsoft's Seattle office could be designated as jacob.seattle.microsoft.com. Here, jacob is the computer name, seattle is the subdomain, and microsoft.com is the parent domain. Another term for a subdomain is a *child domain*.

As you can see, DNS is an integral part of Active Directory technology—so much so, in fact, that you must configure DNS on the network before you can install Active Directory. Working with DNS is covered in Chapter 19. Once you configure DNS, you can install Active Directory by running the Active Directory Installation Wizard (click Start, click Run, type **dcpromo** in the Open field, and then click OK). If there isn't an existing domain, the wizard helps you create a domain and configure Active Directory in a new domain. The wizard can also help you add child domains to existing domain structures.

 Note In the rest of this chapter I'll often use the terms *directory* and *domains* to refer to Active Directory and Active Directory domains, respectively. The exception is when I need to distinguish Active Directory structures from DNS or Windows NT structures.

Getting Started with Active Directory

Active Directory directory service provides both logical and physical structures for network components. Logical structures are

- **Domains**   A group of computers that share a common directory database.
- **Domain trees**   One or more domains that share a contiguous namespace.
- **Domain forests**   One or more domain trees that share common directory information.
- **Organization units**   A subgroup of domains that often mirrors the business or functional structure of the company.

Physical structures are

- **Subnets**   A network group with a specific IP address range and network mask.
- **Sites**   One or more subnets; they're used to configure directory access and replication.

Working with Domain Structures

Logical structures help you organize directory objects and manage network accounts and shared resources. Logical structures include domain forests, domain trees, domains, and organizational units. Sites and subnets, on the other hand, are physical structures that help you map the physical network structure. Physical structures serve to facilitate network communication and to set physical boundaries around network resources.

Understanding Domains

An Active Directory domain is simply a group of computers that share a common directory database. Active Directory domain names must be unique. For example, you can't have two microsoft.com domains, but you could have a microsoft.com parent domain with seattle.microsoft.com and ny.microsoft.com child domains. If the domain is part of a private network, the name assigned to a new domain must not conflict with any existing domain name on the private network. If the domain is part of the global Internet, the name assigned to a new domain must not conflict with any existing domain name throughout the Internet. To ensure uniqueness on the Internet, you must register the parent domain name before using it. Domain registration can be handled through InterNIC (http://www.internic.net) or any designated registrar.

Each domain has its own security policies and trust relationships with other domains. Domains can also span more than one physical location, which means a domain could consist of multiple sites and those sites could have multiple subnets. Within a domain's directory database, you'll find objects defining accounts for users, groups, and computers as well as shared resources, such as printers and folders.

Note   User and group accounts are discussed in Chapter 7. Computer accounts and the various types of computers used in Windows 2000 domains are discussed in "Working with Active Directory Domains" in this chapter.

Understanding Domain Forests and Domain Trees

Each Active Directory domain has a DNS domain name, such as microsoft.com. When one or more domains share the same directory data, they are referred to as a *forest*. The domain names within this forest can be *discontiguous* or *contiguous* in the DNS naming hierarchy.

When domains have a contiguous naming structure, they're said to be in the same domain tree. An example of a domain tree is shown in Figure 5-1. In this example, the root domain msnbc.com has two child domains—seattle.msnbc.com and ny.msnbc.com. These domains in turn have subdomains. All the domains are part of the same tree because they have the same root domain.

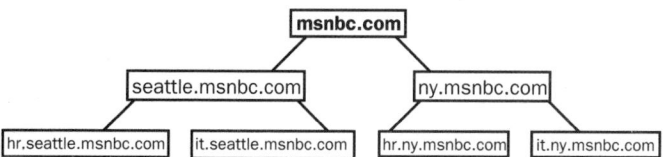

Figure 5-1. *Domains in the same tree share a contiguous naming structure.*

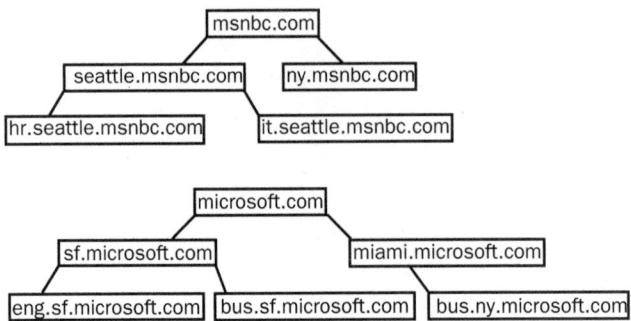

Figure 5-2. *Multiple trees in a forest have discontiguous naming structures.*

If the domains in a forest have discontiguous DNS names, they form separate domain trees within the forest. As shown in Figure 5-2, a domain forest can have one or more domain trees. In this example, the msnbc.com and microsoft.com domains form the roots of separate domain trees in the same forest.

You access domain structures in Active Directory Domains And Trusts, which is shown in Figure 5-3. Active Directory Domains And Trusts is a snap-in for the Microsoft Management Console (MMC) and can also be accessed on the Administrative Tools menu. You'll find separate entries for each root domain. In the figure, the active domain is microsoft.com.

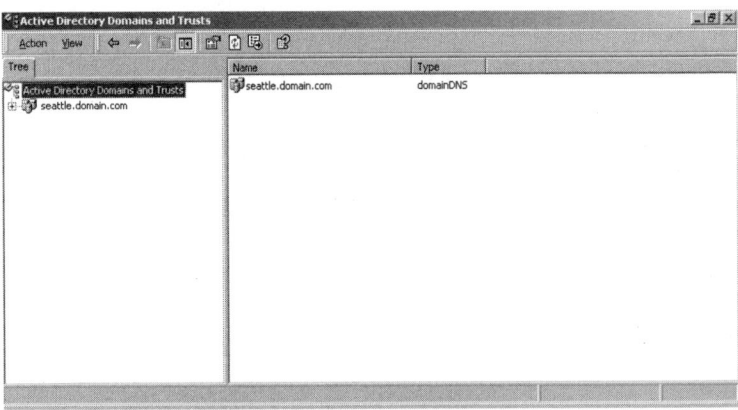

Figure 5-3. *Use Active Directory Domains And Trusts to work with domains, domain trees, and domain forests.*

Understanding Organizational Units

Organizational units are subgroups within domains that often mirror an organization's functional or business structure. You can also think of organizational units as logical containers into which you can place accounts, shared resources, and other organizational units. For example, you could create organizational units named HumanResources, IT, Engineering, and Marketing for the microsoft.com domain. You could later expand this scheme to include child units. Child organizational units for Marketing could include OnlineSales, ChannelSales, and PrintSales.

Objects placed in an organizational unit can only come from the parent domain. For example, organizational units associated with seattle.microsoft.com contain objects for this domain only. You can't add objects from ny.microsoft.com to these containers, but you could create separate organizational units to mirror the business structure of seattle.microsoft.com.

Organizational units are very helpful in organizing the objects around the business or functional structure of the organization. Still, this isn't the only reason to use organizational units. Other reasons to use organizational units are

- Organizational units allow you to assign a group policy to a small set of resources in a domain without applying this policy to the entire domain. This helps you set and manage group policies at the appropriate level in the company.

- Organizational units create smaller, more manageable views of directory objects in a domain. This helps you manage resources more efficiently.

- Organizational units allow you to delegate authority and to easily control administrative access to domain resources. This helps you control the scope of administrator privileges in the domain. You could grant user A administrative authority for one organizational unit and not for others. Meanwhile, you could grant user B administrative authority for all organizational units in the domain.

Organizational units are represented as folders in Active Directory Users And Computers. See Figure 5-4. This utility is a snap-in for the MMC and can also be accessed on the Administrative Tools menu.

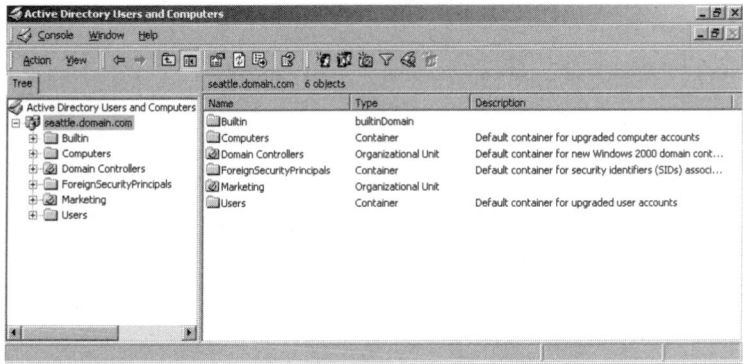

Figure 5-4. *Use Active Directory Users And Computers to manage users, groups, computers, and organizational units.*

Understanding Sites and Subnets

A site is a group of computers in one or more IP subnets. You use sites to map the physical structure of your network. Sites mappings are independent from logical domain structures, and because of this there's no necessary relationship between a network's physical structure and its logical domain structure. With Active Directory, you can create multiple sites within a single domain or create a single site that serves multiple domains. There is also no connection between the IP address ranges used by a site and the domain namespace.

You can think of a subnet as a group of network addresses. Unlike sites, which can have multiple IP address ranges, subnets have a specific IP address range and network mask. Subnet names are shown in the form *network/bits-masks*, such as 192.168.19.9/32. Here, the network address 192.168.19.0 and network mask 255.255.255. are combined to create the subnet name 192.168.19.9/32.

 Note Don't worry, you don't need to know how to create a subnet name. In most cases, you enter the network address and the network mask and then Windows 2000 generates the subnet name for you.

Computers are assigned to sites based on their location in a subnet or a set of subnets. If computers in subnets can communicate efficiently with each other over the network, they're said to be *well connected*. Ideally, sites consist of subnets and computers that are all well connected. If the subnets and computers aren't well connected, you may need to set up multiple sites. Being well connected gives sites several advantages:

- When clients log on to a domain, the authentication process first searches for domain controllers that are in the same site as the client. This means local domain controllers are used first, if possible, which localizes network traffic and can speed up the authentication process.

- Directory information is replicated more frequently *within* sites than *between* sites. This reduces the network traffic load caused by replication while ensuring that local domain controllers get up-to-date information quickly. You can also customize how directory information is replicated using site links. For example, you could designate a bridgehead server to handle replication between sites. This places the bulk of the intersite replication burden on a specific server rather than on any available server in a site.

Sites and subnets are accessed through Active Directory Sites And Services, as shown in Figure 5-5. Since this is a snap-in for the MMC, you can add it to any updateable console. You can access Active Directory Sites And Services on the Administrative Tools menu as well.

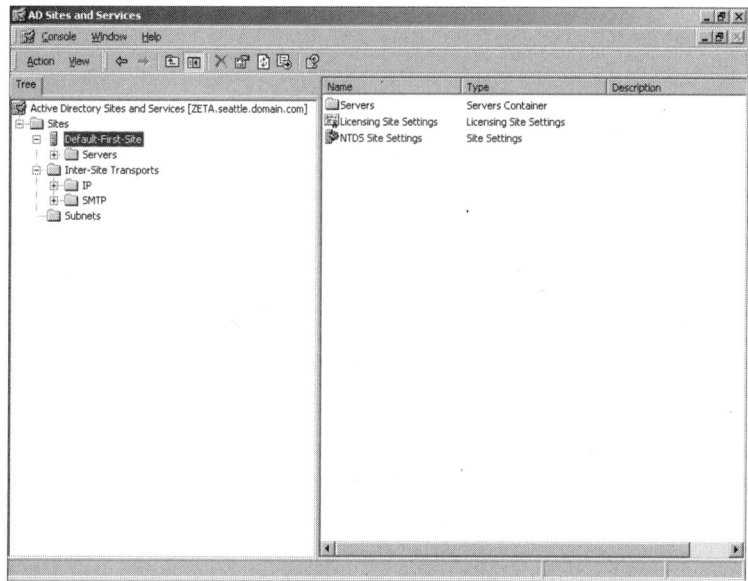

Figure 5-5. *Use Active Directory Sites And Services to manage sites and subnets.*

Working with Active Directory Domains

Although both Active Directory and DNS must be configured on a Windows 2000 network, Active Directory domains and DNS domains have different purposes. Active Directory domains help you manage accounts, resources, and security. DNS domains establish a domain hierarchy that's primarily used for name resolution. Windows 2000 uses DNS to map host names, such as microsoft.com, to numeric TCP/IP addresses, such as 207.149.110.52. To learn more about DNS and DNS domains, see Chapter 19.

Active Directory is designed to work with systems running Windows 2000 as well as systems running Microsoft Windows 95, Microsoft Windows 98, and Microsoft Windows NT. If the necessary client software is installed, Windows 95, Windows 98, and Windows 2000 systems access the network as Active Directory clients. Windows NT systems (and Windows 95 systems (or later) not upgraded with Active Directory client software) access the network as if they were in a Windows NT domain, provided Active Directory's domain operations mode allows this and a Windows NT domain is configured.

Using Windows 2000 with Active Directory

Windows 2000 Professional and Windows 2000 servers can make full use of Active Directory. Systems running Windows 2000 Professional access the network as Active Directory clients and have full use of Active Directory features. As clients, these systems can use transitive trust relationships that exist within the domain tree or forest. A transitive trust is one that isn't established explicitly. Rather, the trust is established automatically based on the forest structure and permissions set in the forest. These relationships allow authorized users to access resources in any domain in the forest.

Systems running Windows 2000 Server provide services to other systems and can act as domain controllers or member servers. A domain controller is distinguished from a member server because it runs Active Directory. You promote member servers to domain controllers by installing Active Directory. You demote domain controllers to member servers by uninstalling Active Directory. You handle both processes through the Active Directory Installation Wizard.

Domains can have one or more domain controllers. When there are multiple domain controllers, the controllers automatically replicate directory data with each other using a multimaster replication model. This model allows any domain controller to process directory changes and then replicate those changes to other domain controllers.

Because of the multimaster domain structure, all domain controllers have equal responsibility by default. You can, however, give some domain controllers precedence over others for certain tasks, such as specifying a bridgehead server that has priority in replicating directory information to other sites. Additionally, some tasks are best performed by a single server. A server that handles this type of task is called an *operations master*. There are five different operations master roles and each can be assigned to a different domain controller. For more information, see the section of this chapter entitled "Understanding Operations Master Roles."

All Windows 2000 computers that join a domain have computer accounts. Like other resources, computer accounts are stored in Active Directory as objects. You use computer accounts to control access to the network and its resources. A computer accesses a domain using its account, which is authenticated before the computer can access the network.

 Tip Windows 2000 uses Active Directory's global catalog to authenticate both computer and user logons. If the global catalog is unavailable, only members of the Domain Admins group can log on to the domain. For more information, see the "Understanding the Directory Structure" section of this chapter.

Using Windows NT with Active Directory

All Windows NT computers must have computer accounts before they can join a domain. To support Windows NT, Active Directory has two domain operations modes:

- **Mixed mode**   When operating in mixed mode, the directory can support both Windows 2000 and Windows NT domains.
- **Native mode**   When operating in native mode, the directory supports only Windows 2000 domains.

Using Mixed Mode Operations

You set the domain operations mode when you install Active Directory on the first Windows 2000 domain controller in a domain. If you're upgrading from a Windows NT domain structure to Windows 2000, this is normally the former primary domain controller (PDC) that has been upgraded to Windows 2000. You upgrade the Windows NT PDC to ensure that it becomes the first controller in the domain and to ensure that existing Security Account Manager (SAM) objects are copied from the registry to the new data store in Active Directory. During the upgrade of the PDC and the installation of Active Directory, you set the operations mode to *mixed* to ensure that other Windows NT systems can still operate in the domain.

In a mixed operations mode, systems that are configured to use Windows NT domains access the network as if they were part of a Windows NT domain. These systems can include Windows 95 and Windows 98 systems that aren't running the Active Directory client, Windows NT workstations, and Windows NT servers. While the role of Windows NT workstations doesn't change, Windows NT servers have a slightly different role. Here, Windows NT servers can act as backup domain controllers (BDCs) or member servers only. The Windows NT domain no longer has a PDC. Instead, the Windows NT domain has a Windows 2000 domain controller that acts as a PDC to replicate read-only copies of Active Directory directory service and to synchronize security changes to any remaining Windows NT BDCs.

The Windows 2000 domain controller acting as a PDC is configured as a PDC emulator operations master. You can assign this role to another Windows 2000 domain controller at any time. A controller acting as a PDC emulator supports two authentication protocols:

- **Kerberos**   Kerberos is a standard Internet protocol for authenticating users and systems and the primary authentication mechanism for Windows 2000.
- **NTLM**   NT Local Area Network (LAN) Manager (NTLM) is the primary Windows NT authentication protocol. It's used to authenticate computers in a Windows NT domain.

Note   Windows 2000 also supports Secure Socket Layer/Transport Layer Security (SSL/TLS) authentication. This authentication mechanism is used with secure Web servers.

Using Native Mode Operations

After upgrading the PDC and other Windows NT systems to Windows 2000, you can change to the native operations mode and then use only Windows 2000 resources. Once you set the native operations mode, however, you can't go back to mixed mode. Because of this, you should only use native operations mode when you're certain that you don't need the old Windows NT domain structure or Windows NT backup domain controllers.

When you change to native mode, you'll notice that

- NTLM replication is no longer supported.
- The PDC emulator can no longer synchronize data with any existing Windows NT BDCs.
- No Windows NT domain controllers can be added to the domain.

Switching to Native Operations Mode
You switch from mixed mode to native mode operations using the Active Directory Domains And Trusts administration utility. This utility is a snap-in for the MMC.

You can access Active Directory Domains And Trusts and switch to native operations mode by completing the following steps:

1. Click Start, point to Programs, point to Administrative Tools, and then select Active Directory Domains And Trusts. As shown in Figure 5-6, this displays Active Directory Domains And Trusts.
2. Right-click the domain you want to administer, and then select Properties.

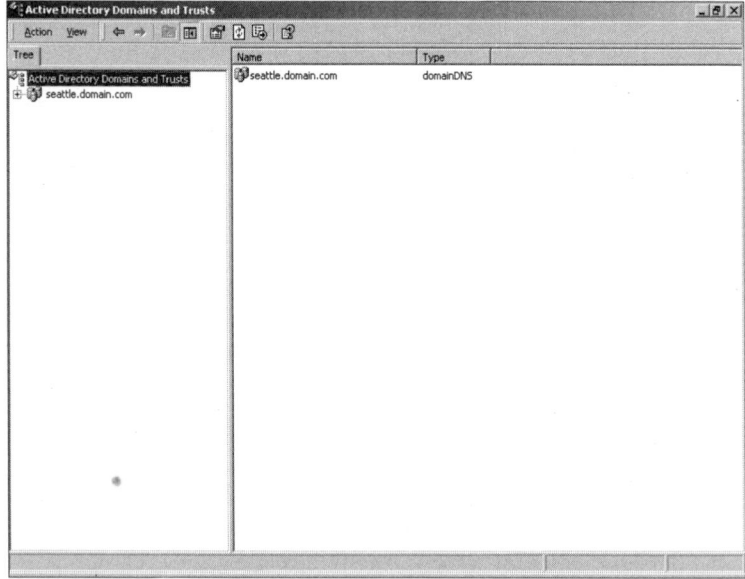

Figure 5-6. *You can add the Active Directory Domains And Trusts snap-in to any console.*

3. The current operations mode is displayed on the General tab (see Figure 5-7). If the domain is using mixed mode, you can change to native mode. However, you can't reverse this action. Consider the implications carefully before you continue.

4. To change to native mode, click Change Mode and then click Yes.

Using Windows 95 and Windows 98 with Active Directory

Systems running Windows 95 and Windows 98 can work with Active Directory in two ways. They can access the network as part of a Windows NT domain, or they can access the network as part of an Active Directory domain. Both techniques depend on a specific network configuration.

Accessing the Network Through a Windows NT Domain

Windows 95 and Windows 98 systems can only access the network as part of a Windows NT domain if Active Directory is running in mixed mode operations, and there is a PDC emulator or BDC available to authenticate the logon.

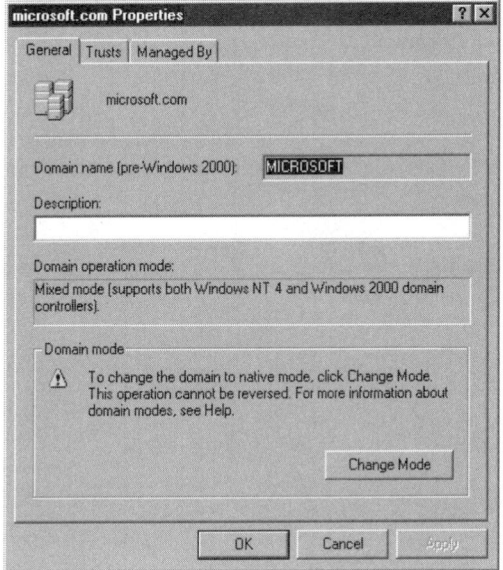

Figure 5-7. *The General tab shows the current operations mode, and you can use its fields to change the operations mode.*

When acting as part of a Windows NT domain, Windows 95 and Windows 98 systems can only access resources available through Windows NT one-way trusts, which must be explicitly established by administrators. This remains true whether the system is using a Windows 2000 domain controller or a Windows NT backup domain controller.

Accessing the Network as an Active Directory Client

Windows 95 and Windows 98 systems can access the network as part of an Active Directory domain as well. To do this, you must install Active Directory client software on the system. With the client software, these systems have full use of Active Directory features and can use transitive trust relationships that exist within the domain tree or forest. Transitive trust relationships allow authorized users to access resources in any domain in the domain tree or forest automatically.

 Tip Transitive trusts are automatically configured during installation of a domain controller, and you may not need to configure explicit trust relationships. Still, Windows 2000 does support explicit trust relationships, and you can establish these relationships if necessary. The main reasons to establish an explicit trust are to enable user authentication in another domain or to simplify the trust path in a complex domain forest.

Installing Active Directory Clients

You install Active Directory client on a Windows 95 or Windows 98 system by completing the following steps:

1. Log on to the Windows 95 or Windows 98 system you want to configure as a client. Then insert the Windows 2000 Server distribution CD-ROM into the CD-ROM drive.

2. Open the Run dialog box by clicking Start and then clicking Run.

3. Type **Clients\Win9X\Dsclient.exe** and click OK. Or click Browse to search the distribution CD-ROM. In the Clients folder, you'll find a subfolder called Win9X. This folder should contain the client executable. Select the client executable, click Open, and then click OK.

4. Running the client executable transfers a few essential files to the client and then starts the Directory Service Client Setup Wizard shown in Figure 5-8. Read the welcome dialog box, and then click Next.

5. Install the client software by clicking Next. The wizard detects the system configuration and then installs the necessary client files on the system.

6. Click Finish to complete the operation and restart the system.

7. Click Start, point to Settings, and then click Control Panel. In the Control Panel, double-click Network.

8. On the Configuration tab, select the Ethernet adapter card entry and then click Properties. Make sure that the TCP/IP settings are configured properly to access the Active Directory domain. Configuring TCP/IP settings is discussed in Chapter 15.

Figure 5-8. *Install the directory service client software using the Directory Service Client Setup Wizard.*

9. On the Identification tab, check the computer name and workgroup information provided. The computer name and workgroup should be set as explained in Chapter 15.

10. If you changed settings, you'll probably need to restart the computer. After the computer restarts, log on to the system using an account with access permissions in the Active Directory domain. You should be able to access resources in the domain.

Note Windows 95 and Windows 98 systems running as clients don't have computer accounts and aren't displayed in Network Neighborhood. You can, however, view session information for Windows 95 and Windows 98 running as Active Directory clients. Start Computer Management, double-click System Tools, double-click Shared Folders, and then select Sessions. Current user and computer sessions are displayed in the view pane. For more information on shared resources, see Chapter 13.

Understanding the Directory Structure

Active Directory has many components and is built on many technologies. Directory data is made available to users and computers through data stores and global catalogs. While most Active Directory tasks affect the data store, global catalogs are equally important. This is because they're used during logon and for information searches. In fact, if the global catalog is unavailable, normal users can't log on to the domain.

You access and distribute Active Directory data using directory access protocols and replication. Directory access protocols allow clients to communicate with computers running Active Directory. Replication is necessary to ensure that updates to data are distributed to domain controllers. While multimaster replication is the primary technique that you use to distribute updates, some data changes can only be handled by individual domain controllers called *operations masters*.

Exploring the Data Store

The data store contains information about objects such as accounts, shared resources, organizational units, and group policies. Another name for the data store is the *directory*, which refers to Active Directory itself.

Domain controllers store the directory in a file called NTDS.DIT. The location of this file is set when Active Directory is installed, and it must be on an NTFS drive formatted for use with Windows 2000. You can also save directory data separately from the main data store. This is true for group policies, scripts, and other types of public information that's stored on the shared system volume (SYSVOL).

Because the data store is a container for objects, the term *publish* is used when you share directory information. For example, you publish information about a printer by sharing the printer over the network. Similarly, you publish information about a folder by sharing the folder over the network.

Domain controllers replicate most changes to the data store in multimaster fashion. As an administrator for a small or medium-sized organization, you'll rarely need to manage replication of the data store. Replication is handled automatically after all, but you can customize it to meet the needs of large organizations or organizations with special requirements.

Not all directory data is replicated. Instead, only public information that falls into one of these three categories is replicated:

- **Domain data** Contains information about objects within a domain. This includes objects for accounts, shared resources, organizational units, and group policies.
- **Configuration data** Describes the topology of the directory. This includes a list of all domains, domain trees, and forests, as well as the locations of the domain controllers and global catalog servers.
- **Schema data** Describes all objects and data types that can be stored in the directory. The default schema provided with Windows 2000 describes account objects, shared resource objects, and more. You can extend the default schema by defining new objects and attributes or by adding attributes to existing objects.

Exploring Global Catalogs

Global catalogs enable network logon by providing universal group membership information when a logon process is initiated. They also enable directory searches throughout all the domains in a forest. A domain controller designated as a global catalog stores a full replica of all objects in the directory for its host domain and a partial replica for all other domains in the domain forest.

Note Partial replicas are used because only certain object properties are needed for logon and search operations. Partial replication also means that less information needs to be circulated on the network, which reduces the amount of network traffic.

By default, the first domain controller installed on a domain is designated as the global catalog. So, if there is only one domain controller in the domain, the domain controller and the global catalog are the same server. Otherwise, the global catalog is on the domain controller that you've configured as such. You can also add additional global catalogs to a domain to help improve response time for logon and search requests. The recommended technique is to have one global catalog per site within a domain.

Domain controllers hosting the global catalog should be well connected to domain controllers acting as infrastructure masters. Infrastructure master is one of the five operations master roles that you can assign to a domain controller. In a domain, the infrastructure master is responsible for updating object references. The infrastructure master does this by comparing its data with that of a global catalog. If the infrastructure master finds outdated data, it requests the updated data from a global catalog. The infrastructure master then replicates the changes to the other domain controllers in the domain. For more information on operations master roles, see the section of this chapter titled "Understanding Operations Master Roles."

When there is only one domain controller in a domain, you can assign the infrastructure master role and the global catalog to the same domain controller. When there are two or more domain controllers in the domain, however, the global catalog and the infrastructure master must be on separate domain controllers. If they aren't, the infrastructure master won't find data that's out of date and, as a result, will never replicate changes. The only exception is when all domain controllers in the domain host the global catalog. In this case, it doesn't matter which domain controller serves as the infrastructure master.

One of the key reasons to configure additional global catalogs in a domain is to ensure that a catalog is available to service logon and directory search requests. Again, if the domain only has one global catalog and the catalog isn't available, normal users can't log on and you can't search the directory. The only users who can log on to the domain when the global catalog is unavailable are members of the Domain Admins group.

Searches in the global catalog are very efficient. The catalog contains information about objects in all domains in the forest. This allows directory search requests to be resolved in a local domain rather than a domain in another part of the network. Resolving queries locally reduces the network load and allows for quicker responses in most cases.

Tip If you notice slow logon or query response times, you may want to configure additional global catalogs. But more global catalogs usually means more replication data being transferred over the network.

Replication and Active Directory

The three types of information stored in the directory are domain data, schema data, and configuration data.

Domain data is replicated to all domain controllers within a particular domain. Schema and configuration information are replicated to all domains in the domain tree or forest. Additionally, all objects in an individual domain, and a subset of object properties in the domain forest, are replicated to global catalogs.

This means that domain controllers store and replicate schema information for the domain tree or forest, configuration information for all domains in the domain tree or forest, and all directory objects and properties for their respective domains.

Domain controllers hosting a global catalog, however, store and replicate schema information for the forest, configuration information for all domains in the forest, a subset of the properties for all directory objects in the forest that is replicated between servers hosting global catalogs only, and all directory objects and properties for their respective domain.

To get a better understanding of replication, consider the following scenario, where you're installing a new network:

1. You start by installing the first domain controller in domain A. The server is the only domain controller and also hosts the global catalog. No replication occurs because there are no other domain controllers on the network.

2. You install a second domain controller in domain A. Because there are now two domain controllers, replication begins. To make sure that data is replicated properly, you assign one domain controller as the infrastructure master and the other as the global catalog. The infrastructure master watches for updates to the global catalog and requests updates to changed objects. The two domain controllers also replicate schema and configuration data.

3. You install a third domain controller in domain A. This server is not a global catalog. The infrastructure master watches for updates to the global catalog, requests updates to changed objects, and then replicates those changes to the third domain controller. The three domain controllers also replicate schema and configuration data.

4. You install a new domain, domain B, and add domain controllers to it. The global catalog hosts in domain A and domain B begin replicating all schema and configuration data, as well as a subset of the domain data in each domain. Replication within domain A continues as previously described. Replication within domain B begins.

Active Directory and LDAP

The Lightweight Directory Access Protocol (LDAP) is a standard Internet communications protocol for TCP/IP networks. LDAP is designed specifically for accessing directory services with the least amount of overhead. LDAP also defines operations that can be used to query and modify directory information.

Active Directory clients use LDAP to communicate with computers running Active Directory whenever they log on to the network or search for shared resources. You can also use LDAP to manage Active Directory.

LDAP is an open standard that can be used by many other directory services. This makes interdirectory communications easier and provides a clearer migration path from other directory services to Active Directory. You can also use Active Directory Service Interfaces (ADSI) to enhance interoperability. ADSI supports the standard APIs for LDAP that are specified in Internet standard Request For Comments (RFC) 1823. You can use ADSI with Windows Script Host to script objects in Active Directory.

Understanding Operations Master Roles

Operations master roles accomplish tasks that are impractical to perform in multimaster fashion. Five different operations master roles are defined; you can assign them to one or more domain controllers. While certain roles can be assigned only once in a domain forest, other roles must be defined once in each domain. The operations master roles are

- **Schema master** Controls updates and modifications to directory schema. To update directory schema, you must have access to the schema master. You can assign only one schema master in a domain forest.

- **Domain naming master** Controls the addition or removal of domains in the forest. To add or remove domains, you must have access to the domain naming master. You can assign only one domain naming master in a domain forest.

- **Relative ID master** Allocates relative IDs to domain controllers. Whenever you create a user, group, or computer object, domain controllers assign a unique security ID to the related object. The security ID consists of the domain's security ID prefix and a unique relative ID, which was allocated by the relative ID master. You must assign one relative ID master in each domain in the forest.

Note The Windows 2000 Resource Kit provides the MOVETREE.EXE utility for moving objects between domains. If you use this utility, you must initiate the move on the relative ID master of the domain that currently contains the object.

- **PDC emulator**   When using mixed mode operations, the PDC emulator acts as a Windows NT primary domain controller (PDC). Its job is to authenticate Windows NT logons, process password changes, and replicate updates to the BDCs. You must assign one relative ID master in each domain in the forest.

- **Infrastructure master**   Updates object references by comparing its directory data with that of a global catalog. If the data is outdated, the infrastructure master requests the updated data from a global catalog and then replicates the changes to the other domain controllers in the domain. You must assign one relative ID master in each domain in the forest.

Operations master roles are assigned automatically in most cases, but you can reassign them. When you install a new network, the first domain controller in the first domain is assigned all the operations master roles. If you later create a new child domain or a root domain in a new tree, the first domain controller in the new domain is automatically assigned operations master roles as well. In a new domain forest, the domain controller is assigned all operations master roles. If the new domain is in the same forest, the assigned roles are relative ID master, PDC emulator, and infrastructure master. The schema master and domain naming master roles remain in the first domain in the forest.

When a domain has only one domain controller, that computer handles all the operations master roles. If you're working with a single site, the default operations master locations should be sufficient. As you add domain controllers and domains, however, you'll probably want to move the operations master roles to other domain controllers.

When a domain has two or more domain controllers, you should configure two domain controllers to handle operations master roles. Here, you would make one domain controller the operations master and the second the standby operations master. The standby operations master is then used if the primary fails. Be sure that the domain controllers are direct replication partners and are well connected.

As the domain structure grows, you may want to split up the operations master roles and place them on separate domain controllers. This can improve the responsiveness of the operations masters. Pay particular attention to the current responsibilities of the domain controller you plan to use.

Best Practice   Two roles that shouldn't be separated are schema master and domain naming master. Always assign these roles to the same server. For the most efficient operations, you'll usually want the relative ID master and PDC emulator to be on the same server as well. But you can separate these roles if necessary. For example, on a large network where peak loads are causing performance problems, you would probably want to place the relative ID master and PDC emulator on separate domain controllers. Additionally, you usually shouldn't place the infrastructure master on a domain controller hosting a global catalog. See the "Exploring Global Catalogs" section of this chapter for details.

Chapter 6

Core Active Directory Service Administration

Core Active Directory directory service administration focuses on key tasks that you'll perform routinely with Active Directory service, such as creating computer accounts or joining computers to a domain. In this chapter you'll learn about the tools you can use to manage Active Directory service as well as specific techniques for managing computers, domain controllers, and organizational units.

Tools for Managing Active Directory Services

Two sets of tools are available for managing Active Directory: Active Directory administration tools and Active Directory support tools.

Active Directory Administration Tools

The Active Directory administrative tools are provided as snap-ins to the Microsoft Management Console (MMC). The key tools you'll use to manage Active Directory are

- **Active Directory Users and Computers** Used to manage users, groups, computers, and organizational units.
- **Active Directory Domains and Trusts** Used to work with domains, domain trees, and domain forests.
- **Active Directory Sites and Services** Used to manage sites and subnets.

If you're running Microsoft Windows 2000 Server, you can add the related snap-ins to any updateable console or access the tools directly on the Administrative Tools menu. If you're using another computer with access to a Windows 2000 domain, the tools won't be available until you install them. One technique for installing these tools was covered in Chapter 1 under "Tools and Configuration," but you could also create a software installation package for the tools that would be distributed and installable through Active Directory.

Another administration tool you may want to use is the Active Directory Schema snap-in. You use Active Directory Schema to manage and modify directory schema. Active Directory Schema is provided in the Windows 2000 Resource Kit, which you can install in the manner explained in Chapter 1 under "Installing the Resource Kit."

Active Directory Support Tools

Active Directory Schema is only one of many Active Directory tools in Windows 2000 Support Tools. A list of some of the most useful tools you can use to configure, manage, and troubleshoot Active Directory is shown in Table 6-1.

Table 6-1. Quick Reference for Active Directory Support Tools

Support Tool	Description
Active Directory Administration Tool (Ldp)	Performs Lightweight Directory Access Protocol (LDAP) operations on Active Directory.
Active Directory Object Manager (movetree)	Moves objects from one domain to another.
Active Directory Replication Monitor (Replmon)	Manages and monitors replication using a graphical user interface.
ADSI Edit	Manages objects in the directory, including the schema directory. Sets access control lists on objects.
DFS File System Utility (dfsutil)	Manages the distributed file system (DFS) and displays DFS information.
Directory Services Management Tool (NTDSUTIL)	Views site, domain, and server information. Manages operations masters.
DNS Server Troubleshooting Tool (dnscmd)	Examines or registers Domain Name Service (DNS) resource records.
Domain Manager (netdom)	Checks site and domain relationships as well as replication structure.
DSACLS	Manages access control lists for objects in Active Directory.
DSAStat	Examines naming contexts on domain controllers to determine differences.
Replication Diagnostics Tool (Repadmin)	Manages and monitors replication using the command line.
Security Descriptor Check Utility (sdcheck)	Checks access control list propagation, replication, and inheritance.
Showaccs	Checks user access permissions on an Active Directory object or resets access control lists to their default state.

(continued)

Table 6-1. *(continued)*

Support Tool	Description
SIDWalker	Sets access control lists on objects previously owned by moved, deleted, or orphaned accounts.

Using the Active Directory Users And Computers Tool

Active Directory Users And Computers is the primary administration tool you'll use to manage Active Directory. You use this utility to handle all user, group, and computer related tasks and to manage organizational units.

Starting Active Directory Users And Computers

You can start Active Directory Users And Computers by selecting its related option on the Administrative Tools menu. You can also add Active Directory Users And Computers as a snap-in to any updateable console. To do that, follow these steps:

1. In MMC, click Console, and then click Add/Remove Snap-In. This opens the Add/Remove snap-In dialog box.

2. On the Standalone tab, click Add.

3. In the Add Snap-In dialog box, click Active Directory Users And Computers, and then click Add.

Getting Started with Active Directory Users And Computers

By default, Active Directory Users And Computers works with the domain your computer is currently connected to. You can access computer and user objects in this domain through the console tree, as shown in Figure 6-1. However, if you can't find a domain controller or if the domain you want to work with isn't shown, you may need to connect to a domain controller in the current domain or a domain controller in a different domain. Other high-level tasks you may want to perform with Active Directory Users And Computers are to view advanced options or search for objects.

When you access a domain in Active Directory Users And Computers, you'll note that a standard set of folders are available. These folders are

- **Builtin**   The list of built-in user accounts
- **Computers**   The default container for computer accounts
- **Domain Controllers**   The default container for domain controllers
- **Users**   The default container for users

You can also add folders for organizational units. In Figure 6-1, I've created two organizational units in the seattle.domain.com domain: ForeignSecurityPrincipals and Marketing.

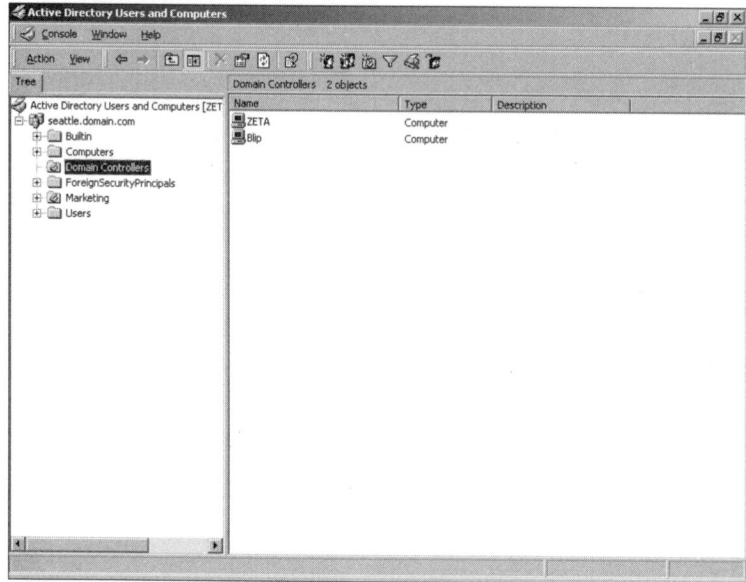

Figure 6-1. *Access Domain Controllers using Active Directory Users And Computers.*

Connecting to a Domain Controller

Connecting to a domain controller serves several purposes. If you start Active Directory Users And Computers and no objects are available, you can connect to a domain controller in order to access user, group, and computer objects in the current domain. You may also want to connect to a domain controller when you suspect replication isn't working properly and want to inspect the objects on a specific controller. Once you're connected, you'd look for discrepancies in recently updated objects.

To connect to a domain controller, complete the following steps:

1. In the console tree, right-click Active Directory Users And Computers. Then select Connect To Domain Controller.

2. You'll see the current domain and domain controller you're working with in the Connect To Domain Controller dialog box shown in Figure 6-2.

3. The Available Controllers In ... list box lists the available controllers in the domain. The default selection is Any Writable Domain Controller. If you

select this option, you'll connect to the domain controller that responds to your request first. Otherwise, choose a specific domain controller to connect to. Click OK.

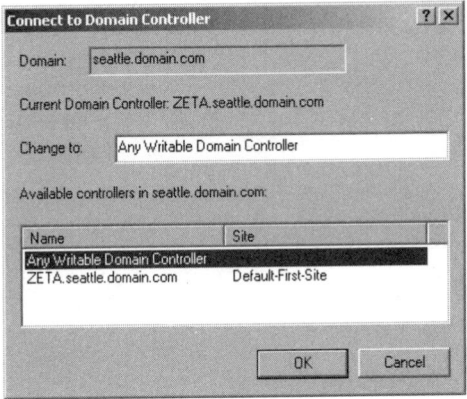

Figure 6-2. *Select a new domain controller to work with using the Connect to Domain Controller dialog box.*

Connecting to a Domain

In Active Directory Users And Computers, you can work with any domain in the forest, provided you have the proper access permissions. You connect to a domain by completing the following steps:

1. In the console tree, right-click Active Directory Users And Computers. Then select Connect To Domain.

2. The Connect To Domain dialog box displays the current (or default) domain. Type a new domain name, and then click OK. Or click Browse, and then select a domain in the Browse For Domain dialog box.

Viewing Advanced Options

Active Directory Users And Computers has advanced options that aren't displayed by default. To access these options, click View and then select Advanced Features. You will now see three additional folders:

- **ForeignSecurityPrincipals** Contains information on objects from a trusted external domain. Normally, these objects are created when an object from an external domain is added to a group in the current domain.

- **LostAndFound** Contains objects that have been orphaned. You can delete or recover them.

- **System** Contains built-in system settings.

Searching for Accounts and Shared Resources

Active Directory Users And Computers has a built-in search feature that allows you to find accounts, shared resources, and other directory objects. You can easily search the current domain, a specific domain, or the entire directory.

You search for directory objects by completing the following steps:

1. In the console tree, right-click the current domain or a specific container that you want to search. Then select Find. This opens the Find Computers dialog box shown in Figure 6-3.

2. Use the Find selection list to choose the type of search. The options are

   - **Users, Contacts, And Groups**   Search for user and group accounts, as well as contacts listed in the directory service.

   - **Computers**   Search for computer accounts by type, name, and owner.

   - **Printers**   Search for printers by name, model, and features.

   - **Shared Folders**   Search for shared folders by name or keyword.

   - **Organizational Units**   Search for organizational units by name.

   - **Custom Search**   Perform an advanced search or LDAP query.

3. Use the In selection list to choose the location to search. If you right-clicked a container, such as Computers, this container is selected by default. To search all objects in the directory, select Entire Directory.

4. After you've typed your search parameters, click Find Now. As shown in Figure 6-4, any matching entries are displayed in the Find view. Double-click an object to view or modify its property settings. Right-click the object to display a shortcut menu that can be used to manage the object.

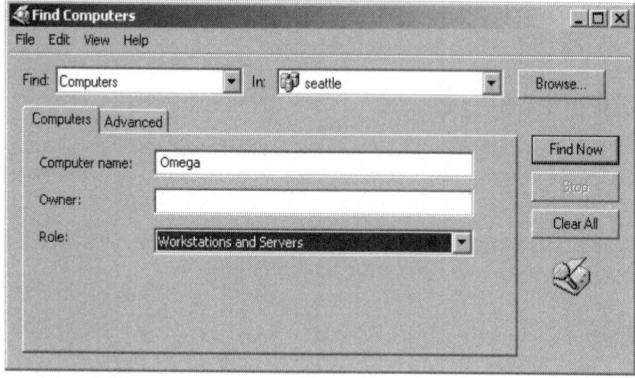

Figure 6-3. *Use the Find Computers dialog box to find resources in Active Directory.*

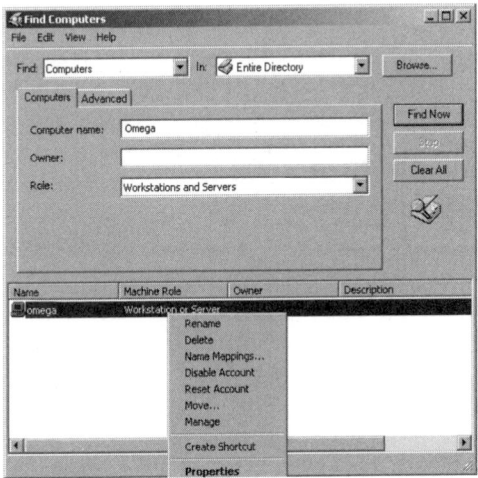

Figure 6-4. *Matching objects are displayed in the Find view, and you can manage them by right-clicking their entry.*

Note The search type determines which fields and tabs are available in the Find dialog box. In most cases you'll simply want to type the name of the object you're looking for in the Name (or Named) field. But other search options are available. For example, with printers, you can search for a color printer, a printer that can print on both sides of the paper, a printer that can staple, and more.

Managing Computer Accounts

Computer accounts are stored in the Active Directory as objects. You use them to control access to the network and its resources. You can add computer accounts to any container displayed in Active Directory Users And Computers. The best containers to use are Computers, Domain Controllers, and any organizational units that you've created.

Note Microsoft Windows 95 and Windows 98 computers access the net- work as Active Directory clients but don't have computer accounts. To learn more about accessing Active Directory domains, see the section of Chapter 5 entitled "Working with Active Directory Domains."

Creating Computer Accounts on a Workstation or Server

The easiest way to create a computer account is to log on to the computer you want to configure and join a domain as described in the "Joining a Computer to a Domain or Workgroup" section. When you do this, the necessary computer account is created automatically and placed in the Computers folder or the Domain Controllers folder, as appropriate. You can also precreate computer accounts in Active Directory Users And Computers.

Creating Computer Accounts in Active Directory Users And Computers

Using Active Directory Users And Computers, you can create computer accounts by following these steps:

1. In the Active Directory Users And Computers console tree, right-click the container in which you want to place the computer account.

2. Click New, and then click Computer. This opens the New Object-Computer dialog box shown in Figure 6-5. Type the client computer name.

3. By default, only members of Domain Admins can join computers to the domain. To allow a different user or group to join the computer to the domain, click Change. Then use the Select User Or Group dialog box to select a user or group account.

 Note You can select any existing user or group account. This allows you to delegate the authority to join this computer account to the domain.

4. If Windows NT systems can use this account, select Allow Pre-Windows 2000 Computers To Use This Account.

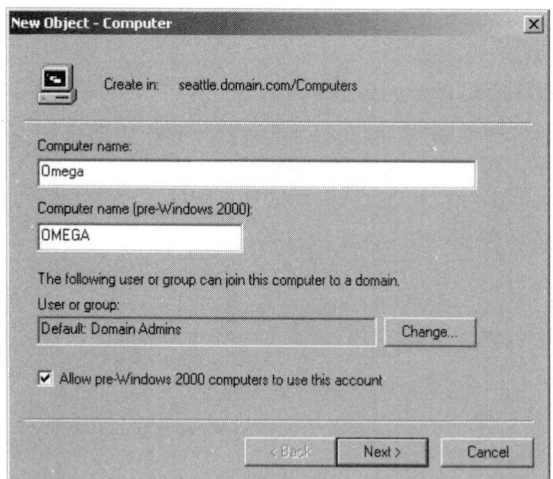

Figure 6-5. *Create new computer accounts using the New Object-Computer dialog box. Back and Next buttons are available only if Remote Installation Services are configured.*

5. Click OK or Next. If you aren't configuring a managed PC, skip steps 6–9. (Managed computers are computers that you can remotely install. Remote Installation Services must be installed.)

6. If you want to configure a managed computer, select This Is A Managed Computer.

7. Type the client computer's globally unique identifier (GUID) into the text entry field, as shown in Figure 6-6.

Note A computer's GUID is supplied by the manufacturer and must be entered in the format {dddddddd-dddd-dddd-dddd-dddddddddddd} where d is a hexadecimal digit, such as {811AC123-BC13-22CD-ABCD-11BB11342112}. To obtain the GUID, you'll need access to the computer. Look for a label on the side of or within the computer case. You may need to access the computer's Basic Input/Output System (BIOS) to find the GUID.

8. Specify which host server will handle the remote installation by selecting one of the following options:

   - **Any Available Remote Installation Server**   Choose this option to allow any server to remotely install the managed PC.

   - **The Following Remote Installation Server**   Choose this option if only a specific server can install the managed PC. Afterward, type the fully qualified DNS name for the host server.

9. Click Next, and then click Finish.

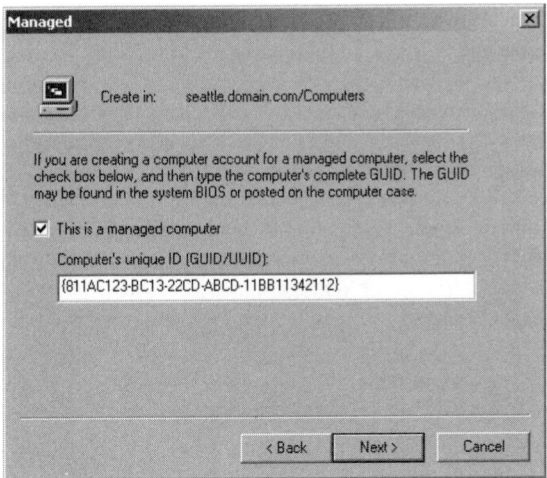

Figure 6-6. *To create an account for a managed PC, you must enter the GUID.*

Note New computers are created as members of the group Domain Computers. When you install Active Directory on a server and the server becomes a domain controller, the computer is moved to the Domain Controllers group. For more information on groups, see Chapters 7 and 8.

Viewing and Editing Computer Account Properties

You can view and edit computer account properties by completing the following steps:

1. Start Active Directory Users And Computers.
2. In the console tree, expand the domain node by clicking the plus sign (+) next to the domain name.
3. Right-click the account you want to work with, and then select Properties. This displays a property dialog box that allows you to view and edit settings.

Deleting, Disabling, and Enabling Computer Accounts

If you no longer need a computer account, you can delete it permanently from Active Directory. Or you can temporarily disable the account and later enable it to be used again.

To delete, disable, or enable computer accounts, complete the following steps:

1. On the Administrative Tools menu, start Active Directory Users And Computers by selecting it.
2. In the console tree, click the container in which the computer account is located. Then right-click the computer.
3. Select Delete to delete the account, and then confirm the deletion by clicking Yes.
4. Select Disable Account to temporarily disable the account, and then confirm the action by clicking Yes. A red circle with an X should indicate that the account is disabled.

 Tip If the account is currently in use, you may not be able to disable it. Try shutting down the computer or disconnecting the computer session in the Sessions folder of Computer Management.

5. Select Enable Account to enable the account so that it can be used again.

Resetting Locked Computer Accounts

Sometimes a computer account may get locked out or a computer session may be frozen. If either happens, you'll need to reset the account by completing the following steps:

1. On the Administrative Tools menu, start Active Directory Users And Computers by selecting it.

2. In the console tree, click the container in which the computer account is located. Then right-click the computer.

3. Select Reset Account. If the account was reset successfully, you should see a confirmation dialog box. Click OK.

Moving Computer Accounts

Computer accounts are normally placed in the Computers, Domain Controllers, or customized organizational unit containers. You can move an account to a different container by completing the following steps:

1. On the Administrative Tools menu, start Active Directory Users And Computers by selecting it.

2. In the console tree, click the container in which the computer account is located.

3. Right-click the computer account you want to move, and then select Move. This displays the Move dialog box shown in Figure 6-7.

4. In the Move dialog box, click the domain node and then click the container to which you want to move the computer. Click OK.

Managing Computers

As the name indicates, you use Computer Management to manage computers. When you're working with Active Directory Users And Computers, you can open Computer Management and connect to a specific computer directly by right-clicking the computer entry in the View pane and selecting Manage.

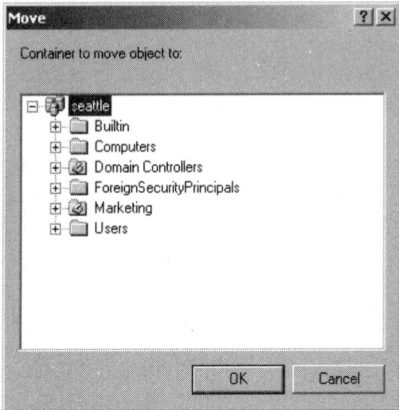

Figure 6-7. *Move computer accounts to different containers using the Move dialog box.*

Joining a Computer to a Domain or Workgroup

Joining a computer to a domain or workgroup allows a Windows NT or Windows 2000 computer to log on and access the network. Windows 95 and Windows 98 computers don't need computer accounts and don't join the network using this technique. With Windows 95 and Windows 98, you must configure the computer as an Active Directory client. For details, see the section of Chapter 5 entitled "Installing Active Directory Clients."

Before you get started, make sure that networking components are properly installed on the computer. These should have been installed during the setup of the operating system. You may also want to refer to Chapter 15 for details on configuring Transmission Control Protocol/Internet Protocol (TCP/IP) connections. If Dynamic Host Configuration Protocol (DHCP), Windows Internet Naming Service (WINS), and DNS are properly installed on the network, workstations don't need to be assigned a static IP address or have a special configuration. The only requirements are a computer name and a domain name, which you can specify when joining the domain.

Joining a Computer with an Existing Network Connection

During installation of the operating system a network connection was probably configured for the computer. Or you may have previously joined the computer to a domain or workgroup. If so, you can join the computer to a new domain or workgroup by completing the following steps:

1. Log on to the workstation or server you want to configure.

2. Start Network And Dial-Up Connections, shown in Figure 6-8. Click Start, point to Settings, and then select Network And Dial-Up Connections.

3. If the computer has existing network or dial-up connections, these connections are displayed. In Figure 6-8, Local Area Connection is an example connection. Double-click the connection to view its status.

4. Click the Network Identification link in the Network And Dial-Up Connections folder. This opens the System Properties dialog box with the Network Identification tab selected, as shown in Figure 6-9.

 Note You can't change the network identification of a domain controller. Because of this, the Network Identification link isn't available. Click Start, point to Settings, and then select Control Panel. In Control Panel, double-click System and then select the Network Identification tab in the System Properties dialog box. You will be able to see the current network identification, but the Network ID and Properties buttons will not be available.

5. Click Properties.

6. To rename the computer, type a new name in the Computer Name field, such as **Zeta**.

7. To join a new domain, in the Member Of panel select Domain and then type the domain name, such as microsoft.com.

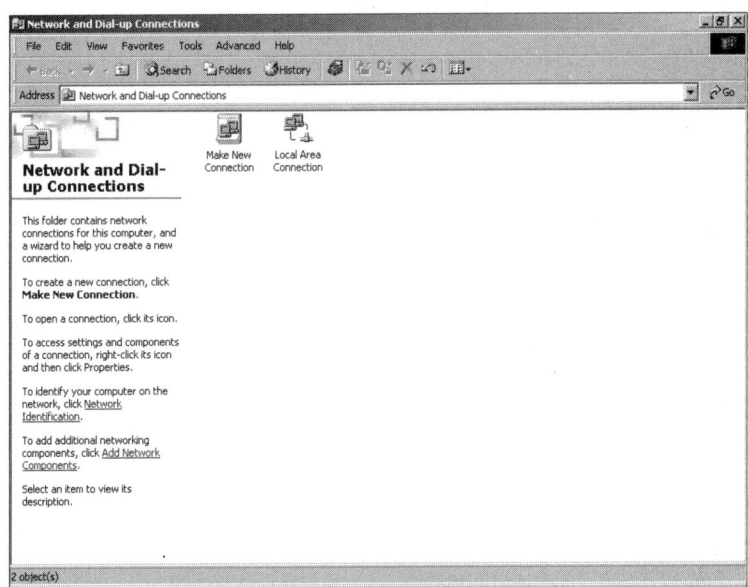

Figure 6-8. *Use Network And Dial-Up Connections to access and configure network connections.*

8. To join a new workgroup, in the Member Of panel select Workgroup and then type the workgroup name, such as TestDevGroup.

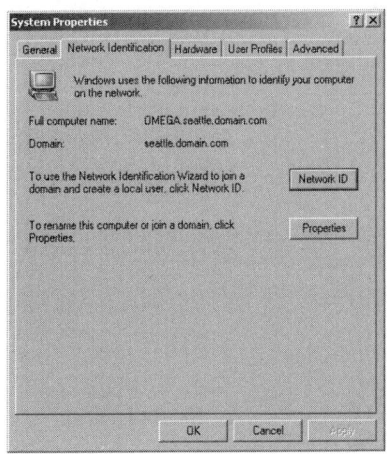

Figure 6-9. *Use the Network Identification tab to change properties or reconfigure the network ID.*

9. If you made changes, click OK. Then when prompted, type the name and password of a user account with permission to make these changes. Click OK again.

10. The changes are made and a new computer account is created, as necessary. If the changes are successful, you'll see a confirmation dialog box stating this. Click OK to reboot the computer.

11. If the changes are unsuccessful, you'll see either a message informing you that they're unsuccessful or a message telling you that the account credentials already exist. This problem can occur when you're changing the name of a computer that's already connected to a domain and when the computer has active sessions in that domain. Close applications that may be connecting to the domain, such as Windows Explorer, that's accessing a shared folder over the network. Then repeat this process.

Joining a Computer Using a New Network Connection

If you didn't configure the networking information during installation or if you simply need to create a new network connection, you can do so by completing the following steps:

1. Log on to the workstation or server you want to configure.

2. To start Network and Dial-Up Connections, click Start, point to Settings, and then select Network And Dial-Up Connections.

3. Click the Network Identification link to open the System Properties dialog box with the Network Identification tab selected, as shown previously in Figure 6-9. As stated previously, this option is not available on domain controllers. You cannot change the connection information for domain controllers.

4. Click Network ID. This starts the Network Identification Wizard. Read the welcome dialog box, and then click Next.

5. As shown in Figure 6-10, the default networking option is to connect the computer to a business network. Since this is what you want to do, click Next.

6. To join a domain, select My Computer Uses A Computer With A Domain, and then click Next.

7. To join a workgroup, select My Computer Uses A Network Without A Domain. Click Next, and then type a workgroup name, such as TestDevGroup. Complete the process by clicking Next and then clicking Finish. Skip the remaining steps.

8. Next, you're asked to gather information that you'll need to join the domain. You'll need to know the name, password, and domain of a user account that can join the computer to the domain, as well as the computer name and computer domain to use. Click Next.

9. As shown in Figure 6-11, type the user name, password, and domain that give you access to files and resources over the network. Click Next.

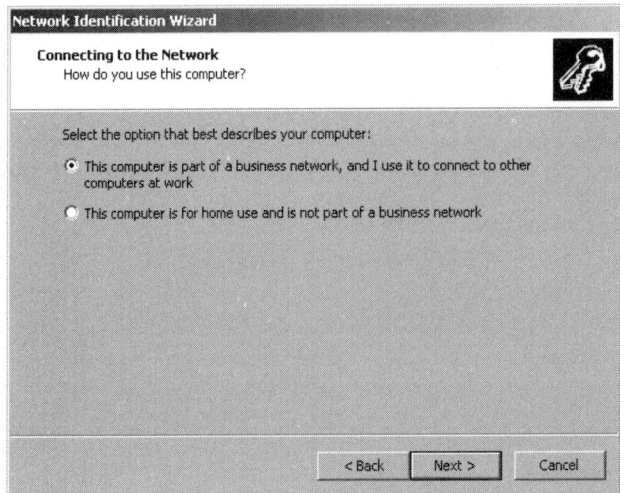

Figure 6-10. *Use the Network Identification Wizard to connect to a business network to access a domain or workgroup over the network.*

10. If the computer name and domain have already been configured and a computer account exists for the computer in this domain, you'll see a prompt asking if you want to join the computer to the domain. Click Yes. Otherwise, type the computer name and computer domain. Then click Next.

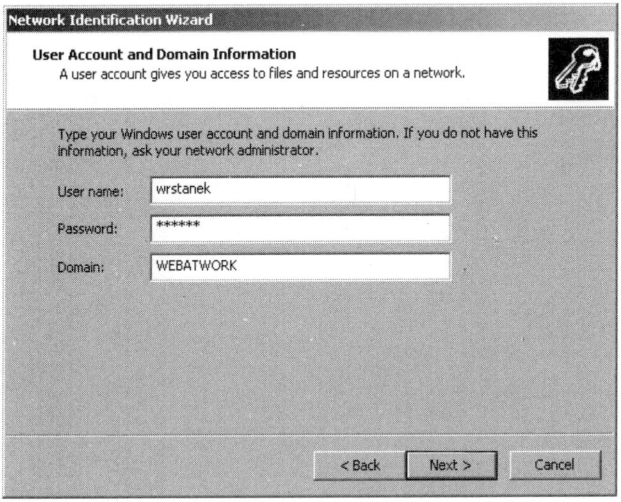

Figure 6-11. *Type user information for access to the network.*

11. If you're prompted for an authorized user account, type the user name, password, and domain of a user account that's authorized to join the computer to the domain.

12. Next, you have the opportunity to authorize a user to access the computer. This allows the user to log on to the computer and to access the computer's resources over the network. If you want to do this, select Add The Following User and then type a user name and user domain, as shown in Figure 6-12. Otherwise, select Do Not Add User At This Time. Keep in mind that you may need to grant access to the computer later.

13. If you authorized a user to access the computer, set the authorization level, as shown in Figure 6-13. Three levels are provided:

   * **Standard User**   Makes the user a power user on the computer and authorizes the user to modify the computer settings and install applications. Standard users are members of the Power Users Group on the local computer.

   * **Restricted User**   Makes the user a normal user on the computer and authorizes the user to access the computer and save documents. The user can't modify the computer settings or install programs. Restricted users are members of the Users Group on the local computer.

   * **Other**   Allows you to set the group membership to any available group on the local computer including Administrators, Backup Operators, and Guests.

14. Click Next, and then click Finish.

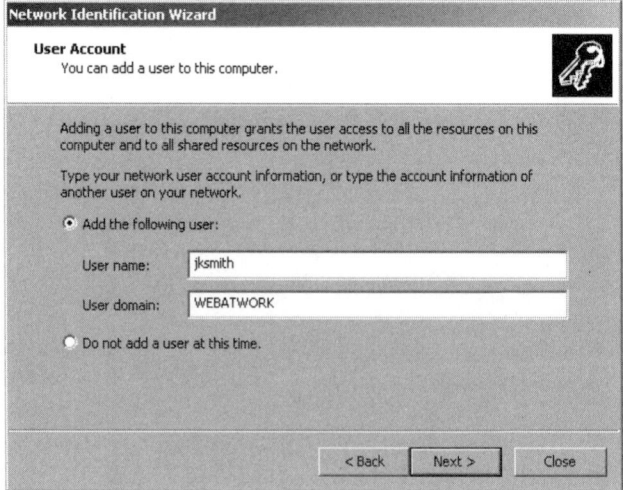

Figure 6-12. *Authorize a user to access the computer.*

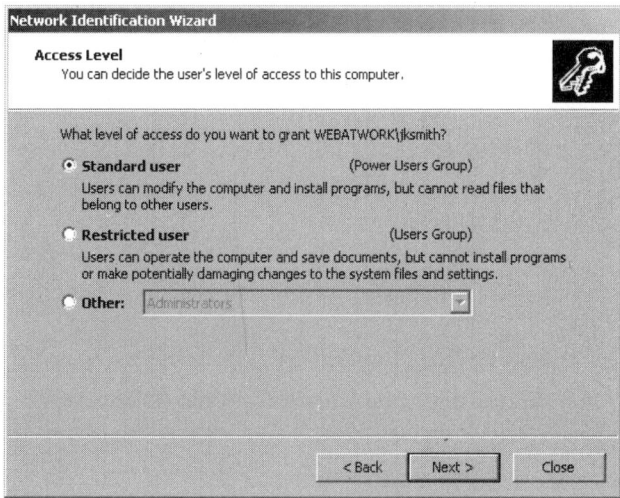

Figure 6-13. *Set the user's authorization level on the local computer.*

Managing Domain Controllers, Roles, and Catalogs

Domain controllers perform many important tasks in Active Directory domains. Many of these tasks were discussed in Chapter 5.

Installing and Demoting Domain Controllers

You install a domain controller by configuring Active Directory on a member server. Later, if you don't want the server to handle controller tasks, you can demote the server. It will then act as a member server again. You install or demote servers following a similar procedure, but before you do you should consider the impact on the network and read the section of Chapter 5 entitled "Understanding the Directory Structure."

As that section explains, when you install a domain controller you may need to transfer operations master roles and reconfigure the global catalog structure. Also, before you can install Active Directory, DNS must be working on the network and you must convert the Active Directory data drive to NTFS 5.0. Converting drive formats is covered in Chapter 10 under "Converting a Volume to NTFS." Similarly, before you demote a domain controller, you should shift any key responsibilities to other domain controllers. This means moving the global catalog off the server and transferring any operations master roles, if necessary.

To install or demote a domain controller, complete the following steps:

1. Log on to the server you want to reconfigure.

2. Click Start, then click Run.

3. Type **dcpromo** and then click OK. This starts the Active Directory Installation Wizard.

4. If the computer is currently a member server, the wizard takes you through the steps needed to install Active Directory directory service. You'll need to specify whether this is a domain controller for a new domain or an additional domain controller for an existing domain.

5. If the computer is currently a domain controller, the Active Directory Installation Wizard takes you through the process of demoting the domain controller. Once it's demoted, the computer acts as a member server.

Viewing and Transferring Domain-Wide Roles

You can use Active Directory Users And Computers to view or change the location of domain-wide operations master roles. At the domain level, you can work with roles for Relative ID (RID) masters, Primary Domain Controller (PDC) emulator masters, and Infrastructure masters.

 Note Operations master roles are discussed in Chapter 5 in the section entitled "Understanding Operations Master Roles." You use Active Directory Domains And Trusts to set the domain naming master role and Active Directory Schema to change the schema master role.

You transfer operations master roles by following these steps:

1. In the console tree, right-click Active Directory Users And Computers. Then select Operations Masters. This opens the Operations Master dialog box shown in Figure 6-14.

2. The RID tab shows the location of the current relative ID master. Click Change, and then select a new domain controller to transfer the role to a new location.

3. The PDC tab shows the location of the current PDC emulator master. Click Change and then select a new domain controller to transfer the role to a new location.

4. The Infrastructure tab shows the location of the current infrastructure master. Click Change, and then select a new domain controller to transfer the role to a new location. Click OK.

Viewing and Transferring Domain Naming Master Role

You can use Active Directory Domains And Trusts to view or change the location of the domain naming master in the domain forest. In Active Directory Domains And Trusts, the root level of the control tree shows the currently selected domain.

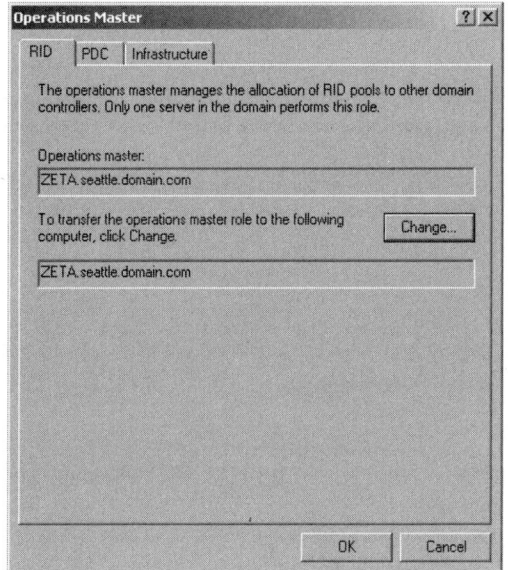

Figure 6-14. *Use the Operations Master dialog box to transfer operations master to new locations or simply view their current location.*

Tip If you need to connect to a different domain, connect to a domain controller following steps similar to those described in the section of this chapter entitled "Connecting to a Domain Controller." The only difference is that you right-click Active Directory Domains And Trusts in the console tree.

You transfer the domain naming master role by following these steps:

1. Start Active Directory Domains And Trusts.

2. In the console tree, right-click Active Directory Domains And Trusts. Then select Operations Master. This opens the Change Operations Master dialog box.

3. The Domain Naming Operations Master field displays the current domain naming master.

4. Click Change and then select a new domain controller. The role is then transferred to this controller.

5. Click Close.

Viewing and Transferring Schema Master Role

You can use Active Directory Schema to view or change the location of the schema master. This utility is provided as a snap-in that is available when the full administrative tool set is installed. You transfer the schema master role by completing the following steps:

1. Once you've installed all of the administrative tools, you can add the Active Directory Schema snap-in to a Microsoft Management Console. Click Start and then click Run.

2. Type **mmc /a** and then click OK.

3. On the console menu, click Add/Remove Snap-In and then click Add.

4. Select Active Directory Schema, click Add, and then click Close. Click OK.

5. In the console tree, right-click Active Directory Schema. Then select Change Domain Controller.

6. Select Any Domain Controller to let Active Directory select the new schema master. Or select Specify Name and type the name of the new schema master, such as zeta.seattle.domain.com.

7. In the console tree, right-click Active Directory Schema and then click Operations Master. Click Change.

Configuring Global Catalogs

Global catalogs have an important role on the network. This role is discussed in the section of Chapter 5 entitled "Understanding the Directory Structure." You configure additional global catalogs by enabling domain controllers to host the global catalog. Additionally, if you have two or more global catalogs within a site, you may want a domain controller to stop hosting the global catalog. You do this by disabling the global catalog on the domain controller.

You enable or disable a global catalog by completing the following steps:

1. Start Active Directory Sites And Services.

2. In the console tree, expand the tree view for the site you want to work with by clicking the plus sign (+) next to the site name.

3. Expand the Servers folder for the site, and then click the server you want to configure to host the global catalog.

4. In the View pane, right-click NTDS Settings and then select Properties.

5. To enable the global catalog, select Global Catalog on the General tab. An example is shown in Figure 6-15.

6. To disable the global catalog, clear Global Catalog on the General tab.

Managing Organizational Units

As discussed in Chapter 5, organizational units help you organize objects, set Group Policy with a limited scope, and more. In this section you'll learn how to create and manage organizational units.

Creating Organizational Units

You usually create organizational units to mirror the business or functional structure of your organization. You can create organizational units as subgroups of a domain or as child units within an existing organizational unit.

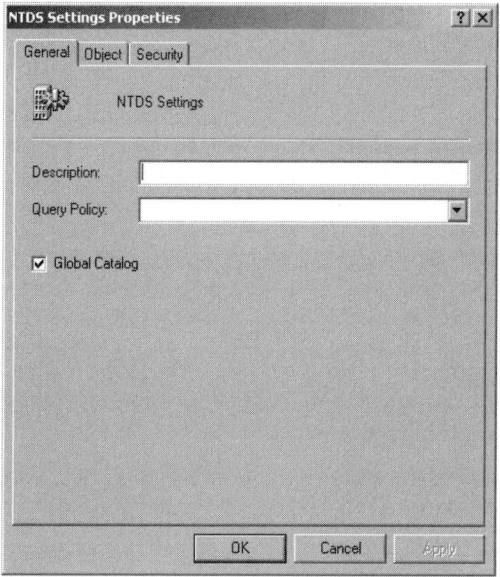

Figure 6-15. *Enable and disable global catalogs through a server's NTDS settings.*

To create an organizational unit, follow these steps:

1. Start Active Directory Users And Computers.

2. In the console tree, expand the domain node by clicking the plus sign (+) next to the domain name.

3. Right-click the domain node or existing organizational unit folder in which you want to add the organizational unit. On the shortcut menu, select New, and then click Organizational Unit.

4. Type the name of the organizational unit. Click OK.

5. You can now move accounts and shared resources to the organizational unit. See the "Moving Computer Accounts" section of this chapter for an example.

Viewing and Editing Organizational Unit Properties

You can view and edit organizational unit properties by completing the following steps:

1. Start Active Directory Users And Computers.

2. In the console tree, expand the domain node by clicking the plus sign (+) next to the domain name.

3. Right-click the organizational unit you want to work with, and then select Properties. This displays a property dialog box that lets you view and edit settings.

Renaming and Deleting Organizational Units

You can rename or delete an organizational unit by completing the following steps:

1. In Active Directory Users And Computers, right-click the organizational unit folder you want to work with.

2. To delete the unit, select Delete. Then confirm the action by choosing Yes.

3. To rename the unit, select Rename. Type a new name for the organizational unit and then press Enter.

Moving Organizational Units

You can move organizational units to different locations within a domain. To do this, complete the following steps:

1. In Active Directory Users And Computers, right-click the organizational unit folder you want to move. Then select Move.

2. In the Move pane, click the domain node. Then click the container to which you want to move the organizational unit. Click OK.

Chapter 7

Understanding
User and Group Accounts

Managing accounts is one of your primary tasks as a Microsoft Windows 2000 administrator. Chapter 3 discussed computer accounts. This chapter examines user and group accounts. User accounts enable individual users to log on to the network and access network resources. Group accounts are used to manage resources for multiple users. The permissions and privileges you assign to user and group accounts determine which actions users can perform, as well as which computer systems and resources they can access.

Although you may be tempted to give users wide access, you need to balance the user's need for job-related resources against your need to protect sensitive resources or privileged information. For example, you wouldn't want everyone in the company to have access to payroll data. Consequently, you'd make sure that only those who need that information have access to it.

The Windows 2000 Security Model

You control access to network resources with the components of the Windows 2000 security model. The key components you need to know about are the ones used for authentication and access controls.

Authentication Protocols

Windows 2000 authentication is implemented as a two-part process. That process consists of interactive logon and network authentication.

When a user logs on to a computer, the interactive logon process authenticates the user's logon, which confirms the user's identity to the local computer and grants access to Active Directory directory service. Afterward, whenever the user accesses network resources, network authentication is used to determine whether the user has permission to do so.

Windows 2000 supports many different network authentication protocols. The key protocols are

- **Kerberos V 5**   A standard Internet protocol for authenticating users and systems. It's the primary authentication mechanism for Windows 2000.

- **NT LAN Manager (NTLM)** The primary Windows NT authentication protocol. It's used to authenticate computers in a Windows NT domain.

- **Secure Socket Layer/Transport Layer Security (SSL/TLS)** The primary authentication mechanism used when accessing secure Web servers.

A key feature of the Windows 2000 authentication model is that it supports Single Sign-On. Single Sign-On works in the following way:

1. A user logs on to the domain by using a logon name and password or by swiping a smart card into a card reader.

2. The interactive logon process authenticates the user's access. With a local account, the credentials are authenticated locally and the user is granted access to the local computer. With a domain account, the credentials are authenticated in Active Directory and the user has access to network resources.

3. Now the user can authenticate to any computer in the domain through the network authentication process. With domain accounts, the network authentication process is automatic (through Single Sign-On). With local accounts, on the other hand, users must provide a user name and password every time they access a network resource.

Access Controls

Active Directory is object-based. Users, computers, groups, shared resources, and many other entities are all defined as objects. Access controls are applied to these objects with security descriptors. Security descriptors do the following:

- List the users and groups that are granted access to objects
- Specify permissions the users and groups have been assigned
- Track events that should be audited for objects
- Define ownership of objects

Individual entries in the security descriptor are referred to as access control entries (ACEs). Active Directory objects can inherit ACEs from their parent objects. This means that permissions for a parent object can be applied to a child object. For example, all members of the Domain Admins group inherit permissions granted to this group.

When working with ACEs, keep the following points in mind:

- Access control entries are created with inheritance enabled by default.
- Inheritance takes place immediately after the ACE is written.
- All access control entries contain information specifying whether the permission is inherited or explicitly assigned to the related object.

Differences Between User and Group Accounts

Windows 2000 provides user accounts and group accounts (of which users can be a member). User accounts are designed for individuals. Group accounts are designed to make the administration of multiple users easier. While you can log on to user accounts, you can't log on to a group account. Group accounts are usually referred to simply as *groups*.

User Accounts

In Windows 2000 two types of user accounts are defined:

- **Domain user accounts**   Users accounts defined in Active Directory are called *domain user accounts*. Through Single Sign-On, domain user accounts can access resources throughout the domain. Domain user accounts are created in Active Directory Users And Computers.

- **Local user accounts**   User accounts defined on a local computer are called *local user accounts*. Local user accounts have access to the local computer only, and they must authenticate themselves before they can access network resources. You create local user accounts with the Local Users And Groups utility.

Note   Only member servers and workstations have local user and group accounts. On the initial domain controller for a domain, these accounts are moved from the local security manager to Active Directory and then become domain accounts.

Logon Names, Passwords, and Public Certificates

All user accounts are identified with a logon name. In Windows 2000, this logon name has two parts:

- **User name**   The text label for the account
- **User domain or workgroup**   The workgroup or domain where the user account exists

For the user WRSTANEK, whose account is created in the MICROSOFT.COM domain, the full logon name for Windows 2000 is `wrstanek@microsoft.com`.

The pre-Windows 2000 logon name is `MICROSOFT\wrstanek`.

When working with Active Directory, you may also need to specify the fully qualified domain name for a user. The fully qualified domain name for a group is the combination of the Domain Name Service (DNS) domain name, the container or organizational unit location, and the group name. For the user Microsoft.com\Users\wrstanek, Microsoft.com is the DNS domain name, Users is the container or organizational unit location, and wrstanek is the user name.

User accounts can also have passwords and public certificates associated with them. Passwords are authentication strings for an account. Public certificates combine a public and private key to identify a user. You log on with a password interactively. You log on with a public certificate using a smart card and a smart card reader.

Security Identifiers and User Accounts

Although Windows 2000 displays user names to describe privileges and permissions, the key identifiers for accounts are security identifiers (SIDs). SIDs are unique identifiers that are generated when accounts are created. SIDs consist of the domain's security ID prefix and a unique relative ID, which was allocated by the relative ID master.

Windows 2000 uses these identifiers to track accounts independently from user names. SIDs serve many purposes. The two most important ones are to allow you to easily change user names and to allow you to delete accounts without worrying that someone may gain access to resources simply by re-creating an account.

When you change a user name, you tell Windows 2000 to map a particular SID to a new name. When you delete an account, you tell Windows 2000 that a particular SID is no longer valid. Afterward, even if you create an account with the same user name, the new account will not have the same privileges and permissions as the previous one. That's because the new account will have a new SID.

Groups

In addition to user accounts, Windows 2000 provides groups. You use groups to grant permissions to similar types of users and to simplify account administration. If a user is a member of a group that can access a resource, that particular user can access the same resource. Thus, you can give a user access to various work-related resources just by making the user a member of the correct group. Note that while you can log on to a computer with a user account, you can't log on to a computer with a group account.

Because different Active Directory domains may have groups with the same name, groups are often referred to by DOMAIN\GroupName, such as WORK\GMarketing for the GMarketing group in the WORK domain. When you work with Active Directory, you may also need to specify the fully qualified domain name for a group. The fully qualified domain name for a group is the concatenation of the DNS domain name, the container or organizational unit location, and the group name. For the group Microsoft.com\Users\Gmarketing, Microsoft.com is the DNS domain name, Users is the container or organizational unit location, and GMarketing is the group name.

Real World   Employees in a marketing department probably need access to all marketing-related resources. Instead of granting access to these resources individually, you could make the users members of a marketing group. That way, they automatically obtain the group's privileges. Later, if a user moves to a different department, you simply remove the user from the group and all access permissions are revoked. Compared to having to revoke access for each individual resource, this technique is pretty easy—so you'll want to use groups whenever possible.

Group Types

In Windows 2000, there are three types of groups:

- **Local groups**   Groups that are defined on a local computer. Local groups are used on the local computer only. You create local groups with the Local Users And Groups utility.

- **Security groups**   Groups that can have security descriptors associated with them. You define security groups in domains using Active Directory Users And Computers.

- **Distribution groups**   Groups that are used as e-mail distribution lists. They can't have security descriptors associated with them. You define distribution groups in domains using Active Directory Users And Computers.

Group Scope

Groups can have different scopes—*domain local, built-in local, global, and universal.* That is, the groups have different areas in which they are valid.

- **Domain local groups**   Groups that are used to grant permissions within a single domain. Members of domain local groups can include only accounts (both user and computer accounts) and groups from the domain in which they are defined.

- **Built-in local groups**   Groups that have a special group scope that have domain local permissions and, for simplicity, are often referred to as *domain local groups.* The difference between built-in local groups and other groups is that built-in local groups can't be created or deleted. You can only modify built-in local groups. References to domain local groups apply to built-in local groups unless otherwise noted.

- **Global groups**   Groups that are used to grant permissions to objects in any domain in the domain tree or forest. Members of global groups can include only accounts and groups from the domain in which they are defined.

- **Universal groups**   Groups that are used to grant permissions on a wide scale throughout a domain tree or forest. Members of global groups include accounts and groups from any domain in the domain tree or forest.

Best Practice Universal groups are very useful in large enterprises where you have multiple domains. If you plan properly, you can use universal groups to simplify system administration. Members of universal groups shouldn't change frequently. Each time you change the members of a universal group, you need to replicate these changes to all the global catalogs in the domain tree or forest. To cut down on changes, assign other groups to the universal group rather than accounts. For more information, see the section entitled "When to Use Domain Local, Global, and Universal Groups."

When you work with groups, there are many things you can and can't do based on the scope of the group. A quick summary of these items is shown in Table 7-1. For complete details on creating groups, see Chapter 8, "Creating User and Group Accounts."

Table 7-1. How Group Scope Affects Group Capabilities

Group Capability	Domain Local Scope	Global Scope	Universal Scope
Native Mode Membership	Accounts, global groups, and universal groups from any domain; domain local groups from the same domain only.	Only accounts from the same domain and global groups from the same domain.	Accounts from any domain, as well as groups from any domain regardless of scope.
Mixed Mode Membership	Accounts and global groups from any domain.	Only accounts from the same domain.	Can't be created in mixed-mode domains.
Member Of	Can be put into other domain local groups and assigned permissions only in the same domain.	Can be put into other groups and assigned permissions in any domain.	Can be put into other groups and assigned permissions in any domain.
Scope Conversion	Can be converted to universal scope, provided it doesn't have as its member another group having domain local scope.	Can be converted to universal scope, provided it's not a member of any other group having global scope.	Can't be converted to any other group scope.

Security Identifiers and Group Accounts

As with user accounts, Windows 2000 uses unique security identifiers to track group accounts. This means that you can't delete a group account, re-create it, and then expect all the permissions and privileges to remain the same. The new group will have a new security identifier and all the permissions and privileges of the old group will be lost.

Windows 2000 creates a security token for each user logon. The security token specifies the user account ID and the SIDs of all the security groups to which the user belongs. The token's size grows as the user is added to additional security groups. This has several consequences:

- The security token must be passed to the user logon process before logon can be completed. Because of this, as the number of security group memberships grows, the logon process takes longer.

- To determine access permissions, the security token is sent to every computer that the user accesses. Because of this, the size of the security token has a direct impact on the network traffic load.

Note Distribution group memberships aren't distributed with security tokens. Because of this, distribution group memberships don't affect the token size.

When to Use Domain Local, Global, and Universal Groups

Domain local, global, and universal groups provide a lot of options for configuring groups in the enterprise. Although these group scopes are designed to simplify administration, poor planning can make these group scopes your worst administration nightmare. Ideally, you'll use group scopes to help you create group hierarchies that are similar to your organization's structure and the responsibilities of particular groups of users. The best uses for domain local, global, and universal groups are as follows:

- **Domain local groups** Groups with domain local scope have the smallest extent. Use groups with domain local scope to help you manage access to resources, such as printers and shared folders.

- **Global groups** Use groups with global scope to help you manage user and computer accounts in a particular domain. Then you grant access permissions to a resource by making the group with global scope a member of the group with domain local scope.

- **Universal groups** Groups with universal scope have the largest extent. Use groups with universal scope to consolidate groups that span domains. Normally, you do this by adding global groups as members. Now when you change membership of the global groups, the changes aren't replicated to all the global catalogs. This is because the membership of the universal group didn't change.

Tip If your organization doesn't have two or more domains, you don't really need to use universal groups. Instead, build your group structure with domain local and global groups. Then, if you ever bring another domain into your domain tree or forest, you can easily extend the group hierarchy to accommodate the integration.

To put this in perspective, consider the following scenario. Say that you have branch offices in Seattle, Chicago, and New York. Each office has its own domain, which is a part of the same domain tree or forest. These domains are called SEATTLE, CHICAGO, and NY. You want to make it easy for any administrator (from any office) to manage network resources, so you create a group structure that is very similar at each location. Although the company has marketing, IT, and engineering departments, let's focus on the structure of the marketing department. At each office, members of the marketing department need access to a shared printer called MarketingPrinter and a shared data folder called MarketingData. You also want users to be able to share and print documents. For example, Bob in Seattle should be able to print documents so that Ralph in New York can pick them up on his local printer, and Bob should also be able to access the quarterly report on the shared folder at the New York office.

To configure the groups for the marketing departments at the three offices, you would follow these steps:

1. Start by creating global groups for each marketing group. On the SEATTLE domain, create a group called GMarketing and add the members of the Seattle marketing department to it. On the CHICAGO domain, create a group called GMarketing and add the members of the Chicago marketing department to it. On the NY domain, create a group called GMarketing and add the members of the New York marketing department to it.

2. In each location, create domain local groups that grant access to the shared printers and shared folders. Call the printer group LocalMarketingPrinter. Call the New York shared folder LocalMarketingData. The SEATTLE, CHICAGO, and NY domains should each have their own local groups.

3. Create a group with universal scope called UMarketing on the domain at any branch office. Add SEATTLE\GMarketing, CHICAGO\Gmarketing, and NY\GMarketing to this group.

4. Add UMarketing to the LocalMarketingPrinter and LocalMarketingData groups at each office. Marketing users should now be able to share data and printers.

Default User Accounts and Groups

When you install Windows 2000, the operating system installs default users and groups. These accounts are designed to provide the basic setup necessary to grow your network. Three types of default accounts are provided:

- **Predefined** User and group accounts installed with the operating system.
- **Built-In** User and group accounts installed with the operating system, applications, and services.
- **Implicit** Special groups created implicitly when accessing network resources; also known as *special identities*.

Note   Although you can modify the default users and groups, you can't delete default users and groups created by the operating system. The reason you can't delete these accounts is that you wouldn't be able to re-create them. The SIDs of the old and new accounts wouldn't match, and the permissions and privileges of these accounts would be lost.

Built-In User Accounts

Built-in user accounts have special uses on Windows 2000. While all Windows 2000 systems have one built-in account called LocalSystem, other built-in user accounts may be available.

The LocalSystem Account

LocalSystem is a pseudo-account for running system processes and handling system-level tasks. The account is available on the local system only. You can't change the settings for the LocalSystem account with the user administration tools. Users can't log on to a computer with this account.

Note   While users can't log on to a computer with the LocalSystem account, certain processes *can* log on using this account. For example, Windows 2000 services can be configured to log on to a computer using the System account. For more information, see the section of Chapter 3 entitled "Managing System Services."

Other Built-In Accounts

When you install add-ons or other applications on a workstation or server, other default accounts may be installed. You can usually delete these accounts.

When you install Internet Information Services, you may find several new accounts, including IUSR_*host* and IWAM_*host*, where *host* is the computer name. The IUSR_*host* account is the built-in account for anonymous access to Internet Information Services. The IWAM_*host* account is used by Internet Information Services to start out of process applications. These accounts are defined in Active Directory when they're configured on a domain. However, they're defined as local users when they're configured on a stand-alone server or workstation. Another built-in account that you may see is TSInternetUser. This account is used by Terminal Services.

Predefined User Accounts

Two predefined user accounts are installed with Windows 2000—Administrator and Guest. With workstations and member servers, predefined accounts are local to the individual system they're installed on.

Predefined accounts have counterparts in Active Directory. These accounts have domain-wide access and are completely separate from the local accounts on individual systems.

The Administrator Account

Administrator is a predefined account that provides complete access to files, directories, services, and other facilities. You can't delete or disable this account. In Active Directory, the Administrator account has domain-wide access and privileges. Otherwise, the Administrator account generally has access only to the local system. Although files and directories can be protected from the Administrator account temporarily, the Administrator account can take control of these resources at any time by changing the access permissions.

 Tip   To prevent unauthorized access to the system or domain, be sure to give the account an especially secure password. Also, because this is a known Windows 2000 account, you may want to rename the account as an extra security precaution.

In most instances you won't need to change the basic settings for this account. However, you may need to change its advanced settings, such as membership in particular groups. By default, the Administrator account for a domain is a member of these groups: Administrators, Domain Admins, Domain Users, Enterprise Admins, Schema Admins, and Group Policy Creator Owners. You'll find more information on these groups in the next section.

 Real World   In a domain environment, you'll use the local Administrator account primarily to manage the system when you first install it. This allows you to set up the system without getting locked out. You probably won't use the account once the system has been installed. Instead, you'll probably want to make your administrators members of the Administrators group. This ensures that you can revoke administrator privileges without having to change the passwords for all the Administrator accounts.

For a system that's part of a workgroup where each individual computer is managed separately, you'll typically rely on this account anytime you need to perform your system administration duties. Here, you probably won't want to set up individual accounts for each person who has administrative access to a system. Instead, you'll use a single Administrator account on each computer.

The Guest Account

Guest is designed for users who need one-time or occasional access. While guests have limited system privileges, you should be very careful about using this account. Whenever you use this account, you open the system to potential security problems. The potential is so great that the account is initially disabled when you install Windows 2000.

Tip If you decide to enable the Guest account, be sure to restrict its use and to change the password regularly. As with the Administrator account, you may want to rename the account as an added security precaution.

Built-In Groups

Built-in groups are installed with all Windows 2000 workstations and servers. Use the built-in groups to grant a user the group's privileges and permissions. You do this by making the user a member of the group. For example, you give a user administrative access to the system by making a user a member of the local Administrators group. You give a user administrative access to the domain by making a user a member of the domain local Administrators group in Active Directory.

The availability of a specific built-in group depends on the current system configuration. Use Table 7-2 to determine the availability of the various built-in groups. Each of these groups is discussed later in the chapter.

Table 7-2. Availability of Built-In Groups Based on the Type of Network Resource

Group Name	Group Type	Active Directory Domain	Windows 2000 Professional or Member Server
Account Operators	Built-In Local	Yes	No
Administrators	Built-In Local, Local	Yes	Yes
Backup Operators	Built-In Local, Local	Yes	Yes
Guests	Built-In Local, Local	Yes	Yes
Power Users	Local	No	Yes
Pre-Windows 2000 Compatible Access	Built-In Local	Yes	No
Print Operators	Built-In Local	Yes	No
Replicator	Built-In Local, Local	Yes	Yes
Server Operators	Built-In Local	Yes	No
Users	Built-In Local, Local	Yes	Yes

Predefined Groups

Predefined groups are installed with Active Directory domains. Use these groups to assign additional permissions to users, computers, and other groups. You do this by making the user a member of the group. Predefined groups include domain local, global, and universal groups. The availability of a specific built-in group depends on the domain configuration.

Use Table 7-3 to determine the availability of the various predefined groups. Key predefined groups are discussed later in this chapter.

Note The group scope for Enterprise Admins and Schema Admins can be either universal or global, depending on the operations mode. In mixed mode, these are global groups. In native mode, these are universal groups.

Table 7-3. Availability of Predefined Groups Based on Domain Configuration

Group Name	Group Type	When Installed
Cert Publishers	Global	By default
DHCP Administrators	Domain Local	With DHCP
DHCP Users	Domain Local	With DHCP
DnsAdmins	Domain Local	With DNS
DnsUpdateProxy	Global	With DNS
Domain Admins	Global	By default
Domain Computers	Global	By default
Domain Controllers	Global	By default
Domain Guests	Global	By default
Domain Users	Global	By default
Enterprise Admins	Universal/Global	By default
Group Policy Creator Owners	Global	By default
RAS and IAS Servers	Domain Local	With remote access services
Schema Admins	Universal/Global	By default
WINS Users	Domain Local	WINS

Implicit Groups and Special Identities

In Windows NT implicit groups were assigned implicitly during logon and were based on how a user accessed a network resource. For example, if a user accessed a resource through interactive logon, the user was automatically a member of the implicit group called Interactive. In Windows 2000, the object-based approach to the directory structure changes the original rules for implicit groups. While you still can't view the membership of special identities, you can grant membership in implicit groups to users, groups, and computers.

To reflect the new role, implicit groups are also referred to as *special identities*. A special identity is a group whose membership can be set implicitly, such as during logon, or explicitly through security access permissions. As with other default groups, the availability of a specific implicit group depends on the current configuration. Use Table 7-4 to determine the availability of the various implicit groups. Implicit groups are discussed later in this chapter.

Table 7-4.   Availability of Implicit Groups Based on the Type of Network Resource

Group Name	Group Type	Active Directory Domain	Windows 2000 Professional or Member Server
Anonymous Logon	Implicit	Yes	Yes
Authenticated Users	Implicit	Yes	Yes
Batch	Implicit	Yes	Yes
Creator Group	Implicit	Yes	Yes
Creator Owner	Implicit	Yes	Yes
Dialup	Implicit	Yes	Yes
Enterprise Domain Controllers	Implicit	Yes	No
Everyone	Implicit	Yes	Yes
Interactive	Implicit	Yes	Yes
Network	Implicit	Yes	Yes
Proxy	Implicit	Yes	No
Restricted	Implicit	Yes	No
Self	Implicit	Yes	No
Service	Implicit	Yes	Yes
System	Implicit	Yes	Yes
Terminal Server User	Implicit	No	Yes

Account Capabilities

When you set up a user account, you can grant the user specific capabilities. You generally assign these capabilities by making the user a member of one or more groups, thus giving the user the capabilities of these groups. You then assign additional capabilities by making a user a member of the appropriate groups. You withdraw capabilities by removing group membership.

In Windows 2000, you can assign various types of capabilities to an account. These capabilities include

- **Privileges**   A type of user right that grants permissions to perform specific administrative tasks. You can assign privileges to both user and group accounts. An example of a privilege is the ability to shut down the system.

- **Logon rights**   A type of user right that grants logon permissions. You can assign logon rights to both user and group accounts. An example of a logon right is the ability to log on locally.

- **Built-in capabilities**   A type of user right that is assigned to groups and includes the automatic capabilities of the group. Built-in capabilities are predefined and unchangeable, but they can be delegated to users with permission to manage objects, organizational units, or other containers. An example of a built-in capability is the ability to create, delete, and manage user accounts. This capability is assigned to administrators and account Operators. Thus, if a user is a member of the Administrators group, the user can create, delete, and manage user accounts.

- **Access permissions** A type of user right that defines the operations that can be performed on network resources. You can assign access permissions to users, computers, and groups. An example of an access permission is the ability to create a file in a directory. Access permissions are discussed in Chapter 13.

As an administrator, you'll be dealing with account capabilities every day. To help track built-in capabilities, refer to the sections that follow. Keep in mind that while you can't change the built-in capabilities of a group, you can change the default rights of a group. For example, an administrator could revoke network access to a computer by removing a group's right to access the computer from the network.

Privileges

A privilege is a type of user right that grants permissions to perform a specific administrative task. You assign privileges through group policies, which can be applied to individual computers, organizational units, and domains. Although you can assign privileges to both users and groups, you'll usually want to assign privileges to groups. In this way, users are automatically assigned the appropriate privileges when they become members of a group. Assigning privileges to groups also makes it easier to manage user accounts.

Table 7-5 provides a brief summary of each of the privileges that can be assigned to users and groups. To learn how to assign privileges, see Chapter 8.

Table 7-5. Windows 2000 Privileges for Users and Groups

Privilege	Description
Act as part of the operating system	Allows a process to authenticate as any user and gain access to resources as any user. Processes that require this privilege should use the LocalSystem account, which already has this privilege.
Add workstations to domain	Allows users to add computers to the domain.
Back up files and directories	Allows users to back up the system regardless of the permissions set on files and directories.
Bypass traverse checking	Allows users to pass through directories while navigating an object path regardless of permissions set on the directories. The privilege doesn't allow the user to list directory contents.

(continued)

Table 7-5. *(continued)*

Privilege	Description
Change the system time	Allows users to set the time for the system clock.
Create a pagefile	Allows users to create and change paging file size for virtual memory.
Create a token object	Allows processes to create token objects that can be used to gain access to local resources. Processes that require this privilege should use the LocalSystem account, which already has this privilege.
Create permanent shared objects	Allows processes to create directory objects in the Windows 2000 object manager. Most components already have this privilege and it's not necessary to specifically assign it.
Debug programs	Allows users to perform debugging.
Enable user and computer accounts to be trusted for delegation	Allows users and computers to change or apply the trusted-for-delegation setting, provided they have write access to the object.
Force shutdown of a remote system	Allows users to shut down a computer from a remote location on the network.
Generate security audits	Allows processes to make security log entries for auditing object access.
Increase quotas	Allows processes to increase the processor quota assigned to other process, provided they have write access to the process.
Increase scheduling priority	Allows processes to increase the scheduling priority assigned to other processes, provided they have write access to the processes.
Load and unload device drivers	Allows users to install and uninstall plug-and-play device drivers. This doesn't affect device drivers that aren't plug-and-play, which can only be installed by administrators.
Lock pages in memory	In Windows NT, allowed processes to keep data in physical memory, preventing the system from paging data to virtual memory on disk. Not used in Windows 2000.
Manage auditing and security log	Allows users to specify auditing options and access the security log. You must turn on auditing in the group policy first.
Modify firmware environment values	Allows users and processes to modify system environment variables.

(continued)

Table 7-5. *(continued)*

Privilege	Description
Profile a single process	Allows users to monitor the performance of nonsystem processes.
Profile system performance	Allows users to monitor the performance of system processes.
Remove computer from docking station	Allows users to unlock a computer
Replace a process-level token	Allows processes to replace the default token for subprocesses.
Restore files and directories	Allows users to restore backed up files and directories, regardless of the permissions set on files and directories.
Shut down the system	Allows users to shut down the local computer.
Synchronize directory service data	Allows users to synchronize directory service data on domain controllers.
Take ownership of files	Allows users to take ownership of any or other objects Active Directory objects.

Logon Rights

A logon right is a type of user right that grants logon permissions. You can assign logon rights to both user and group accounts. As with privileges, you assign logon rights through group policies and you'll usually want to assign logon rights to groups rather than individual users.

Table 7-6 provides a brief summary of each of the logon rights that can be assigned to users and groups. To learn how to assign logon rights, see Chapter 8

Table 7-6. Windows 2000 Logon Rights for Users and Groups

Logon Right	Description
Access this computer from the network	Allows users to connect to the computer over the network. By default, this privilege is granted to Administrators, Everyone, and Power Users.
Deny access to this computer from the network	Denies remote access to the computer.
Deny logon as batch job	Denies the right to log on through a batch job or script.
Deny logon as service	Denies the right to log on as a service.
Deny logon locally	Denies the right to log on to the computer's keyboard.

(continued)

Table 7-6. *(continued)*

Logon Right	Description
Log on as a batch job	Allows users to log on using a batch-queue facility. This capability is not supported in the current release of Windows 2000. By default, this privilege is granted to Administrators.
Log on as a service	Allows a security principal to log on as a service, as a way of establishing a security context. The LocalSystem account always retains the right to log on as a service. Any service that runs under a separate account must be granted this right. By default, this right is not granted to anyone.
Log on locally	Allows users to log on at the computer's keyboard. By default, this right is granted to Administrators, Account Operators, Backup Operators, Print Operators, and Server Operators.

Built-In Capabilities for Groups in Active Directory

The built-in capabilities for groups in Active Directory are fairly extensive. The tables that follow summarize the most common capabilities that are assigned by default. Table 7-7 shows the default user rights for groups in Active Directory domains. This includes both privileges and logon rights. Note that any action that's available to the Everyone group is available to all groups, including the Guests group. This means that although the Guests group doesn't have explicit permission to access the computer from the network, Guests can still access the system because the Everyone group has this right.

Table 7-7. Default User Rights for Groups in Active Directory

User Right	Groups Assigned
Access this computer from the network	Everyone
Add workstations to domain	Administrators
Back up files and directories	Administrators, Server Operators, Backup Operators
Bypass traverse checking	Everyone
Change the system time	Administrators, Server Operators
Create a pagefile	Administrators
Debug programs	Administrators
Force shutdown from a remote system	Administrators, Server Operators
Increase quotas	Administrators

(continued)

Table 7-7. *(contiuned)*

User Right	Groups Assigned
Increase scheduling priority	Administrators
Load and unload device drivers	Administrators
Log on locally	Administrators, Server Operators, Account Operators, Backup Operators, Print Operators
Manage auditing and security log	Administrators
Modify firmware environment variables	Administrators
Profile a single process	Administrators
Profile system performance	Administrators
Remove computer from docking station	Administrators
Restore files and directories	Administrators, Server Operators, Backup Operators
Shut down the system	Administrators, Server Operators, Account Operators, Backup Operators, Print Operators
Take ownership of files or other objects	Administrators

Table 7-8 shows the default user rights for local groups on member servers and workstations. Again, this includes both privileges and logon rights. Note that on these systems, Power Users have privileges that normal users don't.

Table 7-8. Default User Rights for Local Groups

User Right	Groups Assigned
Access this computer from the network	Administrators, Power Users, Everyone
Back up files and directories	Administrators, Backup Operators
Bypass traverse checking	Everyone
Change the system time	Administrators, Power Users
Create a pagefile	Administrators
Debug programs	Administrators
Force shutdown from a remote system	Administrators
Increase quotas	Administrators
Increase scheduling priority	Administrators
Load and unload device drivers	Administrators
Log on locally	Administrators, Backup Operators, Power Users, Users, Everyone, Guests
Manage auditing and security log	Administrators
Modify firmware environment variables	Administrators
Profile a single process	Administrators, Power Users

(continued)

Table 7-8. *(continued)*

User Right	Groups Assigned
Profile system performance	Administrators
Remove computer from docking station	Administrators, Power Users, Users
Restore files and directories	Administrators, Backup Operators
Shut down the system	Administrators, Backup Operators, Power Users, Users
Take ownership of files or other objects	Administrators

Table 7-9 summarizes capabilities that can be delegated to other users and groups. As you study the table, note that restricted accounts include the Administrator user account, the user accounts of administrators, and the group accounts for Administrators, Server Operators, Account Operators, Backup Operators, and Print Operators. Because these accounts are restricted, Account Operators can't create or modify them.

Table 7-9. Other Capabilities for Built-In and Local Groups

Task	Description	Group Normally Assigned
Assign user rights	Allows users to assign user rights to other users	Administrators
Create, delete, and manage user accounts	Allows users to administer domain user accounts	Administrators, Account Operators
Modify the membership of a group	Allows users to add and remove users from domain groups	Administrators, Account Operators
Create and delete groups	Allows users to create a new group and delete existing groups	Administrators, Account Operators
Reset passwords on user accounts	Allows users to reset passwords on user accounts	Administrators, Account Operators
Read all user information	Allows users to view user account information	Administrators, Server Operators, Account Operators
Manage group policy links	Allows users to apply existing group policies to sites, domains, and organizational units for which they have write access to the related objects	Administrators
Manage printers	Allows users to modify printer settings and manage print queues	Administrators, Server Operators, Printer Operators
Create and delete printers	Allows users to create and delete printers	Administrators, Server Operators, Printer Operators

Using Default Group Accounts

The default group accounts are designed to be versatile. By assigning users to the right groups, you can make managing your Windows 2000 workgroup or domain a lot easier. Unfortunately, with so many different groups, understanding the purpose of each isn't easy. To help, let's divide the groups into five categories: groups used by administrators, groups used by operators, groups used by users, groups used by computers, and groups that are implicitly created.

Groups Used by Administrators

An administrator is someone who has wide access to network resources. Administrators can create accounts, modify user rights, install printers, manage shared resources, and more. The main administrator groups are Administrators, Domain Admins, and Enterprise Admins, as compared in Table 7-10.

Table 7-10. Administrators Group Overview

Administrators Group Type	Network Environment	Group Scope	Membership	Account Administration
Administrators	Active Directory domains	Domain Local	Administrator, Domain Admins, Enterprise Admins	Administrators
Administrators	Workgroups, computers not part of a domain	Local	Administrator	Administrators
Domain Admins	Active Directory domains	Global	Administrator	Administrators
Enterprise Admins	Active Directory domains	Global or Universal	Administrator	Administrators

Tip The local group Administrator and the global groups Domain Admins and Enterprise Admins are members of the Administrators group. The Administrator user membership is used to access the local computer. The Domain Admins membership allows other administrators to access the system from elsewhere in the domain. The Enterprise Admins membership allows other administrators to access the system from other domains in the current domain tree or forest. To prevent enterprise-wide access to a domain, you can remove Enterprise Admins from this group.

Administrators is a local group that provides full administrative access to an individual computer or a single domain, depending on its location. Because this account has complete access, you should be very careful about adding users to this group. To make someone an administrator for a local computer or domain, all you need to do is make that person a member of this group. Only members of the Administrators group can modify this account.

Domain Admins is a global group designed to help you administer all the computers in a domain. This group has administrative control over all computers in a domain because it's a member of the Administrators group by default. To make someone an administrator for a domain, make that person a member of this group.

Tip In a Windows 2000 domain, the Administrator local user is a member of Domain Admins by default. This means that if someone logs on to a computer as the administrator and the computer is a member of the domain, the user will have complete access to all resources in the domain. To prevent this, you can remove the local Administrator account from the Domain Admins group.

Enterprise Admins is a global group designed to help you administer all the computers in a domain tree or forest. This group has administrative control over all computers in the enterprise because it's a member of the Administrators group by default. To make someone an administrator for the enterprise, make that person a member of this group.

Tip In a Windows 2000 domain, the Administrator local user is a member of Enterprise Admins by default. This means that if someone logs on to a computer as the administrator and the computer is a member of the domain, the user will have complete access to the domain tree or forest. To prevent this, you can remove the local Administrator account from the Enterprise Admins group.

Groups Used by Operators

Operators are users who have privileges to perform very specific administrative tasks, such as creating accounts or backing up file systems. By default, no other group or user accounts are members of the operator groups. This feature exists primarily to make sure that you grant explicit access to these accounts. Additionally, because these are local groups, operators can only perform the tasks on a specific computer.

The operator groups are Account Operators, Backup Operators, Print Operators, Server Operators, and Replicator Operators, as compared in Table 7-11.

Table 7-11. Operators Group Overview

Operators Group Type	Network Environment	Group Scope	Membership	Account Administration
Account Operators	Active Directory domains	Built-In Local	None	Administrators
Backup Operators	Any server or workstation	Built-In Local, Local	None	Administrators
Print Operators	Active Directory domains	Built-In Local	None	Administrators
Server Operators	Active Directory domains	Built-In Local	None	Administrators
Replicator	Any server or workstation	Built-In Local, Local	None	Administrators, Account Operators, Server Operators

Account Operators is a local group that grants limited account creation privileges to a user. Members of this group can create and modify most types of accounts, including those of users, local groups, and global groups. They can also log on locally to domain controllers. However, Account Operators can't manage the Administrator user account, the user accounts of administrators, or the group accounts Administrators, Server Operators, Account Operators, Backup Operators, and Print Operators. Account Operators also can't modify user rights.

Backup Operators is a local group that enables a user to back up and restore files and directories on workstations and servers in a Windows 2000 domain. Members of this group can log on to a computer, back up or restore files, and shut down the computer. Because of how the account is set up, they can back up files regardless of whether they have read/write access to the files. However, they can't change access permissions of the files or perform other administrative tasks.

Print Operators is a local group for managing network printers. Members of this group can manage printers running in a Windows 2000 domain. They can define which printers are shared, which printers aren't, and other related printer privileges. Print Operators can also log on to a server locally and shut it down.

Server Operators is a local group that allows a user to perform general administrator tasks. These tasks include sharing server resources, performing file backup and recovery, and more. As with other operator accounts, Server Operators can also log on to a server locally and shut it down. Server Operators can perform most common server administration tasks.

Replicator, which is a special group account, is used with the directory replication service. Administrators and operators can set up this service to manage the replication of files and directories in a domain. If you do this, you'll need to set up a special user account for the replication service and make the account a member of this group.

Groups Used by Users

Windows 2000 provides many different types of user accounts. These accounts are designed to meet the needs of diverse networking environments. The user groups are Users, Domain Users, Power Users, Guests, and Domain Guests, as compared in Table 7-12.

Table 7-12. Users Group Overview

Users Group Type	Network Environment	Group Scope	Membership	Account Administration
Users	Active Directory domains, domain member server, or workstation	Built-In Local, Local	Authenticated Users, Domain Users	Administrators, Account Operators
Users	Stand-alone workstation or server	Local	User account selected during installation of the operating system	Administrators
Domain Users	Active Directory domains	Global	Administrators, Guest	Administrators, Account Operators
Power Users	Domain member server or workstation	Local	Interactive; user account selected during installation of the operating system	Administrators
Power Users	Stand-alone workstation or server	Local	User account selected during installation of the operating system	Administrators
Guest	Active Directory domains	Built-In Local	Domain Guests, Guest	Administrators, Account Operators
Guest	Domain member server or workstation; stand-alone workstation or server	Local	Guest	Administrators
Domain Guest	Active Directory domains	Global	Guest	Administrators, Account Operators

Users are the people who do most of their work on a single Windows 2000 workstation. Because of this, members of the Users group have more restrictions than privileges. By default, members of the Users group can't log on locally to a Windows 2000 server acting as a domain controller. However, they can access the controller's resources over the network.

On Windows 2000 workstations, members of the Users group can log on to a workstation locally, keep a local profile, lock the workstation, and shut down the workstation. Users can also create local groups and manage those groups.

In Windows 2000 domains, implicitly authenticated users and the global Domain Users are members of this group by default. For workgroups or isolated workstations, there are no predefined members of this group.

Domain Users is a global group for users in Active Directory domains. When you create new domain users, they're automatically added to this group. By default, the local Administrator and Guest accounts are members of this group.

Power Users exist only on computers that aren't domain controllers. Power Users have all the privileges of members of the Users group, as well as a few additional privileges, such as the capability to modify computer settings and install programs.

To give users of a Windows 2000 workstation extra control, Microsoft recommends that you make them members of the Power Users group. This allows users to perform limited administration on their workstations.

Guests are users with very limited privileges. Members of the Guests group can access the system and its resources remotely, but they can't perform most other tasks.

In Active Directory domains, the members of this group are Domain Guests and the local Guest user. On nondomain controllers, the only member is Guest.

 Note Keep in mind that any action available to the Everyone group is available to the Guests group. This means that if someone is a member of the local Guests account, that person can perform any task that anyone in the Everyone group can.

Domain Guests are users with guest privileges throughout a domain. By default, the local Guest user is a member of this account. Therefore, anytime you create a local guest account in a Windows 2000 domain, the guest user gains access to the entire domain.

Groups Used by Computers

Windows 2000 provides two types of user accounts for computers. These accounts are designed to set permissions for member servers, workstations, and domain controllers. The computer groups are Domain Computers and Domain Controllers, as compared in Table 7-13.

Table 7-13. Computers Group Overview

Computers Group Type	Network Environment	Group Scope	Membership	Account Administration
Domain Computers	Active Directory domains	Global	All member servers and workstations in the domain	Administrators, Account Operators
Domain Controllers	Active Directory domains	Global	All domain controllers in a domain	Administrators, Account Operators

You use Domain Computers to identify and set default permissions for member servers and workstations in a domain. By default, Domain Computers have more restrictions than they have capabilities. This configuration reflects their role in the domain environment.

You use Domain Controllers to identify and set default permissions for domain controllers in a domain. By default, Domain Controllers have more capabilities than restrictions. This configuration reflects their high-priority role in the domain environment.

Implicit Groups and Identities

Windows 2000 defines a set of special identities that you can use to assign permissions in certain situations. You usually assign permissions implicitly to special identities. However, you can assign permissions to special identities when you modify Active Directory objects. The special identities include

- **The Anonymous Logon identity**   Any user accessing the system through anonymous logon has the Anonymous Logon identity. This identity is used to allow anonymous access to resources, such as a Web pages published on the corporate presence servers.

- **The Authenticated Users identity**   Any user accessing the system through a logon process has the Authenticated Users identity. This identity is used to allow access to shared resources within the domain, such as files in a shared folder that should be accessible to all the workers in the organization.

- **The Batch identity**   Any user or process accessing the system as a batch job (or through the batch queue) has the Batch identity. This identity is used to allow batch jobs to run schedule tasks, such as a nightly cleanup job that deletes temporary files.

- **The Creator Group identity**   Windows 2000 uses this group to automatically grant access permissions to users who are members of the same group(s) as the creator of a file or a directory.

- **The Creator Owner identity**   The person who created the file or the directory is a member of this group. Windows 2000 uses this group to automatically grant access permissions to the creator of a file or directory.

- **The Dial-Up identity**   Any user accessing the system through a dial-up connection has the Dial-Up identity. This identity is used to distinguish dial-up users from other types of authenticated users.

- **The Enterprise Domain Controllers identity**   Domain controllers with enterprise-wide roles and responsibilities have the Enterprise Domain Controllers identity. This identity allows them to perform certain tasks in the enterprise using transitive trusts.

- **The Everyone identity**   All interactive, network, dial-up, and authenticated users are members of the Everyone group. This group is used to give wide access to a system resource.

- **The Interactive identity**   Any user logged on to the local system has the Interactive identity. This identity is used to allow *only* local users to access a resource.

- **The Network identity**   Any user accessing the system through a network has the Network identity. This identity is used to allow *only* remote users to access a resource.

- **The Proxy identity**   Users and computers accessing resources through a proxy have the Proxy identity. This identity is used when proxies are implemented on the network.

- **The Restricted identity**   Users and computers with restricted capabilities have the Restricted identity. On a member server or workstation, a local user who is a member of the Users group (rather than the Power Users group) has this identity.

- **The Self identity**   The Self identity refers to the object itself and allows the object to modify itself.

- **The Service identity**   Any service accessing the system has the Service identity. This identity grants access to processes being run by Windows 2000 services.

- **The System identity**   The Windows 2000 operating system itself has the System identity. This identity is used when the operating system needs to perform a system-level function.

- **The Terminal Server User identity**   Any user accessing the system through terminal services has the Terminal Server User identity. This identity allows terminal server users to access terminal server applications and to perform other necessary tasks with terminal services.

Chapter 8

Creating User and Group Accounts

A key part of your job as an administrator is to create user accounts, and this chapter will show you how to do that.

User accounts allow Microsoft Windows 2000 to track and manage information about users, including permissions and privileges. When you create user accounts, the primary account administration tools you use are

- Active Directory Users And Computers, which is designed to administer accounts throughout an Active Directory domain.

- Local Users And Groups, which is designed to administer accounts on a local computer.

Creating domain accounts as well as local users and groups is covered in this chapter.

User Account Setup and Organization

The most important aspects of account creation are account setup and organization. Without the appropriate policies, you could quickly find that you need to rework all your user accounts. So before you create accounts, determine the policies you'll use for setup and organization.

Account Naming Policies

A key policy you'll need to set is the naming scheme for accounts. User accounts have *display names* and *logon names*. The display name (or full name) is the name displayed to users and the name referenced in user sessions. The logon name is the name used to log on to the domain. Logon names were discussed briefly in the section of Chapter 7 entitled "Logon Names, Passwords, and Public Certificates."

Rules for Display Names
In Windows 2000, the display name is normally the concatenation of the user's first name and last name, but you can set it to any string value. The display names must follow these rules:

- Local display names must be unique on a workstation.

- Display names must be unique throughout a domain.
- Display names must be no more than 64 characters long.
- Display names can contain alphanumeric characters and special characters.

Rules for Logon Names

Logon names must follow these rules:

- Local logon names must be unique on a workstation and global logon names must be unique throughout a domain.
- Logon names can be up to 104 characters. However, it isn't practical to use logon names that are longer than 64 characters.
- A Microsoft Windows NT version 4.0 or earlier logon name is given to all accounts, which by default is set to the first 20 characters of the Windows 2000 logon name. The Windows NT version 4.0 or earlier logon name must be unique throughout a domain.
- Users logging on to the domain from Windows 2000 computers can use their Windows 2000 logon name or their Windows NT version 4.0 or earlier logon name, regardless of the domain operations mode.
- Logon names can't contain certain characters. Invalid characters are

  " / \ [ ] : ; | = , + * ? < >

- Logon names can contain all other special characters, including spaces, periods, dashes, and underscores. But it's generally not a good idea to use spaces in account names.

 Note Although Windows 2000 stores user names in the case that you enter, user names aren't case sensitive. For example, you can access the Administrator account with the user name Administrator or administrator. Thus, user names are case aware but not case sensitive.

Naming Schemes

You'll find that most small organizations tend to assign logon names that use the user's first or last name. But you can have several Toms, Dicks, and Harrys in an organization of any size. So rather than having to rework your logon naming scheme when you run into problems, select a good naming scheme now and make sure other administrators use it. For naming accounts, you should use a consistent procedure that allows your user base to grow and limits the possibility of name conflicts and ensures that your accounts have secure names that aren't easily exploited. If you follow these guidelines, the types of naming schemes you may want to use include:

- **User's first name and last initial** You take the user's first name and combine it with the first letter of the last name to create the logon name. For William Stanek, you would use *williams* or *bills*. This naming scheme isn't practical for large organizations.

- **User's first initial and last name**   You take the user's first initial and combine it with the last name to create the logon name. For William Stanek, you would use *wstanek*. This naming scheme isn't practical for large organizations, either.

- **User's first initial, middle initial, and last name**   You combine the user's first initial, middle initial, and last name to create the logon name. For William R. Stanek, you would use *wrstanek*.

- **User's first initial, middle initial, and first five characters of the last name**   You combine the user's first initial, middle initial, and the first five characters of the last name to create the logon name. For William R. Stanek, you would use *wrstane*.

- **User's first name and last name**   You combine the user's first and last name. To separate the names, you could use the underscore character (_) or hyphen (-). For William Stanek, you could use *william_stanek* or *william-stanek*.

Tip   In tight security environments, you can assign a numeric code for the logon name. This numeric code should be at least 20 characters long. Combine this strict naming method with smart cards and smart card readers to allow users to quickly log on to the domain. Don't worry, users can still have a display name that humans can read.

Password and Account Policies

Windows 2000 accounts use passwords and public certificates to authenticate access to network resources. This section focuses on passwords.

Secure Passwords

A password is a case-sensitive string that can contain up to 104 characters with Active Directory directory service and up to 14 characters with Windows NT Security Manager. Valid characters for passwords are letters, numbers, and symbols. When you set a password for an account, Windows 2000 stores the password in an encrypted format in the account database.

But simply having a password isn't enough. The key to preventing unauthorized access to network resources is to use *secure* passwords. The difference between an average password and a secure password is that secure passwords are difficult to guess and crack. You make passwords difficult to crack by using combinations of all the available character types—including lowercase letters, uppercase letters, numbers, and symbols. For example, instead of using **happydays** for a password you would use **haPPy2Days&**, **Ha******y!dayS**, or even **h*****PPY%d*****ys**.

Unfortunately, no matter how secure you initially make a user's password, eventually the user usually chooses the password. Because of this, you'll want to set account policies. Account policies are a subset of the policies configurable as a group policy.

Setting Account Policies

As you know from previous discussions, you can apply group policies at various levels within the network structure. You manage local group policies in the manner discussed in the section of Chapter 4 entitled "Managing Local Group Policies." You manage global group policies as explained in the section of Chapter 4 entitled "Managing Site, Domain, and Unit Policies."

Once you access the group policy container you want to work with, you can set account policies by completing the following steps:

1. As shown in Figure 8-1, access the Account Policies node by working your way down the console tree. Expand Computer Configuration, then Windows Settings, and then Security Settings.

2. You can now manage account policies through the Password Policy, Account Lockout Policy, and Kerberos Policy nodes.

 Note Kerberos policies aren't used with local computers. Kerberos policies are only available with group policies that affect sites, domains, and organizational units.

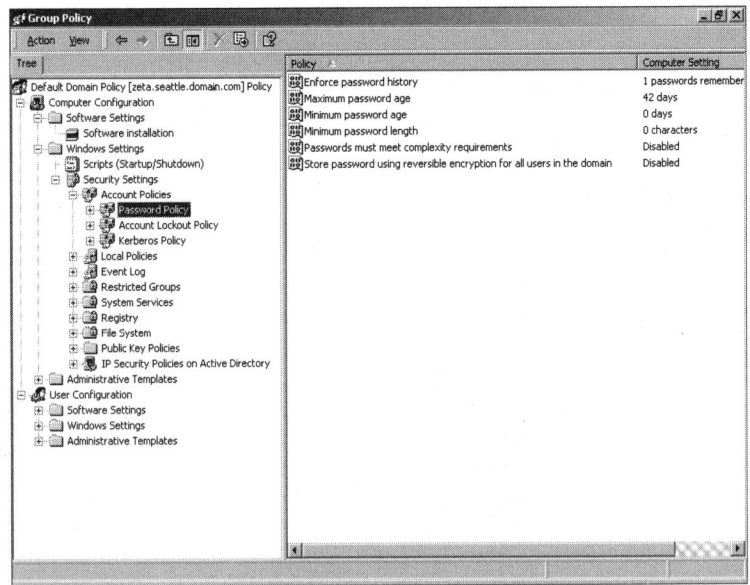

Figure 8-1. *Use entries in the Account Policies node to set policies for passwords and general account use. The console tree shows the name of the computer or domain you're configuring. Be sure this is the appropriate network resource to configure.*

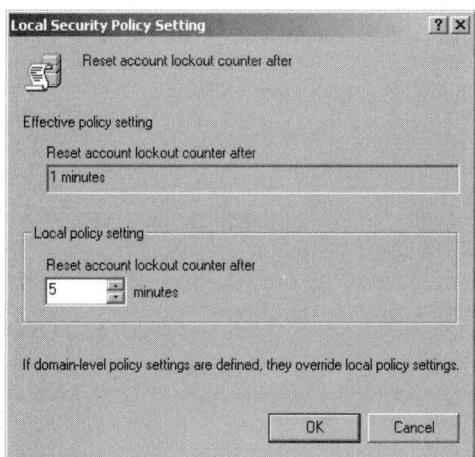

Figure 8-2. *With local policies, you'll see the effective policy as well as the local policy.*

3. To configure a policy, double-click its entry or right-click on it and select Security. This opens a Properties dialog box for the policy.

4. For a local policy, the Properties dialog box is similar to the one shown in Figure 8-2. The effective policy for the computer is displayed but you can't change it. You can change the local policy settings, however. Use the fields provided to configure the local policy. For a local policy, skip the remaining steps; those steps apply to global group policies.

Note   Site, domain, and organizational unit policies have precedence over local policies.

5. For a site, domain, or organizational unit, the Properties dialog box is similar to the one shown in Figure 8-3.

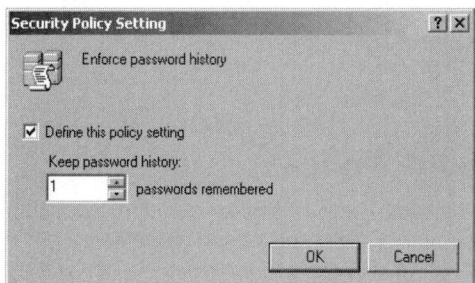

Figure 8-3. *Define and configure global group policies using their Properties dialog box.*

6. All policies are either defined or not defined. That is, they are either configured for use or not configured for use. A policy that isn't defined in the current container could be inherited from another container.

7. Select or clear the Define This Policy Setting check box to determine whether a policy is defined.

 Tip Policies can have additional fields for configuring the policy. Often, these fields are option buttons labeled Enabled and Disabled. Enabled turns on the policy restriction. Disabled turns off the policy restriction.

Specific procedures for working with account policies are discussed in the sections of the chapter entitled "Configuring Password Policies," "Configuring Account Lockout Policies," and "Configuring Kerberos Policies." This chapter's next section, "Viewing Effective Policies," will teach you more about viewing the effective policy on a local computer.

Viewing Effective Policies

When working with account policies and user rights assignment, you'll often want to view the effective policy on a local system. The effective policy is the policy being enforced and, as discussed in Chapter 4 under "Group Policy Management," the effective policy depends on the order in which you apply the policies.

To view the effective policy on a local system, complete the following steps:

1. Access the local policy for the system you want to work with, as explained in the section of Chapter 4 entitled "Managing Local Group Policies." Or select Local Policy Settings on the Administrative Tools menu (if these tools are installed and you're currently logged on to the computer you want to examine).

2. Access the policy node that you want to examine. Figure 8-4 shows the Password Policy node.

3. With local policies, the Computer Setting column is replaced by a Local Setting column and an Effective Setting column. The Local Setting column shows the local policy settings. The Effective Setting column shows the policy settings that are being enforced on the local computer.

4. If there are policy conflicts that you want to track down, review the sections of Chapter 4 entitled "In What Order Are Multiple Policies Applied?" and "When Are Group Policies Applied?"

Configuring Account Policies

As you learned in the previous section, there are three types of account policies: password policies, account lockout policies, and Kerberos policies. The sections that follow show you how to configure each one of these policies.

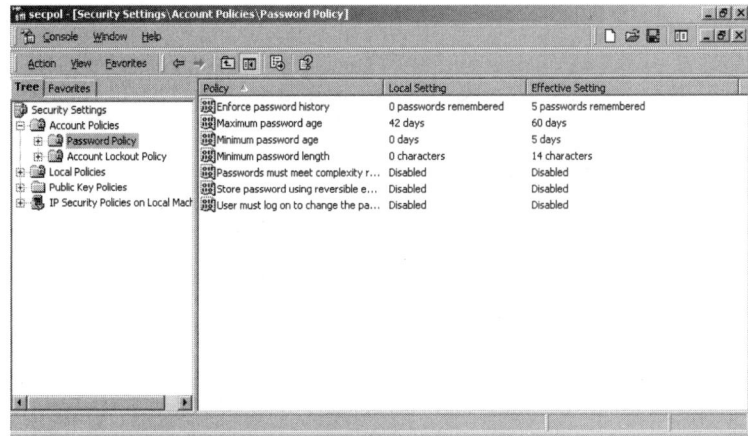

Figure 8-4. *Local policies show the effective setting as well as the local setting.*

Configuring Password Policies

Password policies control security for passwords and they include

- Enforce Password History
- Maximum Password Age
- Minimum Password Age
- Minimum Password Length
- Passwords Must Meet Complexity Requirements
- Store Password Using Reversible Encryption For All Users In The Domain

The uses of these policies are discussed in the following sections.

Enforce Password History

Enforce Password History sets how frequently old passwords can be reused. You can use this policy to discourage users from changing back and forth between a set of common passwords. Windows 2000 can store up to 24 passwords for each user in the password history. By default, Windows 2000 stores one password in the password history.

To disable this feature, set the size of the password history to zero. To enable this feature, set the size of the password history using the Passwords Remember field. Windows 2000 will then track old passwords using a password history that is unique for each user, and users won't be allowed to reuse any of the stored passwords.

Note To discourage users from cheating Enforce Password History, you shouldn't allow them to change passwords immediately. This will prevent users from changing their passwords several times to get back to their old passwords.

Maximum Password Age

Maximum Password Age determines how long users can keep a password before they have to change it. The aim is to periodically force users to change their passwords. When you use this feature, set a value that makes sense for your network. Generally, you use a shorter period when security is very important and a longer period when security is less important.

The default expiration date is 42 days, but set it to any value from 0 to 999. A value of zero specifies that passwords don't expire. Although you may be tempted to set no expiration date, users should change passwords regularly to ensure the network's security. Where security is a concern, good values are 30, 60, or 90 days. Where security is less important, good values are 120, 150, or 180 days.

 Note Windows 2000 notifies users when they're getting close to the password expiration date. Anytime the expiration date is less than 30 days away, users see a warning when they log on that they have to change their password within so many days.

Minimum Password Age

Minimum Password Age determines how long users must keep a password before they can change it. You can use this field to prevent users from cheating the password system by entering a new password and then changing it right back to the old one.

By default, Windows 2000 lets users change their passwords immediately. To prevent this, set a specific minimum age. Reasonable settings are from three to seven days. In this way, you make sure that users are less inclined to switch back to an old password but are able to change their passwords in a reasonable amount of time if they want to.

Minimum Password Length

Minimum Password Length sets the minimum number of characters for a password. If you haven't changed the default setting, you'll want to do so immediately. The default is to allow empty passwords (passwords with zero characters), which is definitely not a good idea.

For security reasons, you'll generally want passwords of at least eight characters. The reason for this is that long passwords are usually harder to crack than short ones. If you want greater security, set the minimum password length to 14 characters.

Passwords Must Meet Complexity Requirements

Beyond the basic password and account policies, Windows 2000 includes facilities for creating additional password controls. These facilities are available in the password filters, which can be installed on a domain controller. If you've installed a password filter, enable Passwords Must Meet Complexity Requirements. Passwords are then required to meet the filter's security requirement.

For example, the standard Windows NT filter (PASSFILT.DLL) enforces the use of secure passwords that follow these guidelines:

- Passwords must be at least six characters long.

- Passwords can't contain the user name, such as stevew, or parts of the user's full name, such as Steve.

- Passwords must use three of the four available character types: lowercase letters, uppercase letters, numbers, and symbols.

Store Password Using Reversible Encryption

Passwords in the password database are encrypted. This encryption can't normally be reversed. If you want to allow the encryption to be reversed, enable Store Password Using Reversible Encryption For All Users In The Domain. Passwords are then stored with reversible encryption and can be recovered in case of emergency. Forgetting a password in not an emergency situation. Any administrator can change user passwords.

Configuring Account Lockout Policies

Account lockout policies control how and when accounts are locked out of the domain or the local system. These policies are

- Account Lockout Threshold
- Account Lockout Duration
- Reset Account Lockout Threshold After

Account Lockout Threshold

Account Lockout Threshold sets the number of logon attempts that are allowed before an account is locked out. If you decide to use lockout controls, you should set this field to a value that balances the need to prevent account cracking against the needs of users who are having difficulty accessing their accounts.

The main reason users may not be able to access their accounts properly the first time is that they forgot their passwords. If this is the case, it may take them several attempts to log on properly. Workgroup users could also have problems accessing a remote system where their current passwords don't match the passwords the remote system expects. If this happens, several bad logon attempts may be recorded by the remote system before the user ever gets a prompt to enter the correct password. The reason is that Windows 2000 may attempt to automatically log on to the remote system. In a domain environment, this normally doesn't happen because of the Single Log-On feature.

You can set the lockout threshold to any value from 0 to 999. The lockout threshold is set to zero by default, which means that accounts won't be locked out because of invalid logon attempts. Any other value sets a specific lockout threshold. Keep in mind that the higher the lockout value, the higher the risk that a hacker may be able to break into your system. A reasonable range of values for this threshold is between 7 and 15. This is high enough to rule out user error and low enough to deter hackers.

Account Lockout Duration

If someone violates the lockout controls, Account Lockout Duration sets the length of time the account is locked. You can set the lockout duration to a specific length of time using a value between 1 and 99,999 minutes or to an indefinite length of time by setting the lockout duration to zero.

The best security policy is to lock the account indefinitely. When you do, only an administrator can unlock the account. This will prevent hackers from trying to access the system again and will force users who are locked out to seek help from an administrator, which is usually a good idea. By talking to the user, you can determine what the user is doing wrong and help the user avoid problems.

 Tip When an account is locked out, access the Properties dialog box for the account in Active Directory Users And Computers. Then click the Account tab and clear the Account Is Locked Out check box. This unlocks the account.

Reset Account Lockout Threshold After

Every time a logon attempt fails, Windows 2000 raises the value of a threshold that tracks the number of bad logon attempts. Reset Account Lockout Threshold After determines how long the lockout threshold is maintained. This threshold is reset in one of two ways. If a user logs on successfully, the threshold is reset. If the waiting period for Reset Account Lockout Threshold After has elapsed since the last bad logon attempt, the threshold is also reset.

By default, the lockout threshold is maintained for one minute, but you can set any value from 1 to 99,999 minutes. As with Account Lockout Threshold, you need to select a value that balances security needs against user access needs. A good value is from one to two hours. This waiting period should be long enough to force hackers to wait longer than they want to before trying to access the account again.

 Note Bad logon attempts to a workstation against a password-protected screen saver don't increase the lockout threshold. Similarly, if you lock a server or workstation using Ctrl+Alt+Delete, bad logon attempts against the Unlock dialog box don't count.

Configuring Kerberos Policies

Kerberos version 5 is the primary authentication mechanism used in an Active Directory domain. To verify the identification of users and network services, Kerberos uses service tickets and user tickets. As you might expect, service tickets are used by Windows 2000 service processes and user tickets are used by user processes. Tickets contain encrypted data that confirm the identity of the user or service.

You can control ticket duration, renewal, and enforcement through the following policies:

- Enforce User Logon Restrictions
- Maximum Lifetime For Service Ticket
- Maximum Lifetime For User Ticket
- Maximum Lifetime For User Ticket Renewal
- Maximum Tolerance For Computer Clock Synchronization

These policies are discussed in the sections that follow.

Caution   Only administrators with an intimate understanding of Kerberos security should change these policies. If you change these policies to inefficient settings, you may cause serious problems on the network. In most cases the default Kerberos policy settings work just fine.

Enforce User Logon Restrictions

Enforce User Logon Restrictions ensures that any restrictions placed on a user account are enforced. For example, if the user's logon hours are restricted, this policy is what enforces the restriction. By default, the policy is enabled and should only be disabled in rare circumstances.

Maximum Lifetime

Maximum Lifetime For Service Ticket and Maximum Lifetime For User Ticket set the maximum duration for which a service or user ticket is valid. By default, service tickets have a maximum duration of 41,760 minutes and user tickets have a maximum duration of 720 hours.

You can change the duration of tickets. For service tickets, the valid range is from 0 to 99,999 minutes. For user tickets, the valid range is from 0 to 99,999 hours. A value of zero effectively turns off expiration. Any other value sets a specific ticket lifetime.

A ticket that expires can be renewed, provided the renewal takes place within the time set for Maximum Lifetime For User Ticket Renewal. By default, the maximum renewal period is 60 days. You can change the renewal period to any value from 0 to 99,999 days. A value of zero effectively turns off the maximum renewal period and any other value sets a specific renewal period.

Maximum Tolerance

Maximum Tolerance For Computer Clock Synchronization is one of the few Kerberos policies that you may need to change. By default, computers in the domain must be synchronized within five minutes of each other. If they aren't, authentication fails.

If you have remote users that log on to the domain without synchronizing their clock to the network timeserver, you may need to adjust this value. You can set any value from 0 to 99,999.

Configuring User Rights Policies

Chapter 7 covered built-in capabilities and user rights. Although you can't change built-in capabilities for accounts, you can administer user rights for accounts. Normally, you apply user rights to users by making them members of the appropriate group or groups. You can also apply rights directly, and you do this by managing the user rights for the user's account.

 Note Any user who is a member of a group that's assigned a certain right also has that right. For example, if the Backup Operators group has the right and TJSMITH is a member of this group, TJSMITH has this right as well. Keep in mind that changes you make to user rights can have a far-reaching effect. Because of this, only experienced administrators should make changes to the user rights policy.

You assign user rights through the Local Policies node of Group Policy. As the name implies, local policies pertain to a local computer. However, you can configure local policies and then import them into Active Directory. You can also configure these local policies as part of an existing Group Policy for a site, domain, or organizational unit. When you do this, the local policies apply to computer accounts in the site, domain, or organizational unit.

To administer user rights policies, complete the following steps:

1. Access the group policy container you want to work with, and then access the Local Policies node by working your way down the console tree. Expand Computer Configuration, Windows Settings, and then Local Policies.

2. Expand User Rights Assignment, shown in Figure 8-5, You can now manage user rights.

   To configure user rights assignment, double-click a user right or right-click on it and select Security. This opens a Properties dialog box.

3. You can now configure the user rights as described in Steps 1–4 of the section of this chapter entitled "Configuring User Rights Locally" or Steps 1–7 of the following section, "Configuring User Rights Globally."

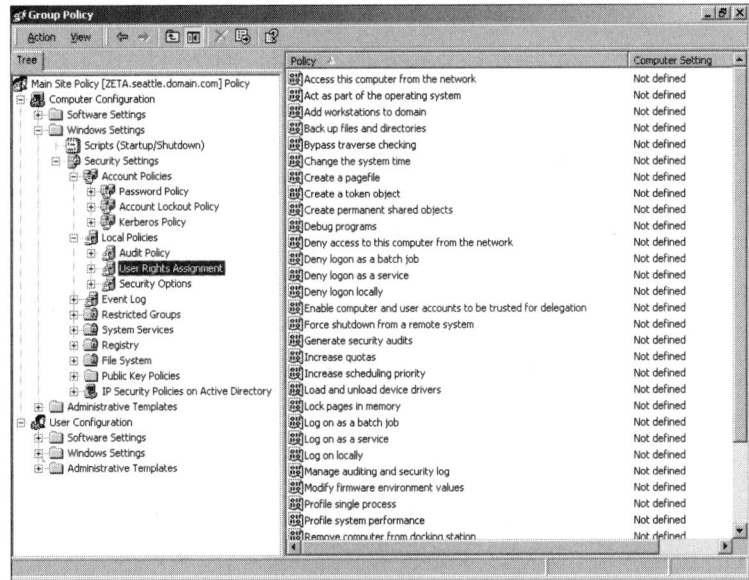

Figure 8-5. *Use User Rights Assignment to configure user rights for the current group policy container.*

Configuring User Rights Globally

For a site, domain, or organizational unit, you configure individual user rights by completing the following steps:

1. Open the Properties dialog box for the user right, shown in Figure 8-6.

Note All policies are either defined or not defined. That is, they are either configured for use or not configured for use. A policy that isn't defined in the current container could be inherited from another container.

2. Select Define These Policy Settings to define the policy.

   To apply the right to a user or group, click Add. Then, in the Group Name dialog box, click Browse. This opens the Select Users Or Groups dialog box shown in Figure 8-7. You can now apply the right to users and groups. The fields of this dialog box are used as follows:

   • **Look In** To access account names from other domains, click the Look In list box. You should now see a list that shows the current domain, trusted domains, and other resources that you can access. Select Entire Directory to view all the account names in the directory.

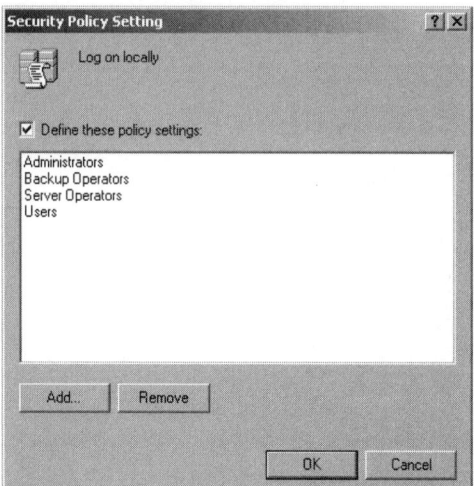

Figure 8-6. *Define the user right and then apply the right to users and groups.*

 Note Only domains that have been designated as trusted are available in the Look In drop-down menu. Because of the transitive trusts in Windows 2000, this usually means that all domains in the domain tree or forest are listed. A transitive trust is one that isn't established explicitly. Rather, the trust is established automatically based on the forest structure and permissions set in the forest.

- **Name** The Name column shows the available accounts of the currently selected domain or resource.
- **Add** Add selected names to the selection list.
- **Check Names** Validate the user and group names entered into the selection list. This is useful if you type names in manually and want to ensure that they're available.

3. After you select the account names to add to the group, click OK. The Group Name dialog box should now show the selected accounts. Click OK again.

4. The Properties dialog box is updated to reflect your selections. If you made a mistake, select a name and remove it by clicking Remove.

5. When you're finished granting the right to users and groups, click OK.

Configuring User Rights Locally

For local computers, you apply user rights by completing the following steps:

1. Open the Properties dialog box for the user right, shown in Figure 8-8.

2. The effective policy for the computer is displayed, but you can't change it. However, you can change the local policy settings. Use the fields provided

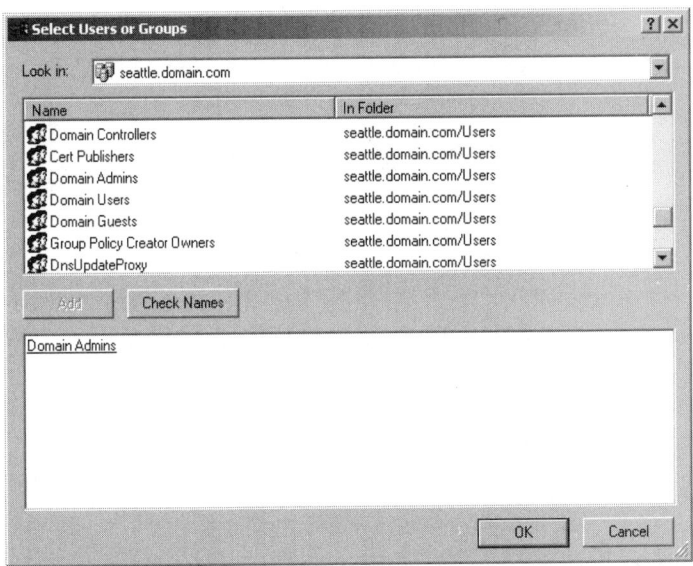

Figure 8-7. *Use the Select Users Or Groups dialog box to apply the user right to users and groups.*

to configure the local policy. Remember that site, domain, and organizational unit policies have precedence over local policies.

3. The Assigned To column shows current users and groups that have been given a user right. Select or clear the related check boxes under the Local Policy Setting column to apply or remove the user right.

You can apply the user right to additional users and groups by clicking Add. This opens the Select Users Or Groups dialog box shown previously in Figure 8-7. You can now add users and groups.

Adding a User Account

You need to create a user account for each user who wants to use your network resources. You create domain user accounts with Active Directory Users And Computers. You create local user accounts with Local Users And Groups.

Creating Domain User Accounts

Generally, there are two ways to create new domain accounts:

- **Create a completely new user account**   Create a completely new account by right-clicking on the container in which you want to place the user account, pointing to New, and then selecting User. This opens the New Object - User Wizard shown in Figure 8-9. When you create a new account, the default system settings are used.

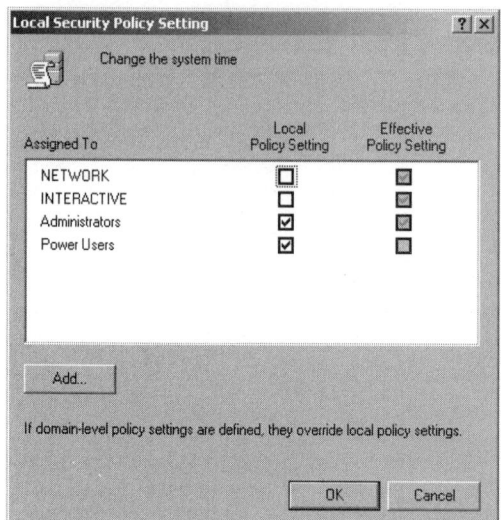

Figure 8-8. *Define the user right and then apply the right to users and groups.*

- **Base the new account on an existing account** Right-click the user account you want to copy in Active Directory Users And Computers, and then select Copy. This starts the Copy Object - User Wizard, which is essentially the same as the New User dialog box. However, when you create a copy of an account, the new account gets most of its environment settings from the existing account. For more information on copying accounts, see the section of Chapter 9 entitled "Copying Domain User Accounts."

Once either the New Object - User or the Copy Object - User Wizard is started, you can create the account by completing the following steps:

1. As shown in Figure 8-9, the first wizard dialog box lets you configure the user display name and logon name.

2. Type the user's first and last name in the fields provided. The first and last names are used to create the Full Name, which is the user's display name.

3. Make changes to the Full Name field as necessary. For example, you may want to type the name in LastName FirstName MiddleInitial format or in FirstName MiddleInitial LastName format. The Full Name must be unique in the domain and must be 64 characters or less.

4. In User Logon Name, type the user's logon name. Then use the drop-down list to select the domain the account is to be associated with. This sets the fully qualified logon name.

5. The first 20 characters of the logon name are used to set the Windows NT version 4.0 or earlier logon name. This logon name must be unique in the domain. If necessary, change the Windows NT version 4.0 or earlier logon name.

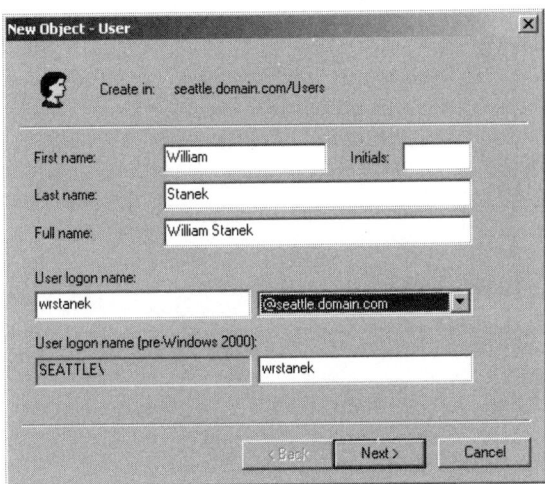

Figure 8-9. *Configure the user display and logon names.*

6. Click Next. Then configure the user's password using the dialog box shown in Figure 8-10. The options for this dialog box are used as follows:

- **Password** The password for the account. This password should follow the conventions of your password policy.

- **Confirm Password** A field to ensure that you assign the account password correctly. Simply reenter the password to confirm it.

- **User Must Change Password At Next Logon** If selected, the user must change the password upon logon.

- **User Cannot Change Password** If checked, the user can't change the password.

- **Password Never Expires** If selected, the password for this account never expires. This setting overrides the domain account policy. Generally, it's not a good idea to set a password so it doesn't expire because this defeats the purpose of having passwords in the first place.

- **Account Is Disabled** If checked, the account is disabled and can't be used. Use this field to temporarily prevent anyone from using an account.

7. Click Next, and then click Finish to create the account. If there are problems creating the account, you'll see a warning and you'll need to use the Back button to retype information in the user name and password dialog boxes, as necessary.

Once the account is created, you can set advanced properties for the account as discussed later in the chapter.

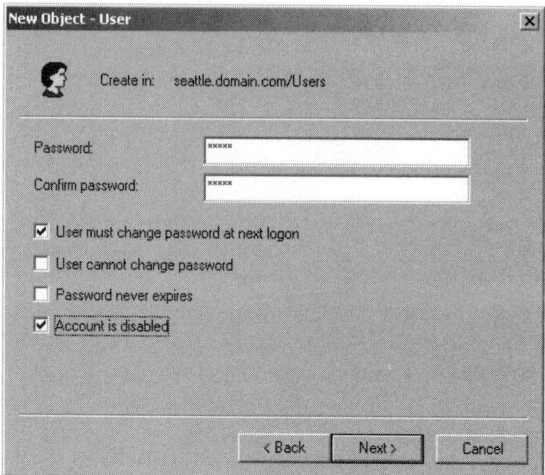

Figure 8-10. *Configure the user's password.*

Creating Local User Accounts

You create local user accounts with Local Users And Groups. You can access this utility and create an account by completing the following steps:

1. Choose Start, then Programs, then Administrative Tools, and then Computer Management. Or select Computer Management in the Administrative Tools folder.

2. Right-click the Computer Management entry in the console tree and select Connect To Another Computer on the shortcut menu. You can now choose the system whose local accounts you want to manage. Domain controllers don't have local users and groups.

3. Expand the System Tools node by clicking the plus sign (+) next to it and then choose Local Users And Groups.

4. Right-click Users and then select New User. This opens the New User dialog box shown in Figure 8-11. Each of the fields in the dialog box are used as follows:

   - **Username** The logon name for the user account. This name should follow the conventions for the local user name policy.

   - **Full Name** The full name of the user, such as William R. Stanek.

   - **Description** A description of the user. Normally you'd type the user's job title, such as Webmaster. You could also type the user's job title and department.

   - **Password** The password for the account. This password should follow the conventions of your password policy.

   - **Confirm Password** A field to ensure that you assign the account password correctly. Simply reenter the password to confirm it.

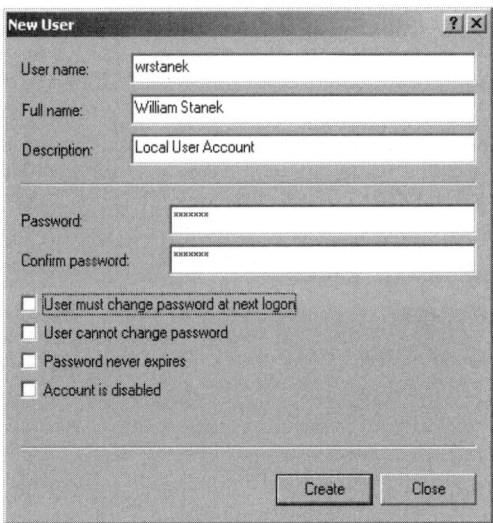

Figure 8-11. *Configuring a local user account is different than configuring a domain user account.*

- **User Must Change Password At Next Logon** If selected, the user must change the password upon logon.
- **User Cannot Change Password** If checked, the user can't change the password.
- **Password Never Expires** If selected, the password for this account never expires. This setting overrides the local account policy.
- **Account Is Disabled** If checked, the account is disabled and can't be used. Use this field to temporarily prevent anyone from using an account.

5. Click Create when you're finished configuring the new account.

Adding a Group Account

You use group accounts to manage privileges for multiple users. You create global group accounts in Active Directory Users And Computers. You create local group accounts in Local Users And Groups.

As you set out to create group accounts, remember that you create group accounts for similar types of users. Following this, the types of groups you may want to create include the following:

- **Groups for departments within the organization** Generally, users who work in the same department need access to similar resources. Because of this, you can create groups that are organized by department, such as Business Development, Sales, Marketing, or Engineering.

- **Groups for users of specific applications** Often, users will need access to an application and resources related to the application. If you create application-specific groups, you can be sure that users get proper access to the necessary resources and application files.

- **Groups for roles within the organization** Groups could also be organized by the user's role within the organization. For example, executives probably need access to different resources than supervisors and general users. Thus, by creating groups based on roles within the organization, you can ensure that proper access is given to the users that need it.

Creating a Global Group

To create a global group, complete the following steps:

1. Start Active Directory Users And Computers. Right-click the container in which you want to place the user account. Afterward, point to New, and then select Group. This opens the New Object - Group dialog box shown in Figure 8-12.

2. Type a name for the group. Global group account names follow the same naming rules as display names for user accounts. They aren't case sensitive and can be up to 64 characters long.

3. The first 20 characters of the group name are used to set the Windows NT version 4.0 or earlier group name. This group name must be unique in the domain. If necessary, change the Windows NT version 4.0 or earlier group name.

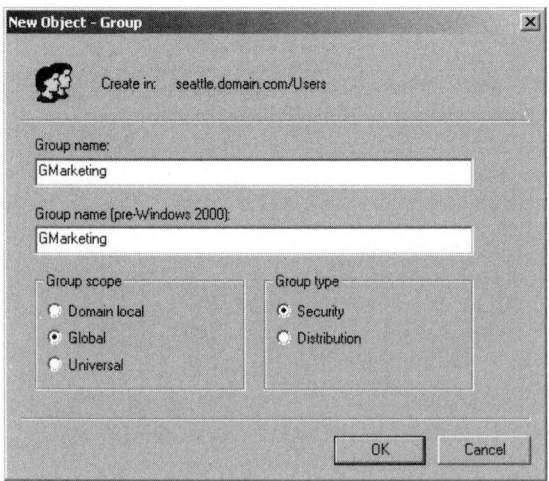

Figure 8-12. *The New Object - Group dialog box allows you to add a new global group to the domain.*

4. Select a group scope, either Domain Local, Global, or Universal.

5. Select a group type, either Security or Distribution.

6. Click OK to create the group. Once the account is created, you can add members and set additional properties, as discussed later in the chapter.

Creating a Local Group and Assigning Members

You create local groups with Local Users And Groups. You can access this utility and create a group by completing the following steps:

1. Choose Start, then Programs, then Administrative Tools, and then Computer Management. Or select Computer Management in the Administrative Tools folder.

2. Right-click the Computer Management entry in the console tree and select Connect To Another Computer on the shortcut menu. You can now choose the system whose local accounts you want to manage. Domain controllers don't have local users and groups.

3. Expand the System Tools node by clicking the plus sign (+) next to it and then choose Local Users And Groups.

4. Right-click Groups and then select New Group. This opens the New Group dialog box shown in Figure 8-13.

   After you type a name and description of the group, use the Add button to add names to the group. This opens the Select Users Or Groups dialog box, which was shown previously in Figure 8-7. You can now add members to the group. You can use the fields of this dialog box as follows:

   • **Look In**   To access account names from other computers and domains, click the Look In list box. You should now see a list that shows the current computer, trusted domains, and other resources that you can access. Select Entire Directory to view all the account names in the directory.

   • **Name**   The Name column shows the available accounts of the currently selected domain or resource.

   • **Add**   Add selected names to the selection list.

   • **Check Names**   Validate the user and group names entered into the selection list. This is useful if you type names in manually and want to make sure that they're available.

5. After you select the account names to add to the group, click OK.

6. The New Group dialog box is updated to reflect your selections. If you made a mistake, select a name and remove it by clicking Remove.

7. Click Create when you're finished adding or removing group members.

Figure 8-13. *The New Group dialog box allows you to add a new local group to a computer.*

Handling Global Group Membership

You use Active Directory Users And Computers to configure group membership. When working with groups keep the following points in mind:

- All new domain users are members of the group Domain Users, and their primary group is specified as Domain Users.

- All new domain workstations and member services are members of Domain Computers, and their primary group is Domain Computers.

- All new domain controllers are members of Domain Controllers and their primary group is Domain Controllers.

Active Directory Users And Computers gives you several ways to manage group membership. You can

- Manage individual membership
- Manage multiple memberships
- Set primary group membership for individual users and computers

Managing Individual Membership

You can add or remove group membership for any type of account by completing the following steps:

1. Double-click the user, computer, or group entry in Active Directory Users And Computers. This opens the account's Properties dialog box.
2. Select the Member Of tab.

3. To make the account a member of a group, click Add. This opens the Select Groups dialog box, which is the same as the Select Users Or Groups dialog box discussed in previous examples. You can now choose groups that the currently selected account should be a member of.

4. To remove the account from a group, select a group and then click Remove.

5. Click OK.

Managing Multiple Memberships

Another way to manage group membership is to use a group's Properties dialog box to add or remove multiple accounts. To do this, follow these steps:

1. Double-click the user or computer entry in Active Directory Users And Computers. This opens the account's Properties dialog box.

2. Select the Members tab.

3. To add accounts to the group, click Add. This opens the Select Users Or Groups dialog box. You can now choose users, computers, and groups that should be members of this currently selected group.

4. To remove members from a group, select an account and then click Remove.

5. Click OK.

Setting the Primary Group for Users and Computers

Primary groups are used by users who access Windows 2000 through services for Macintosh. When a Macintosh user creates files or directories on a Windows 2000 system, the primary group is assigned to these files or directories. All user and computer accounts must have a primary group regardless of whether the accounts access Windows 2000 systems through Macintosh. This group must be a group with global or universal scope, such as the global group Domain Users or the global group Domain Computers. To set the primary group, complete the following steps:

1. Double-click the user, computer, or group entry in Active Directory Users And Computers. This opens the account's Properties dialog box.

2. Select the Member Of tab.

3. Select a group with global or universal scope in the Member Of list box.

4. Click Set Primary Group.

All users must be a member of at least one primary group. You can't revoke membership in a primary group without first assigning the user to another primary group. To do this, complete the following steps:

1. Select a different group with global or universal scope in the Member Of list box, and then click Set Primary Group.

2. In the Member Of list box, click the former primary group and then click Remove. The group membership is now revoked.

Chapter 9

Managing Existing
User and Group Accounts

In a perfect world, you could create user and group accounts and never have to touch them again. Unfortunately, we live in the real world. After you create accounts, you'll spend a lot of time managing them. This chapter provides guidelines and tips to make that task easier.

Managing User Contact Information

Active Directory is a directory service. When you create user accounts, those accounts can have detailed contact information associated with them. The contact information is then available to anyone in the domain tree or forest and can be used to search for users and to create address book entries.

Setting Contact Information

You can set contact information for a user account by completing the following steps:

1. Double-click the user name in Active Directory Users And Computers. This opens the account's Properties dialog box.

2. Select the General tab, shown in Figure 9-1. Use the following fields to set general contact information:

   - **First Name, Initials, Last Name**   Sets the user's full name.
   - **Display Name**   Sets the user's display name as seen in logon sessions and in Active Directory.
   - **Description**   Sets a description of the user.
   - **Office**   Sets the user's office location.
   - **Telephone Number**   Sets the user's primary business telephone number. If the user has other business telephone numbers that you want to track, click Other and then use the Phone Number (Others) dialog box to enter additional phone numbers.
   - **E-Mail**   Sets the user's business e-mail address.

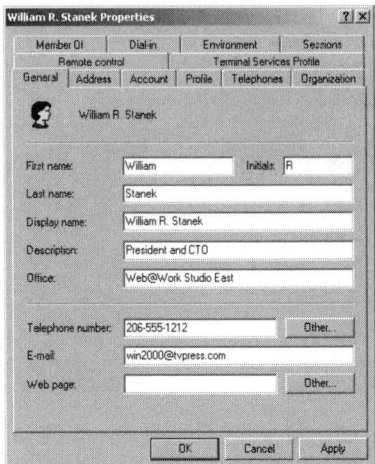

Figure 9-1. *Use the General tab to configure general contact information for the user. This information can then be used in searches and address books.*

* **Web Page** Sets the Uniform Resource Locator (URL) of the user's home page, which can be either on the Internet or on the company intranet. If the user has other Web pages that you want to track, click Other and then use the Web Page Address (Others) dialog box to enter additional Web page addresses.

 Tip The E-Mail and Web Page fields must be filled in if you want to use the Send Mail and Open Home Page features of Active Directory Users And Computers. For more information, see the section in this chapter entitled "Updating User and Group Accounts."

3. Select the Address tab. Use the fields provided to set the user's business or home address. You'll usually want to enter the user's business address. In this way, you can track the business locations and mailing addresses of users at various offices.

 Note You need to consider privacy issues before you enter users' home addresses. Discuss the matter with your Human Resources and Legal departments. You may also want to get user consent prior to releasing home addresses.

4. Select the Telephones tab. Type the primary telephone numbers that should be used to contact the user, such as home, pager, mobile, fax and IP phone.

5. Other numbers can be configured for each type of telephone number. Click the associated Others button and then use the dialog box provided to enter additional phone numbers.

6. Select the Organization tab. As appropriate, type the user's title, department, and company.

7. To specify the user's manager, click Change and then select the user's manager in the Select User Or Contact dialog box. When you specify a manager, the user shows up as a direct report in the manager's account.

8. Click Apply or OK to apply the changes.

Searching for Users and Creating Address Book Entries

Active Directory makes it easy for you to find users in the directory and then create address book entries using search results. Normally, these are tasks that you'll need to help users with. You do that by completing the following steps:

1. Click Start, point to Search, and then click For People. This opens the dialog box shown in Figure 9-2.

2. Click the Look In list box, select Active Directory, and then type the name or e-mail address of the user you want to search for.

3. Click Find Now to begin the search. If matches are found, the search results are displayed. Otherwise, type new search parameters and search again.

4. You can view an account's properties by selecting a display name and then clicking Properties.

5. You can add contact information to an address book by selecting a display name and then clicking Add To Address Book.

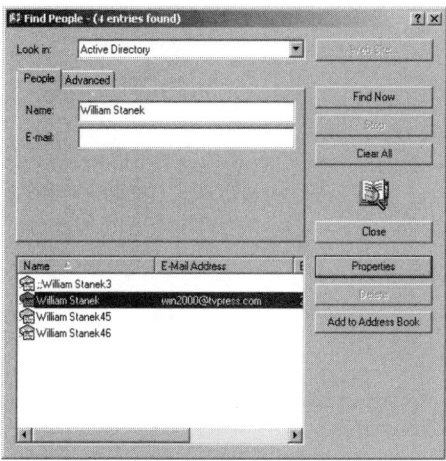

Figure 9-2. *Search for users in Active Directory, and then use the results to create address book entries.*

Configuring the User's Environment Settings

User accounts can also have profiles, logon scripts, and home directories associated with them. To configure these optional settings, double-click a display name in Active Directory Users And Computers and then select the Profile tab, shown in Figure 9-3. In the Profile tab you can set the following fields:

- **Profile Path** The path to the user's profile. Profiles provide the environment settings for users. Each time a user logs on to a computer, that user's profile is used to determine desktop and control panel settings, the availability of menu options and applications, and more. Setting the profile path is covered later in this chapter in the section entitled "Managing User Profiles."

- **Logon Script** The path to the user's logon script. Logon scripts are batch files that run whenever a user logs on. You use logon scripts to set commands that should be executed each time a user logs on. Chapter 4 discusses logon scripts in detail.

- **Local Path** The directory the user should use for storing files. Here, you assign a specific directory for the user's files. If the directory is available to the network, the user can access the directory from any computer on the network.

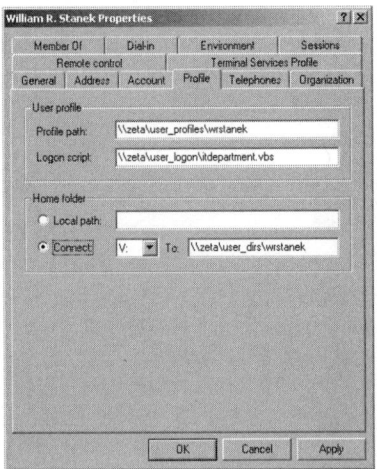

Figure 9-3. *The Profile tab allows you to create a user profile. Profiles let you configure the network environment for a user.*

System Environment Variables

System environment variables often come in handy when you're setting up the user's environment, especially when you work with logon scripts. You'll use environment variables to specify path information that can be dynamically assigned. The environment variables you'll use the most are the following:

- **%SystemRoot%** The base directory for the Microsoft Windows 2000 operating system, such as C:\WIN2000. Use it with the Profile tab of the user's Properties dialog box and logon scripts.

- **%UserName%** The user account name, such as WRSTANEK. Use it with the Profile tab of the user's Properties dialog box and logon scripts.

- **%HomeDrive%** The drive letter of the user's home directory, such as C:. Use it with logon scripts.

- **%HomePath%** The full path to the user's home directory on the respective home drive, such as \USERS\MKG\GEORGEJ. Use it with logon scripts.

- **%Processor_Architecture%** The processor architecture of the user's computer, such as x86. Use it with logon scripts.

Figure 9-4 shows how you might use environment variables when creating user accounts. Note that by using the *%UserName%* variable, you allow the system to determine the full path information on a user-by-user basis. If you use this technique, you can use the same path information for multiple users and all the users will have unique settings.

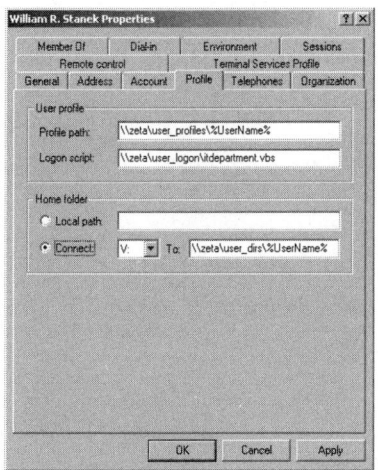

Figure 9-4. *When you use the Profile tab, environment variables can save you typing, especially when you create an account based on another account.*

Logon Scripts

Logon scripts set commands that should be executed each time a user logs on. You can use logon scripts to set the system time, network drive paths, network printers, and more. Although you can use logon scripts to execute one-time commands, you shouldn't use them to set environment variables. Any environment settings used by scripts aren't maintained for subsequent user processes. Also, you shouldn't use logon scripts to specify applications that should run at startup. You should set startup applications by placing the appropriate shortcuts in the user's Startup folder.

Normally, logon scripts contain Windows 2000 commands. However, logon scripts can be

- Windows Script Host files with the .VBS, .JS, or other valid script file extensions
- Batch files with the .BAT extension
- Command files with the .CMD extension
- Executable programs with the .EXE extension

One user or many users can use a single logon script, and as the administrator, you control which users use which scripts. As the name implies, logon scripts are accessed when users log on to their accounts. You can specify a logon script by completing the following steps:

1. Access the user's Properties dialog box in Active Directory Users And Computers, and then choose the Profile tab.

2. Enter the path to the logon script in the Logon Script field. Be sure to set the full path to the logon script, such as \\ZETA\USER_LOGON\ENG.VBS.

 Note You can specify logon and logoff scripts using other techniques. For complete details, see the section in Chapter 4 entitled "User and Computer Script Management."

Creating logon scripts is easier than you might think, especially when you use the Windows 2000 command language. Just about any command you can type into a command prompt can be set to run in a logon script. The most common tasks you'll want logon scripts to handle are to set the default printers and network paths for users. You can set this information with the NET USE command. The following NET USE commands define a network printer and a network drive:

```
net use lpt1: \\zeta\deskjet
```

```
net use g: \\gamma\corp\files
```

If these commands were in the user's logon script, the user would have a network printer on LPT1 and a network drive on G.

Assigning Home Directories

Windows 2000 lets you assign a home directory for each user account. Users can use this directory to store and retrieve their personal files. Many applications use the home directory as the default for File Open and Save As operations, which helps users find their resources easily. The command prompt also uses the home directory as the initial current directory.

Home directories can be located on a user's local hard disk drive or on a shared network drive. On a local drive, the directory is only accessible from a single workstation. On the other hand, shared network drives can be accessed from any computer on the network, which makes for a more versatile user environment.

Tip   Although users can share home directories, it's not a good idea. You'll usually want to provide each user with a unique home directory.

You don't need to create the user's home directory ahead of time. Active Directory Users And Computers automatically creates the directory for you. But if there's a problem creating the directory, Active Directory Users And Computers will instruct you to create it manually.

To specify a local home directory:

1. Access the user's Properties dialog box in Active Directory Users And Computers, and then choose the Profile tab.
2. Click the Local Path option button, and then enter the path to the home directory in the associated field. Here's an example: **C:\Home\\%*UserName*%**.

To specify a network home directory, complete the following steps:

1. Access the user's Properties dialog box in Active Directory Users And Computers, and then choose the Profile tab.
2. Click the Connect option button, and then select a drive letter for the home directory. For consistency, you should use the same drive letter for all users. Also, be sure to select a drive letter that won't conflict with any currently configured physical or mapped drives. To avoid problems, you may want to use Z as the drive letter.
3. Type the complete path to the home directory using the Universal Naming Convention (UNC) notation, such as: **\\GAMMA\USER_DIRS\\%*UserName*%**. You include the server name in the drive path to ensure that the user can access the directory from any computer on the network.

Note   If you don't assign a home directory, Windows 2000 uses the de- fault local home directory. On systems where Windows 2000 is installed as an upgrade, this directory is \Users\Default. Otherwise, this directory is the root directory.

Setting Account Options and Restrictions

Windows 2000 provides many ways to control user accounts and their access to the network. You can define logon hours, permitted workstations for logon, dial-in privileges, and more.

Managing Logon Hours

Windows 2000 allows you to control when users can log on to the network. You do this by setting their valid logon hours. You can use logon hour restrictions to tighten security and prevent system cracking or malicious conduct after normal business hours.

During valid logon hours, users can work as they normally do. They can log on to the network and access network resources. During restricted logon hours, users can't work. They can't log on to the network or make connections to network resources. If users are logged on when their logon time expires, what follows depends on the account policy you've set for them. Generally, one of two things happens to the user:

- **Forcibly disconnected** You can set a policy that tells Windows 2000 to forcibly disconnect Windows 2000 users when their logon hours expire. If this policy is set, remote Windows 2000 users are disconnected from all network resources and logged off the system when their hours expire.

- **Not disconnected** Users aren't disconnected from the network when they enter the restricted hours. Instead, Windows 2000 simply doesn't allow them to make any new network connections.

Configuring Logon Hours

To configure the logon hours, follow these steps:

1. Access the user's Properties dialog box in Active Directory Users And Computers and then choose the Account tab.

2. Click the Logon Hours button. You can now set the valid and invalid logon hours using the Logon Hours dialog box shown in Figure 9-5. Logon Hours features are listed in Table 9-1.

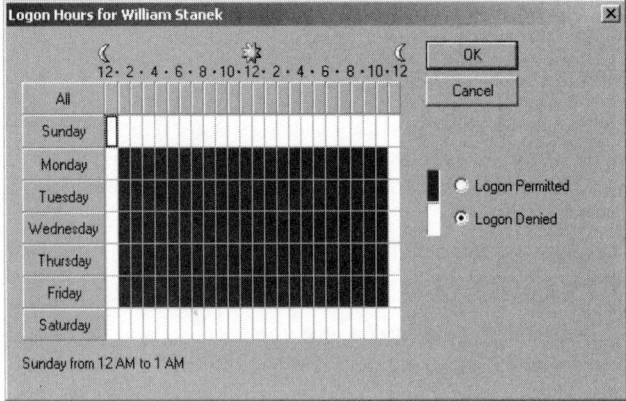

Figure 9-5. *Configure logon hours for users using the fields provided.*

In this dialog box each hour of the day or night is a field that you can turn on and off.

- Hours that are allowed are filled in with a dark bar—you can think of these hours as being turned on.

- Hours that are disallowed are blank—you can think of these hours as being turned off.

To change the setting for an hour, click it. Then select either the Logon Permitted or Logon Denied option button.

Table 9-1. Logon Hours Features

Feature	Function
All button	Allows you to select all the time periods.
Day of week buttons	Allow you to select all the hours in a particular day.
Hour buttons	Allow you to select a particular hour for all the days of the week.
Logon Permitted	Sets the allowed logon hours.
Logon Denied	Sets the disallowed logon hours.

Tip   When you set logon hours, you'll save yourself a lot of work in the long run if you give users a moderately restricted time window. For example, rather than explicit 9–5 hours, you may want to allow a few hours on either side of the normal work hours. This will let the early birds onto the system and allow the night owls to keep working until they finish for the day.

Enforcing Logon Hours

If you want to forcibly disconnect users when their logon hours expire, complete the following steps:

1. Access the group policy container you want to work with, as detailed in Chapter 4 in the section entitled "Managing Site, Domain, and Unit Policies."

2. Access the Security Options node, shown in Figure 9-6, by working your way down through the console tree. Expand Computer Configuration, Windows Settings, and then Security Settings. In Security Settings, expand Local Policies and then select Security Options.

3. Double-click Automatically Log Off Users When Logon Time Expires. This opens a Properties dialog box for the policy.

4. Select the Define This Policy Setting check box and then click Enabled. This turns on the policy restriction and enforces the logon hours. Click OK.

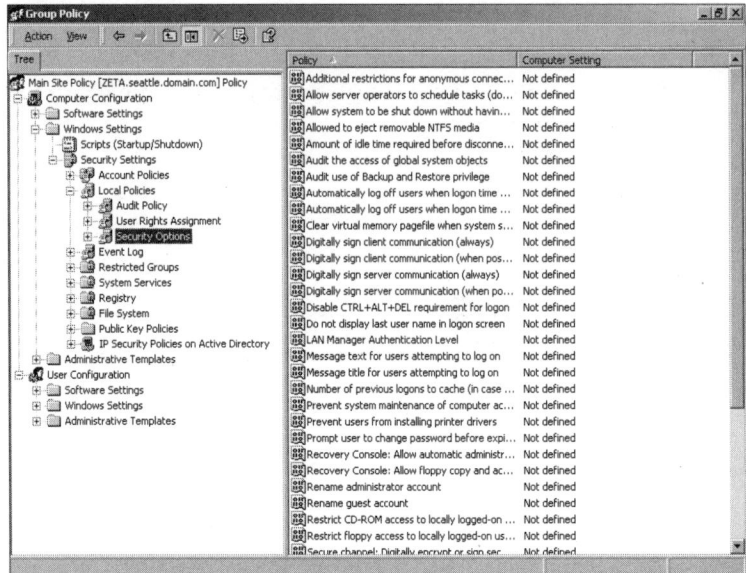

Figure 9-6. *Access the Security Options node in Group Policy.*

Setting Permitted Logon Workstations

Windows 2000 has a formal policy that allows users to log on to systems locally. This policy controls whether or not a user can sit at the computer's keyboard and log on. By default, on Windows 2000 workstations you can use any valid user account, including the guest account, to log on locally.

As you might imagine, allowing users to log on to any workstation is a big security no-no. Unless you restrict workstation use, anyone who obtains a user name and password can use it to log on to any workstation in the domain. By defining a permitted workstation list, you close the opening in your domain and reduce the security risk. Now not only must hackers find a user name and password, they must also find the permitted workstations for the account.

 Note The permitted logon workstation restrictions only affect Microsoft Windows 2000 and Windows NT computers in the domain. If there are any Microsoft Windows 95 or Windows 98 computers in the domain, they aren't subject to the restrictions, which means you only need a valid user name and password to log on to these systems.

For domain users, you define permitted logon workstations by completing the following steps:

1. Access the user's Properties dialog box in Active Directory Users And Computers, and then choose the Account tab.

2. Open the Logon Workstations dialog box by clicking the Log On To button.

3. Select The Following Computers option button, shown in Figure 9-7.

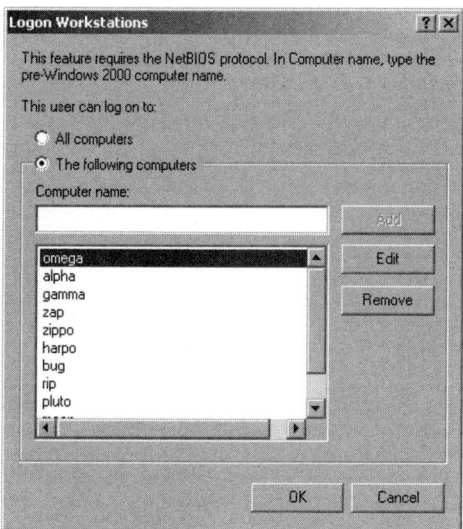

Figure 9-7. *To restrict access to workstations, specify the permitted logon workstations.*

4. Type the name of a permitted workstation and then click Add. Repeat this procedure to specify additional workstations.

5. If you make a mistake, select the erroneous entry and then click Edit or Remove, as appropriate.

Setting Dial-In Privileges

Windows 2000 lets you set dial-in privileges for accounts using the Dial-In tab of the user's Properties dialog box. As shown in Figure 9-8, dial-in privileges are controlled through Remote Access Policy by default. This is the preferred method of controlling remote access. You can explicitly grant or deny dial-in privileges by selecting Allow Access or Deny Access. In any event, before users can dial in to the network, you'll need to complete the following steps:

1. Install Remote Access Services using Configure Your Server.

2. To enable remote access connections, configure the group policy for a site, domain, or organizational unit. You do this using the Network Dial-Up And Connections node. Expand User Configuration, Administrative Templates, and then Network. Then select Network Dial-Up And Connections.

3. Configure remote access using Routing And Remote Access. In Computer Management, expand Services And Applications, and then select Routing And Remote Access.

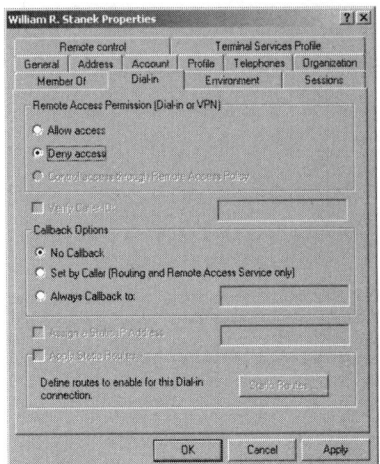

Figure 9-8. *Dial-in privileges control remote access to the network.*

After you grant a user permission to access the network remotely, configure the following additional dial-in parameters using the Dial-In tab of the user's Properties dialog box (see Figure 9-8). Complete the following steps:

1. If the user must dial in from a specific phone number, select Verify Caller-ID and then type the telephone number from which this user is required to log on. Your telephone system must support Caller ID for this feature to work.

2. Define callback parameters using the following options:

    • **No Callback**   Allows the user to dial in directly and remain connected. The user pays the long-distance telephone charges, if applicable.

    • **Set By Caller**   Allows the user to dial in directly, and then the server prompts the user for a callback number. Once the number is entered, the user is disconnected and the server dials the user back at the specified number to reestablish the connection. The company pays the long-distance telephone charges, if applicable.

 Note   You shouldn't assign callback for users who dial in through a switchboard. The switchboard may not allow the user to properly connect to the network.

    • **Always Callback To**   Allows you to set a predefined callback number for security purposes. When a user dials in, the server calls back the preset number. The company pays the long-distance telephone charges, if applicable, and reduces the risk of an unauthorized person accessing the network.

Note You shouldn't use preset callback numbers with multilinked lines. The multilinked lines won't function properly.

3. If necessary, you can also assign static IP addresses and static routes for dial-in connections using Assign A Static IP Address and Apply Static Routes, respectively. For more information on IP addresses and routing, see Chapter 15.

Setting Account Security Options

The Account tab of the user's Properties dialog box has many options designed to help you maintain a secure network environment. Use these options to control how user accounts are used and what options are available. The options are:

- **User Must Change Password At Next Logon**   Forces the user to change his or her password when they log on next.

- **User Cannot Change Password**   Doesn't allow the user to change the account password.

- **Password Never Expires**   Ensures the account password never expires, which overrides the normal password expiration period.

Caution Selecting this option creates a security risk on the network. While you may want to use Password Never Expires with administrator accounts, you shouldn't use this option with normal user accounts in most cases.

- **Store The Password Using Reversible Encryption**   Saves password as encrypted clear text.

- **Account Is Disabled**   Disables the accounts, which prevents the user from accessing the network and logging on.

- **Smart Card Is Required For Interactive Logon**   Requires the user to log on to a workstation using a smart card. The user can't logon to the workstation by typing a logon name and password at the keyboard.

- **Account Is Trusted For Delegation**   Specifies that the user may need object management privileges in Active Directory and that the user is trusted to perform any permissible actions on objects that the user has been delegated the authority to work with.

Note Most users don't need to be trusted for delegation. Only users with special privileges or Active Directory management needs should be granted this permission.

- **Account Is Sensitive And Cannot Be Delegated**   Specifies that the user can't be trusted for delegation. You may want to set this option for all normal user accounts to prevent these users from manipulating Active Directory objects unless specifically permitted to by you or other authorized administrators.

- **Use DES Encryption Types For This Account** Specifies that the user account will use DES (Data Encryption Standard) encryption.

- **Do Not Require Kerberos Preauthentication** Specifies that the user account doesn't need Kerberos preauthentication to access network resources. Preauthentication is a part of the Kerberos version 5 security procedure. The option to log on without it is available in order to allow authentication from clients using a previous, or nonstandard, implementation of Kerberos.

Managing User Profiles

User profiles contain settings for the network environment, such as desktop configuration and menu options. Problems with a profile can sometimes prevent a user from logging on. For example, if the display size in the profile isn't available on the system being used, the user may not be able to log on properly. In fact, the user may get nothing but a blank screen. You could reboot the machine, go into VGA (Video Graphics Adapter) mode, and then reset the display manually, but solutions for profile problems aren't always this easy and you may need to update the profile itself.

Windows 2000 provides several ways to manage user profiles:

- You can assign profile paths in Active Directory Users And Computers.

- You can copy, delete, and change the type of an existing local profile with the System utility in the Control Panel.

- You can set system policies that prevent users from manipulating certain aspects of their environment.

Local, Roaming, and Mandatory Profiles

In Windows 2000 every user has a profile. Profiles control startup features for the user's session, the types of programs and applications that are available, the desktop settings, and a lot more. Each computer that a user logs on to has a copy of the user's profile. Because this profile is stored on the computer's hard disk, users who access several computers will have a profile on each one of them. Another computer on the network can't access a locally stored profile, called a *local profile,* and, as you might expect, this has some drawbacks. For example, if a user logs on to three different workstations, the user could have three very different profiles on each system. As a result, the user may get confused about what network resources are available on a given system.

To solve the problem of multiple profiles and reduce confusion, you may want to create a profile that can be accessed by other computers. This type of profile is called a *roaming profile.* With a roaming profile, users can access the same profile no matter which computer they're using within the domain. Roaming profiles are server-based and can only be stored on a Windows 2000 server. When a user with a roaming profile logs on, the profile is downloaded, which creates a local copy on the user's computer. When the user logs off, changes to the profile are updated both on the local copy and on the server.

As an administrator, you can control user profiles or let users control their own profiles. One reason to control profiles yourself is to make sure that all users have a common network configuration, which can reduce the number of environment-related problems.

Profiles controlled by administrators are called *mandatory profiles*. Users who have a mandatory profile can only make transitory changes to their environment. Here, any changes that users make to the local environment aren't saved, and the next time they log on they are back to the original profile. The idea is that if users can't permanently modify the network environment, they can't make changes that cause problems. A key drawback to mandatory profiles is that the user can only log on if the profile is accessible. If, for some reason, the server that stores the profile is inaccessible and a cached profile *isn't* accessible, the user won't be able to log on. If the server is inaccessible but a cached profile *is* accessible, the user will receive a warning message and will be logged onto the local Windows 2000 system using the system's cached profile.

Creating Local Profiles

In Windows 2000, user profiles are maintained either in a default directory or in the location set by the Profile Path field in the user's Properties dialog box. The default location for profiles depends on the workstation configuration in the following way:

- **Windows 2000 Upgrade Installation** The user profile is located at *%SystemRoot%*\Profiles\ *%UserName%*\NTUSER.DAT, where *%SystemRoot%* is the root directory for the operating system, such as C:\WINNT, and *%UserName%* is the user name, such as wrstanek.

- **New Installation of Windows 2000** The user profile is located at *%SystemDrive%*\Documents and Settings\ *%UserName%.%UserDomain%*\ NTUSER.DAT, such as F:\Documents and Settings\WRSTANEK. WEBATWORK\NTUSER.DAT. If the user logs on to a domain controller, the profile may be located at *%SystemDrive%*\Documents and Settings\ *%UserName%*.<Logon Server>, such as F:\Documents and Settings\WRSTANEK. ZETA\NTUSER.DAT.

If you don't change the default location, the user will have a local profile.

Creating Roaming Profiles

Roaming profiles are stored on Windows 2000 servers. If you want a user to have a roaming profile, you must set a server-based location for the profile directory by completing the following steps:

1. Create a shared directory on a Windows 2000 server and make sure that the group Everyone has access to it.

2. Access the user's Properties dialog box in Active Directory Users And Computers, and then choose the Profile tab. Enter the path to the shared directory in the Profile Path field. The path should have the form \\server name\profile folder name\user name. An example is \\ZETA\USER_PROFILES\GEORGEJ, where ZETA is the server name, USER_PROFILES is the shared directory, and GEORGEJ is the user name.

3. The roaming profile is then stored in the NTUSER.DAT file in the designated directory, such as \\ZETA\USER_PROFILES\GEORGEJ\NTUSER.DAT.

 Note You don't usually need to create the profile directory. The directory is created automatically when the user logs on.

4. As an optional step, you can create a profile for the user or copy an existing profile to the user's profile folder. If you don't create an actual profile for the user, the next time the user logs on, the user will use the default local profile. Any changes the user makes to this profile will be saved when the user logs off. Thus, the next time the user logs on, the user can have a personal profile.

Creating Mandatory Profiles

Mandatory profiles are stored on Windows 2000 servers. If you want a user to have a mandatory profile, you define the profile as follows:

1. Follow steps 1–3 in the previous section, "Creating Roaming Profiles."

2. Create a mandatory profile by renaming the NTUSER.DAT file as *%USERNAME%*\NTUSER.MAN. Now when the user logs on the next time, the user will have a mandatory profile.

 Note NTUSER.DAT contains the registry settings for the user. When you change the extension for the file to NTUSER.MAN, you tell Windows 2000 to create a mandatory profile.

Using the System Utility to Manage Local Profiles

To manage local profiles, you'll need to log on to the user's computer. Afterward, you can use the System utility in the Control Panel to manage local profiles. To view current profile information, start the System utility, and then click the User Profiles tab.

As shown in Figure 9-9, the User Profiles tab displays various information about the profiles stored on the local system. You can use this information to help you manage profiles. The fields have the following meanings:

- **Name** The name of the local profile, which generally includes the name of the originating domain or computer and the user account name. For example, the name WEBATWORK\WRSTANEK tells you that the original profile is from the domain WEBATWORK and the user account is WRSTANEK.

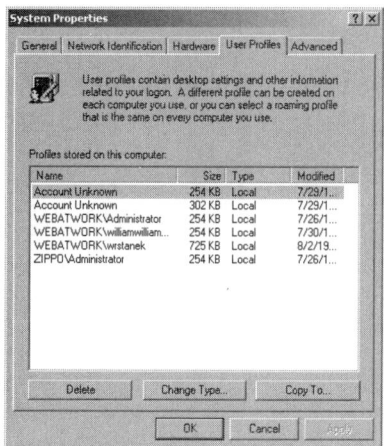

Figure 9-9. *The User Profiles tab in the System Properties dialog box lets you manage existing local profiles.*

If you delete an account but don't delete the associated profile, you may also see an entry that says Account Deleted or Account Unknown. Don't worry, the profile is still available for copying if you need it.

- **Size**   The size of the profile. Generally, the larger the profile, the more the user has customized the environment.
- **Type**   The profile type, which is either local or roaming.
- **Modified**   The date when the profile was last modified.

Creating a Profile by Hand

In some cases, you may want to create the profile by hand. You do this by logging on to the user account, setting up the environment, and then logging out. As you might guess, creating accounts in this manner is time-consuming. A better way to handle account creation is to create a base user account. Here, you create the base user account, set up the account environment, and then use this account as the basis of other accounts.

Copying an Existing Profile to a New User Account

If you have a base user account or a user account that you want to use in a similar manner, you can copy an existing profile to the new user account. To do this, you'll use the System Control Panel utility. You do that by completing the following steps:

1. Start the System Control Panel utility and open the User Profile tab.

2. Select the existing profile you want to copy using the Profiles Stored On This Computer list box (see Figure 9-9).

3. Copy the profile to the new user's account by clicking on the Copy To button. Next, enter the path to the new user's profile directory in the Copy

Profile To field (see Figure 9-10). For example, if you were creating the pro-file for our user, GEORGEJ, you would type **\\ZETA\USER_PROFILES\ GEORGEJ**.

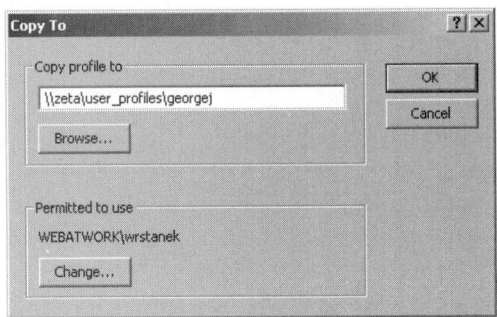

Figure 9-10. *Use the Copy To dialog box to enter the location of the profile di-rectory and to assign access permissions to the user.*

4. Now you need to give the user permission to access the profile. Click the Change button in the Permitted To Use area, and then use the Select User Or Object dialog box to grant access to the new user account.

5. Close the Copy To dialog box by clicking OK. Windows 2000 will then copy the profile to the next location.

 Tip If you know the name of the user or group you want to use, you can type it directly into the Name field. This will save you time.

Copying or Restoring a Profile

When you work with workgroups where each computer is managed separately, you'll often have to copy a user's local profile from one computer to another. Copying a profile allows users to maintain environment settings when they use different computers. Of course, in a Windows 2000 domain you can use a roam-ing profile to create a single profile that can be accessed from anywhere within the domain. The catch is that sometimes you may need to copy an existing local profile over the top of a user's roaming profile (when the roaming profile is corrupt) or you may need to copy an existing local profile to a roaming profile in another domain.

You can copy an existing profile to a new location by doing the following:

1. Log on to the user's computer, and then start the System Control Panel util-ity and open the User Profile tab.

2. Select the existing profile you want to copy using the Profiles Stored On This Computer list box.

3. Copy the profile to the new location by clicking the Copy To button, and then enter the path to the new profile directory in the Copy Profile To field. For example, if you're creating the profile for JANEW, you could type: **\\GAMMA\USERPROFILES\ JANEW**.

4. Now you need to give the user permission to access the profile. Click the Change button in the Permitted To Use area, and then use the Select User Or Group dialog box to grant access to the appropriate user account.

5. When you're finished, close the Copy To dialog box by clicking OK. Windows 2000 will then copy the profile to the new location.

Deleting a Local Profile and Assigning a New One

Profiles are accessed when a user logs on to a computer. Windows 2000 uses local profiles for all users who don't have roaming profiles. Generally, local profiles are also used if the local profile has a more recent modification date than the user's roaming profile. Because of this, there are times when you may need to delete a user's local profile. For example, if a user's local profile becomes corrupt, you can delete the profile and assign a new one. Keep in mind that when you delete a local profile that isn't stored anywhere else on the domain, you can't recover the user's original environment settings.

To delete a user's local profile, complete the following steps:

1. Log on to the user's computer.

2. Start the System utility and then click the User Profiles tab.

3. Select the profile you want to delete and then click Delete. When asked to confirm that you want to delete the profile, click Yes.

Note You can't delete a profile that's in use. If the user is logged on to the local system (the computer you're deleting the profile from), the user will need to log off. In some instances Windows 2000 marks profiles as in use when they are not. This is typically a result of an environment change for the user that hasn't been properly applied. To correct this, you may need to reboot the computer.

Now the next time the user logs on, Windows 2000 will do one of two things. Either the operating system will give the user the default local profile for that system or it'll retrieve the user's roaming profile stored on another computer. To prevent the use of either of these profiles, you'll need to assign the user a new profile. To do this you can

- Copy an existing profile to the user's profile directory. Copying profiles is covered in the next section.

- Update the profile settings for the user in Active Directory Users And Computers. Setting the profile path is covered in this chapter in the section entitled "Configuring the User's Environment Settings."

Changing the Profile Type

With roaming profiles, the System utility lets you change the profile type on the user's computer. To do this, select the profile and then click Change Type. The options in this dialog box allow you to

- **Change a roaming profile to a local profile** If you want the user to always work with the local profile on this computer, set the profile for local use. Here, all changes to the profile are made locally and the original roaming profile is left untouched.

- **Change a local profile (that was defined originally as a roaming profile) to a roaming profile** The user will use the original roaming profile for the next logon. Afterward, Windows 2000 will treat the profile like any other roaming profile, which means that any changes to the local profile will be copied to the roaming profile.

 Note If these options aren't available, the user's original profile is defined locally.

Updating User and Group Accounts

Active Directory Users And Computers is the tool to use when you want to update a domain user or group account. If you want to update a local user or group account, you'll need to use Local Users And Groups.

Renaming User and Group Accounts

To rename an account, complete the following steps:

1. Access Active Directory Users And Computers or Local Users And Groups, whichever is appropriate for the type of account you're renaming.

2. Right-click the account name, and then choose Rename. Type the new account name when prompted.

SIDs

When you rename a user account, you give the account a new label. As discussed in Chapter 7, user names are meant to make managing and using accounts easier. Behind the scenes, Windows 2000 uses SIDs (security identifiers) to identify, track, and handle accounts independently from user names. SIDs are unique identifiers that are generated when accounts are created.

Because SIDs are mapped to account names internally, you don't need to change the privileges or permissions on the renamed account. Windows 2000 simply maps the SID to the new account names as necessary.

One common reason for changing the name of a user account is that the user gets married. For example, if Jane Williams (JANEW) gets married, she may want her user name to be changed to Jane Marshall (JANEM). When you change the user name from JANEW to JANEM, all associated privileges and permissions will reflect the name change. Thus, if you view the permissions on a file that JANEW had access to, JANEM will now have access (and JANEW will no longer be listed).

Changing Other Information

When you change JANEW to JANEM, the user properties and names of files associated with the account aren't changed. This means you should update the account information. The information you *may* need to change includes:

- **Display Name** Change the user account's Display Name in Active Directory Users And Computers.

- **User Profile Path** Change the Profile Path in Active Directory Users And Computers, and then rename the corresponding directory on disk.

- **Logon Script Name** If you use individual logon scripts for each user, change the Logon Script Name in Active Directory Users And Computers, and then rename the logon script on disk.

- **Home Directory** Change the home directory path in Active Directory Users And Computers, and then rename the corresponding directory on disk.

Note Changing directory and file information for an account when a user is logged on may cause problems. So you may want to update this information after hours or ask the user to log off for a few minutes and then log back on.

Copying Domain User Accounts

Creating domain user accounts from scratch every time can be tedious. Instead of starting anew each time, you may want to use an existing account as a starting point. To do this, follow these steps:

1. Right-click the account you want to copy in Active Directory Users And Computers, and then choose Copy. This opens the Copy Object – User dialog box.

2. Create the account as you would any other domain user account. Then update the properties of the account, as appropriate.

As you might expect, when you create a copy of an account, Active Directory Users And Computers doesn't retain all the information from the existing account. Instead, Active Directory Users And Computers tries to copy only the information you'll need and to discard the information that you'll need to update. The properties that are retained include

- City, state, zip code, and country values set on the Address tab

- Department and company set on the Organization tab

- Account options set using the Account Options fields on the Account tab

- Logon hours and permitted logon workstations

- Account expiration date
- Group account memberships
- Profile settings
- Dial-in privileges

 Note If you used environment variables to specify the profile settings in the original account, the environment variables are used for the copy of the account as well. For example, if the original account used the *%UserName%* variable, the copy of the account will also use this variable.

Deleting User and Group Accounts

Deleting an account permanently removes the account. Once you delete an account, you can't create an account with the same name to get the same permissions. That's because the SID for the new account won't match the SID for the old account.

Because deleting built-in accounts can have far-reaching effects on the domain, Windows 2000 doesn't let you delete built-in user accounts or group accounts. You *could* remove other types of accounts by selecting them and pressing the Del key or by right-clicking and selecting Delete. When prompted, click OK and then click Yes.

With Active Directory Users And Computers, you can select multiple accounts by doing one of the following:

- Select multiple user names for editing by holding down the Ctrl key and clicking the left mouse button on each account you want to select.
- Select a range of user names by holding down the Shift key, selecting the first account name, and then clicking on the last account in the range.

 Note When you delete a user account, Windows 2000 doesn't delete the user's profile, personal files, or home directory. If you want to delete these files and directories, you'll have to do it manually.

Changing and Resetting Passwords

As an administrator, you'll often have to change or reset user passwords. This usually happens when users forget their passwords or their passwords expire.

To change or reset a password, complete the following steps:

1. Access Active Directory Users And Computers or Local Users And Groups, whichever is appropriate for the type of account you're renaming.
2. Right-click the account name, and then choose Reset Password or Set Password, as appropriate.

3. Type a new password for the user and confirm it. The password should conform to the password policy set for the computer or domain.

4. Double-click the account name, and then clear Account Is Disabled and Account Is Locked Out, whichever is appropriate and necessary. In Active Directory Users And Computers, these check boxes are on the Account tab.

Enabling User Accounts

User accounts can become disabled for several reasons. If a user forgets the password and tries to guess it, the user may exceed the account policy for bad logon attempts. Or another administrator could have disabled the account while the user was on vacation. Or the account could have expired. What to do when an account is disabled, locked out, or expired is described below.

Account Disabled

When an account is disabled, complete the following steps:

1. Access Active Directory Users And Computers or Local Users And Groups, whichever is appropriate for the type of account you're renaming.

2. Right-click the user's account name, and then select Enable Account.

Account Locked Out

When an account is locked out, complete the following steps:

1. Access Active Directory Users And Computers or Local Users And Groups, whichever is appropriate for the type of account you're renaming.

2. Double-click the user's account name, and then clear the Account Is Locked Out check box. In Active Directory Users And Computers, this check box is on the Account tab.

Note If users frequently get locked out of their accounts, consider adjusting the account policy for the domain. Here, you may want to increase the value for acceptable bad logon attempts and reduce the duration for the associated counter. For more information on setting account policy, see the section of Chapter 8 entitled "Configuring Account Policies."

Account Expired

Only domain accounts have an expiration date. Local user accounts do not have an expiration date.

When a domain account is expired, complete the following steps:

1. Access Active Directory Users And Computers.

2. Double-click the user's account name, and then select the Account tab.

3. In the Account Expires panel, select End Of and then click the down arrow on the related field. This displays a calendar that you can use to set a new expiration date.

Troubleshooting Logon Problems

The previous section listed ways in which accounts can become disabled. Beyond the typical reasons for an account being disabled, some system settings can also cause access problems. Specifically, you should look for the following:

- **User gets a message that says that the user can't log on interactively** The user right to log on locally isn't set for this user and the user isn't a member of a group that has this right.

  The user may be trying to log on to a server or domain controller. If so, keep in mind that the right to log on locally applies to all domain controllers in the domain. Otherwise, this right only applies to the single workstation.

  If the user should have access to the local system, configure the Logon Locally user right as described in the section of Chapter 8 entitled "Configuring User Rights Policies."

- **User gets a message that the system could not log the user on** If you've already checked the password and account name, you may want to check the account type. The user may be trying to access the domain with a local account. If this isn't the problem, the global catalog server may be unavailable and as a result, only users with administrator privileges can log on to the domain.

- **User has a mandatory profile and the computer storing the profile is unavailable** When a user has a mandatory profile, the computer storing the profile must be accessible during the logon process. If the computer is shut down or otherwise unavailable, users with mandatory profiles won't be able to log on.

- **User gets a message saying the account has been configured to prevent the user from logging on to the workstation** The user is trying to access a workstation that isn't defined as a permitted logon workstation. If the user should have access to this workstation, change the logon workstation information as described in the section of this chapter entitled "Setting Permitted Logon Workstations."

Part III
Microsoft Windows 2000 Data Administration

This part of the book, Part III, covers Microsoft Windows 2000 data administration. Chapter 10 starts by explaining how to add hard disk drives to a system and how to partition drives. It then discusses common tasks for managing file systems and drives, such as defragmenting disks and encrypting data. Chapter 11 covers tools for managing volume sets and RAID (redundant array of independent disks) arrays. It also provides detailed advice on repairing damaged arrays. Chapter 12 focuses on managing files and directories and the associated tasks. Chapter 13 shows you how to enable file, drive, and directory sharing for remote network and Internet users. Chapter 14 explores data backup and recovery and explains how to manage media pools.

Chapter 10

Managing File Systems and Drives

A hard disk drive is the most common storage device used on network workstations and servers. Users depend on hard disk drives to store their word-processing documents, spreadsheets, and other types of data. Drives are organized into file systems that users can access either locally or remotely as follows:

- **Local file systems** Installed on a user's computer and don't require remote network connections to access. An example of a local file system is the C drive available on most workstations and servers. You access the C drive using the file path C:\.

- **Remote file systems** Accessed, on the other hand, through a network connection to a remote resource. You can connect to a remote file system using the Map Network Drive feature of Windows Explorer.

Wherever disk resources are located, it's your job as a system administrator to manage them. The tools and techniques you use to manage file systems and drives are discussed in this chapter. Chapter 11 looks at volume sets and fault tolerance. Chapter 12 tells you how to manage files and directories.

Adding Hard Disk Drives

Before you make a hard disk drive available to users, you'll need to configure it and consider the way it will be used. Microsoft Windows 2000 makes it possible to configure hard disk drives in a variety of ways. The technique you choose depends primarily on the type of data you're working with and the needs of your network environment. For general user data stored on workstations, you may want to configure individual drives as stand-alone storage devices. In that case, user data is stored on a workstation's hard disk drive, where it can be accessed and stored locally.

Although storing data on a single drive is convenient, it isn't the most reliable way to store data. To improve reliability and performance, you may want a set of drives to work together. Windows 2000 supports drive sets and arrays using RAID (redundant array of independent disks) technology, which is built into the operating system. RAID arrays are usually installed on Windows 2000 servers instead of workstations.

Physical Drives

Whether you use individual drives or drive sets, you'll need physical drives. Physical drives are the actual hardware devices that are used to store data. The amount of data a drive can store depends on its size and whether it uses compression. Typical drives have capacities of 2 GB to 25 GB. The two drive types most commonly used on Windows 2000 are SCSI (Small Computer Systems Interface) and IDE (Integrated Drive Electronics).

The terms SCSI and IDE designate the interface type used by the hard disk drives. This interface is used to communicate with a drive controller. SCSI drives use SCSI controllers. IDE drives use IDE controllers. In general, you'll find that SCSI drives are more expensive than IDE drives but are faster and offer more options.

 Note You'll see lots of acronyms associated with SCSI and IDE drives. Don't let these acronyms confuse you. For SCSI drives, you'll see references to Ultra SCSI, Wide SCSI, SCSI-2, and SCSI-3. The SCSI-2 and SCSI-3 are successors to the original SCSI specification. These newer versions use the ultra or wide SCSI interface and offer performance enhancements over standard SCSI. EIDE, on the other hand, is an enhanced version of IDE that offers performance enhancements over standard IDE. One of the more recent specifications for enhanced IDE is the Ultra DMA (ATA-4) specification. So, ironically, references to EIDE, Ultra DMA, and Ultra ATA may all refer to the same type of drive. The focus here is on the standard SCSI and IDE interfaces.

SCSI Drives

With SCSI you can connect up to seven drives to a single controller. Each drive connected to the primary controller is given a numeric designator from 0 to 6. This designator is the drive's SCSI ID, meaning drive 0 is SCSI ID 0, drive 1 is SCSI ID 1, and so on. The drive controller itself is usually designated as SCSI ID 7. Designators for drives on secondary controllers start where the first controller leaves off. For example, if the first controller has seven drives, the first drive on the second controller would normally be SCSI ID 8.

Generally, you set a drive's SCSI ID number before you install it. You do this by using the jumpers on the back of the drive. Instead of jumpers, some drives have a push button or similar mechanism for setting the SCSI ID. If you change the ID of a SCSI device, you must turn the drive off and then back on. This ensures that the change takes effect.

SCSI devices are connected to the controller in a daisy chain, with each device serially in a single line. The first and last device in the chain must be terminated properly. Typically, the SCSI controller terminates the first device itself, and the last device in the chain uses an actual terminator.

Before you can use a hard disk drive, it must be low-level formatted. With SCSI, the manufacturer normally performs this task before shipping the drive. If you need to do a low-level format on site, you'll usually find that the manufacturer has supplied a utility for this. If necessary, use this utility to format the drive.

IDE Drives

With IDE you can connect up to two drives to a controller. Each drive connected to the primary controller is given a numeric designator from 0 to 1. The first drive has a designator of 0. The second drive has a designator of 1. Designators for drives on secondary controllers start where the first controller leaves off. For example, if the first controller has two drives, the first drive on the second controller normally would have a designator of 3.

As with SCSI drives, you should set an IDE drive's designator before you install it. If this is the first IDE drive on a controller, you must set it up as the master device. If there are two drives on a controller, you must set up one drive as a master device and the other as a slave device. Generally, if you're installing a new drive, the existing drive becomes the master device and the new drive becomes the slave device.

Note   Generally, you can't perform a low-level formatting of an IDE drive. The manufacturer performs this task before shipping the drive.

Preparing a Drive for Use

Once you install a drive, you'll need to configure it for use. You configure the drive by partitioning it and creating file systems in the partitions, as needed. A partition is a section of a physical drive that functions as if it were a separate unit. After you create a partition, you can create a file system in the partition.

Using Disk Management

You'll use the Disk Management tool to configure drives. Disk Management makes it easy to work with the internal and external drives on a local or remote system. To start Disk Management and connect to a local or remote system, follow these steps:

1. Run Computer Management by going to Start, selecting Programs, then Administrative Tools, and then Computer Management.

2. You're automatically connected to the local computer on which you're running Computer Management. To manage hard disk drives on another computer, right-click the Computer Management entry in the console tree and select Connect To Another Computer on the shortcut menu. You can now choose the system whose drives you want to manage.

Tip   If you receive an error message from the Logical Disk Manager, read the message and click OK. A failed connection to the Logical Disk Manager Service usually means that this service or the related administrative service isn't started on the local or remote system. If necessary, start Logical Disk Manager and Logical Disk Manager Administrative Service as described in the section of Chapter 3 entitled "Starting, Stopping, and Pausing Services." Network policies and trusts can affect your ability to administrate computers remotely as well.

3. In Computer Management, expand Storage and then select Disk Management. You can now manage the drives on the local or remote system.

Disk Management has three views: Volume List, Graphical view, and Disk List.

 Note Before you work with Disk Management, there are several things you should know. If you create a partition but don't format it, the partition will be labeled as Free Space. If you haven't assigned a portion of the disk to a partition, this section of the disk is labeled Unallocated.

In Figure 10-1, the Volume List view is in the upper-right corner and the Graphical view is in the lower-right corner. This is the default configuration. You can change the view for the top or bottom pane as follows:

- To change the top view, select View, choose Top, and then select the view you want to use.

- To change the bottom view, select View, choose Bottom, and then select the view you want to use.

- To hide the bottom or top view, select View, choose Top or Bottom, and then select Hidden.

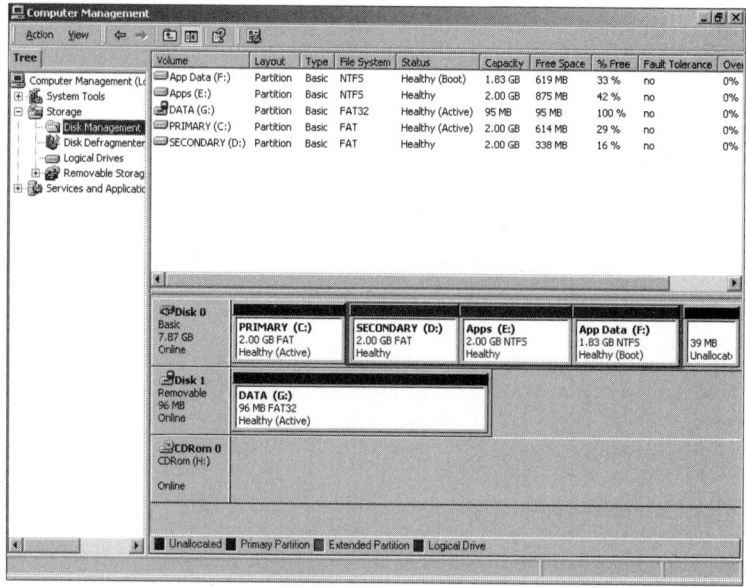

Figure 10-1. *In Disk Management the upper view provides a detailed summary of all the drives on the computer and the lower view provides an overview of the same drives by default.*

The Volume List View

Within Disk Management, the Volume List view provides a detailed summary of all the drives on the computer. Clicking a column label, such as Name, allows you to sort the disk information based on that column. The column labels are used as follows:

- **Volume**   The drive letter and name of the volume, such as Primary (C).
- **Layout**   The layout of the drive, such as a partition or volume.
- **Type**   The drive type, such as basic or dynamic.
- **File System**   The file system type, such as FAT (file allocation table), FAT32, or NTFS (Windows NT file system).
- **Status**   The status of the volume, such as healthy or unhealthy.
- **Capacity**   The amount of data the volume can hold.
- **Free Space**   The amount of free space in megabytes.
- **% Free**   The amount of free space as a percentage of total drive capacity.
- **Fault Tolerance**   Whether the drive uses Windows 2000 fault tolerant features, such as mirroring or striping.
- **Overhead**   The total additional drive space required as a result of the fault tolerant feature used.

Note   Volume sets and fault tolerance are discussed in Chapter 11.

The Graphical View

Within Disk Management, the Graphical view provides a graphical overview of all the physical and logical drives installed on the system. In this example, there are three disk devices installed on the system: Disk 0, a fixed drive of 7.87 GB; Disk 1, a removable drive; and CDRom 0, a CD-ROM device. Disk 0 is further broken down into sections: a primary partition, three logical drives, and a section of free space. The information provided for these drive sections could tell you the following: drive letter and text label for the partition or volume; the file system type, such as FAT, FAT32, or NTFS; the size of the drive section in megabytes; and the status of partitions or volumes, such as healthy or unhealthy.

Summary information for the physical disk devices includes the disk number and device type, such as basic, removable, or CD-ROM; the disk capacity; and the status of the disk device, such as online or offline.

The Disk List View

Within Disk Management, the Disk List view summarizes information about physical drives. The summary includes the disk number and device type, such as basic, removable, or CD-ROM; the disk capacity; the size of unallocated space on the disk (if any); the status of the disk device, such as online or offline; and the device interface type, such IDE or SCSI.

More Detailed Drive Information

From the Disk Management window, you can get more detailed information on a drive section by right-clicking it and then selecting Properties from the pop-up menu. When you do this, you'll see a dialog box much like the one shown in Figure 10-2. This is the same dialog box that you can access from Windows Explorer (by selecting the top-level folder for the drive and then choosing Properties from the File menu). The information provided on the General tab of the Properties dialog box tells you the following:

- The drive letter for the section.
- The text label for the section (known as a volume label).
- The disk type. A local disk is a disk on the current computer system. A network drive is a disk located on a remote computer system that is accessible through a network connection. You may also see floppy, CD-ROM, and RAM drive types.
- The file system type, such as FAT, FAT32, or NTFS.
- The amount of used space on the disk.
- The amount of free space on the disk.
- The total capacity of the disk.

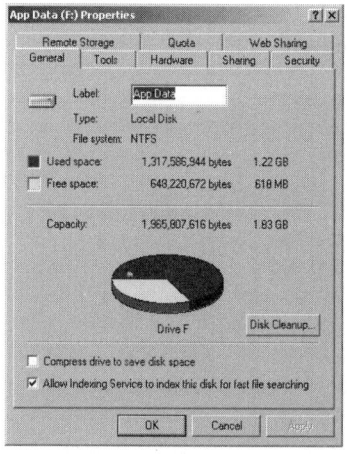

Figure 10-2. *The General tab of the Properties dialog box provides detailed information about a drive.*

Installing and Checking for a New Drive

Hot swapping is a feature that allows you to remove devices without shutting off the computer. Typically, hot swappable drives are installed and removed from the front of the computer. If your computer supports hot swapping of drives, you can install drives to the computer without having to shut down. After you do this, access Disk Management and from the Action menu select Rescan Disks. New disks found are added as basic disks. If a disk you've added isn't found, reboot.

If the computer doesn't support hot swapping of drives, you must turn the computer off and then install the new drives. Afterward you can scan for new disks as described previously.

Understanding Drive Status

Knowing the drive status is useful when you install new drives or troubleshoot drive problems. Disk Management shows the drive status in the Graphical and Volume List views. Table 10-1 summarizes the most common status values.

Table 10-1. Common Drive Status Values and Their Meaning

Status	Description	Resolution
Online	The normal disk status. It means the disk is accessible and doesn't have problems. Both dynamic disks and basic disks display this status.	The drive doesn't have any known problems.
Online (Errors)	I/O errors have been detected on a dynamic disk.	You can try to correct temporary errors using the REACTIVATE DISK command.
Offline	The dynamic disk isn't accessible and may be corrupted or temporarily unavailable. If the disk name changes to Missing, the disk can no longer be located or identified on the system.	Check for problems with the drive, its controller, and cables. Make sure that the drive has power and is connected properly. Use the REACTIVATE DISK command to bring the disk back online (if possible).
Foreign	The dynamic disk has been moved to your computer but hasn't been imported for use. A failed drive brought back online may sometimes be listed as Foreign.	Use the IMPORT FOREIGN DISKS command to add the disk to the system.
Unreadable	The disk isn't accessible currently, which can occur when rescanning disks. Both dynamic and basic disks display this status.	If the drives aren't being scanned, the drive may be corrupt or have I/O errors. Use the RESCAN DISK command to correct the problem (if possible). You may also want to reboot the system.

(continued)

Table 10-1. *(continued)*

Status	Description	Resolution
Unrecognized	The disk is of an unknown type and can't be used on the system. A drive from a non-Windows system may display this status.	You can't use the drive on the computer. Try a different drive.
No Media	No media have been inserted into the CD-ROM or removable drive. Only CD-ROM and removable disk types display this status.	Insert a CD-ROM, floppy, or removable disk to bring the disk online.

Working with Basic and Dynamic Disks

Windows 2000 supports two types of disk configurations:

- **Basic** The standard disk type used in previous versions of Windows. Basic disks are divided into partitions and can be used with previous versions of Windows.

- **Dynamic** An enhanced disk type for Windows 2000 that can be updated without having to restart the system (in most cases). Dynamic disks are divided into volumes and can only be used with Windows 2000.

Using Basic and Dynamic Disks

When you upgrade to Windows 2000, disks with partitions are initialized as basic disks. When you install Windows 2000 on a new system with unpartitioned drives, you have the option of initializing the drives as either basic or dynamic.

Basic drives support all the fault tolerant features found in Windows NT 4.0. You can use basic drives to maintain existing driving, mirroring, and striping configurations and to delete these configurations. However, you can't create fault tolerant drives using the basic disk type. You'll need to upgrade to dynamic disks and then create volumes that use mirroring or striping. The fault tolerant features and the ability to modify disks without having to restart the computer are the key capabilities that distinguish basic and dynamic disks. Other features available on a disk depend on the disk formatting.

You can use both basic and dynamic disks on the same computer. The catch is that volume sets must use the same disk type. For example, if you have mirrored drives C and D that were created under Windows NT 4.0, you can use these drives under Windows 2000. If you want to upgrade C to the dynamic disk type, you must also upgrade D. To learn how to upgrade a disk from basic to dynamic, see the section of this chapter entitled "Changing Drive Types."

Special Considerations for Basic and Dynamic Disks

Whether you're working with basic or dynamic disks, you need to keep in mind three special types of drive sections:

- **System** The system partition or volume contains the hardware-specific files needed to load the operating system. On Compaq Alpha-based computers, the system partition or volume must be formatted for the FAT file system. The system partition or volume can't be part of a striped, spanned, or RAID-5 volume.

- **Boot** The boot partition or volume contains the operating system and its support files. The system and boot partition or volume can be the same.

- **Active** The active partition or volume is the drive section from which the computer starts. When the computer uses multiple operating systems, the active drive section must contain the startup files for all operating systems loaded on the computer and it must be a primary partition on a basic disk. If you only use Windows 2000, the active drive section must be a simple volume on a dynamic disk (which can be the same volume as the system volume).

Marking an Active Partition

You can mark a partition as active by completing the following steps:

1. Make sure that the necessary startup files are on the primary partition that you want to make the active partition. For Windows NT and Windows 2000, these files are BOOT.INI, NTDETECT.COM, NTLDR, and BOOTSECT.DOS. You may also need NTBOOTDD.SYS.

2. Access Disk Management.

3. Right-click the primary partition you want to mark as active, and then select Mark Partition Active.

Note You can't mark volumes as active. When you upgrade a basic disk containing the active partition to a dynamic disk, this partition becomes a simple volume that is active automatically.

Changing Drive Types

Basic disks are designed to be used with previous versions of Windows. Dynamic disks are designed to let you take advantage of the latest Windows 2000 features. You can't use dynamic disks with previous versions of Windows, but you can use dynamic disks with other operating systems, such as Unix. To do this, you need to create a separate volume for the non-Windows operating system. You can't use dynamic disks on portable computers.

Windows 2000 provides the tools you need to upgrade a basic disk to a dynamic disk and to change a dynamic disk back to a basic disk. When you upgrade to a dynamic disk, partitions are changed to volumes of the appropriate type automatically. You can't change these volumes back to partitions. Instead, you must delete the volumes on the dynamic disk and then change the disk back to a basic disk. Deleting the volumes destroys all the information on the disk.

Upgrading a Basic Disk to a Dynamic Disk

Before you upgrade a basic disk to a dynamic disk, you should make sure that you don't need to boot the computer to a previous version of Windows. You should also make sure that the disk has 1 MB of free space at the end of the disk. While Disk Management reserves this free space when creating partitions and volumes, disk management tools on other operating systems might not. As a result, the upgrade will fail. Other considerations you should make before upgrading are as follows:

- You can't upgrade drives that use sector sizes larger than 512 bytes. If the drive has large sector sizes, you'll need to reformat before upgrading.

- You can't upgrade removable media to dynamic disks. You can only configure removable media drives as basic drives with primary partitions.

- You can't upgrade a disk if the system or boot partition is part of spanned, striped, mirrored, or RAID-5 volume. You'll need to stop the spanning, mirroring, or striping before you upgrade.

- You can upgrade disks with other types of partitions that are part of spanned, striped, mirrored, or RAID-5 volumes. These volumes become dynamic volumes of the same type. However, you must upgrade all drives in the set together.

To upgrade a basic disk to a dynamic disk, complete the following steps:

1. In Disk Management, right-click a basic disk that you want to upgrade, either in the Disk List view or in the left pane of the Graphical view. Then select Upgrade To Dynamic Disk.

2. In the Upgrade To Dynamic Disk dialog box, select the check boxes for the disks you want to upgrade. If you're upgrading a spanned, striped, mirrored, or RAID-5 volume, be sure to select all the basic disks in this set. You must upgrade the set together. Click OK when you're ready to continue.

3. As shown in Figure 10-3, the Disks To Upgrade dialog box shows the disks you're upgrading. The buttons and columns on this dialog box contain the following information:

   - **Name** Shows the disk number.
   - **Disk Contents** Shows the type and status of partitions, such as boot, active, or in use.

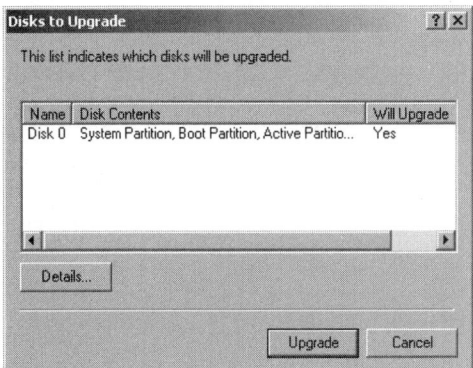

Figure 10-3. *In the Disks To Upgrade dialog box, notice the Disk Contents and Will Upgrade columns before continuing.*

- **Will Upgrade**   Specifies whether the drive will be upgraded. If the drive doesn't meet the criteria, it won't be upgraded, and you may need to take corrective action, as described previously.
- **Details**   Shows the volumes on the selected drive.
- **Upgrade**   Starts the upgrade operation.

4. If you're ready to begin the upgrade, click Upgrade. Disk Management warns you that once you upgrade you won't be able to boot previous versions of Windows from volumes on the selected disks. Click Yes to continue.

5. Disk Management will restart the computer if a selected drive contains the boot partition, system partition, or a partition in use.

Changing a Dynamic Disk Back to a Basic Disk

Before you can change a dynamic disk back to a basic disk, you must delete all dynamic volumes on the disk. Once you do this, right-click the disk and select the REVERT TO BASIC DISK command. This changes the dynamic disk to a basic disk and you can then create new partitions and logical drives on the disk.

Reactivating Dynamic Disks

If the status of a dynamic disk displays as Online (Errors) or Offline, you can often reactivate the disk to correct the problem. You reactivate a disk by completing the following steps:

1. In Disk Management, right-click the dynamic disk you want to reactivate, and then select Reactivate Disk. Confirm the action when prompted.

2. If the drive status doesn't change, you may need to reboot the computer. If this still doesn't resolve the problem, check for problems with the drive, its controller, and the cables. Also, make sure that the drive has power and is connected properly.

Rescanning Disks

Rescanning all drives on a system updates the drive configuration information on the computer. It can sometimes resolve problems with drives that show a status of Unreadable. Because the drive configuration may change as a result of the rescan, you may need to update the BOOT.INI file for the computer, as discussed later in this chapter in the section entitled "Updating the Boot Disk."

You rescan disks on a computer by selecting Rescan Disk from Disk Management's Action menu.

 Real World Take a screenshot of the disk configuration in Disk Management before scanning and after scanning to double-check the configuration for changes. On my primary server, the original configuration had a floppy drive on A; logical drives on C, D, E, and F; a removable drive on G; and a CD-ROM drive on H. After rescanning, the removable drive was on B, and as a result, the number of the boot partition changed (and Windows 2000 gave no notification of this change).

During reboot of the system, Windows 2000 stated incorrectly that the NTOSKRNL.EXE file needed to be restored on the Windows 2000 root folder. Using the emergency boot disk created as explained in Chapter 14, you could modify the BOOT.INI file and recover the system. Without the emergency boot disk, you'd need to repair the Windows 2000 installation using the Windows 2000 Setup Boot Disks. Creating the Windows 2000 setup disks is also covered in Chapter 14.

Moving a Dynamic Disk to a New System

Windows 2000 makes the task of moving drives to a new system a lot easier. If you want to move a dynamic drive to a new computer, follow these steps:

1. Access Disk Management on the system where the dynamic drives are currently installed.

2. Check the status of the drives and ensure that they're marked as healthy. If the status isn't healthy, you should repair partitions and volumes, as necessary, before you move the disk drives.

3. Remove drive letters and drive paths that reference the drives, as described in the section of this chapter entitled "Assigning Drive Letters and Paths."

4. If the drives are hot-swappable and this feature is supported on both systems, remove the drives, and then install them on the destination computer. Otherwise, turn off both computers. Remove the drives from the original system and then install them on the new system. When you're finished, turn the computers back on.

5. On the destination computer, from the Action menu select Rescan Disks. When the scan finishes, right-click any disk marked Foreign, and then click Import Foreign Disks.

Using Basic Disks and Partitions

When you install a new computer or update an existing computer, you'll often need to partition the drives on the computer. You partition drives using Disk Management. Use partitions when you need to boot the computer to Microsoft Windows 95, Windows 98, or Windows NT as well as Microsoft Windows 2000.

Caution   Before you make any changes to hard disk drives, consider the consequences. Changing partition information for drives may result in data loss, and improper configuring of partitions may even prevent system boot. To prevent some configuration problems, Windows 2000 restricts the operations you can perform on system or boot partitions.

Understanding Drive Partitions

Windows 2000 uses two types of partitions—primary and extended.

- **Primary partitions**   Drive sections that you can access directly for file storage. Each physical drive can have up to four primary partitions. You make a primary partition accessible to users by creating a file system on it.

- **Extended partitions**   Unlike primary partitions, you can't access these directly. Instead, you can configure extended partitions with one or more logical drives that are used to store files. Being able to divide extended partitions into logical drives allows you to divide a physical drive into more than four sections.

On Windows 2000 a physical drive can have up to four primary partitions and up to one extended partition. This allows you to configure drives in one of two ways: using one to four primary partitions or using one to three primary partitions and one extended partition.

Note   With MS-DOS, a physical drive can have only one primary partition. This partition is the boot partition. If you plan to boot a Windows 2000 system in MS-DOS, you should use only one primary partition and then use an extended partition to create additional logical drives.

Assigning Drive Letters

After you partition a drive, you format the partitions to assign drive letters. This is a high-level formatting that creates the file system structure rather than a low-level formatting that sets up the drive for initial use.

You're probably very familiar with the C drive used by Windows 2000. Well, the C drive is simply the designator for a disk partition. If you partition a disk into multiple sections, each section can have its own drive letter. You use the drive letters to access file systems in various partitions on a physical drive. Unlike MS-DOS, which assigns drive letters automatically starting with the letter C, Windows 2000 lets you specify drive letters. Generally, the drive letters C through Z are available for your use.

Note The drive letter A is usually assigned to the system's floppy drive. If the system has a second floppy drive, the letter B is assigned to it, so you can only use the letters C through Z. Don't forget that CD-ROMs, Zip drives, and other types of media drives need drive letters as well. The total number of drive letters you can use at one time is 24. If you need additional volumes, you can create them using drive paths.

Assigning Drive Paths

In Windows NT 4.0, you could only have 24 active volumes. To get around this limitation, Windows 2000 allows you to mount disks to drive paths. A drive path is set as a folder location on another drive. For example, you could mount additional drives as E:\data1, E:\data2, and E:\data3.

Drive paths can be used with basic and dynamic disks. The only restriction for drive paths is that you mount them on empty folders that are on NTFS drives.

Color Coding Partitions

To help you differentiate between primary partitions and extended partitions with logical drives, Disk Management color codes the partitions. For example, primary partitions may be color coded with a dark blue band and logical drives in extended partitions may be color coded with a light blue band. The key for the color scheme is shown at the bottom of the Disk Management window. You can change the colors using the View Settings dialog box. From Disk Management's View menu, select the Settings option.

Creating Partitions and Logical Drives

In Disk Management you create partitions and logical drives by completing the following steps:

1. In the Disk Management Graphical view, right-click an area marked Unallocated and then choose Create Partition. This starts the Create Partition Wizard. Read the welcome dialog box, and then click Next. As shown in Figure 10-4, you can now select a partition type.

2. Select Primary Partition to create a primary partition. Each physical drive can have up to four primary partitions. A primary partition can fill an entire disk or be sized as appropriate for the workstation or server you're configuring.

3. Select Extended Partition to create an extended partition. Each physical drive can have one extended partition. This extended partition can contain one or more logical drives, which are simply sections of the partition with their own file system.

 Note If a drive already contains an extended partition, the Extended Partition option won't be available. You'll need to delete the existing extended partition and create a new one, which will result in data loss. Note also that you can only create primary partitions on removable drives.

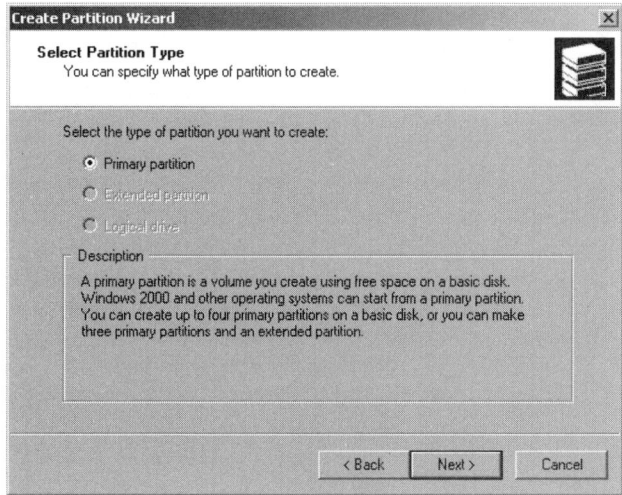

Figure 10-4. *In the Create Partition Wizard select a partition type, and then click Next.*

4. Select Logical Drive if you want to create a logical drive within an extended partition.

Tip   Although you can size the logical drive any way you want, you may want to take a moment to consider how you'll use logical drives on the current workstation or server. Generally, you use logical drives to divide a large drive into manageable sections. With this in mind, you may want to divide a 21 GB extended partition into 3 logical drives of 7 GB each.

5. Next you should see the Specify Partition Size dialog box shown in Figure 10-5. This dialog box specifies the minimum and maximum size for the partition in megabytes and lets you size the partition within these limits. Size the partition using the Amount Of Disk Space To Use field.

6. Specify whether you want to assign a drive letter or path. These options are used as follows:

   • **Assign A Drive Letter**   To assign a drive letter, choose this option, and then select an available drive letter in the selection list provided.

   • **Mount This Volume To An Empty Folder That Supports Drive Paths**   To assign a drive path, choose this option, and then type the path to an existing folder or click Browse to search for or create a folder.

   • **Do Not Assign A Drive Letter Or Drive Path**   To create the partition without assigning a drive letter or path, choose this option. You can assign a drive letter or path later, if necessary.

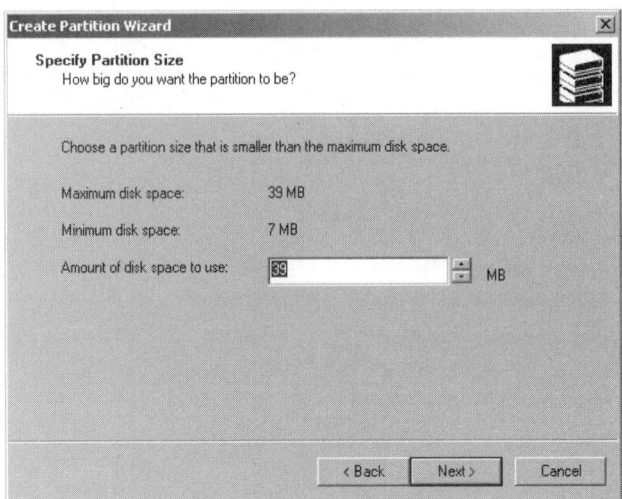

Figure 10-5. *Size the primary partition within the minimum and maximum size limits and then click Next.*

7. Determine whether the partition should be formatted in the Format Partition dialog box, shown in Figure 10-6. If you elect to format the partition, follow the steps described in the following section, "Formatting Partitions."

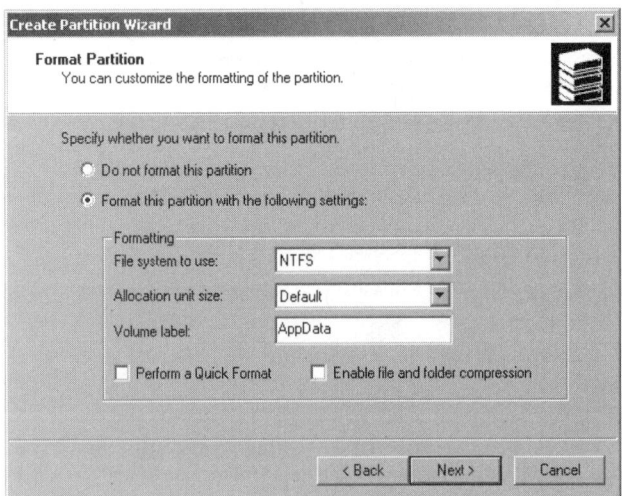

Figure 10-6. *Format a partition by specifying its file system type and volume label.*

8. Click Next and then click Finish. If you add partitions to a physical drive that contains the Windows 2000 operating system, you may inadvertently change the number of the boot partition. As Figure 10-7 shows, Windows 2000 will display a prompt warning you that the number of the boot partition will change. Click Yes.

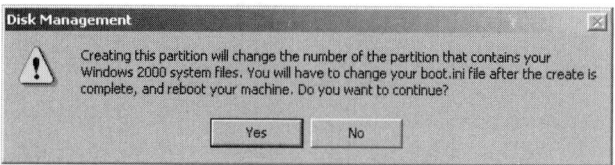

Figure 10-7. *If you update the physical drive containing the operating system, you may need to update the BOOT.INI file.*

9. Disk Management then creates the partition, assigns a drive letter or path, as appropriate, and formats the partition, as appropriate. If you saw a warning prompt previously, you may see another warning prompt telling you to edit the BOOT.INI file. Edit the BOOT.INI file and update the designator for the boot partition as described in the section in this chapter entitled "Updating the Boot Disk." Then immediately reboot the computer.

Formatting Partitions

Formatting creates a file system in a partition and permanently deletes any existing data. This is a high-level formatting that creates the file system structure rather than a low-level formatting that initializes a drive for use. To format a partition, right-click the partition, and then chose Format. This opens the Format dialog box shown in Figure 10-8. If you compare Figures 10-6 and 10-8, you'll see that the available fields are essentially the same. Because of this, you format a drive using the Create Partition Wizard and the Format dialog box using the same techniques. You use the formatting fields as follows:

- **Volume Label**   Specifies a text label for the partition. This label is the partition's volume name.

- **File System**   Specifies the file system type as FAT, FAT32, or NTFS. FAT is the file system type supported by MS-DOS and Microsoft Windows 3.1, Windows 95, and Windows 98. NTFS is the native file system type for Windows NT and Windows 2000. The section of Chapter 12 entitled "Windows 2000 File Structures" tells you more about NTFS and the advantages of using it with Windows 2000.

- **Allocation Unit Size**   Specifies the cluster size for the file system. This is the basic unit in which disk space is allocated. The default allocation unit size is based on the size of the volume and is set dynamically prior to formatting. To override this feature, you can set the allocation unit size to a specific value. If you use lots of small files, you may want to use a smaller cluster size, such as 512 or 1024 bytes. With these settings, small files use less disk space.

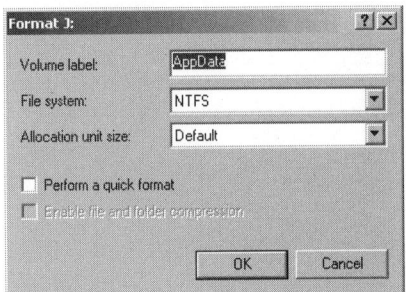

Figure 10-8. *Format a partition by specifying its file system type and volume label.*

 Tip If you create a file system as FAT or FAT32, you can later convert it to NTFS by using the Convert utility. You can't, however, convert NTFS partitions to FAT. Often you'll want your boot partition to be FAT and other partitions to be NTFS. With Intel x86 systems, having your system partitions as FAT is often a good idea. This gives you freedom to boot the system under MS-DOS, if necessary.

With RISC (Reduced Instruction Set Computing)–based systems, you don't have the option of using NTFS. The boot partition must be FAT. For details on creating partitions, see the section of this chapter entitled "Understanding Drive Partitions."

- **Perform A Quick Format** Tells Windows 2000 to format without checking the partition for errors. With large partitions, this option can save you a few minutes. However, it's more prudent to check for errors, which allows Disk Management to mark bad sectors on the disk and lock them out.

- **Enable File And Folder Compression** Turns on compression for the disk. Built-in compression is only available for NTFS. Under NTFS, compression is transparent to users and compressed files can be accessed just like regular files. If you select this option, files and directories on this drive are compressed automatically. For more information on compressing drives, files, and directories, see the section entitled "Compressing Drives and Data."

When you're ready to proceed, click OK. Because formatting a partition destroys any existing data, Disk Management gives you one last chance to abort the procedure. Click OK to start formatting the partition. Disk Management changes the status of the drive to reflect the formatting and the percentage of completion. When formatting is complete, the drive status will change to reflect this.

Updating the Boot Disk

When you add partitions to a physical drive that contains the Windows 2000 operating system, the number of the boot partition may change. If this happens, you'll need to update the system's BOOT.INI file. Normally, this file is located on the C drive.

The BOOT.INI file contains entries that look like this:

```
[boot loader]

timeout=30

default=multi(0)disk(0)rdisk(0)partition(3)\WIN2000

[operating systems]

multi(0)disk(0)rdisk(0)partition(3)\WIN2000="Microsoft Windows
2000 Server" /fastdetect

multi(0)disk(0)rdisk(0)partition(2)\WINNT="Windows NT Server
Version 4.00"

multi(0)disk(0)rdisk(0)partition(2)\WINNT="Windows NT Server
Version 4.00

[VGA mode]" /basevideo /sos

multi(0)disk(0)rdisk(0)partition(1)\WINNT="Windows NT Workstation
Version 4.00"

multi(0)disk(0)rdisk(0)partition(1)\WINNT="Windows NT Workstation
Version 4.00 [VGA mode]" /basevideo /sos
```

Entries like this tell Windows NT where to find the operating system:

```
multi(0)disk(0)rdisk(0)partition(3)\WIN2000
```

The designators for this entry are used as follows:

- **multi(0)** Designates the controller for the drive, which in this case is controller 0. If the secondary mirror is on a different controller, enter the number of the controller. Controllers are numbered from 0 to 3.

Note   The format for the BOOT.INI entries is the ARC (Advanced RISC Computer) name format. On SCSI systems that don't use SCSI BIOS (basic input/output system), the first field in the entry is scsi(n), where *n* is the controller number.

- **disk(0)** Designates the SCSI bus adapter, which in this case is adapter 0. On most systems, this is always 0. The exception is for systems with multiple bus SCSI adapters. These systems use the scsi(n) syntax.
- **rdisk(0)** Designates the ordinal number of the disk on the adapter, which in this case is drive 0. With SCSI drives that use SCSI BIOS, you'll see numbers from 0 to 6. With other SCSI drives, this is always 0. With IDE, you'll see either 0 or 1. In most cases, you'll need to change this field—so be sure to enter the number of the secondary mirror drive.

- **partition(3)** Designates the partition that contains the operating system, which in this case is 3.

If the boot partition for Window 2000 changed from 3 to 4, you would update the BOOT.INI file shown earlier as follows:

```
[boot loader]

timeout=30

default=multi(0)disk(0)rdisk(0)partition(4)\WIN2000

[operating systems]

multi(0)disk(0)rdisk(0)partition(4)\WIN2000="Microsoft Windows
2000 Server" /fastdetect

multi(0)disk(0)rdisk(0)partition(2)\WINNT="Windows NT Server
Version 4.00"

multi(0)disk(0)rdisk(0)partition(2)\WINNT="Windows NT Server
Version 4.00

[VGA mode]" /basevideo /sos

multi(0)disk(0)rdisk(0)partition(1)\WINNT="Windows NT Workstation
Version 4.00"

multi(0)disk(0)rdisk(0)partition(1)\WINNT="Windows NT Workstation
Version 4.00 [VGA mode]" /basevideo /sos
```

Managing Existing Partitions and Drives

Disk Management provides many ways to manage existing partitions and drives. Use these features to assign drive letters, delete partitions, set the active partition, and more. In addition, Windows 2000 provides other utilities to carry out common tasks such as converting a volume to NTFS or checking a drive for errors.

Assigning Drive Letters and Paths

Drives can be assigned one drive letter and one or more drive paths, provided the drive paths are mounted on NTFS drives. Drives don't have to be assigned a drive letter or path. A drive with no designators is considered to be unmounted and can be mounted by assigning a drive letter or path at a later date. You need to unmount a drive before moving it to another computer.

To manage drive letters and paths, right-click the drive you want to configure in Disk Management, and then choose Change Drive Letter And Path. This opens the dialog box shown in Figure 10-9. You can now:

- **Add a drive path** Click Add, select Mount In This NTFS Folder, and then type the path to an existing folder or click Browse to search for or create a folder.

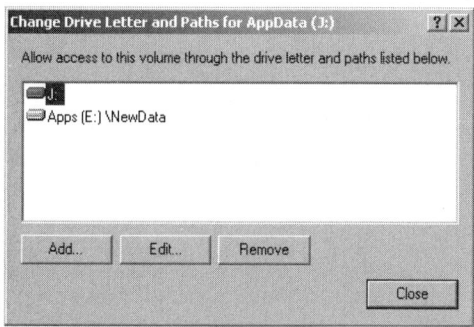

Figure 10-9. *Use this dialog box to change the drive letter and path assignment.*

- **Remove a drive path**   Select the drive path to remove, click Remove, and then click Yes.

- **Assign a drive letter**   Click Add, select Assign A Drive Letter, and then choose an available letter to assign to the drive.

- **Change the drive letter**   Select the current drive letter, and then click Edit. Select Assign A Drive Letter, and then choose a different letter to assign to the drive.

- **Remove a drive letter**   Select the current drive letter, click Remove, and then click Yes.

Note   If you try to change the letter of a drive that's in use, Windows 2000 displays a warning. You'll need to exit programs that are using the drive and try again or allow Disk Management to force the change by clicking Yes when prompted.

Changing or Deleting the Volume Label

The volume label is a text descriptor for a drive. Because this label is displayed when the drive is accessed in various Windows 2000 utilities, such as Windows Explorer, you can use the label to help provide information about the contents of a drive. You can change or delete a volume label using Disk Management or Windows 2000 Explorer.

Using Disk Management, you can change or delete a label by doing this:

1. Right-click the partition, and then choose Properties.

2. In the General tab of the Properties dialog box, use the Label field to type a new label for the volume or delete the existing label. Click OK.

Using Windows Explorer, you can change or delete a label by doing this:

1. Right-click the drive icon and then choose Properties.

2. In the General tab of the Properties dialog box, use the Label field to type a new label for the volume or delete the existing label. Click OK.

Deleting Partitions and Drives

To change the configuration of an existing drive that is fully allocated, you may need to delete existing partitions and logical drives. Deleting a partition or a drive removes the associated file system, and all data in the file system is lost. So before you delete a partition or a drive, you should back up any files and directories the partition or drive contains.

You can delete a primary partition or logical drive by doing this:

1. In Disk Management, right-click the partition or drive you want to delete, and then choose Delete Partition or Delete Logical Drive, as appropriate.

2. Confirm that you want to delete the partition by clicking Yes.

3. If you delete a partition on a physical drive that contains the Windows 2000 operating system, the number of the boot partition may change. If so, you'll need to update the BOOT.INI file as described in the section of this chapter entitled "Updating the Boot Disk." Be sure to note the new partition number to use.

To delete an extended partition, do this:

1. Delete all the logical drives on the partition following the steps outlined above.

2. You should now be able to select the extended partition area itself and delete it.

Converting a Volume to NTFS

Windows 2000 provides a utility for converting FAT volumes to NTFS. This utility, called Convert (CONVERT.EXE), is located in the *%SystemRoot%* folder. When you convert a volume using this tool, the file and directory structure is preserved and no data is lost. Keep in mind, however, that Windows 2000 doesn't provide a utility for converting NTFS to FAT. The only way to go from NTFS to FAT is to delete the partition by following the steps outlined in the previous section and then to recreate the partition as a FAT volume.

The Convert Utility Syntax

Convert is a command-line utility run at the Command prompt. If you want to convert a drive, use the follow syntax:

```
convert volume /FS:NTFS
```

where *volume* is the drive letter followed by a colon, drive path, or volume name. For example, if you wanted to convert the D drive to NTFS, you would use the following command:

```
convert D: /FS:NTFS
```

The complete syntax for Convert is shown in Table 10-2.

Table 10-2. Convert Syntax and Usage

Syntax

```
convert volume /FS:NTFS [/V]
```

The options and switches for Convert are used as follows:

volume	Sets the volume to work with.
/FS:NTFS	Converts to NTFS.
/V	Sets verbose mode.

Syntax

```
convert c:\drive1 /FS:NTFS /V
```

Using the Convert Utility

Before you use the Convert utility, double-check to see if the partition is being used as the active boot partition or a system partition containing the operating system. With Intel x86 systems, you can convert the active boot partition to NTFS. Doing so requires that the system gain exclusive access to this partition, which can only be obtained during startup. Thus, if you try to convert the active boot partition to NTFS, Windows 2000 displays a prompt asking if you want to schedule the drive to be converted the next time the system starts. If you click Yes, you can restart the system to begin the conversion process.

Tip Often it'll take several restarts of a system to completely convert the active boot partition. Don't panic. Let the system proceed with the conversion.

RISC-based systems are hardware configured and don't use an active boot partition. RISC computers, however, do use a system partition that contains the necessary files for the operating system. This partition must be a FAT file system, so you shouldn't convert the system partition to NTFS on RISC-based computers.

Before the Convert utility actually converts a drive to NTFS, the utility checks to see if the drive has enough free space to perform the conversion. Generally, Convert needs a block of free space that is roughly equal to 25 percent of the total space used on the drive. For example, if the drive stores 100 MB of data, Convert needs about 25 MB of free space. If there isn't enough free space, Convert aborts and tells you that you need to free up some space. On the other hand, if there is enough free space, Convert initiates the conversion. Be patient. The conversion process takes several minutes (longer for large drives). Don't access files or applications on the drive while the conversion is in progress.

Checking a Drive for Errors and Bad Sectors

The Windows 2000 utility for checking the integrity of a disk is Check Disk (CHKDSK.EXE). You'll find this utility in the *%SystemRoot%* folder. Use Check

Disk to check for and optionally repair problems found on FAT, FAT32, and NTFS volumes.

While Check Disk can check for and correct many types of errors, the utility primarily looks for inconsistencies in the file system and its related metadata. One of the ways Check Disk locates errors is by comparing the volume bitmap to the disk sectors assigned to files in the file system. But beyond this, the usefulness of Check Disk is rather limited. For example, Check Disk can't repair corrupted data within files that appear to be structurally intact.

Running Check Disk from the Command Line

You can run Check Disk from the command line or within other utilities. At the Command prompt you can test the integrity of the E drive by typing the command

```
chkdsk E:
```

To find and repair errors that are found in the E drive, use the command

```
chkdsk /f E:
```

 Note Check Disk can't repair volumes that are in use. If the volume is in use, Check Disk displays a prompt that asks if you want to schedule the volume to be checked the next time you restart the system. Answer Yes to the prompt to schedule this.

The complete syntax for Check Disk is shown as Table 10-3.

Table 10-3. Check Disk Syntax and Usage

Syntax

```
chkdsk [volume[[path]filename]]] [/F] [/V] [/R] [/X] [/I] [/C] [/L[:size]]
```

The options and switches for Check Disk are used as follows:

volume	Sets the volume to work with.
filename	FAT only: Specifies files to check for fragmentation.
/F	Fixes errors on the disk.
/V	On FAT/FAT32: Displays the full path and name of every file on the disk.
	On NTFS: Displays cleanup messages, if any.
/R	Locates bad sectors and recovers readable information (implies /F).
/L:size	NTFS only: Changes the log file size.
/X	Forces the volume to dismount first if necessary (implies /F).

(continued)

Table 10-3. *(continued)*
Syntax

/I	NTFS only: Performs a minimum check of index entries.
/C	NTFS only: Skips checking of cycles within the folder structure.

Running Check Disk Interactively

You can also run Check Disk interactively by using either Windows Explorer or Disk Management.

Using Disk Management, access Check Disk by doing the following:

1. Right-click the drive, and then choose Properties.
2. In the Tools tab of the Properties dialog box, click Check Now.

Using Windows 2000 Explorer, access Check Disk by doing the following:

1. Right-click the drive, and then choose Properties.
2. In the Tools tab of the Properties dialog box, click Check Now.

Figure 10-10 shows the dialog box for the interactive version of Check Disk. Use this dialog box to check a disk for errors and then to repair them if you like.

- To check for errors without repairing them, click Start without selecting either of the check boxes.
- To check for errors and fix them, make the appropriate selections in the check boxes to fix file system errors or to recover bad sectors, or both.

Defragmenting Disks

Anytime you add files to or remove files from a drive, the data on the drive can become fragmented. When a drive is fragmented, large files can't be written to a single continuous area on the disk. As a result, the operating system must write the file to several smaller areas on the disk, which means more time is spent reading the file from the disk. To reduce fragmentation, you should periodically analyze and defragment disks using Disk Defragmenter.

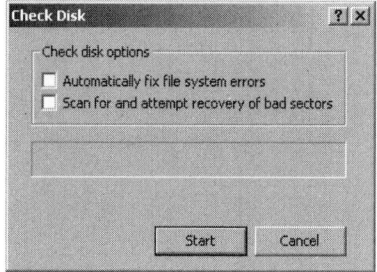

Figure 10-10. *Check Disk is available by clicking the Check Now button on the Properties dialog box. Use it to check a disk for errors and repair them, if you wish.*

You can analyze a disk to determine the level of fragmentation and defragment a disk by completing the following steps:

1. In Computer Management, expand Storage, and then select Disk Defragmenter.

2. Select the logical drive or volume that you want to work with by clicking it, as shown in Figure 10-11.

3. To analyze the amount of fragmentation on a partition or volume, click Analyze. The progress of the analysis is shown in the Analysis Display area. Fragmented files, contiguous files, system files, and free space are highlighted in different colors using the color code shown at the bottom of the display area. You can pause or stop the analysis if necessary.

4. When the analysis is complete, Disk Defragmenter recommends a course of action based on the amount of fragmentation. If there is a lot of fragmentation, you'll be prompted to defragment the disk. Otherwise you'll be told the disk doesn't need to be defragmented.

5. To defragment the disk, click Defragment. The progress of the defragment operation is shown in the Defragmentation Display area. You can pause or stop the operation, if necessary.

6. To view a report of the analysis or defragmentation, click View Report.

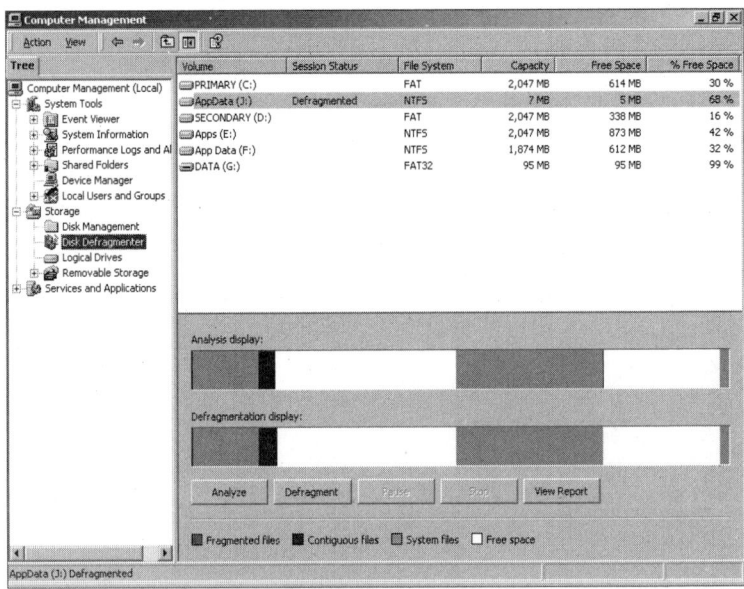

Figure 10-11. *Disk Defragmenter analyzes and defragments disks efficiently. The more frequently data is updated on drives, the more often you'll need to run this utility.*

Compressing Drives and Data

When you format a drive for NTFS, Windows 2000 allows you to turn on the built-in compression feature. With built-in compression, all files and directories stored on a drive are automatically compressed when they're created. Because this compression is transparent to users, compressed data can be accessed just like regular data. The difference is that you can store more information on a compressed drive than you can on an uncompressed drive.

Compressing Directories and Files

If you decide not to compress a drive, Windows 2000 lets you selectively compress directories and files. To compress a file or directory, complete these steps:

1. Right-click the file or directory that you want to compress, and then select Properties.

2. In the General tab of the related property dialog box, click Advanced. Select Compress Contents To Save Disk Space, shown in Figure 10-12. Click OK twice.

For an individual file, Windows 2000 marks the file as compressed and then compresses it. For a directory, Windows 2000 marks the directory as compressed and then compresses all the files in it. If the directory contains subfolders, Windows 2000 displays a dialog box that allows you to compress all the subfolders associated with the directory. Simply select Apply Changes To This Folder, Subfolders, And Files and then click OK. Once you compress a directory, any new files added or copied to the directory are compressed automatically.

Note   If you move an uncompressed file from a different drive, it's compressed. However, if you move an uncompressed file to a compressed folder on the same NTFS drive, the file isn't compressed. Note also that you can't encrypt compressed files.

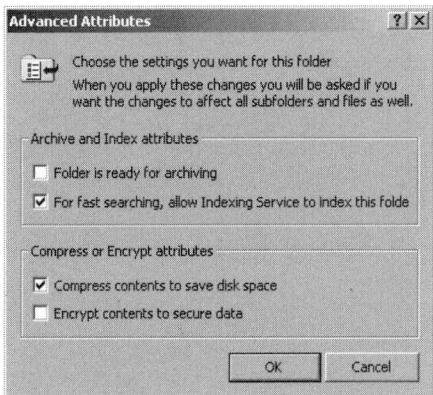

Figure 10-12. *With NTFS, you can compress a file or directory by selecting the Compress check box in the Advanced Attributes dialog box.*

Expanding Compressed Directories and Files

If you decide later that you want to expand a compressed file or directory, reverse the process by completing the following steps:

1. Right-click the file or directory in Windows Explorer.
2. In the General tab of the related property dialog box, click Advanced. Clear the Compress Contents To Save Disk Space check box. Click OK twice.

With files, Windows 2000 removes compression and expands the file. With directories, Windows 2000 expands all the files within the directory. If the directory contains subfolders, you'll also have the opportunity to remove compression from the subfolders. To do this, select Apply Changes To This Folder, Subfolders, And Files when prompted and then click OK.

 Tip Windows 2000 also provides command-line utilities for compressing and decompressing your data. The compression utility is called Compact (COMPACT.EXE). The decompression utility is called Expand (EXPAND.EXE).

Encrypting Drives and Data

Windows 2000 supports file encryption of data on NTFS volumes. Encryption allows users to store data in encrypted format. Files in encrypted format can only be read by the person who encrypted the file. Before other users can read an encrypted file, the file must be decrypted by the user. Otherwise, encrypted files can be copied, moved, and renamed just like any other file—and these actions don't affect the encryption of the data.

The process that handles encryption and decryption is called the Encrypting File System (EFS). The default setup for EFS allows users to encrypt files without needing special permission. Files are encrypted using a public/private key that is automatically generated by EFS on a per user basis.

 Tip The encryption algorithm used is the expanded Data Encryption Standard (DESX), which is enforced using 56-bit encryption by default. For stricter security, North American users can order the Enhanced CryptoPAK from Microsoft. The Enhanced CryptoPAK provides 128-bit encryption. Files that use 128-bit encryption can only be used on a system that supports 128-bit encryption. Administrators designated as Recovery Agents can decrypt files, if necessary.

Encrypting Directories and Files

With NTFS volumes, Windows 2000 lets you select files and folders for encryption. When you encrypt files, the file data is converted to an encrypted format that can only be read by the person who encrypted the file. Users can only encrypt files if they have the proper access permissions. When you encrypt folders, the folder is marked as encrypted, but actually only the files within it are encrypted. All files that are created in or added to a folder marked as encrypted are encrypted automatically.

To encrypt a file or directory, complete the following steps:

1. Right-click the file or directory that you want to encrypt, and then select Properties.

2. In the General tab of the related property dialog box, click Advanced. Then select Encrypt Contents To Secure Data. Click OK twice.

Note You can't encrypt compressed files, system files, or read-only files. If you try to encrypt compressed files, the files are automatically uncompressed and then encrypted. If you try to encrypt system files, you'll get an error.

For an individual file, Windows 2000 marks the file as encrypted and then encrypts it. For a directory, Windows 2000 marks the directory as encrypted and then encrypts all the files in it. If the directory contains subfolders, Windows 2000 displays a dialog box that allows you to encrypt all the subfolders associated with the directory. Simply select Apply Changes To This Folder, Subfolders, And Files and then click OK.

Note On NTFS volumes, files remain encrypted even when they're moved, copied, and renamed. If you copy or move an encrypted file to a FAT or FAT32 drive, the file is automatically decrypted before being copied or moved. Thus, you must have proper permissions to copy or move the file.

Decrypting Files and Directories

If you decide later that you want to decrypt a file or directory, reverse the process by completing the following steps:

1. Right-click the file or directory in Windows Explorer.

2. In the General tab of the related property dialog box, click Advanced. Clear Encrypt Contents To Secure Data. Click OK twice.

With files, Windows 2000 decrypts the file and restores it to its original format. With directories, Windows 2000 decrypts all the files within the directory. If the directory contains subfolders, you'll also have the opportunity to remove encryption from the subfolders. To do this, select Apply Changes To This Folder, Subfolders, And Files when prompted and then click OK.

Tip Windows 2000 also provides a command-line utility for encrypting and decrypting your data. This utility is called Cipher (CIPHER.EXE). Typing CIPHER at the command line by itself shows you the encryption status of all folders in the current directory.

Chapter 11

Administering Volume Sets and RAID Arrays

When you work with Microsoft Windows 2000 servers, you'll often need to perform advanced disk setup procedures, such as creating a volume set or setting up a RAID array. The following are some of the tasks that you can perform with Disk Manager.

- With a *volume set*, you can create a single volume that spans multiple drives. Users can access this volume as if it were a single drive, regardless of how many drives the actual volume is spread over. A volume that is on a single drive is referred to as a *simple* volume. A volume that spans multiple drives is referred to as a *spanned* volume.

- With *RAID arrays*, you can protect important business data and, sometimes, improve the performance of drives. RAID is an acronym for redundant array of independent disks. Windows 2000 supports three different levels of RAID: 0, 1, and 5. You implement RAID arrays as mirrored, striped, and striped with parity volumes.

In Windows 2000, volumes are designed to be used with dynamic disks. If you created volumes under Microsoft Windows NT 4.0, you'll need to upgrade the basic drives containing the volumes to dynamic drives and then manage the volumes as you would any other Windows 2000 volume. If you don't do this, your management options for the volumes are limited.

Volume sets and RAID arrays are created on dynamic drives and are only accessible to Windows 2000 and later. Because of this, if you dual boot a computer to a previous version of Windows, the dynamic drives are unavailable. However, computers running previous versions of Windows can access the drives over the network—just like any other network drive.

Using Volumes and Volume Sets

You create and manage volumes in much the same way as partitions. A volume is a drive section that can be used to store data directly.

 Note With spanned and striped volumes on basic disks, you can delete the volume but you can't create or extend volumes. With mirrored volumes on basic disks, you can delete, repair, and resync the mirror. You can also break the mirror. With striped with parity volumes (RAID 5) on basic disks, you can delete or repair the volume but you can't create new volumes.

Volume Basics

As Figure 11-1 shows, Disk Management color codes volumes by type, much like partitions. Volumes also have a specific

- **Layout** Volume layouts include simple, spanned, mirrored, striped, and striped with parity.

- **Type** Volumes always have the type dynamic.

- **File system** As with partitions, each volume can have a different file system type, such as FAT (file allocation table), FAT 32, or NTFS (Windows NT file system).

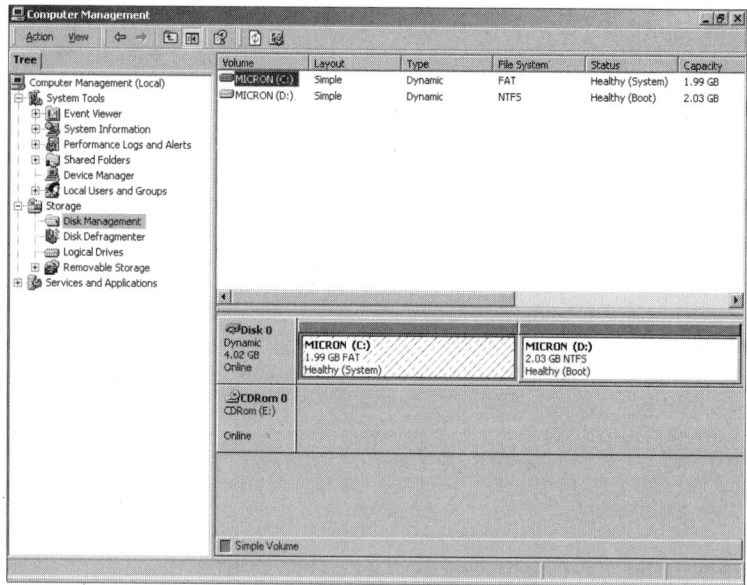

Figure 11-1. *Disk Management displays volumes much like partitions.*

- **Status** The state of the drive. For details on drive state, see the section of Chapter 10 entitled "Understanding Drive Status."
- **Capacity** The total storage size of the drive.

An important advantage of dynamic volumes over basic volumes is your ability to make changes to volumes and drives without having to restart the system (in most cases). Volumes also let you take advantage of the fault tolerance enhancements of Windows 2000. While you can't use dynamic drives with previous versions of Windows, you can install other operating systems and dual boot a Windows 2000 system. To do this, you must create a separate volume for the other operating system. For example, you could install Windows 2000 on volume C and Linux on volume D.

With volumes, you can

- Assign drive letters, as discussed in the section of Chapter 10 entitled "Assigning Drive Letters."
- Assign drive paths, as discussed in the section of Chapter 10 entitled "Assigning Drive Paths."
- Create any number of volumes on a disk as long as you have free space.
- Create volumes that span two or more disks and, if necessary, configure fault tolerance.
- Extend volumes to increase the capacity of the volume.
- Designate Active, System, and Boot volumes, as described in the section of Chapter 10 entitled "Special Considerations for Basic and Dynamic Disks."

Understanding Volume Sets

With volume sets, you can create volumes that span several drives. To do this, you use free space on different drives to create what users see as a single volume. Files are stored on the volume set segment by segment, with the first segment of free space being used first to store files. When this segment fills up, the second segment is used, and so on.

You can create a volume set using free space on up to 32 hard disk drives. The key advantage to volume sets is that they let you tap into unused free space and create a usable file system. The key disadvantage is that if any hard disk drive in the volume set fails, the volume set can no longer be used—which means that essentially all the data on the volume set is lost.

Creating Volumes and Volume Sets

You create volumes and volume sets by completing the following steps:

1. In the Disk Management Graphical view, right-click an area marked Unallocated on a dynamic disk and then choose Create Volume. This starts the Create Volume Wizard. Read the welcome dialog box, and then click Next.

2. As shown in Figure 11-2, select Simple Volume to create a volume on a single disk or Spanned Volume to create a volume set on multiple disks. Simple volumes can be formatted as FAT, FAT 32, or NTFS. To make management easier, you should format volumes that span multiple disks as NTFS. NTFS formatting allows you to expand the volume set, if necessary.

 Note If you find that you need more space on a volume, you can extend simple and spanned volumes. You do this by selecting an area of free space and adding it to the volume. You can extend a simple volume within the same disk. You can also extend a simple volume onto other disks. When you do this, you create a spanned volume, which must be formatted as NTFS.

3. You should see the Select Disks dialog box shown in Figure 11-3. Use this dialog box to select dynamic disks that are a part of the volume and to size the volume segments on those disks.
4. Available dynamic disks are shown in the All Available Dynamic Disks list box. Select a disk in this list box, and then click Add >> to add the disk to the Selected Dynamic Disks list box. If you make a mistake, you can remove disks from the Selected Dynamic Disks list box by selecting the disk and then clicking <<Remove.
5. Select a disk in the Selected Dynamic Disks list box, and then use the For Selected Disk ... MB combo box to specify the size of the volume on the selected disk. The Maximum field shows you the largest area of free space available on the selected disk. The Total Volume Size field shows you the total disk space selected for use with the volume.

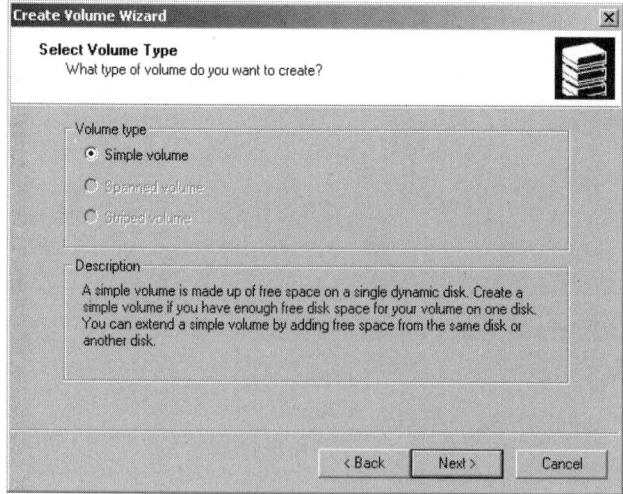

Figure 11-2. *Select a volume type, and then click Next.*

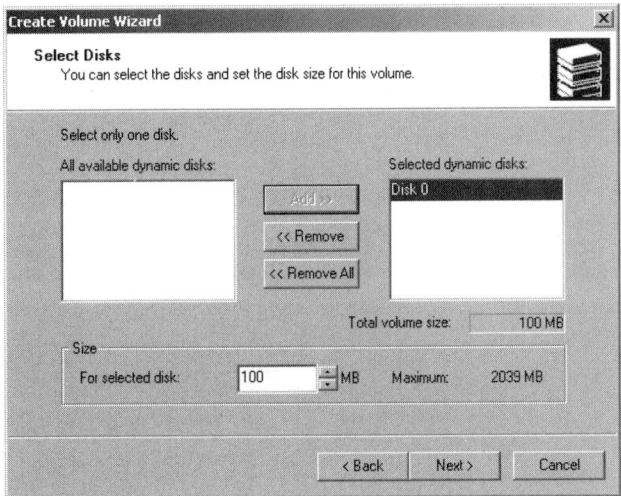

Figure 11-3. *Use the Select Disks dialog box to select disks to be a part of the volume, and then size the volume on each disk.*

Tip Although you can size the volume set any way you want, you may want to take a moment to consider how you'll use volume sets on the current workstation or server. Simple and spanned volumes aren't fault tolerant. Rather than creating one monstrous volume with all the available free space, you may want to create several smaller volumes.

6. Specify whether you want to assign a drive letter or path. These options are used as follows:

   • **Assign A Drive Letter** To assign a drive letter, choose this option and then select an available drive letter in the selection list provided.

   • **Mount This Volume To An Empty Folder That Supports Drive Paths** To assign a drive path, choose this option and then type the path to an existing folder or click Browse to search for or create a folder.

   • **Do Not Assign A Drive Letter Or Drive Path** To create the volume without assigning a drive letter or path, choose this option. You can assign a drive letter or path later, if necessary.

7. As shown in Figure 11-4, determine whether the volume should be formatted. If you elect to format the volume, follow the steps described in the section of Chapter 10 entitled "Formatting Partitions."

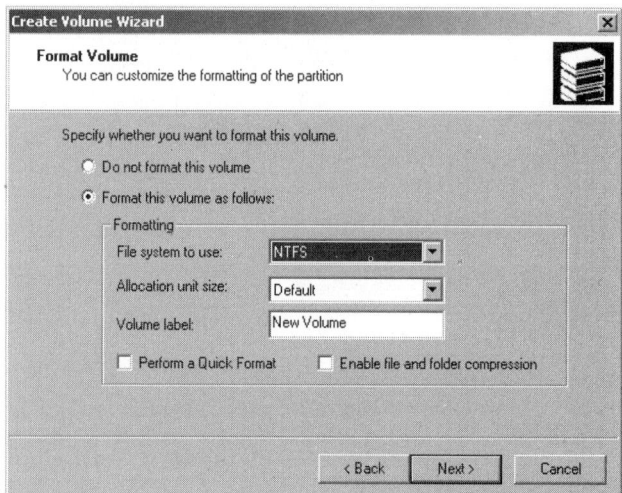

Figure 11-4. *Format a volume by specifying its file system type and volume label.*

8. Click Next, and then click Finish. If you add volumes to a physical drive that contains the Windows 2000 operating system, you may inadvertently change the number of the boot volume. Read the warning prompts and then make any necessary changes to the BOOT.INI file as described in Chapter 10 under "Updating the Boot Disk."

Deleting Volumes and Volume Sets

You use the same technique to delete all volumes, whether they're simple, spanned, mirrored, striped, or striped with parity. Deleting a volume set removes the associated file system and data. So before you delete a volume set you should back up any files and directories that the volume set contains.

To delete volumes, follow these steps:

1. In Disk Management, right-click any volume in the set and then choose Delete Volume. You can't delete a portion of a spanned volume without deleting the entire volume.

2. Confirm that you want to delete the volume by clicking Yes.

3. If you delete a volume on a physical drive that contains the Windows 2000 operating system, the number of the boot partition may change. If so, you'll

need to update the BOOT.INI file as described in the section of Chapter 10 entitled "Updating the Boot Disk."

Extending a Simple or Spanned Volume

Windows 2000 provides several ways to extend NTFS volumes that aren't part of a mirror set or a stripe set. You can extend a simple volume and you can extend existing volume sets. When you extend volumes, you add free space to them.

Note   When extending volume sets, there are many things you can't do.
You can't extend boot or system volumes. You can't extend volumes that use mirroring or striping. You can't extend a volume onto more than 32 disks, either. Additionally, you can't extend FAT or FAT 32 volumes—you must first convert them to NTFS. And you can't extend simple or spanned volumes that were upgraded from basic disks. As you work with volume sets, please keep these exceptions in mind.

To extend an NTFS volume, complete the following steps:

1. In Disk Management, right-click the simple or spanned volume that you want to extend, and then select Extend Volume. This starts the Extend Volume Wizard. Read the welcome dialog box, and then click Next.

2. You can now select dynamic disks that are a part of the volume, and size the volume segments on those disks as described in steps 5–7 of the "Creating Volumes and Volume Sets" section of this chapter.

Note   A volume set that spans multiple drives can't be mirrored or
striped. Only simple volumes can be mirrored or striped.

3. Click Next and then click Finish.

Managing Volumes

You manage volumes much like you manage partitions. You can

- Assign drive letters and paths
- Change or delete volume labels
- Convert a volume to NTFS
- Check a drive for errors and bad sectors
- Defragment disks
- Compress drives and data
- Encrypt drives and data

Follow the techniques outlined in the section of Chapter 10 entitled "Managing Existing Partitions and Drives."

Improved Performance and Fault Tolerance with RAIDs

You'll often want to give important data increased protection from drive failures. To do this, you can use RAID technology to add fault tolerance to your file systems. With RAID 1 you increase data integrity and availability by creating copies of the data. With RAID 5, you increase data integrity by creating a volume with data and parity striped intermittently across three or more physical disks. You can also use RAID to improve the performance of your disks. However, the data integrity feature is not available with RAID 0.

Different implementations of RAID technology are available. These implementations are described in terms of levels. Currently, the most widely implemented RAID levels are 0, 1, 2, 3, 4, 5, 6, 7, 10, and 53. Each RAID level offers different features. Windows 2000 supports RAID levels 0, 1, and 5.

- Use RAID 0 to improve the performance of your drives. You can also use RAID 0 to gain more space by combining leftover sections on two or more physical drives.

- Use RAID 1 and 5 to provide fault tolerance for data.

Table 11-1 provides a brief overview of the supported RAID levels. This support is completely software-based and is only available on Windows 2000 servers.

Table 11-1. Windows 2000 Server Support for RAID

RAID Level	RAID Type	Description	Major Advantages
0	Disk striping	Two or more volumes, each on a separate drive, are configured as a stripe set. Data is broken into blocks, called stripes, and then written sequentially to all drives in the stripe set.	Speed/Performance
1	Disk mirroring	Two volumes on two drives are configured identically. Data is written to both drives. If one drive fails, there's no data loss because the other drive contains the data. (Doesn't include disk striping.)	Redundancy. Better write performance than disk striping with parity.
5	Disk striping with parity	Uses three or more volumes, each on a separate drive, to create a stripe set with parity error checking. In the case of failure, data can be recovered.	Fault tolerance with less overhead than mirroring. Better read performance than disk mirroring.

The most common RAID levels in use on Windows 2000 servers are level 1 disk mirroring and level 5 disk striping with parity. Disk mirroring is the least expensive way to increase data protection with redundancy. Here you use two identically sized volumes on two different drives to create a redundant data set. If one of the drives fails, you can still obtain the data from the other drive.

On the other hand, disk striping with parity requires more disks—a minimum of three—but offers fault tolerance with less overhead than disk mirroring. If any of the drives fail, the data can automatically be recovered by combining blocks of data on the remaining disks with a parity record. Parity is a method of error checking that uses a special algorithm to create a value that could be used to recover lost data. You use this parity sector to recover data in case of hard drive failure.

Implementing RAID on Windows 2000 Servers

For server systems, Windows 2000 supports disk mirroring, disk striping, and disk striping with parity. How to implement these RAID techniques is discussed in the sections that follow.

Note Some operating systems, such as MS-DOS, don't support RAID. If you dual boot your system to one of these noncompliant operating systems, your RAID-configured drives will be unusable.

Implementing RAID 0: Disk Striping

RAID level 0 is disk striping. With disk striping, two or more volumes—each on a separate drive—are configured as a stripe set. Data written to the stripe set is broken into blocks that are called *stripes*. These stripes are written sequentially to all drives in the stripe set. You can place volumes for a stripe set on up to 32 drives, but in most circumstances sets with two to five volumes offer the best performance improvements over non-RAID volumes because data from multiple drives is simultaneously accessed. Beyond this, the performance improvement decreases significantly.

The major advantage of disk striping is speed. Data can be accessed on multiple disks using multiple drive heads, which improves performance considerably. However, this performance boost comes with a price tag. As with volume sets, if any hard disk drive in the stripe set fails, the stripe set can no longer be used, which means that essentially all data in the stripe set is lost. You'll need to recreate the stripe set and restore the data from backups. Data backup and recovery are discussed in Chapter 14.

Note The boot and system volumes can't be part of a striped set. Don't use disk striping with these volumes.

When you create stripe sets, you'll want to use volumes that are approximately the same size. Disk Management bases the overall size of the stripe set on the smallest volume size. Specifically, the maximum size of the stripe set is a multiple of the smallest volume size. For example, if you have three physical drives and if the smallest volume is 50 MB, the maximum size for the stripe set is 150 MB.

To maximize performance of the stripe set, there are several things you can do:

- Use disks that are on separate disk controllers. This allows the system to simultaneously access the drives.

- Don't use the disks containing the stripe set for other purposes. This allows each disk to dedicate its time to the stripe set.

You create a stripe set by completing the following steps:

1. In the Disk Management Graphical view, right-click an area marked Unallocated on a dynamic disk and then choose Create Volume. This starts the Create Volume Wizard. Read the welcome dialog box, and then click Next.

2. Select Striped Volume as the volume type. Create the volume as described previously in this chapter in the section entitled "Creating Volumes and Volume Sets." The key difference is that you need at least two dynamic disks to create a striped volume.

3. Once you create a striped volume, you can use the volume just like any other volume. You can't expand a stripe set once it's created. Because of this, you should carefully consider the setup before you implement it.

Implementing RAID 1: Disk Mirroring

RAID level 1 is disk mirroring. With disk mirroring, you use identically sized volumes on two different drives to create a redundant data set. Here, the drives are written with identical sets of information, and if one of the drives fails, you can still obtain the data from the other drive.

Disk mirroring offers about the same fault tolerance as disk striping with parity. Because mirrored disks don't need to write parity information, they can offer better write performance in most circumstances. However, disk striping with parity usually offers better read performance because read operations are spread over multiple drives.

The major drawback to disk mirroring is that it effectively cuts the amount of storage space in half. For example, to mirror a 5 GB drive, you need another 5 GB drive. That means you use 10 GB of space to store 5 GB of information.

 Note Unlike with disk striping, with disk mirroring you can mirror any volume. This means you can mirror the boot and system volumes if you want.

As with disk striping, you'll often want the mirrored disks to be on separate disk controllers. This provides increased protection against failure of the disk controller. If one of the disk controllers fails, the disk on other controller is still available. Technically, when you use two separate disk controllers to duplicate data, you're using a technique known as *disk duplexing*. Figure 11-5 shows the difference between the two techniques. Disk mirroring typically uses a single drive controller, but disk duplexing uses two drive controllers.

If one of the mirrored drives in a set fails, disk operations can continue. Here, when users read and write data, the data is written to the remaining disk. You'll need to break the mirror before you can fix the mirror. To learn how, see the section of this chapter entitled "Managing RAIDs and Recovering from Failures."

Creating a Mirror Set in Disk Management
You create a mirror set by completing the following steps:

1. In the Disk Management Graphical view, right-click an area marked Unallocated on a dynamic disk, and then choose Create Volume. This starts the Create Volume Wizard. Read the welcome dialog box, and then click Next.

2. Select Mirrored Volume as the volume type. Create the volume as described previously in the section of this chapter entitled "Creating Volumes and Volume Sets." The key difference is that you must create two identically sized volumes and these volumes must be on separate dynamic drives.

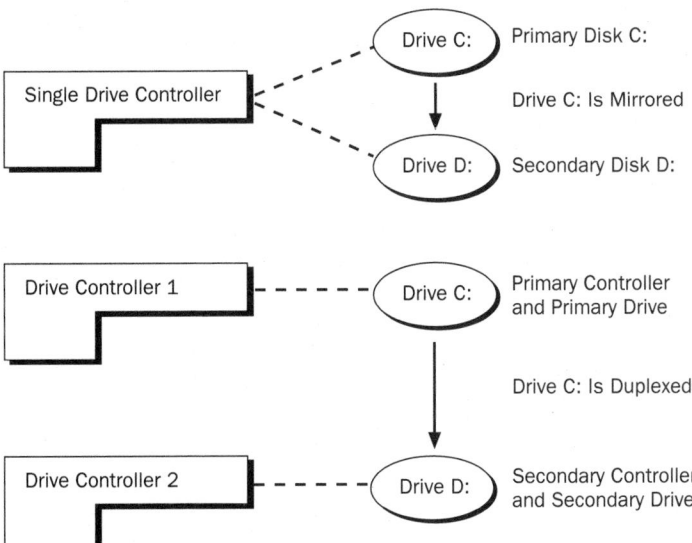

Figure 11-5. *While disk mirroring typically uses a single drive controller to create a redundant data set, disk duplexing uses two drive controllers. Otherwise, the techniques are essentially the same.*

3. As with other RAID techniques, mirroring is transparent to users. Users see the mirrored set as a single drive that they can access and use like any other drive.

 Note The status of a normal mirror is Healthy. During the creation of a mirror, you may see a status of Initializing. This tells you that Disk Management is setting up the mirror.

Mirroring an Existing Volume

Rather than creating a new mirrored volume, you can use an existing volume to create a mirrored set. To do this, the volume you want to mirror must be a simple volume, and you must have an area of unallocated space on a second dynamic drive of equal or larger space than the existing volume.

In Disk Management, you mirror an existing volume by completing the following steps:

1. Right-click the simple volume you want to mirror, and then select Add Mirror. This starts the Add Mirror Wizard.

2. Use the wizard dialog boxes to select and configure the second volume in the mirrored set. The steps you follow are similar to those outlined in the "Creating Volumes and Volume Sets" section of this chapter.

Implementing RAID 5: Disk Striping with Parity

RAID level 5 is disk striping with parity. With this technique, you need a minimum of three hard disk drives to set up fault tolerance. The volumes on these drives are sized identically by Disk Management. Although you can place volumes for a stripe set on up to 32 drives, in most circumstances sets with two to five volumes offer the best performance improvements. Beyond this, the performance improvement decreases significantly.

RAID 5 is essentially an enhanced version of RAID 1—with the key addition of fault tolerance. Fault tolerance ensures that the failure of a single drive won't bring down the entire drive set. Instead, the set continues to function with disk operations directed at the remaining volumes in the set.

To allow for fault tolerance, RAID 5 writes parity checksums with the blocks of data. If any of the drives in the stripe set fails, you can use the parity information to recover the data. (This process, called regenerating the striped set, is covered in the section of this chapter entitled "Managing RAIDs and Recovering from Failures.") If two disks fail, however, the parity information isn't sufficient to recover the data, and you'll need to rebuild the striped set from backup.

 Note The boot and system volumes can't be part of a striped set. Don't use disk striping with parity on these volumes.

Creating a Stripe Set with Parity in Disk Management

In Disk Management, you can create a stripe set with parity by completing the following steps:

1. In the Disk Management Graphical view, right-click an area marked Unallocated on a dynamic disk and then choose Create Volume. This starts the Create Volume Wizard. Read the welcome dialog box, and then click Next.

2. Select RAID-5 Volume as the volume type. Create the volume as described previously in the section of this chapter entitled "Creating Volumes and Volume Sets." The key difference is that you need to select free space on three separate dynamic drives.

3. Once you create a stripe set, users can use the set just like they would a normal drive. Keep in mind that you can't expand a stripe set once it's created by adding more disks or replacing one of the disks with a larger drive. Because of this, you should carefully consider the setup before you implement it.

Managing RAIDs and Recovering from Failures

Managing mirrored drives and stripe sets is somewhat different from managing other drive volumes, especially when it comes to recovering from failure. The techniques you'll need to manage RAID arrays and to recover from failure are covered in this section.

Breaking a Mirrored Set

You may want to break a mirror for two reasons:

- If one of the mirrored drives in a set fails, disk operations can continue. Here, when users read and write data, these operations use the remaining disk. Still, at some point you'll need to fix the mirror, and to do this you must first break the mirror and then reestablish it.

- If you no longer want to mirror your drives, you may also want to break a mirror. This allows you to use the disk space for other purposes.

Note   Although breaking a mirror doesn't delete the data in the set, you should always back up the data before you perform this procedure. This ensures that if you have problems, you can recover your data.

In Disk Management, you can break a mirrored set by following these steps:

1. Right-click one of the volumes in the mirrored set, and then choose Break Mirror.

2. Confirm that you want to break the mirror by clicking Yes. This creates two independent volumes.

Resynchronizing and Repairing a Mirrored Set

Windows 2000 automatically synchronizes mirrored volumes on dynamic drives. However, data on mirrored drives can get out of sync. For example, if one of the drives goes offline, data is only written to the drive that's online.

You can resynchronize and repair mirrored sets on basic and dynamic disks, but you must rebuild the set using the same disk type. To resynchronize a failed mirror set, complete the following steps:

1. You need to get both drives in the mirrored set online. The status of the mirrored set should read Failed Redundancy. The corrective action you take depends on the status of the failed volume.

2. If the status is Missing or Offline, make sure that the drive has power and is connected properly. Afterward, start Disk Management, right-click the failed volume and select Reactivate Disk. The drive's status should change to Re-generating and then to Healthy. If the volume doesn't return to the Healthy status, right-click the volume and then click Resynchronize Mirror.

3. If the status is Online (Errors), right-click the failed volume and select Reactivate Disk. The drive's status should change to Regenerating and then to Healthy. If the volume doesn't return to the Healthy status, right-click the volume and then click Resynchronize Mirror.

4. If one of the drives shows as Unreadable, you may need to rescan the drives on the system by selecting Rescan Disks from Disk Management's Action menu. If the drive status doesn't change, you may need to reboot the computer.

5. If one of the drives still won't come back online, right-click the failed volume and then select Remove Mirror. Next, right-click the remaining volume in the original mirror and then select Add Mirror. You'll now need to mirror the volume on an unallocated area of free space. If you don't have free space, you'll need to create space by deleting other volumes or replacing the failed drive.

Repairing a Mirrored System Volume to Enable Boot

The failure of a mirrored drive may prevent your system from booting. Typically, this happens when you're mirroring the system or boot volume, or both, and the primary mirror drive has failed. To correct this problem, you need to replace the failed drive and then use an emergency boot disk for the system or a similarly configured system to enable system boot. This should not be confused with the emergency repair disk, which is mainly used to fix registry corruption. Creating an emergency boot disk is covered in Chapter 14.

Editing BOOT.INI for the Mirror

Once you have an emergency boot disk, you need to edit the BOOT.INI file it contains so that the operating system loads from the secondary mirror. This file contains entries that look like this:

```
[boot loader] timeout=30
default=multi(0)disk(0)rdisk(0)volume(2)\WIN2000 [operating
```

```
systems]  multi(0)disk(0)rdisk(0)volume(2)\WIN2000="Windows
2000Server"
```

If the secondary mirror drive was on drive 2, you could update the BOOT.INI file shown earlier as follows:

```
[boot  loader]  timeout=30
default=multi(0)disk(0)rdisk(1)volume(2)\WIN2000 [operating
systems]  multi(0)disk(0)rdisk(1)volume(2)\WIN2000=""Windows
2000Server"
```

Note   For a more detailed explanation of BOOT.INI, see the section of Chapter 10 entitled "Updating the Boot Disk."

Booting and Rebooting the System

Once you update the BOOT.INI file, you can use the emergency boot disk to boot your system. When the system boots, you'll need to complete the following steps:

1. Break the mirror set and then re-create the mirror on the drive you replaced, which is usually drive 0. Right-click the remaining volume that was part of the original mirror and then select Add Mirror. Next, follow the technique described in the "Mirroring an Existing Volume" section of this chapter.

2. When the mirror is completely rebuilt, use Disk Management to break the mirror again. Make sure that the primary drive in the original mirror set has the drive letter that was previously assigned to the complete mirror. If it doesn't, assign the appropriate drive letter.

3. Right-click the original system volume, and then select Add Mirror. Now re-create the mirror.

4. Update BOOT.INI so that the original system volume is used during startup.

Removing a Mirrored Set

In Disk Management, you can remove one of the volumes from a mirrored set. When you do this, all data on the removed mirror is deleted and the space it used is marked as Unallocated.

To remove a mirror, complete the following steps:

1. In Disk Management, right-click one of the volumes in the mirrored set and then choose Remove Mirror.

2. Confirm the action when prompted. All data on the removed mirror is deleted.

Repairing a Stripe Set Without Parity

A stripe set without parity doesn't have fault tolerance. If a drive that is part of a stripe set fails, the entire stripe set is unusable. Before you try to restore the stripe set, you should repair or replace the failed drive. Afterward, you need to re-create the stripe set and then recover the data contained on the stripe set from backup.

Regenerating a Stripe Set with Parity

With RAID 5 you can recover the stripe set if a single drive fails. You'll know that a stripe set with parity drive has failed because the status of the set changes to Failed Redundancy and the status of the individual volume changes to Missing, Offline, or Online (Errors).

You can repair RAID 5 on basic and dynamic disks, but you must rebuild the set using the same disk type. To resolve problems with the RAID 5 set, complete the following steps:

1. You need to get all drives in the RAID 5 set online. The status of the set should read Failed Redundancy. The corrective action you take depends on the status of the failed volume.

 Note If possible, you should back up the data before you perform this procedure. This ensures that if you have problems, you can recover your data.

2. If the status is Missing or Offline, make sure that the drive has power and is connected properly. Afterward, start Disk Management, right-click the failed volume, and select Reactivate Disk. The drive's status should change to Regenerating and then to Healthy. If the status of the drive doesn't return to Healthy, right-click the volume and select Regenerate Parity.

3. If the status is Online (Errors), right-click the failed volume and select Reactivate Disk. The drive's status should change to Regenerating and then to Healthy. If the status of the drive doesn't return to Healthy, right-click the volume and select Regenerate Parity.

4. If one of the drives shows as Unreadable, you may need to rescan the drives on the system by selecting Rescan Disks from Disk Management's Action menu. If the drive status doesn't change, you may need to reboot the computer.

5. If one of the drives still won't come back online, you need to repair the failed region of the RAID 5 set. Right-click the failed volume and then select Remove Volume. You now need to select an unallocated space on a separate dynamic disk for the RAID 5 set. This space must be at least as large as the region to repair, and it can't be on a drive that's already being used by the RAID 5 set. If you don't have enough space, the Repair Volume command is unavailable, and you'll need to free space by deleting other volumes or replacing the failed drive.

Chapter 12

Managing
Files and Directories

Microsoft Windows 2000 provides a robust environment for working with files and directories. At the core of this environment are the two basic types of file system:

- FAT (file allocation table), available in 16-bit and 32-bit versions
- NTFS (Windows NT file system), available in 4.0 and 5.0 versions

When you work with files and directories on a Windows 2000 system, you'll usually work with one of these file system types. To help you better administer FAT and NTFS volumes, this chapter explains how to perform common file and directory tasks. It also offers ways of troubleshooting problems.

Windows 2000 File Structures

This section covers the essential information you'll need to work with files. An understanding of file basics can make your job as an administrator a lot easier.

Major Features of FAT and NTFS

What you can or can't do with files and directories in Windows 2000 depends on the file system type. Windows 2000 servers and workstations provide direct support for FAT and NTFS.

FAT Volumes

FAT volumes rely on an allocation table to keep track of the status of files and directories. Although FAT is adequate for most file and directory needs, it's rather limited. Two versions of FAT are supported on Windows 2000:

- **FAT 16**   The version of FAT widely used on Microsoft Windows NT 4.0. FAT 16 supports a 16-bit file allocation table and is usually referred to simply as FAT. You'll get optimal performance with volumes that are less than 2 GB.

- **FAT 32**   The version of FAT introduced with Windows 95 operating system (OS) release 2 and Windows 98. FAT 32 supports a 32-bit file allocation table and is usually referred to as FAT 32. FAT 32 supports smaller cluster sizes than FAT and can allocate space more efficiently. On Windows 2000, FAT 32 supports volumes up to 32 GB.

Table 12-1 provides a brief comparison of FAT 16 and FAT 32 features.

Table 12-1. FAT and FAT 32 Features Comparison

Feature	FAT	FAT32
File allocation table size	16-bit	32-bit
Maximum volume size	4 GB; best 2 GB or less	2 TB; limited in Windows 2000 to 32 GB
Maximum file size	2 GB	4 GB
Operating systems supported	MS-DOS, all versions of Windows	Windows 95 OSR2, Windows 98, and Windows 2000
Supports small cluster size	No	Yes
Supports NTFS 4.0 features	No	No
Supports NTFS 5.0 features	No	No
Use on floppy disks	Yes	Yes
Use on removable disks	Yes	Yes

Using NTFS

NTFS offers a robust environment for working with files and directories. There are two versions of NTFS:

- **NTFS 4.0**   The version used with Windows NT 4.0. It features full support for local and remote access controls on files and directories as well as support for Windows compression. It doesn't support most Windows 2000 file system features.

- **NTFS 5.0**   The version used with Windows 2000. It features full support for new Windows 2000 features, such as Active Directory directory service, disk quotas, and encryption. It is only supported by Windows 2000 and minimally by Windows NT 4.0 with Service Pack 4 or later.

 Note   If you created NTFS volumes on Windows NT 4.0 and upgraded to Windows 2000, the volumes aren't upgraded automatically to NTFS 5.0. You must specifically choose to upgrade the volumes during installation of the operating system or when you install Active Directory on a Windows 2000 server.

Table 12-2 provides a brief comparison of NTFS 4.0 and NTFS 5.0. Windows NT 4.0 systems with Service Pack 4 or later can access NTFS 5.0 files and directories, provided they don't use any of the new NTFS features.

Table 12-2. NTFS 4.0 and NTFS 5.0 Features Comparison

Feature	NTFS 4.0	NTFS 5.0
Maximum volume size	32 GB	2 TB
Maximum file size	32 GB	Only limited by volume size
Operating systems supported	Windows NT 4.0, Windows 2000	Windows 2000 and Windows NT 4.0 minimally
Advanced file access permissions	Yes	Yes
Supports Windows compression	Yes	Yes
Supports Windows encryption	No	Yes
Supports Active Directory structures	No	Yes
Supports sparse files	No	Yes
Supports remote storage	No	Yes
Supports disk quotas	No	Yes
Use on floppy disks	No	No
Use on removable disks	Yes	Yes

File Naming

Windows 2000 file naming conventions apply to both files and directories. For simplicity, the term "file naming" is often used to refer to both files *and* directories. Although Windows 2000 file names are case-aware, they aren't case-sensitive. This means that you can save a file named MyBook.doc and the file name will be displayed in the correct case. However, you can't save a file called mybook.doc to the same directory.

Both NTFS and FAT support long file names—up to 255 characters. You can name files using just about any of the available characters, including spaces. However, there are some characters you can't use. They are

? * / \ :   < > |

Tip Using spaces in file names can cause access problems. Anytime you reference the file name, you may need to enclose the file name within quotation marks. Also, if you plan to publish the file on the Web, you may need to remove the spaces from the file name or convert them to the underscore character (_) to ensure that Web browsers have easy access to the file.

The following file names are all acceptable:

- My Favorite Short Story.doc
- My_Favorite_Short_Story.doc

- My..Favorite..Short..Story.doc
- My Favorite Short Story!!!.doc

Accessing Long File Names Under MS-DOS

Under MS-DOS and 16-bit FAT file systems, file and directory names are restricted to eight characters with a three-character file extension, such as CHAPTER4.TXT. This naming convention is often referred to as the 8.3 file-naming rule or the standard MS-DOS file-naming rule. Because of this rule, when you work with files at the Command prompt you may have problems accessing files and directories.

To support access to long file names, abbreviated file names are created for all files and directories on a system. These file names conform to the standard MS-DOS file-naming rule. You can see the abbreviated file names using the command

```
dir /X
```

A typical abbreviated file name looks like this:

```
PROGRA~1.DOC
```

How Windows 2000 Creates an Abbreviated File Name

When Windows 2000 creates an abbreviated file name from a long file name, it uses the following rules:

- Any spaces in the file name are removed. The file name My Favorite Short Story.doc becomes MyFavoriteShortStory.doc.

- All periods in the file name are removed (with the exception of the period separating the file name from the file extension). The file name My..Favorite..Short..Story.doc becomes MyFavoriteShortStory.doc.

- Invalid characters under the standard MS-DOS naming rule are replaced with the underscore character (_). The file name My[Favorite]ShortStory.doc becomes My_Favorite_ShortStory.doc.

- All remaining characters are converted to uppercase. The file name, My Favorite Short Story.doc, becomes MYFAVORITESHORTSTORY.DOC.

Afterward, the rules of truncation are applied to create the standard MS-DOS file name.

The Rules of Truncation

To make the file conform to the 8.3 naming convention, the file name and file extension are truncated, if necessary. The rules for truncation are as follows:

- The file extension is truncated to the first three characters. The file name Mary.text becomes MARY.TEX.

- The file name is truncated to the first six characters (this is the file's root name) and a unique designator is appended. The unique designator follows the convention ~n, where *n* is the number of the file with the six-character file name. Following this, the file name My Favorite Short Story.doc becomes MYFAVO~1.DOC. The second file in this directory that is truncated to MYFAVO becomes MYFAVO~2.DOC.

Note The file name truncation rule described here is the one you'll usually see, and you won't often have to worry about anything else. However, if you have a lot of files with similar names, you may see another convention used to create the short file name.

Specifically, if more than four files use the same six-character root, additional file names are created by combining the first two characters of the file name with a four-character hash code and then appending a unique designator. A directory could have files named MYFAVO~1.DOC, MYFAVO~2.DOC, MYFAVO~3.DOC, and MYFAVO~4.DOC. Additional files with this root could be named MY3140~1.DOC, MY40C7~1.DOC, and MYEACC~1.DOC.

Exploring Files and Directories

Windows Explorer is the tool of choice for working with files and directories. You can also use My Computer and My Network Places to perform many file manipulation tasks. Access My Computer and My Network Places by double-clicking their icons on the Windows 2000 desktop.

Note For brevity, this section focuses primarily on using Windows Explorer. However, you can apply similar techniques to My Computer and My Network Places.

Using Windows Explorer

To run Windows Explorer, go to Start, choose Programs, choose Accessories, and then select Windows Explorer. You can now use Windows Explorer to browse local and remote resources.

Windows Explorer Views and Toolbars

Windows Explorer can use multiple viewing panes. These panes include

- **Explorer Bar** Shows different views depending on the current action. The available views are Folders, Search, History, and Favorites. Folders is the default view.
- **Contents** Shows the contents of a selected folder or the results of a search.
- **Tip Of The Day** Displays helpful pointers for working with Windows 2000.

As Figure 12-1 shows, individual folders can have custom views as well. By default, Windows Explorer displays only the Explorer Bar and the Contents view. To modify the view panes, you can

- **Display other views on the Explorer Bar**   Select View, choose Explorer Bar, and then select the view you want to use.

- **Display the Tip Of The Day**   Select View, choose Explorer Bar, and then select Tip Of The Day.

- **Remove the Explorer Bar or Tip Of The Day**   Click Close (the X in the upper left or upper right corner of the pane).

To change the settings for the Contents view, you use the View menu as well. Selected items are enabled. Cleared items are disabled. The main options you want to use are

- **Toolbar**   Allows you to add and remove toolbars.

- **Status Bar**   Adds a status bar that displays information about objects that are selected.

- **List**   Displays a list of files and folders instead of the detailed listings or file icons.

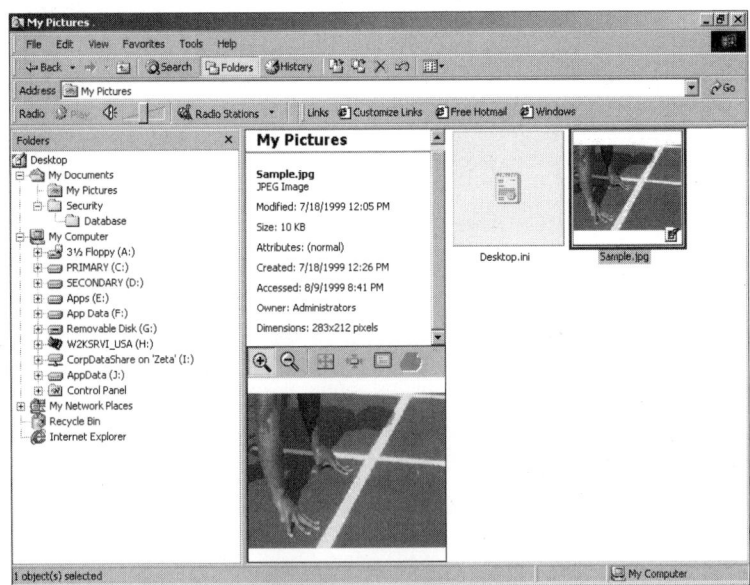

Figure 12-1. *My Pictures has a custom view. You can customize Windows Explorer folders to use a similar view or other views to suit your needs. Your settings are saved when you exit Windows.*

- **Details** Displays detailed listings for files and folders. The detailed view adds file size, file type, and modification date to the Contents panel.

- **Small Icons** Displays small icons for files and folders.

- **Large Icons** Displays large icons for files and folders.

- **Arrange Icons** Allows you to arrange files and folders by name, type, size, and date. In detailed view, clicking on the column headers has the same effect.

- **Thumbnails** Allows you to view a miniature version of an image that you can use for quick browsing.

Understanding Windows Explorer Icons

Each icon displayed in Windows Explorer has a purpose. Key icons displayed in the Folders pane are used as follows:

- **Desktop** A top-level folder that stores files, folders, and shortcuts on the Windows desktop. This folder is at the same level in the hierarchy as My Network Places and My Computer.

- **My Computer** A top-level folder containing all local resources and folders available to the computer.

- **My Network Places** The top-level folder for the network. Click this to browse network resources.

- **Recycle Bin** A folder that stores files and directories that have been deleted. If the system is configured to use the Recycle Bin, you can recover files from this folder before they're permanently removed.

- **My Documents** A folder used to store personal files. In My Documents you'll find the My Pictures folder, which has special features for previewing images.

- **Drives** Storage devices that are identified with unique icons and drive letters. Windows 2000 shows hard disk drives, floppy disk drives, removable disk drives, and CD-ROMs.

- **Network Drives** A remote network resource that's connected to the system.

- **Open Folders** Folders that have been accessed by clicking them. Open folders show their contents in the Contents pane.

- **Closed Folders** Folders that have not been accessed. Closed folders don't display their contents.

Tip To expand a folder without displaying its contents in the Contents pane, click the plus (+) symbol next to the folder. This technique allows you to browse folders on remote systems faster than usual.

You can also use this technique when you're copying files. Here, you display the contents of the folder you want to copy in the Contents pane, and then browse for the destination folder in the Folders pane. When you find it, you copy the source files to the folder.

Displaying Hidden and Compressed Files in Windows Explorer

As an administrator, you'll often want to see system files, such as DLLs (dynamic-link library files), and files that have or haven't been compressed. By default, however, Windows Explorer doesn't display hidden file types or differentiate between compressed and uncompressed files. To override the initial settings, from the Tools menu select Folder Options, and then click the View tab. You can now configure new settings using the dialog box shown in Figure 12-2.

- To display hidden files, click Show Hidden Files And Folders.

- To always display file extensions, clear the Hide File Extensions For Known File Types check box.

- To display operating system files, clear the Hide Protected Operating System Files check box.

- To highlight compressed files and folders, select the Display Compressed Files And Folders With Alternate Color check box.

Customizing Folder Views

When Web content is enabled, Windows Explorer supports customizable views for all folders on a Windows 2000 system. You can change the look and feel of the view on individual folders or on all folders on a system.

Working with Folder Templates

Windows Explorer uses template files to determine what each folder looks like in the Contents pane. It creates these templates as HTML documents and you can edit them just like any Web document. The technologies used to create the templates are HTML (Hypertext Markup Language), CSS (cascading style sheets), and scripts. Scripts are used to customize the folders and make them more interactive. Normally, scripts are written in JavaScript but can also be written in VBScript. The predefined templates are

- **Standard**   A full-featured template that shows document previews and summaries.

- **Classic (Icons Only)**   A quick and efficient no-frills view.

- **Simple**   A basic view that has some Web-enabled features but doesn't use scripts.

- **Image Preview**   A view with special features for previewing images.

Folder view settings you use are seen by all users who access the system, either locally or remotely. The default view for most folders is Standard. You can change the view by customizing the folder, provided you have write permissions on the folder. If you like a particular view, you can apply it to all your folders on the system as well. To do this, you must have ownership of the folder.

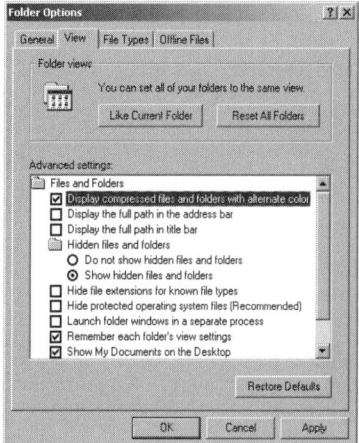

Figure 12-2. *Set options for Windows Explorer using the Folder Options dialog box.*

Note In Standard view, a preview window displays viewable documents and images. In order to do this, the operating system starts the necessary application control, reads the document or image, and then displays a preview of the document or image.

In addition to being able to change folder templates, you can also add backgrounds and comments to folders. Backgrounds are displayed behind all the icons and text in a folder. Comments are displayed in the folder's summary pane, and you can use them to explain what the folder contains. The changes you make for backgrounds and comments are added to the current folder's template as a customization.

Enabling Web Content for Folders

Folder templates are used only when Web content is enabled for folders. The enabling or disabling of this feature is based on options set in Windows Explorer, which are different for each user who logs on to a computer. To enable or disable Web content for folders, complete the following steps:

1. In Windows Explorer, from the Tools menu select Folders Options.

2. In the General tab, select Enable Web Content In Folders to enable Web content or select Use Windows Classic Folders to disable Web content.

3. Click OK.

Configuring Custom Folder Views

To configure custom views for folders, follow these steps:

1. In Windows Explorer, select the folder you want to customize. If you want to customize all the folders on a system, select any folder, and then when you complete this operation, follow the instructions in the section of this chapter entitled "Setting Views for Multiple Folders."

2. Choose the Customize This Folder option of the View menu. This starts the Customize This Folder Wizard. Read the welcome dialog box, and then click Next.

3. Select the type of customization you want to make, shown in Figure 12-3:

   • **Choose Or Edit An HTML Template For This Folder**   Select this option to select or create a new template for the folder.

   • **Modify Background Picture And Filename Appearance**   Select this option to add background colors and images to a folder.

   • **Add Folder Comment**   Select this option to type a descriptive comment for the folder.

4. If you choose to work with templates, use the Change Folder Template dialog box to select a new template. The available options are: Standard, Classic (Icons Only), Simple, and Image Preview. If you want to edit the template file, select I Want To Edit This Template.

 Caution   Template files are written using advanced scripting technologies. If you have experience working with these technologies, you'll find it easy to modify the template files. You'll find it easy to modify the template files—but be very careful. Incorrect edits may make the template unusable, and you'll need to repeat this procedure to assign a new template to the folder.

5. If you chose to work with backgrounds, use the Modify Background And Filename Appearance dialog box to select background and text settings. You can choose a predefined background picture by using the list box provided or by clicking Browse to find an image to use. After you select an image, you can change the foreground and background colors used with file names by clicking Text and Background (see Figure 12-4).

6. If you chose to add a comment, use the Add Folder Comment dialog box to type a comment for the folder. If you plan on applying the template to all folders on the system, you may want to leave this blank for now.

7. Click Next, and then click Finish. The folder view is then applied to the current folder.

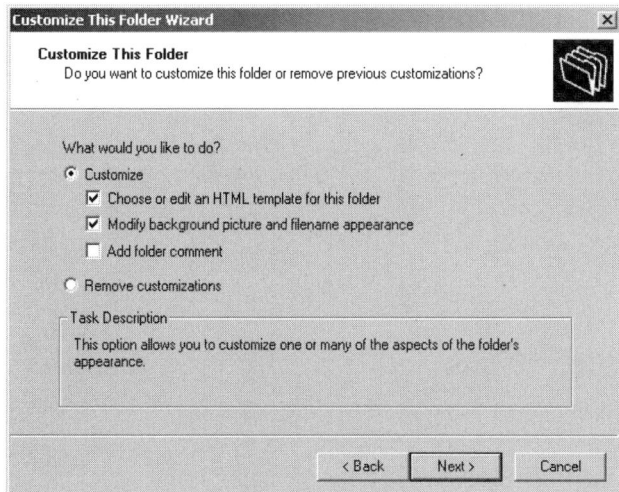

Figure 12-3.   *Use the Customize This Folder Wizard to choose a folder template to use. Folder templates are created with HTML, CSS, and scripts.*

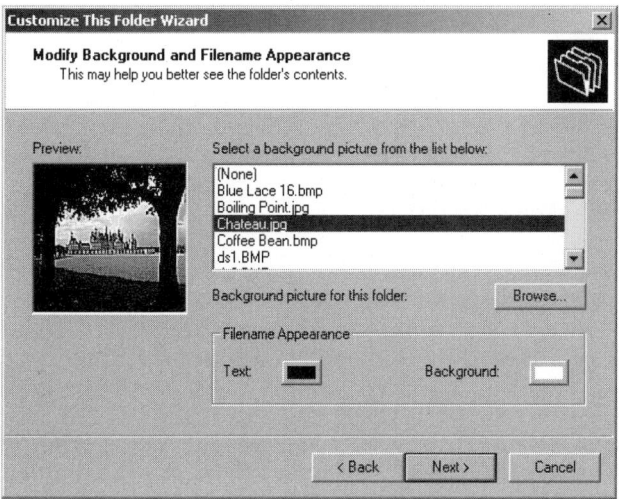

Figure 12-4.   *Select a background picture and modify the file name appearance.*

Setting Views for Multiple Folders

Using the Folder Options dialog box, you can apply a custom view to all your folders on a system or restore the default view to all your folders on a system. To do that, complete the following steps:

1. In Windows Explorer, select the folder you want to work with. You can apply the view settings for this folder to all your folders on a system.

2. From the Tools menu choose Folder Options, and then select the View tab.

3. To apply the current folder view to all your folders on a system, click Like Current Folder.

4. To restore all your folders to their default view, click Reset All Folders.

Formatting Floppy Disks and Other Removable Disks

Windows Explorer makes it easy to work with floppy and other removable disks. You can format disks by following these steps:

1. Insert the floppy or other removable disk you want to format.

2. Right-click the floppy or other removable disk icon in Windows Explorer's Folders pane.

3. From the pop-up menu select Format, and then use the Format dialog box to set the formatting options. For floppy disks, the only available file system type is FAT. For other removable disks, such as Zip, you can use FAT, FAT 32, or NTFS.

 Note   If you format removable disks as NTFS volumes, they are format-ted as NTFS 5.0 volumes. Unlike Windows NT 4.0, Windows 2000 allows you to eject volumes formatted as NTFS at any time. Click Eject on the removable disk drive or right-click the drive icon in Windows Explorer, and then select Eject.

4. Click Start to begin formatting the floppy or other removable disk.

Copying Floppy Disks

To copy a floppy disk, follow these steps:

1. Right-click the floppy disk icon in Windows Explorer's Folders pane, and then from the pop-up menu choose Copy Disk.

2. Use the Copy Disk dialog box to select the source and destination drives. In the Copy From area, select the drive you want to use as the source. In the Copy To area, select the drive you want to use as the destination. If you have only one floppy disk drive, the source and destination drive will be the same (as shown in Figure 12-5).

3. Click Start when you're ready to begin copying, and then insert the source and destination disks when prompted. The progress bar in the lower area of the Copy Disk dialog box shows the progress of the copy operation.

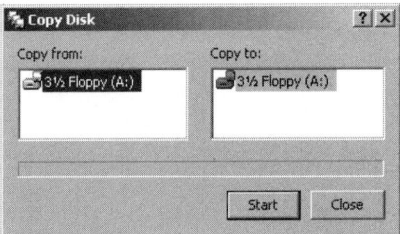

Figure 12-5. *Use the Copy Disk dialog box to select the source and destination drives.*

Managing Files

Windows 2000 provides many ways to manage files. The most common file operations are *copy* and *move*. You can copy or move files *within* windows— such as within Windows Explorer—and *between* windows—such as copying a file from Windows Explorer to the My Network Places window. You can also copy or move files to and from the desktop.

Selecting Files and Directories

In Windows Explorer you can select individual and multiple files in a variety of ways. You select individual files by clicking them with the mouse. You select multiple files by

- Holding down the CTRL key and then clicking the left mouse button on each file or folder you want to select.
- Holding down the SHIFT key, selecting the first file or folder, and then clicking the last file or folder.

Copying Files and Folders by Dragging

To copy or move items to any open window or visible area on the desktop, complete the following steps:

1. Select the item(s) you want to copy or move.

2. Hold down the mouse button and drag the item(s) to the new location.

3. If you drag the file or folder to a new location on a different drive, it's copied automatically. To move the file instead, hold down the SHIFT key as you drag the file or folder.

4. If you drag the file or folder to a new location on the same drive, Windows 2000 will try to move the item instead. To prevent this, hold down the CTRL key as you drag the file or folder.

Note To copy a file, the source and destination location must be visible. This means you may need to open multiple versions of Windows Explorer or multiple windows and expand the folders within these windows, as necessary.

Copying Files and Folders to Locations That Aren't Displayed

You may also need to copy items to locations that aren't currently displayed. To do this, follow these steps:

1. Select the item(s) you want to copy.

2. Hold down the mouse button and drag the item(s) into the Folders pane.

3. Slowly drag the items up to the last visible folder at the top of the pane (or down to the last visible folder at the bottom of the pane). You should be able to scroll up or down slowly through the existing tree structure.

4. When you find the destination folder, release the mouse button. If it's on a different drive, the item is copied. Otherwise, it's moved.

Copying and Pasting Files

I prefer to move files around by copying and pasting. When you copy and paste files, you don't have to worry about whether the file will be copied or moved. You simply copy files to the clipboard and paste them anywhere you like. You can even paste copies of files in the same folder—something you can't do by dragging.

To copy and paste files, follow these steps:

1. Select the item(s) you want to copy.

2. Right-click and from the pop-up menu select Copy. You could also select Copy from the Edit menu or press CTRL+C.

3. Access the destination location, then right-click, and from the pop-up menu select Paste. You could also select Paste from the Edit menu or press CTRL+V.

 Note Windows 2000 may not let you copy files and folders to special windows. For example, you generally can't copy a file and then paste it into the My Computer window. Similarly, you may not be able to copy items in special folders and paste them into other windows.

Moving Files by Cutting and Pasting

To move files by cutting and pasting, follow these steps:

1. Select the item(s) you want to move.

2. Right-click and from the pop-up menu select Cut. You could also select Cut from the Edit menu or press CTRL+X.

3. Access the destination location, then right-click, and from the pop-up menu select Paste. You could also select Paste from the Edit menu or press CTRL+V.
4. When prompted to move the selected items, click OK.

Note   When you use the CUT and PASTE commands, Windows 2000 doesn't delete the item(s) from the original location immediately. The CUT command simply places a copy of the item(s) on the clipboard. After you use the PASTE command to paste the file to the new location, the file is deleted from the old location.

Renaming Files and Directories

To rename a file or directory, follow these steps:

1. Right-click the file or directory name, and then from the pop-up menu select Rename. Or select the file or directory name, and then from the File menu select Rename.
2. The resource name is now editable. Type the new name for the resource.
3. Press ENTER or click the resource's icon.

Deleting Files and Directories

To delete files and directories, follow these steps:

1. Select the items to be deleted.
2. Press the DELETE key or choose Delete from the File menu. Alternatively, you could choose Delete from the pop-up menu.

Note   By default, Windows Explorer puts deleted items in the Recycle Bin. To delete the files permanently, you need to empty the Recycle Bin. To delete a file immediately and bypass the Recycle Bin, press down the SHIFT key, and then press the DELETE key or choose Delete from the File menu.

Creating Folders

In Windows Explorer you can create a folder by following these steps:

1. In the Folders pane, select the directory that will contain the new folder.
2. In the Contents pane, right-click, and then from the New menu select Folder. A new folder is added to the Contents pane. The folder name is initialized to New Folder and selected for editing.
3. Edit the name of the folder and press ENTER.

Examining Drive Properties

Windows Explorer, My Computer, and My Network Places all let you examine the properties of your drives. This includes logical drives, floppy disk drives, removable disk drives, network drives, and CD-ROM drives.

To examine drive properties you can do either of two things:

- Right-click the drive's icon. From the pop-up menu select Properties.
- Select the drive by clicking on it. From the File menu select Properties.

Figure 12-6 shows the Properties dialog box for a logical drive. Some of the tabs shown are only available for NTFS. For example, on NTFS you can use the Security tab to set access permissions, auditing, and ownership.

The exact number of tabs available depends on the type of drive. Table 12-3 provides a quick overview of how the tabs are used and when they're available.

Table 12-3. Availability and Description of Drive Property Tabs

Tab	Availability	Description
General	All drive types	Provides an overview of drive configuration and drive space.
Tools	Hard disk drives, floppy disk drives, and removable disk drives	Provides access to drive tools for error checking, defragmentation, and backup.
Hardware	Hard disk drives, floppy disk drives, and removable disk drives	Provides access to device properties and troubleshooting features.
Sharing	All local drives	Allows you to share the drive with remote users.
Security	NTFS drives	Sets access permissions, auditing, and ownership.
Remote Storage	NTFS drives	Manages remote storage.
Quota	NTFS drives	Configures disk usage for users on a per disk basis.
Web Sharing	All local drives	Allows you to share the drive with a local Web server. (Available when the system has Internet Information Server or Personal Web Server installed.)

Examining File and Folder Properties

Windows Explorer, My Computer, and My Network Places all let you examine the properties of files and folders. There are two ways you can do this:

- Right-click the file or folders icon. From the pop-up menu select Properties.
- Select the file or folder by clicking on it. From the File menu select Properties.

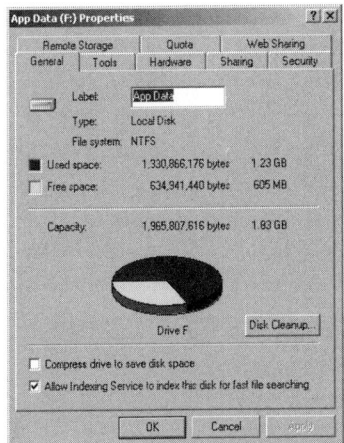

Figure 12-6. *The Properties dialog box provides a quick overview of the drive. The number of tabs available depends on the type of drive.*

Figure 12-7 shows the Properties dialog box for a folder on NTFS. The General tab provides an overview of the folder and allows you to set its attributes. Folder and file attributes include

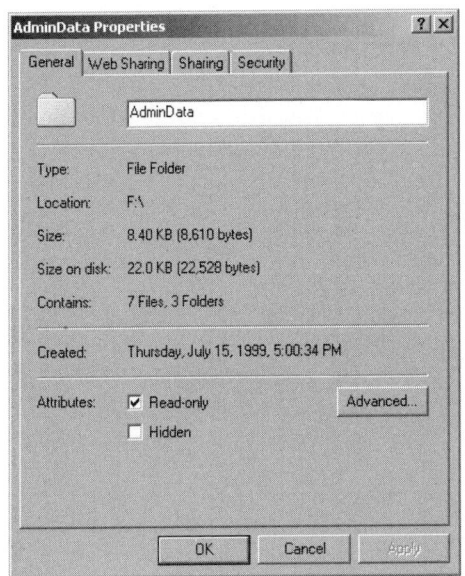

Figure 12-7. *The file and folder Properties dialog boxes are similar. The availability of tabs depends on the file system type and the file type.*

- **Read-Only** Shows whether the file or folder is read-only. You can't modify or accidentally delete read-only files and folders.

- **Hidden** Determines whether the file is displayed in file listings. You can override this by telling Windows Explorer to display hidden files.

- **Advanced** Allows you to set compression, encryption, and archiving for the file.

With file and folder properties, the availability of tabs depends on the type of file or folder. Table 12-4 provides a quick overview of how the common tabs are used and when they're available.

Table 12-4. Availability and Description of Common File and Folder Tabs

Tab	Availability	Description
General	All files and folders	Provides an overview of the item and lets you set its attributes.
Web Sharing	All local folders	Allows you to share the folder with a local Web server. (Available when the system has Internet Information Services installed.)
Sharing	All local folders	Allows you to share the folder with remote users.
Security	NTFS files and folders	Sets access permissions, auditing, and ownership.
Summary	Win32 DLL and executable files	Provides editable summary, authoring, and revision information.
Version	Win32 DLL and executable files	Allows you to check the file version, description, copyright, and other key information.

 Note When you register a new file type, the file type can create entries that add and remove property tabs. For example, with most image files, you'll see additional tabs. These tabs can include Keywords, Description, Caption, Origin, and Credits. Adobe Photoshop adds another tab called Photoshop Image, which can provide a thumbnail for the image that allows you to view it without having to open it.

Chapter 13

Data Sharing, Security, and Auditing

Data sharing allows remote users to access network resources, such as files, folders, and drives. When you share a folder or a drive, you make all of its files and subfolders available to a specified set of users. If you want to control access to specific files and subfolders within a shared folder, you can only do it with Windows NT file system (NTFS) volumes. On NTFS volumes you use access control lists to grant or deny access to files and folders.

Object security applies to all resources on NTFS volumes. It includes files, folders, and Active Directory directory service objects. Normally, only administrators have the right to manage Active Directory objects, but you can delegate to users the authority to manage Active Directory objects. When you do, you make information in Active Directory available for viewing and modification by designated users. You control these users' permissions through access control lists. By auditing access to objects, you can closely monitor network activity and ensure that only authorized users are accessing resources.

Sharing Folders on Local and Remote Systems

You use shares to control access for remote users. Permissions on shared folders have no effect on users who log on locally to a server or to a workstation that has shared folders.

- To grant remote users access to files *across the network*, you use standard folder sharing.

- To grant remote users access to files *from the Web*, you use Web sharing. This is only available if the system has Internet Information Services installed.

Viewing Existing Shares

You can view the shared folders on a local or remote computer by completing the following steps:

1. In Computer Management, connect to the computer you want to work with.

2. In the console tree, expand System Tools and Shared Folders, and then select Shares. The current shares on the system are displayed, as shown in Figure 13-1.

3. The columns of the Shares node provide the following information:

- **Shared Folder** Name of the shared folder
- **Shared Path** Complete path to the folder on the local system
- **Type** What kind of computers can use the share

Note An entry of "Windows" means that all Microsoft Windows clients can use the share as well as other permitted clients, such as Macintosh users. An entry of "Macintosh" means that only Macintosh clients can use the share.

- **# Client Redirections** Number of clients currently accessing the share
- **Comment** Description of the share

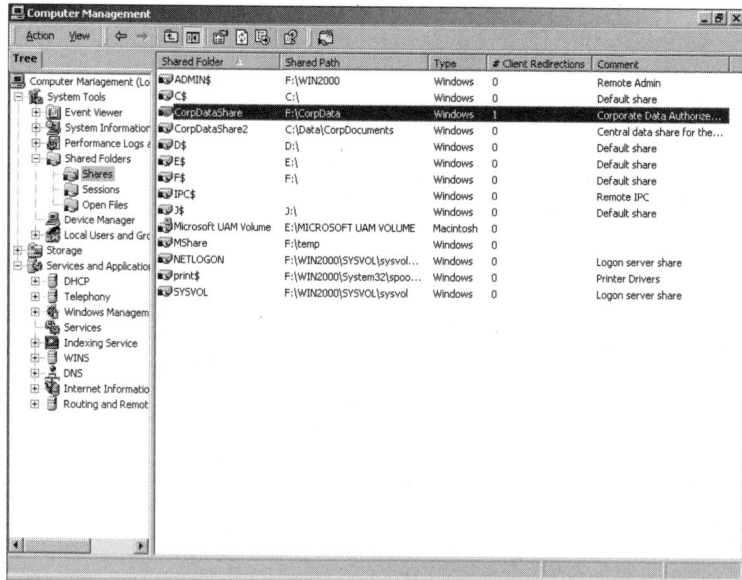

Figure 13-1. *Available shares are listed in the Shared Folders node.*

Creating Shared Folders

Microsoft Windows 2000 provides two ways to share folders: You can share local folders using Windows Explorer or you can share local and remote folders using Computer Management.

Because Computer Management allows you to work with and manage shared resources on any of your network computers, it's usually the best tool to use. To share folders on a Windows 2000 server, you must be a member of the Administrators or the Server Operators group. To share a folder on a Windows 2000 workstation, you must be a member of the Administrators or the Power Users group.

In Computer Management you share a folder by completing the following steps:

1. Right-click Computer Management in the console tree, and then select Connect To Another Computer. Then use the Select Computer dialog box to choose the computer you want to work with.

2. In the console tree, expand System Tools and Shared Folders, and then select Shares. The current shares on the system are displayed.

3. Right-click Shares, and then select New File Share. This opens the Create Shared Folder Wizard shown in Figure 13-2.

4. In the Folder To Share field, type the local file path to the folder you want to share. The file path must be exact, such as C:\Data\CorpDocuments. If you don't know the full path, click Browse, and then use the Browse For Folder dialog box to find the folder you want to share.

Tip If the file path doesn't exist, the wizard can create the necessary path for you. Click Yes when prompted to create the necessary folders.

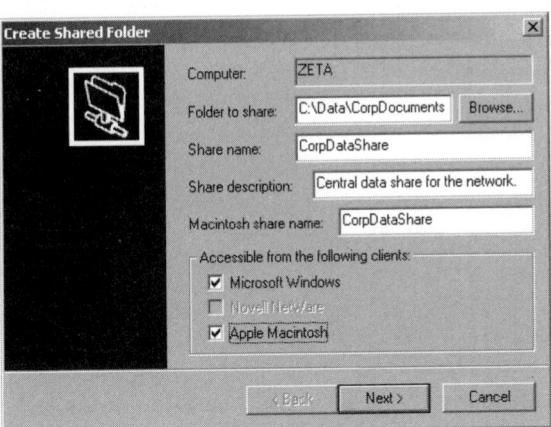

Figure 13-2. *Use the Create Shared Folder Wizard to create a new share on the selected computer. Client accessibility options are displayed only when File Services For Macintosh are installed.*

5. Type a name for the share. This is the name of the folder to which users will connect. Share names must be unique for each system.

 Note MS-DOS and Windows 3.1 computers only access shares that follow the standard 8.3 naming convention. To ensure that the share is accessible to users on these systems, you should follow the 8.3 naming convention. For example, instead of using the name PrimaryShare, you would use PRIMARY.SHR or something similar. See Chapter 12 for more information on this naming convention.

6. If you like, you can type a description of the share. Then, when you view shares on a particular computer, the description is displayed in Computer Management.

7. Optionally, specify the types of clients that will access the computer:

- Microsoft Windows
- Novell Netware
- Apple Macintosh

 Note Shares for Apple Macintosh and Novell Netware must be created on NTFS. File Server For Macintosh is the service that makes files available to Macintosh users. These services must be installed and running if you want to share resources with users on these systems. Use Configure Your Server to configure the computer as a file server. In Configure Your Server you can also use Optional Components under the Advanced entry to start the Windows Components Wizard. Then use the wizard to add the Other Network File And Print Services component.

8. If you selected Apple Macintosh as a client type, you can change the default share name for Macintosh users by typing a new name in the Macintosh Share Name field.

9. Click Next, and then set basic permissions for the share. You'll find helpful pointers in the "Managing Share Permissions" section of this chapter. As shown in Figure 13-3, the available options are

- **All Users Have Full Control** Gives users full control over the share, which means that users can perform any necessary task with the shared files and folders. Full control allows users to create, modify, and delete files and folders. On NTFS it also gives users the right to change permissions and take ownership of files and folders.

- **Administrators Have Full Control; Other Users Have Read-Only Access** Gives administrators complete control over the share. Other users can only view files and read data. They can't create, modify, or delete files and folders.

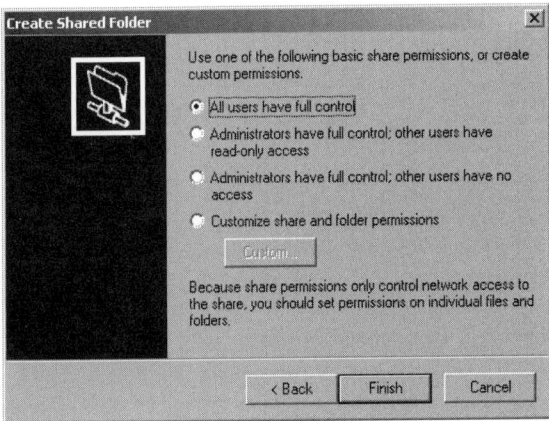

Figure 13-3. *Set permissions for the share.*

- **Administrators Have Full Control; Other Users Have No Access** Gives administrators complete control over the share but denies access to other users. Use this option if you want to create the share and grant user permissions later or if you want to create an administrative share.

- **Customize Share And Folder Permissions** Allows you to configure access for specific users and groups, which is usually the best technique to use. Setting share permissions is discussed fully later in this chapter in the section entitled "Managing Share Permissions."

10. Click Finish, and you're done.

Note If you view the shared folder in Windows Explorer, you'll see that the folder icon now includes a hand to indicate a share. Through Computer Management, you can also view shared resources. To learn how, see the section of this chapter entitled "Sharing Folders on Local and Remote Systems."

Creating Additional Shares on an Existing Share

Individual folders can have multiple shares. Each share can have a different name and a different set of access permissions. To create additional shares on an existing share, simply follow the steps for creating a share outlined in the previous section—with these changes:

- In Step 3: When you name the share, make sure that you use a different name.

- In Step 6: When you add a description for the share, use a description that explains what the share is used for (and how it's different from the other share(s) for the same folder).

Creating a Web Share

If the system you're currently logged on to has Internet Information Services installed on it, you can create shares that are accessible from Web browsers. To create Web shares, follow these steps:

1. In Windows Explorer, right-click the local folder you want to share, and then from the pop-up menu select Properties.

2. In the Properties dialog box, click the Web Sharing tab, which is shown in Figure 13-4.

3. Use the Share On drop-down list box to select the local Web site on which you want to share the folder.

4. If this is the first share for this folder, select the Share This Folder option button to display the Edit Alias dialog box. Otherwise, click Add. Figure 13-5 shows the Edit Alias dialog box.

5. In the Alias field, type an alias for the folder. The alias is the name you'll use to access the folder on the Web server. This name must be unique and must not conflict with existing folders used by the Web server. For example, if you type the alias **MyDir**, you could access the folder as *http://localhost/MyDir/*.

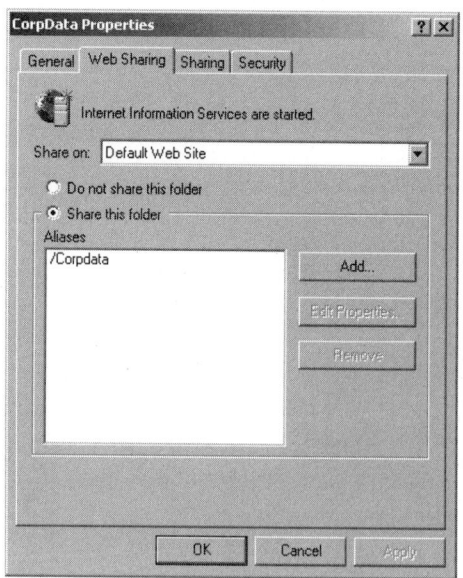

Figure 13-4. *Use the Web Sharing tab to create a Web share.*

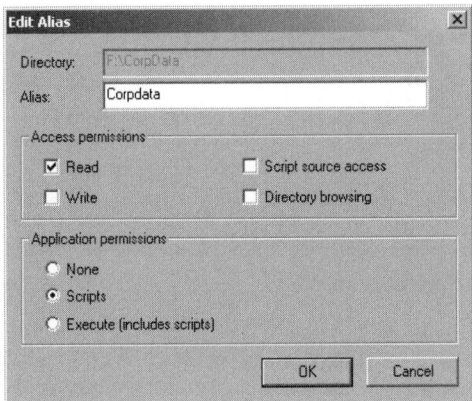

Figure 13-5. *The Edit Alias dialog box allows you to set the alias and access permissions for the folder.*

6. Set access permissions for the folder. The available check boxes are used as follows:

- **Read** Allows Web users to read files in the folder.
- **Write** Allows Web users to write data in the folder.
- **Script Source Access** Allows Web users to access the source code for scripts.
- **Directory Browsing** Allows Web users to browse the folder and its subfolders.

7. Set application permissions for the folder. The available check boxes are used as follows:

- **None** Disallows the execution of programs and scripts.
- **Scripts** Allows scripts in the folder to be run from the Web.
- **Execute (Includes Scripts)** Allows programs and scripts in the folder to be executed from the Web.

8. Click OK when you're finished.

9. To further restrict access to contents of a shared folder on an NTFS volume, set file and folder permissions as outlined in the section of this chapter entitled "File and Folder Permissions."

Note Web shares are subject to the access controls enforced by the Web server and Windows 2000. If you have problems accessing a share, check the Web server permissions first and then the Windows 2000 file and folder permissions.

Managing Share Permissions

Share permissions set the maximum allowable actions available within a shared folder. By default, when you create a share, everyone with access to the network has full control over the share's contents. With NTFS volumes you can use file and folder permissions to further constrain actions within the share as well as share permissions. With file allocation table (FAT) volumes, share permissions provide the only access controls.

The Different Share Permissions

Share permissions available, from the most restrictive to the least restrictive, are

- **No Access**   No permissions are granted for the share.
- **Read**   With this permission, users can
  - View file and subfolder names.
  - Access the subfolders of the share.
  - Read file data and attributes.
  - Run program files.
- **Change**   Users have Read permissions and the additional ability to
  - Create files and subfolders.
  - Modify files.
  - Change attributes on files and subfolders.
  - Delete files and subfolders.
- **Full Control**   Users have Read and Change permissions, as well as the following additional capabilities on NTFS volumes:
  - Change file and folder permissions.
  - Take ownership of files and folders.

 Note   Only NTFS volumes have file and folder permissions or (sometimes and) file and folder ownership.

You can assign share permissions to users and groups. You can even assign permissions to implicit groups. For details on implicit groups, see the section of Chapter 7 entitled "Implicit Groups and Special Identities."

Viewing Share Permissions

To view share permissions, follow these steps:

1. In Computer Management, connect to the computer on which the share is created.
2. In the console tree, expand System Tools and Shared Folders, and then select Shares.

3. Right-click the share you want to view, and then select Properties.

4. In the Share Properties dialog box, click the Share Permissions tab, shown in Figure 13-6. You can now view the users and groups that have access to the share and the type of access they have.

Configuring Share Permissions

In Computer Management, you can add user, computer, and group permissions to shares by completing the following steps:

1. Right-click the share you want to manage, and then select Properties.

2. In the Share Properties dialog box, click the Share Permissions tab.

3. Choose Add. This opens the Select Users, Contacts, Computers, Or Groups dialog box shown in Figure 13-7. You can now grant access to users, contacts, computers, or groups. You can use the fields of this dialog box as follows:

   • **Look In**   This drop-down list box allows you to access account names from other domains. Click Look In to see a list of the current domain, trusted domains, and other resources that you can access. Select Entire Directory to view all the account names in the folder.

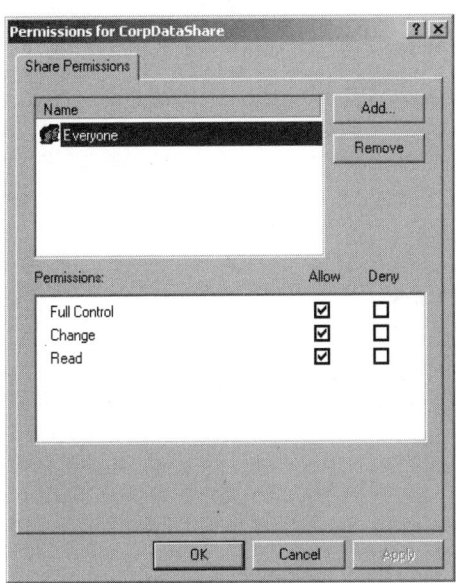

Figure 13-6. *The Share Permissions tab shows which users and groups have access to the share and what type of access they have.*

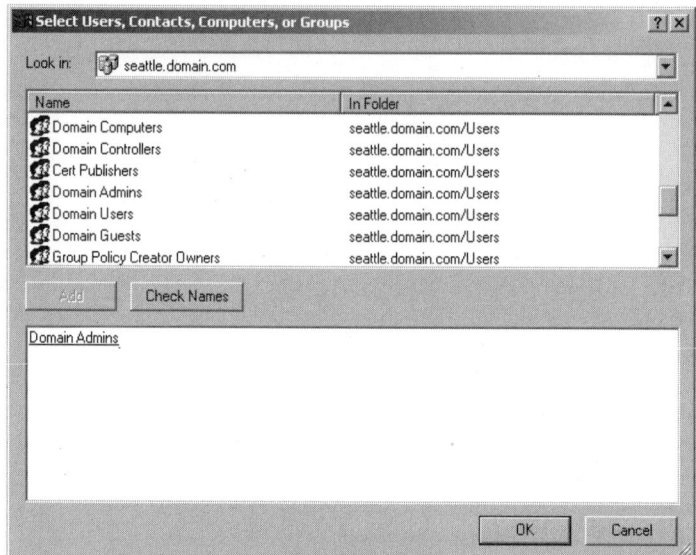

Figure 13-7. *Add users and groups to the share using the Select Users, Contacts, Computers, Or Groups dialog box.*

 Note Only domains that have been designated as trusted are available in the Look In drop-down list box. Because of the transitive trusts in Windows 2000, this usually means that all domains in the domain tree or forest are listed.

- **Name** This column shows the available accounts of the currently selected domain or resource.
- **Add** This button adds selected names to the selection list.
- **Check Names** This button validates the user and group names entered into the selection list. This is useful if you type names in manually and want to make sure that they are available.

4. Click OK. The users and groups are added to the Name list for the share.
5. Configure access permissions for each user, contact, computer, and group by selecting an account name and then allowing or denying access permissions. Keep in mind that you're setting the maximum allowable permissions for a particular user, contact, computer, or group.
6. Click OK when you're finished. To assign additional security permissions for NTFS, see the section of this chapter entitled "File and Folder Permissions."

Modifying Existing Share Permissions

You can change the share permissions you assign to users, contacts, computers, and groups by using the Share Properties dialog box. In Computer Management, follow these steps:

1. Right-click the share you want to manage, and then select Properties.
2. In the Share Properties dialog box, click the Share Permissions tab.
3. In the Name list box, select the user, contact, computer, or group you want to modify.
4. Use the fields in the Permissions area to allow or deny permissions.
5. Repeat for other users, contacts, computers, or groups, and then click OK when you're finished.

Removing Share Permissions for Users and Groups

You also remove share permissions assigned to users, contacts, computers, and groups with the Share Permissions dialog box. In Computer Management, follow these steps:

1. Right-click the share you want to manage, and then select Properties.
2. In the Share Properties dialog box, click the Share Permissions tab.
3. In the Name list box, select the user, contact, computer, or group you want to remove, and then choose Remove.
4. Repeat for other users or groups, as necessary, and then click OK when you're finished.

Managing Existing Shares

As an administrator, you'll often have to manage shared folders. The common administrative tasks of managing shares are covered in this section.

Understanding Special Shares

When you install Windows 2000, the operating system creates special shares automatically. These shares are also known as *Administrative shares* and *Hidden shares*. These shares are designed to help make system administration easier. You can't set access permissions on special shares; Windows 2000 assigns access permissions. However, you can delete special shares if you're certain the shares aren't needed.

Which special shares are available depends on your system configuration. Table 13-1 lists special shares you may see and how they are used.

Table 13-1. Special Shares Used by Windows 2000

Special Share Name	Description	Usage
ADMIN$	Used during remote administration of a system. Provides access to the operating system %SystemRoot%.	On workstations and servers, administrators and backup operators can access these shares. On domain controllers, server operators also have access.
FAX$	Supports network faxes.	Used by FAX clients when sending faxes.
IPC$	Supports named pipes during remote IPC access.	Used by programs when performing remote administration and when viewing shared resources.
NETLOGON	Supports the Net Logon service.	Used by the Net Logon service when processing domain logon requests. Everyone has Read access.
Microsoft UAM Volume	Supports Macintosh file and printer services.	Used by File Server For Macintosh and Print Server For Macintosh.
PRINT$	Supports shared printer resources by providing access to printer drivers.	Used by shared printers. Everyone has Read access. Administrators, server operators, and printer operators have full control.
SYSVOL	Supports Active Directory.	Used to store data and objects for Active Directory.
Driveletter$	Allows administrators to connect to the root folder of a drive. These shares are shown as C$, D$, E$, and so on.	On workstations and servers, Administrators and backup operators can access these shares. On domain controllers, server operators also have access.

Connecting to Special Shares

Special shares end with the $ symbol. Although these shares aren't displayed in Windows Explorer, administrators and certain operators can connect to them. To connect to a special share, follow these steps:

1. In Windows Explorer, from the Tools menu, select Map Network Drive. This opens the dialog box shown in Figure 13-8.

2. In the Drive field, select a free drive letter. This drive letter is used to access the special share.

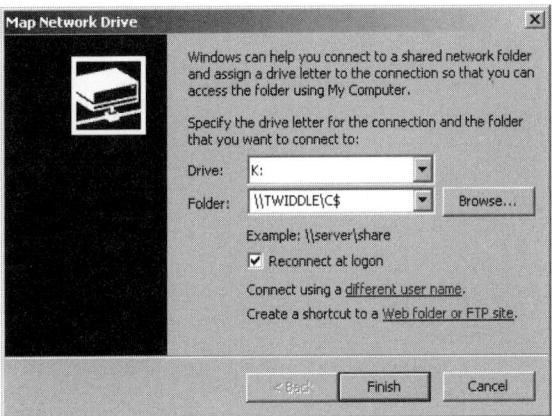

Figure 13-8. *Connect to special shares by mapping them with the Map Network Drive dialog box.*

3. In the Folder field, type the Universal Naming Convention (UNC) path to the desired share. For example, to access the C$ share on a server called Twiddle, you would use the path **TWIDDLE\C$**.

4. Click OK.

Once you connect to a special share, you can access it as you would any other drive. Because special shares are protected, you don't have to worry about ordinary users accessing these shares. The first time you connect to the share, you may be prompted for a user name and password. If you are, provide that information.

Viewing User and Computer Sessions

Computer Management can track all connections to shared resources on a Windows 2000 system. Whenever a user or computer connects to a shared resource, a connection is listed in the Sessions node.

To view connections to shared resources, follow these steps:

1. In Computer Management, connect to the computer on which the share is created.

2. In the console tree, expand System Tools and Shared Folders, and then select Sessions.

3. As shown in Figure 13-9, you can now view connections to shares for users and computers.

The Sessions node provides important information about user and computer connections. The columns of this node provide the following information:

- **User** The names of users or computers connected to shared resources. Computer names are shown with a $ suffix to differentiate them from users.

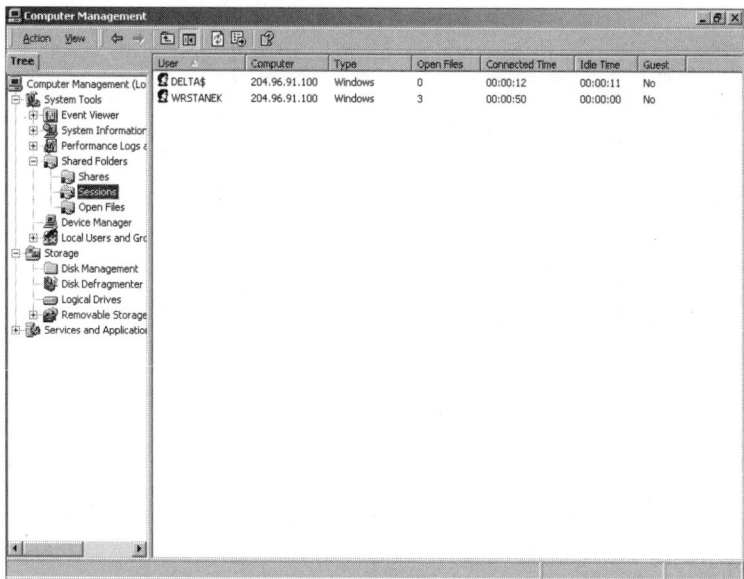

Figure 13-9. *Viewing user and computer connections.*

- **Computer** The IP address of the computer being used.
- **Type** The type of computer being used.
- **Open Files** The number of files the user is actively working with. For more detailed information, access the Open Files node.
- **Connected Time** The time that has elapsed since the connection was established.
- **Idle Time** The time that has elapsed since the connection was last used.
- **Guest** Whether the user is logged on as a guest.

Managing Sessions and Shares

Managing sessions and shares is a common administrative task. Before you shut down a server or an application running on a server, you may want to disconnect users from shared resources. You may also need to disconnect users when you plan to change access permissions or delete a share entirely. Another reason to disconnect users is to break locks on files. You disconnect users from shared resources by ending the related user sessions.

Ending individual sessions To disconnect individual users from shared resources, follow these steps:

1. In Computer Management, connect to the computer on which the share is created.

2. In the console tree, expand System Tools and Shared Folders, and then select Sessions.

3. Right-click the user sessions you want to end, and then choose Close Session.

4. Click OK to confirm the action.

Ending all sessions To disconnect all users from shared resources, follow these steps:

1. In Computer Management, connect to the computer on which the share is created.

2. In the console tree, expand System Tools and Shared Folders, and then right-click Sessions.

3. Choose Disconnect All Sessions, and then click OK to confirm the action.

Note Keep in mind that you're disconnecting users from shared resources and not from the domain. You can only force users to log off once they've logged on to the domain through logon hours and group policy. Thus, disconnecting users doesn't log them off·the network. It simply disconnects them from the shared resource.

Managing Open Resources

Anytime users connect to shares, the individual file and object resources they're actively working with are displayed in the Open Files node. The Open Files node may show the files the user has open but isn't currently editing.

You can access the Open Files node by completing the following steps:

1. In Computer Management, connect to the computer on which the share is created.

2. In the console tree, expand System Tools and Shared Folders, and then select Open Files. This displays the Open Files node, shown in Figure 13-10.

The Open Files node The Open Files node provides the following information about resource usage:

- **Open File** The file or folder path to the open file on the local system. May also be a named pipe, such as \PIPE\spools, which is used for printer spooling.

- **Accessed By** The name of the user accessing the file.

- **Type** The type of computer being used.

- **# Locks** The number of locks on the resource.

- **Open Mode** The access mode used when the resource was opened, such as Read, Write, or Write+Read mode.

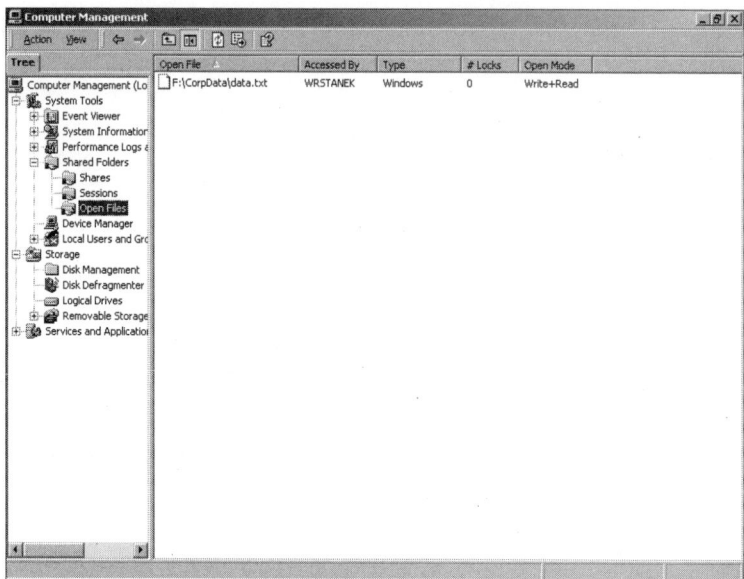

Figure 13-10. *You can manage open resources using the Open Files node.*

Close an open file To close an open file on a computer's shares, follow these steps:

1. In Computer Management, connect to the computer you want to work with.

2. In the console tree, expand System Tools and Shared Folders, and then select Open Files.

3. Right-click the open file you want to close, and then choose Close Open File.

4. Click OK to confirm the action.

Close all open files To close all open files on a computer's shares, follow these steps:

1. In Computer Management, connect to the computer on which the share is created.

2. In the console tree, expand System Tools and Shared Folders, and then right-click Open Files.

3. Choose Disconnect All Open Files, and then click OK to confirm the action.

Stop Sharing Files and Folders

To stop sharing a folder, follow these steps:

1. In Computer Management, connect to the computer on which the share is created and then access the Shares node.

2. Right-click the share you want to remove, and then choose Stop Sharing. Click OK to confirm the action.

Caution You should never delete a folder containing shares without first stopping the shares. If you fail to stop the shares, Windows 2000 will attempt to reestablish the shares the next time the computer is started, and the resulting error will be logged in the System event log.

Connecting to Network Drives

Users can connect to a network drive and to shared resources available on the network. This connection is shown as a network drive that users can access like any other drive on their systems.

Note When users connect to network drives, they're subject not only to the permissions set for the shared resources, but also to Windows 2000 file and folder permissions. Differences in these permission sets are usually the reason users may not be able to access a particular file or subfolder within the network drive.

Mapping a Network Drive

On Windows 2000 you connect to a network drive by mapping to it. On other systems, you connect to a network drive using the procedure specific to the operating system.

To connect to a shared resource on Windows 2000, follow these steps:

1. While the user is logged on, start Windows Explorer on the user's computer.

2. From the Tools menu, select Map Network Drive. This opens the Map Network Drive dialog box.

3. Using the Drive field, you can now create a network drive for a shared resource. Select a free drive letter to create a network drive that can be accessed in Windows Explorer and My Computer. Select (None) to create a network drive without assigning a drive letter. This drive is opened in its own Windows Explorer window and can't be accessed from My Computer.

4. In the Folder field, type the UNC path to the desired share. For example, to access a share called DOCS on a server called ROMEO, you would use the path **\\ROMEO\DOCS.** If you don't know the share location, click Browse to search for available shares.

5. If you want the network drive to be automatically connected in subsequent sessions, select Reconnect At Logon. Otherwise, clear this check box and double-click the network drive when you want to connect.

6. To connect using a different user name from the logon name, click Different User Name, and then type a user name and password for the connection.

7. Click OK.

 Tip On other operating systems, such as Novell NetWare, you could use the UNC from the command line as follows:

Net Use K: \\Server1\Public

If you would like to make this mapping permanent, then add /Persistent: yes to the end of the Net Use statement:

Net Use K: \\Server1\Public /Persistent:yes

This will ensure that the system will try to access the Public folder on Server1 every time you log on to the system.

Disconnecting a Network Drive

To disconnect a network drive, follow these steps:

1. While the user is logged on, start Windows Explorer on the user's computer.
2. From the Tools menu, select Disconnect Network Drive. This opens the Disconnect Network Drive dialog box.
3. Select the drive you want to disconnect, and then click OK.

Object Management, Ownership, and Inheritance

Windows 2000 takes an object-based approach to describing resources and managing permissions. Objects that describe resources are defined on NTFS volumes and in Active Directory. With NTFS volumes, you can set permissions for files and folders. With Active Directory, you can set permissions for other types of objects, such as users, contacts, computers, and groups. You can use these permissions to control access with precision.

Objects and Object Managers

Whether defined on an NTFS volume or in Active Directory, each type of object has an object manager and primary management tools. The object manager controls object settings and permissions. The primary management tools are the tools of choice for working with the object. Objects, their managers, and management tools are summarized in Table 13-2.

Table 13-2. Windows 2000 Objects

Object Type	Object Manager	Management Tool
Files and folders *(continued)*	NTFS	Windows Explorer

Table 13-2. *(continued)*

Object Type	Object Manager	Management Tool
Shares	Server service	Windows Explorer; Computer Management
Registry keys	Windows registry	Registry Editor
Services	Service controllers	Security Configuration Tool Set
Printers	Print spooler	Printers in Control Panel

Object Ownership and Transfer

It's important to understand the concept of object ownership. In Windows 2000 the object owner isn't necessarily the creator of the object. Instead, the object owner is the person who has direct control over the object. Object owners can grant access permissions and give other users permission to take ownership of the object.

As an administrator, you can take ownership of objects on the network. This ensures that authorized administrators can't be locked out of files, folders, printers, and other resources. Once you take ownership of files, however, you can't return ownership to the original owner (in most cases). This prevents administrators from accessing files and then trying to hide the fact.

The way ownership is assigned initially depends on the location of the resource being created. In most cases, however, the Administrators group is listed as the current owner and the actual creator of the object is listed as a person who can take ownership.

Ownership can be transferred in several ways:

- If Administrators is initially assigned as the owner, the creator of the object can take ownership, provided he or she does this before someone else takes ownership.

- The current owner can grant the Take Ownership permission to other users, allowing those users to take ownership of the object.

- An administrator can take ownership of an object, provided the object is under his or her administrative control.

To take ownership of an object, follow these steps:

1. Start the management tool for the object. For example, if you want to work with files and folders, start Windows Explorer.

2. Right-click the object you want to take ownership of.

3. From the pop-up menu, select Properties, and then in the Properties dialog box click the Security tab.

4. Display the Access Control Settings dialog box by clicking the Advanced button. Then select the Owner tab, shown in Figure 13-11.

5. Click the new owner in the Change Owner To list box, and then click OK.

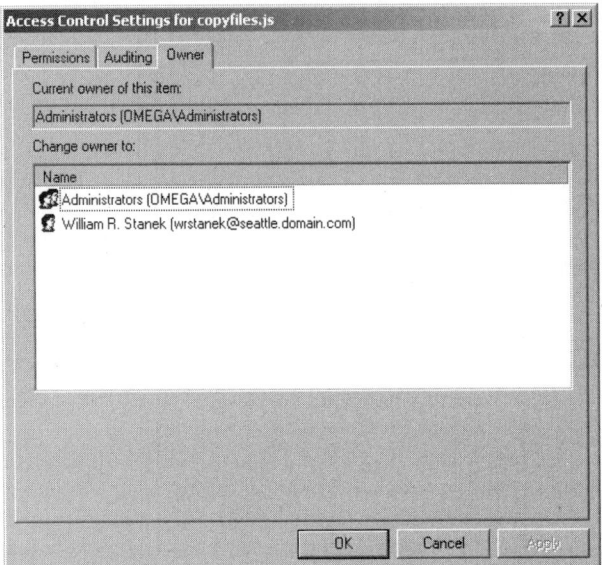

Figure 13-11. *Use the Owner tab to change ownership of a file.*

Object Inheritance

Objects are defined using a parent-child structure. A parent object is a top-level object. A child object is an object defined below a parent object in the hierarchy. For example, the folder C:\ is the parent of the folders C:\data and C:\backups. Any subfolders created in C:\data or C:\backups are children of these folders and grandchildren of C:\.

Child objects can inherit permissions from parent objects. In fact, all Windows 2000 objects are created with inheritance enabled by default. This means that child objects automatically inherit the permissions of the parent. Because of this, the parent object permissions control access to the child object. If you want to change permissions on a child object, you must

- Edit the permissions of the parent object.

- Stop inheriting permissions from the parent object, and then assign permissions to the child object.

- Select the opposite permission to override the inherited permission. For example, if the parent allows the permission, you would deny it on the child object.

To start or stop inheriting permissions from a parent object, follow these steps:

1. Start the management tool for the object. For example, if you want to work with files and folders, start Windows Explorer.
2. Right-click the object you want to work with.
3. From the pop-up menu, select Properties, and then in the Properties dialog box click the Security tab.
4. Display the Access Control Settings dialog box by clicking Advanced.
5. In the Permissions tab, select or clear Allow Inheritable Permissions From Parent To Propagate To This Object.

File and Folder Permissions

On NTFS volumes, you can set security permissions on files and folders. These permissions grant or deny access to the files and folders. You can view security permissions for files and folders by completing the following steps:

1. In Windows Explorer, right-click the file or folder you want to work with.
2. From the pop-up menu, select Properties, and then in the Properties dialog box click the Security tab.
3. In the Name list box, select the user, contact, computer, or group whose permissions you want to view. If the permissions are dimmed, it means the permissions are inherited from a parent object.

Understanding File and Folder Permissions

The basic permissions you can assign to files and folders are summarized in Table 13-3. File permissions include Full Control, Modify, Read & Execute, Read, and Write. Folder permissions include Full Control, Modify, Read & Execute, List Folder Contents, Read, and Write.

Anytime you work with file and folder permissions, you should keep the following in mind:

- Read is the only permission needed to run scripts. Execute permission doesn't matter.
- Read access is required to access a shortcut and its target.
- Giving a user permission to write to a file but not to delete it doesn't prevent the user from deleting the file's contents. A user can still delete the contents.
- If a user has full control over a folder, the user can delete files in the folder regardless of the permission on the files.

Table 13-3. File and Folder Permissions Used by Windows 2000

Permission	Meaning for Folders	Meaning for Files
Read	Permits viewing and listing of files and subfolders	Permits viewing or accessing of the file's contents
Write	Permits adding of files and subfolders	Permits writing to a file
Read & Execute	Permits viewing and listing of files and subfolders as well as executing of files; inherited by files and folders	Permits viewing and accessing of the file's contents as well as executing of the file
List Folder Contents	Permits viewing and listing of files and subfolders as well as executing of files; inherited by folders only	N/A
Modify	Permits reading and writing of files and subfolders; allows deletion of the folder	Permits reading and writing of the file; allows deletion of the file
Full Control	Permits reading, writing, changing, and deleting of files and subfolders	Permits reading, writing, changing and deleting of the file

The basic permissions are created by combining special permissions in logical groups. Table 13-4 shows special permissions used to create the basic permissions for files. Using advanced permission settings, you can assign these special permissions individually, if necessary. As you study the special permissions, keep the following in mind:

- If no access is specifically granted or denied, the user is denied access.

- Actions that users can perform are based on the sum of all the permissions assigned to the user and to all the groups the user is a member of. For example, if the user GeorgeJ has Read access and is a member of the group Techies that has Change access, GeorgeJ will have Change access. If Techies is in turn a member of Administrators, which has Full Control, GeorgeJ will have complete control over the file.

Table 13-4. Special Permissions for Files

Special Permissions	Full Control	Modify	Read & Execute	Read	Write
Traverse Folder/Execute File	X	X	X		
List Folder/Read Data	X	X	X	X	
Read Attributes	X	X	X	X	
Read Extended Attributes	X	X	X	X	
Create Files/Write Data	X	X			X
Create Folders/Append Data	X	X			X

(continued)

Table 13-4. *(continued)*

Special Permissions	Full Control	Modify	Read & Execute	Read	Write
Write Attributes	X	X			X
Write Extended Attributes	X	X			X
Delete Subfolders and Files	X				
Delete	X	X			
Read Permissions	X	X	X	X	X
Change Permissions	X				
Take Ownership	X				

Table 13-5 shows special permissions used to create the basic permissions for folders. As you study the special permissions, keep the following in mind:

- When you set permissions for parent folders, you can force all files and subfolders within the folder to inherit the permissions. You do this by selecting Reset Permissions On All Child Objects And Enable Propagation Of Inheritable Permissions.

- When you create files in folders, these files inherit certain permission settings. These permission settings are shown as the default file permissions.

Table 13-5. Special Permissions for Folders

Special Permissions	Full Control	Modify	Read & Execute	List Folder Contents	Read	Write
Traverse Folder / Execute File	X	X	X	X		
List Folder /Read Data	X	X	X	X	X	
Read Attributes	X	X	X	X	X	
Read Extended Attributes	X	X	X	X	X	
Create Files / Write Data	X	X				X
Create Folders / Append Data	X	X				X
Write Attributes	X	X				X
Write Extended Attributes	X	X				X
Delete Subfolders and Files	X					
Delete	X	X				
Read Permissions	X	X	X	X	X	X
Change Permissions	X					
Take Ownership	X					

Setting File and Folder Permissions

To set permissions for files and folders, follow these steps:

1. In Windows Explorer, right-click the file or folder you want to work with.

2. From the pop-up menu, select Properties, and then in the Properties dialog box click the Security tab, shown in Figure 13-12.

3. Users or groups that already have access to the file or folder are listed in the Name list box. You can change permissions for these users and groups by doing the following:

   - Select the user or group you want to change.
   - Use the Permissions list box to grant or deny access permissions.

 Tip Inherited permissions are shaded. If you want to override an inherited permission, select the opposite permission.

4. To set access permissions for additional users, contacts, computers, or groups, click Add. This displays the Select Users, Computers, Or Groups dialog box shown in Figure 13-13.

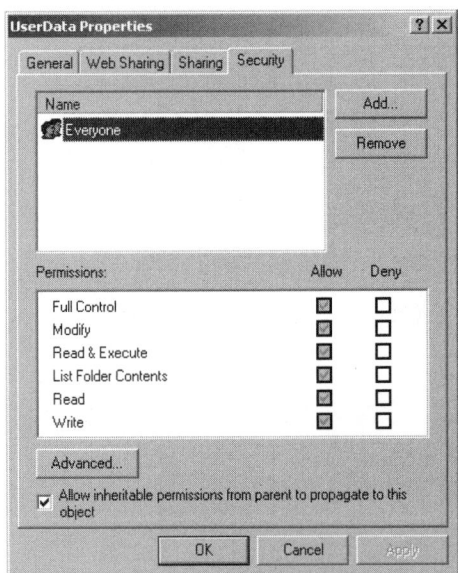

Figure 13-12. *Use the Security tab to configure basic permissions for the file or folder.*

5. Use the Select Users, Computers, Or Groups dialog box to select the users, computers, or groups for which you want to set access permissions. You can use the fields of this dialog box as follows:

- **Look In**   This drop-down list box allows you to access account names from other domains. Click Look In to see a list of the current domain, trusted domains, and other resources that you can access. Select Entire Directory to view all the account names in the folder.

- **Name**   This column shows the available accounts of the currently selected domain or resource.

- **Add**   This button adds selected names to the selection list.

- **Check Names**   This button validates the user, contact, and group names entered into the selection list. This is useful if you type names in manually and want to make sure they're available.

6. In the Name list box, select the user, computer, or group you want to configure, and then use the fields in the Permissions area to allow or deny permissions. Repeat for other users, computers, or groups.

7. Click OK when you're finished.

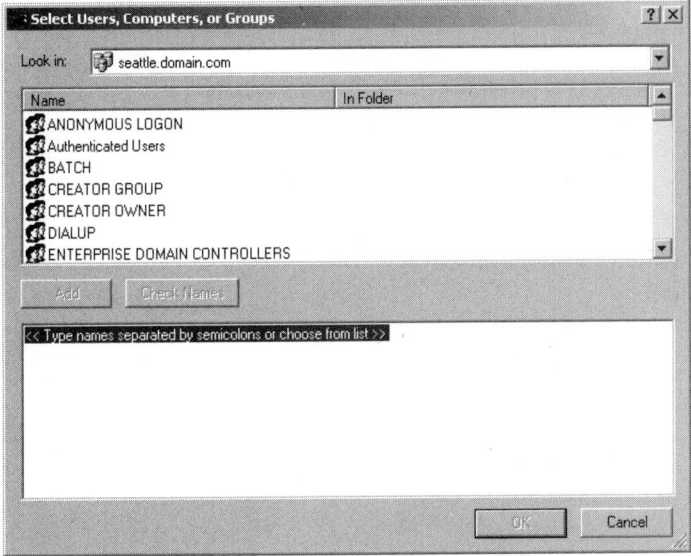

Figure 13-13. *Select users, computers, and groups that should be granted or denied access.*

Auditing System Resources

Auditing is the best way to track what's happening on your Windows 2000 systems. You can use auditing to collect information related to resource usage, such as file access, system logon, and system configuration changes. Anytime an action occurs that you've configured for auditing, the action is written to the system's security log, where it's stored for your review. The security log is accessible from Event Viewer.

Note For most auditing changes, you'll need to be logged on using an account that is a member of the Administrators group or be granted the Manage Auditing And Security Log right in Group Policy.

Setting Auditing Policies

Auditing policies are essential to ensure the security and integrity of your systems. Just about every computer system on the network should be configured with some type of security logging. You configure auditing policies with Group Policy. Through Group Policy, you can set auditing policies for an entire site, domain, or organizational unit. You can also set policies for an individual workstation or server.

Once you access the Group Policy container you want to work with, you can set auditing policies by completing the following steps:

1. As shown in Figure 13-14, access the Audit Policy node by working your way down through the console tree. Expand Computer Configuration, Windows Settings, Security Settings, and Local Policies. Then select Audit Policy.

2. The auditing options are

   - **Audit Account Logon Events** Tracks events related to user logon and logoff.

   - **Audit Account Management** Tracks account management by means of Active Directory Users And Computers. Events are generated anytime user, computer, or group accounts are created, modified, or deleted.

   - **Audit Directory Service Access** Tracks access to the Active Directory. Events are generated any time users or computers access the directory.

   - **Audit Logon Events** Tracks events related to user logon, logoff, and remote connections to network systems.

   - **Audit Object Access** Tracks system resource usage for files, directories, shares, printers, and Active Directory objects.

   - **Audit Policy Change** Tracks changes to user rights, auditing, and trust relationships.

- **Audit Privilege Use** Tracks the use of user rights and privileges, such as the right to back up files and directories.

Note The Audit Privilege Use policy doesn't track system access–related events, such as the use of the right to log on interactively or the right to access the computer from the network. These events are tracked with Logon and Logoff auditing.

- **Audit Process Tracking** Tracks system processes and the resources they use.
- **Audit System Events** Tracks system startup, shutdown, and restart, as well as actions that affect system security or the security log.

3. To configure an auditing policy, double-click its entry or right-click and select Security. This opens a Properties dialog box for the policy.

4. Select Define These Policy Settings, and then select either the Success check box or the Failure check box, or both. Success logs successful events, such as successful logon attempts. Failure logs failed events, such as failed logon attempts.

5. Click OK when you're finished.

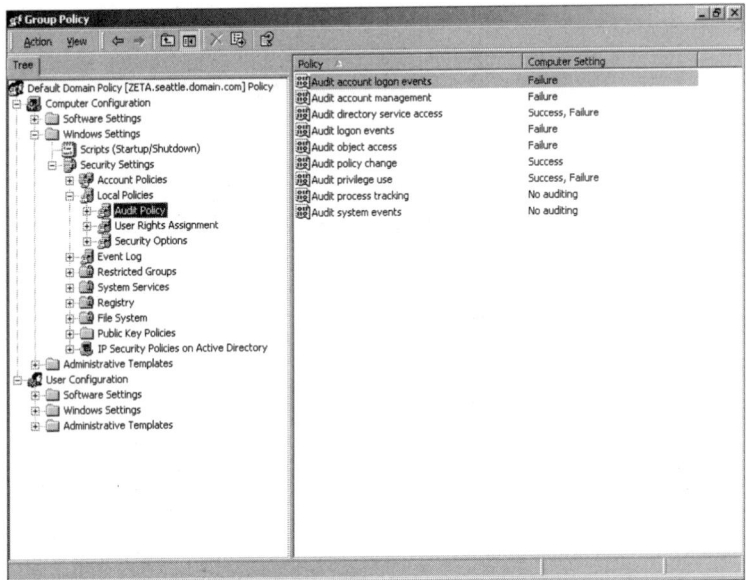

Figure 13-14. *Set auditing policies using the Audit Policy node in Group Policy.*

Auditing Files and Folders

If you configure a group policy to enable the Audit Object Access option, you can set the level of auditing for individual folders and files. This allows you to control precisely how folder and file usage is tracked. Auditing of this type is only available on NTFS volumes.

You can configure file and folder auditing by completing the following steps:

1. In Windows Explorer, right-click the file or folder to be audited, and then from the pop-up menu select Properties.

2. Choose the Security tab, and then click Advanced.

3. In the Access Control Settings dialog box, select the Auditing tab, shown in Figure 13-15.

4. If you want to inherit auditing settings from a parent object, ensure that Allow Inheritable Auditing Entries From Parent To Propagate To This Object is selected.

5. If you want child objects of the current object to inherit the settings, select Reset Auditing Entries On All Child Objects And Enable Propagation Of Inheritable Auditing Entries.

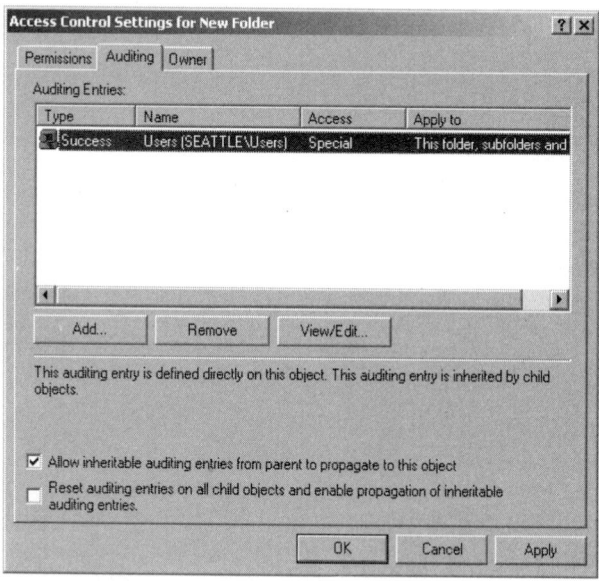

Figure 13-15. *Once you audit object access, you can use the Auditing tab to set auditing policies on individual files and folders.*

6. Use the Auditing Entries list box to select the users, groups, or computers whose actions you want to audit. To remove an account, select the account in the Auditing Entries list box, and then click Remove.

7. To add specific accounts, click Add, and then use the Select Users, Contacts, Computers, Or Groups dialog box to select an account name to add. When you click OK, you'll see the Auditing Entry For New Folder dialog box, shown in Figure 13-16.

Note If you want to audit actions for all users, use the special group Everyone. Otherwise, select the specific user groups or users, or both, that you want to audit.

8. As necessary, use the Apply Onto drop-down list box to specify where objects are audited.

9. Select the Successful or Failed check boxes, or both, for each of the events you want to audit. Successful logs successful events, such as successful file reads. Failed logs failed events, such as failed file deletions. The events you can audit are the same as the special permissions listed in Table 13-5—except you can't audit synchronizing of offline files and folders.

10. Choose OK when you're finished. Repeat this process to audit other users, groups, or computers.

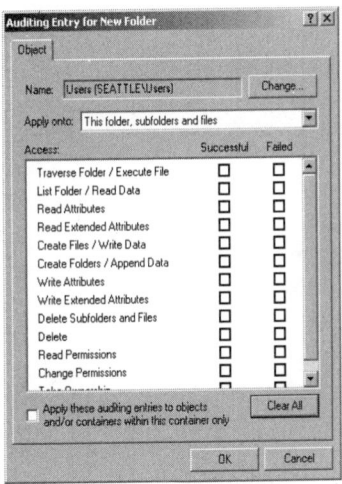

Figure 13-16. *Use the Auditing Entry For New Folder dialog box to set auditing entries for a user, contact, computer, or group.*

Auditing Active Directory Objects

If you configure a group policy to enable the Audit Directory Service Access option, you can set the level of auditing for Active Directory objects. This allows you to control precisely how object usage is tracked.

To configure object auditing, follow these steps:

1. In Active Directory Users And Computers, access the container for the object.

2. Right-click the object to be audited, and then from the pop-up menu select Properties.

3. Choose the Security tab, and then click Advanced.

4. In the Access Control Settings dialog box, select the Auditing tab. To inherit auditing settings from a parent object, make sure that Allow Inheritable Auditing Entries From Parent To Propagate To This Object is selected.

5. Use the Auditing Entries list box to select the users, contacts, groups, or computers whose actions you want to audit. To remove an account, select the account in the Auditing Entries list box, and then click Remove.

6. To add specific accounts, click Add, and then use the Select Users, Contacts, Computers, Or Groups dialog box to select an account name to add. When you click OK, the Auditing Entry For dialog box is displayed.

7. Use the Apply Onto drop-down list box to specify where objects are audited.

8. Select the Successful or Failed check boxes, or both, for each of the events you want to audit. Successful logs successful events, such as successful file reads. Failed logs failed events, such as failed file deletions.

9. Choose OK when you're finished. Repeat this process to audit other users, contacts, groups, or computers.

Chapter 14

Data Backup and Recovery

Because data is the heart of the enterprise, it's crucial for you to protect it. And to protect your organization's data, you need to implement a data backup and recovery plan. Backing up files can protect against accidental loss of user data, database corruption, hardware failures, and even natural disasters. It's your job as an administrator to make sure that backups are performed and that backup tapes are stored in a secure location.

Creating a Backup and Recovery Plan

Data backup is an insurance plan. Important files are accidentally deleted all the time. Mission-critical data can become corrupt. Natural disasters can leave your office in ruin. With a solid backup and recovery plan, you can recover from any of these. Without one, you're left with nothing to fall back on.

Figuring Out a Backup Plan

It takes time to create and implement a backup and recovery plan. You'll need to figure out what data needs to be backed up, how often the data should be backed up, and more. To help you create a plan, consider the following:

- **How important is the data on your systems?** The importance of data can go a long way in helping you determine if you need to back it up—as well as when and how it should be backed up. For critical data, such as a database, you'll want to have redundant backup sets that extend back for several backup periods. For less important data, such as daily user files, you won't need such an elaborate backup plan, but you'll need to back up the data regularly and ensure that the data can be recovered easily.

- **What type of information does the data contain?** Data that doesn't seem important to you may be very important to someone else. Thus, the type of information the data contains can help you determine if you need to back up the data—as well as when and how the data should be backed up.

- **How often does the data change?** The frequency of change can affect your decision on how often the data should be backed up. For example, data that changes daily should be backed up daily.

- **How quickly do you need to recover the data?** Time is an important factor in creating a backup plan. For critical systems, you may need to get back online swiftly. To do this, you may need to alter your backup plan.

- **Do you have the equipment to perform backups?** You must have backup hardware to perform backups. To perform timely backups, you may need several backup devices and several sets of backup media. Backup hardware includes tape drives, optical drives, and removable disk drives. Generally, tape drives are less expensive but slower than other types of drives.

- **Who will be responsible for the backup and recovery plan?** Ideally, someone should be a primary contact for the organization's backup and recovery plan. This person may also be responsible for performing the actual backup and recovery of data.

- **What is the best time to schedule backups?** Scheduling backups when system use is as low as possible will speed the backup process. However, you can't always schedule backups for off-peak hours. So you'll need to carefully plan when key system data is backed up.

- **Do you need to store backups off-site?** Storing copies of backup tapes off-site is essential to recovering your systems in the case of a natural disaster. In your off-site storage location, you should also include copies of the software you may need to install to reestablish operational systems.

The Basic Types of Backup

There are many techniques for backing up files. The techniques you use will depend on the type of data you're backing up, how convenient you want the recovery process to be, and more.

If you view the properties of a file or directory in Windows Explorer, you'll note an attribute called Archive. This attribute often is used to determine whether a file or directory should be backed up. If the attribute is on, the file or directory may need to be backed up. The basic types of backups you can perform include

- **Normal/full backups** All files that have been selected are backed up, regardless of the setting of the archive attribute. When a file is backed up, the archive attribute is cleared. If the file is later modified, this attribute is set, which indicates that the file needs to be backed up.

- **Copy backups** All files that have been selected are backed up, regardless of the setting of the archive attribute. Unlike a normal backup, the archive attribute on files isn't modified. This allows you to perform other types of backups on the files at a later date.

- **Differential backups** Designed to create backup copies of files that have changed since the last normal backup. The presence of the archive attribute indicates that the file has been modified and only files with this attribute are backed up. However, the archive attribute on files isn't modified. This allows you to perform other types of backups on the files at a later date.

- **Incremental backups** Designed to create backups of files that have changed since the most recent normal or incremental backup. The presence of the archive attribute indicates that the file has been modified and only files with this attribute are backed up. When a file is backed up, the archive attribute is cleared. If the file is later modified, this attribute is set, which indicates that the file needs to be backed up.

- **Daily backups** Designed to back up files using the modification date on the file itself. If a file has been modified on the same day as the backup, the file will be backed up. This technique doesn't change the archive attributes of files.

In your backup plan you'll probably want to perform full backups on a weekly basis and supplement this with daily, differential, or incremental backups. You may also want to create an extended backup set for monthly and quarterly backups that includes additional files that aren't being backed up regularly.

Tip You'll often find that weeks or months can go by before anyone notices that a file or data source is missing. This doesn't mean the file isn't important. Although some types of data aren't used often, they're still needed. So don't forget that you may also want to create extra sets of backups for monthly or quarterly periods, or both, to ensure that you can recover historical data over time.

Differential and Incremental Backups

The difference between differential and incremental backups is extremely important. To understand the distinction between them, examine Table 14-1. As it shows, with differential backups you back up all the files that have changed since the last full backup (which means that the size of the differential backup grows over time). With incremental backups, you only back up files that have changed since the most recent full or incremental backup (which means the size of the incremental backup is usually much smaller than a full backup).

Table 14-1. Incremental and Differential Backup Techniques

Day of Week	Weekly Full Backup with Daily Differential Backup	Weekly Full Backup with Daily Incremental Backup
Sunday	A full backup is performed.	A full backup is performed.
Monday	A differential backup contains all changes since Sunday.	An incremental backup contains changes since Sunday.
Tuesday	A differential backup contains all changes since Sunday.	An incremental backup contains changes since Monday.
Wednesday	A differential backup contains all changes since Sunday.	An incremental backup contains changes since Tuesday.
Thursday	A differential backup contains all changes since Sunday.	An incremental backup contains changes since Wednesday.
Friday	A differential backup contains all changes since Sunday.	An incremental backup contains changes since Thursday.
Saturday	A differential backup contains all changes since Sunday.	An incremental backup contains changes since Friday.

Once you determine what data you're going to back up and how often, you can select backup devices and media that support these choices. These are covered in the next section.

Selecting Backup Devices and Media

Many tools are available for backing up data. Some are fast and expensive. Others are slow but very reliable. The backup solution that's right for your organization depends on many factors, including

- **Capacity** The amount of data that you need to back up on a routine basis. Can the backup hardware support the required load given your time and resource constraints?
- **Reliability** The reliability of the backup hardware and media. Can you afford to sacrifice reliability to meet budget or time needs?
- **Extensibility** The extensibility of the backup solution. Will this solution meet your needs as the organization grows?
- **Speed** The speed with which data can be backed up and recovered. Can you afford to sacrifice speed to reduce costs?
- **Cost** The cost of the backup solution. Does it fit into your budget?

Common Backup Solutions

Capacity, reliability, extensibility, speed, and cost are the issues driving your backup plan. If you understand how these issues affect your organization, you'll be on track to select an appropriate backup solution. Some of the most commonly used backup solutions include

- **Tape drives** Tape drives are the most common backup devices. Tape drives use magnetic tape cartridges to store data. Magnetic tapes are relatively inexpensive but aren't highly reliable. Tapes can break or stretch. They can also lose information over time. The average capacity of tape cartridges ranges from 100 MB to 2 GB. Compared with other backup solutions, tape drives are fairly slow. Still, the selling point is the low cost.
- **Digital audio tape (DAT) drives** DAT drives are quickly replacing standard tape drives as the preferred backup devices. DAT drives use 4 mm and 8 mm tapes to store data. DAT drives and tapes are more expensive than standard tape drives and tapes, but they offer more speed and capacity. DAT drives that use 4 mm tapes can typically record over 30 MB per minute and have capacities of up to 16 GB. DAT drives that use 8 mm tapes can typically record more than 10 MB per minute and have capacities of up to 36 GB (with compression).
- **Auto-loader tape systems** Auto-loader tape systems use a magazine of tapes to create extended backup volumes capable of meeting the high-capacity needs of the enterprise. With an auto-loader system, tapes within the magazine are automatically changed as needed during the backup or recovery process. Most auto-loader tape systems use DAT tapes. The typical sys-

tem uses magazines with between 4 and 12 tapes. The main drawback to these systems is the high cost.

- **Magnetic optical drives**   Magnetic optical drives combine magnetic tape technology with optical lasers to create a more reliable backup solution than DAT. Magnetic optical drives use 3.5-inch and 5.25-inch disks that look similar to floppies but are much thicker. Typically, magnetic optical disks have capacities of between 1 GB and 4 GB.

- **Tape jukeboxes**   Tape jukeboxes are similar to auto-loader tape systems. Jukeboxes use magnetic optical disks rather than DAT tapes to offer high-capacity solutions. These systems load and unload disks stored internally for backup and recovery operations. Their key drawback is the high cost.

- **Removable disks**   Removable disks, such as Iomega Jaz, are increasingly being used as backup devices. Removable disks offer good speed and ease of use for a single drive or single system backup. However, the disk drives and the removable disks tend to be more expensive than standard tape or DAT drive solutions.

- **Disk drives**   Disk drives provide the fastest way to back up and restore files. With disk drives, you can often accomplish in minutes what takes a tape drive hours. So when business needs mandate a speedy recovery, nothing beats a disk drive. The drawbacks to disk drives, however, are relatively high costs and less extensibility.

Before you can use a backup device, you must install it. When you install backup devices other than standard tape and DAT drives, you need to tell the operating system about the controller card and drivers that the backup device uses. For detailed information on installing devices and drivers, see the section of Chapter 2 entitled "Managing Hardware Devices and Drivers."

Buying and Using Tapes

Selecting a backup device is an important step toward implementing a backup and recovery plan. But you also need to purchase the tapes or disks, or both, that will allow you to implement your plan. The number of tapes you need depends on how much data you'll be backing up, how often you'll be backing up the data, and how long you'll need to keep additional data sets.

The typical way to use backup tapes is to set up a rotation schedule whereby you rotate through two or more sets of tapes. The idea is that you can increase tape longevity by reducing tape usage and at the same time reduce the number of tapes you need to ensure that you have historic data on hand when necessary.

One of the most common tape rotation schedules is the 10-tape rotation. With this rotation schedule, you use 10 tapes divided into two sets of 5 (one for each weekday). As shown in Table 14-2, the first set of tapes is used one week and the second set of tapes is used the next week. On Fridays, full backups are scheduled. On Mondays through Thursdays, incremental backups are scheduled. If you add a third set of tapes, you can rotate one of the tape sets to an off-site storage location on a weekly basis.

Table 14-2. Using Incremental Backups

Day of Week	Tape Set 1	Tape Set 2
Friday	Full backup on Tape 5	Full backup on Tape 5
Monday	Incremental backup on Tape 1	Incremental backup on Tape 1
Tuesday	Incremental backup on Tape 2	Incremental backup on Tape 2
Wednesday	Incremental backup on Tape 3	Incremental backup on Tape 3
Thursday	Incremental backup on Tape 4	Incremental backup on Tape 4

 Tip The 10-tape rotation schedule is designed for the 9 to 5 workers of the world. If you're in a 24 x 7 environment, you'll definitely want extra tapes for Saturday and Sunday. In this case, use a 14-tape rotation with two sets of 7 tapes. On Sundays, schedule full backups. On Mondays through Saturdays, schedule incremental backups.

Backing Up Your Data

Microsoft Windows 2000 provides a backup utility, called Backup, for creating backups on local and remote systems. You use Backup to archive files and folders, restore archived files and folders, access media pools reserved for Backup, access remote resources through My Network Places, create snapshots of the system state for backup and restore, schedule backups through the Task Scheduler, and create emergency repair disks.

Getting Started with the Backup Utility

You can access Backup in several different ways, including

- In Computer Management, expand System Tools, and then in the console tree click System Information. The menu should be updated to include Tools. Click the Tools menu, choose Windows, and then select Backup.
- Click the Start menu, and then click Run. In the Run dialog box, type **ntbackup,** and then click OK.
- Click the Start menu, click Programs, click Accessories, click System Tools, and then click Backup.

Figure 14-1 shows the main window for the Backup utility. As you can see, Backup has four tabs that provide easy access to key features. These tabs are

- **Welcome**   Introduces Backup and provides buttons for starting the Backup Wizard, the Restore Wizard, and the Emergency Repair Disk creation utility.
- **Backup**   Provides the main interface for selecting data to back up. You can back up data on local drives and mapped network drives.
- **Restore**   Provides the main interface for restoring archived data. You can restore data to the original location or to an alternate location anywhere on the network.

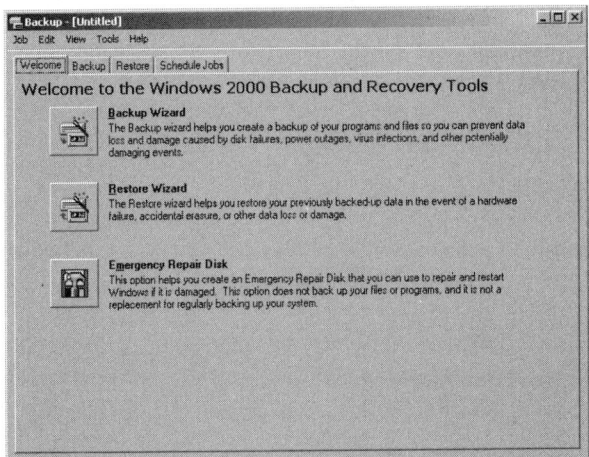

Figure 14-1. *The Windows 2000 Backup utility provides a user-friendly interface for backup and restore.*

- **Schedule Jobs** Provides a month-by-month job schedule for backups. You can view executed jobs as well as jobs scheduled for future dates.

You must have certain permissions and user rights to back up and restore files. Members of the Administrators and the Backup Operators groups have full authority to back up and restore any type of file, regardless of who owns the file and the permissions set on it. File owners and those that have been given control over files can also back up files, but only those that they own or those for which they have Read, Read and Execute, Modify, or Full Control permissions.

Note Keep in mind that while local accounts can only work with local systems, domain accounts have domain-wide privileges. Therefore, a member of the local administrators group can only work with files on the local system, but a member of the domain administrators group could work with files throughout the domain.

Backup provides extensions for working with special types of data, including

- **System state data** Includes essential system files needed to recover the local system. All computers have system state data, which must be backed up in addition to other files to restore a complete working system.

- **Exchange server data** Includes the Exchange information store and data files. You must back up this data if you want to be able to recover Exchange server. Only systems running Microsoft Exchange Server have this type of data.

- **Removable Storage data** Is stored in %SystemRoot%\System32\ Ntmsdata. If you back up this data, you can use the advanced restore option Restore Removable Storage Database to recover the Removable Storage configuration.

- **Remote Storage data** Is stored in %SystemRoot%\System32\Remote-storage. If you back up this data, you can restore Remote Storage by copying the data back to this directory.

Setting Default Options for Backup

You create backups using the Backup utility's Backup tab or the Backup Wizard. Both techniques make use of default options set for the Backup utility. You can view or change the default options by clicking Tools, and then selecting Options. As Figure 14-2 shows, there are five categories of default options: General, Restore, Backup Type, Backup Log, and Exclude Files. Each of these option categories is examined in the sections that follow.

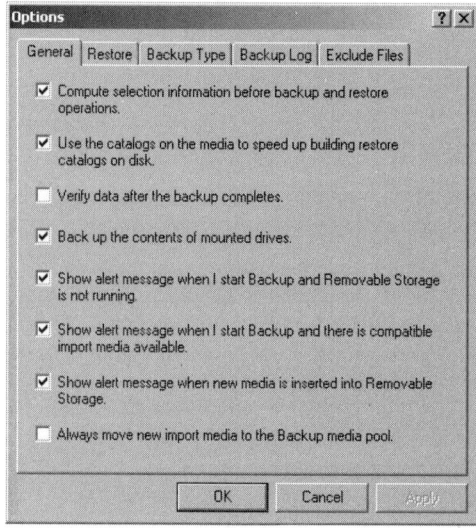

Figure 14-2. *Setting default options for the Backup utility.*

General Backup Options

General options control the default behavior of Backup. You can work with these options using the fields in the General tab of the Options dialog box. The available options are summarized in Table 14-3.

Table 14-3. General Backup Options

Option	Description
Compute Selection Information Before Backup And Restore Operations	Calculates the number of files and bytes involved prior to the backup/restore procedure. Otherwise, this data is calculated during the backup/restore procedure.

(continued)

Table 14-3. *(continued)*

Option	Description
Use The Catalogs On The Media To Speed Up Building Restore Catalogs On Disk	Allows you to use archive logs on the media rather than scan the entire archive to determine what files are included. Clear this option if the catalog is missing, damaged, or otherwise unavailable.
Verify Data After The Backup Completes	Checks the archive data against the original data to ensure that the data is the same. If the data isn't the same, there may be a problem with the backup media and you should run the backup again using different media.
Back Up The Contents Of Mounted Drives	Allows you to back up data on mounted network drives. Otherwise, only the path information for mounted drives will be backed up.
Show Alert Message When I Start Backup And Removable Storage Is Not Running	Displays an alert if you start Backup and the Removable Storage service isn't running. It's a good option to use if you work with removable media.
Show Alert Message When I Start Backup And There Is Compatible Import Media Available	Displays an alert if you start Backup and there is new media available in the import media pool. It's useful if you work with removable media.
Show Alert Message When New Media Is Inserted Into Removable Storage	Displays an alert when Removable Storage detects new media. It's useful if you work with removable media.
Always Move New Import Media To Backup Pools	Allows Removable Storage to move new media to the backup media pool automatically. Select this option if you use Removable Storage and you want new media to be available to Backup.

Setting Restore and Backup Options

The list of general options is quite extensive but, for the most part, the list doesn't control the behavior of the actual backup or restore operation. Table 14-4 summarizes options for controlling backup and restore behavior. The first column shows the tab where the option is available. This is followed by option names and descriptions.

Table 14-4. Restore, Backup Type, and Backup Log Options

Tab	Option	Description
Restore	Do Not Replace The Files On My Computer (Recommended)	Select this option if you don't want to copy over existing files.

(continued)

Table 14-4. *(continued)*

Tab	Option	Description
	Replace The File On Disk Only If the File On Disk Is Older	Select this option to replace older files on disk with newer files from the backup.
	Always Replace The File On My Computer	Select this option to replace all files on disk with files from the backup.
Backup Type	Default Backup Type	Select this option to set the default backup type. Available types are Normal, Copy, Differential, Incremental, and Daily.
Backup Log	Detailed	Select this option to log all operations, including the names of files.
	Summary	Select this option to log only key information and backup failure.
	None	Select this option to disable logging.

Viewing and Setting Backup Exclusions

Many types of system files are excluded from backups by default. You manage exclusions in the Options dialog box, which you access by selecting Options from the Tools menu in Backup.

Viewing exclusions In Backup you can view file exclusions by clicking the Exclude Files tab in the Options dialog box. File exclusions are based on file ownership and can be set for all users as well as the user currently logged on to the system (see Figure 14-3).

Creating exclusions To exclude additional files, follow these steps:

1. In the Options dialog box, choose the Exclude Files tab.

2. If you want to exclude files that are owned by any user, click Add New under the Files Excluded For All Users list. This displays the Add Excluded Files dialog box shown in Figure 14-4.

3. If you want to exclude only files that you own, click Add New under the Files Excluded For User Administrator list. This displays the Add Excluded Files dialog box.

4. You can exclude files by registered file type by clicking a file type in the Registered File Type list box. Or you can exclude files by custom file type by typing a period and then the file extension in the Custom File Mask box. For example, you could choose .DOC or type the customer type .WBK.

5. Enter a drive or file path in Applies To Path. Files will then be restricted from all subfolders of that path unless you clear the Applies To All Subfolders check box. For example, if you use C:\ and select Applies To All Subfolders, all files ending with the designated file extension are excluded wherever they occur on the C drive. Click OK.

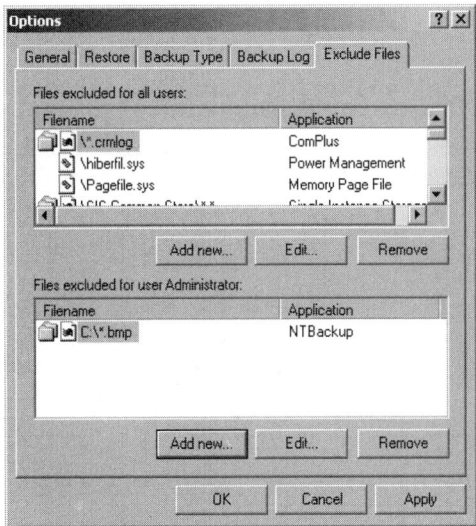

Figure 14-3. *Viewing existing file exclusions for users.*

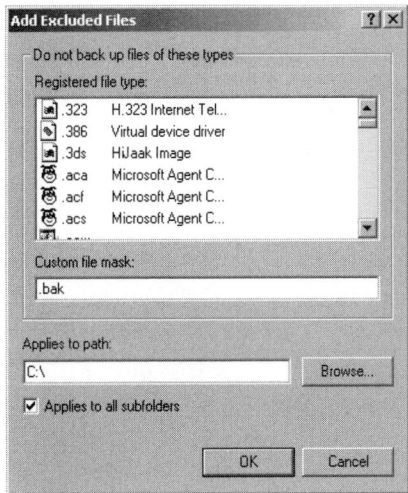

Figure 14-4. *Setting file exclusions for users.*

Changing exclusions To change existing exclusions, follow these steps:

1. In the Options dialog box, choose the Exclude Files tab.

2. Select an existing exclusion you want to edit, and then click Edit. You can now edit the file exclusion.

3. Select an existing exclusion you want to remove, and then click Remove. The exclusion is removed. Click Apply when you're finished.

Backing Up Data with the Backup Wizard

The procedures you use to work with the Backup Wizard are similar to those you use to back up data manually. You start and work with the wizard by completing the following steps:

1. Start Backup. In the Welcome tab, click Backup Wizard, and then click Next.

 Note You can select files in the Backup tab and then start the Backup Wizard. If you do this, you'll be given the opportunity to back up the selected files only. Clicking Yes takes you directly to the dialog box. Clicking No clears the selected files and starts the wizard as usual.

2. Select what you want to back up. The options are

   * **Back Up Everything On My Computer** Back up all data on the computer, including the system state data.

   * **Back Up Selected Files, Drives, Or Network Data** Only back up data you select.

   * **Only Back Up The System State Data** Create a backup of the system state data.

 Note For Windows 2000 Professional and servers that aren't domain controllers, system state data includes essential boot and system files, the Windows registry, and the COM+ class registration database. For domain controllers, system state data includes Active Directory directory service data and files stored on the system volume (Sysvol) as well.

3. Click next. If you wanted to select data to back up, choose the items you want to back up:

   * You make selections by selecting or clearing the check boxes associated with a particular drive or folder. When you select a drive's check box, all the files and folders on the drive are selected. When you clear a drive's check box, all the files and folders on the drive are cleared.

   * If you want to work with individual files and folders on a drive, click the plus sign (+) to the right of the drive icon. You can now select and clear individual directories and files by clicking their associated check boxes. When you do this, the drive's check box shows a shaded checkmark. This indicates that you haven't selected all the files on the drive.

4. Click Next, and then select the Backup Media Type. Choose File if you want to back up to a file. Choose a storage device if you want to back up files and folders to a tape or removable disk.

Tip   When you write backups to a file, the backup file normally has the .BKF file extension. However, you can use another file extension if you want. Also, keep in mind that Removable Storage is used to manage tapes and removable disks. If no media are available, you'll be prompted to allocate media to the Backup media pool. Follow the instructions given in the section of this chapter entitled "Managing Media Pools."

5. In Backup Media Or File Name, select the backup file or media you want to use. If you're backing up to a file, type a path and file name for the backup file or click Browse to find a file. If you're backing up to a tape or removable disk, choose the tape or disk you want to use.

6. Click Next. Click Advanced if you want to override default options or schedule the backup to be run as a job. Then follow steps 7–12. Otherwise, skip to step 13.

7. Select the type of backup to perform. The available types are Normal, Copy, Differential, Incremental, and Daily.

8. To back up data that has been designated for Remote Storage, select Backup Migrated Remote Storage Data. Placeholder files for Remote Storage are then archived with the backup, which ensures that you can recover an entire file system with necessary Remote Storage references intact.

9. You can now set these options for verification and compression:

   - **Verify Data After Backup**   Instructs Backup to verify data after the backup procedure is completed. If selected, every file on the backup tape is compared to the original file. Verifying data can protect against write errors or failures.

   - **Use Hardware Compression, If Available**   Allows Backup to compress data as it's written to the storage device. The option is only available if the device supports hardware compression, and only compatible drives can read the compressed information, which may mean that only a drive from the same manufacturer can recover the data.

10. Set options for copying data to the designated file, tape, or removable disk. To add the backup after existing data, select Append This Backup To The Media. To overwrite existing data, select Replace The Data On The Media With This Backup. If you're overwriting data, you can specify that only the owner and an administrator can access the archive file by selecting Allow Only The Owner And Administrator Access.

11. Next, type a backup label and a media label, if desired. The backup label applies to the current backup only. The media label sets the label for a tape or removable disk.

Note   The media label is only changed when you're writing to a blank tape or overwriting existing data.

12. Determine when the backup will run. Select Now to run the backup now or select Later to schedule the backup for a specific run date. If you want to schedule the backup for a later date, type and confirm your password when prompted. Afterward, type a job name, click Set Schedule, and then set a run schedule as explained in the section of Chapter 4 entitled "Scheduling Tasks."

13. Click Finish to start the backup using the default backup options. This starts the backup operation. You can cancel the backup by clicking Cancel in the Set Information and Backup Progress dialog boxes.

14. During backup operations, the Backup utility behaves differently depending on the type and status of a file. If a file is open, the utility generally attempts to back up the last saved version. If the file is locked by an exclusive lock, it isn't backed up at all. The utility also doesn't back up any files on the exclusion list and only backs up system state data if you've elected to do so.

15. When the backup is completed, click Close to complete the process or click Report to view the backup log.

 Tip If you don't want to view the backup log now or if you scheduled backups for later, you can read the backup log later. Backup logs are written as ASCII text files and are stored in %USERPROFILE%\Local Settings\Microsoft\WindowsNT\ NTBackup\Data. To find the backup log you want to use, check the time/date stamp on the backup log file. Backup logs are named in the format backup##.log, where backup01.log is the initial log created by Backup.

Backing Up Files Without the Wizard

You don't have to use a wizard to back up files. You can configure backups manually by completing the following steps:

1. Start Backup, and then click the Backup tab, shown in Figure 14-5.

2. Clear any existing selections in the Backup tab by selecting New from the Job menu and clicking Yes when prompted.

3. Choose the data you want to back up:

   • You make selections by selecting or clearing the check boxes associated with a particular drive or folder. When you select a drive's check box, all files and folders on the drive are selected. When you clear a drive's check box, all files and folders on the drive are cleared.

   • If you want to work with individual files and folders on a drive, click the plus sign (+) to the right of the drive icon. You can now select and clear individual directories and files by clicking their associated check boxes. When you do this, the drive's check box shows a shaded checkmark. This indicates that you haven't selected all the files on the drive.

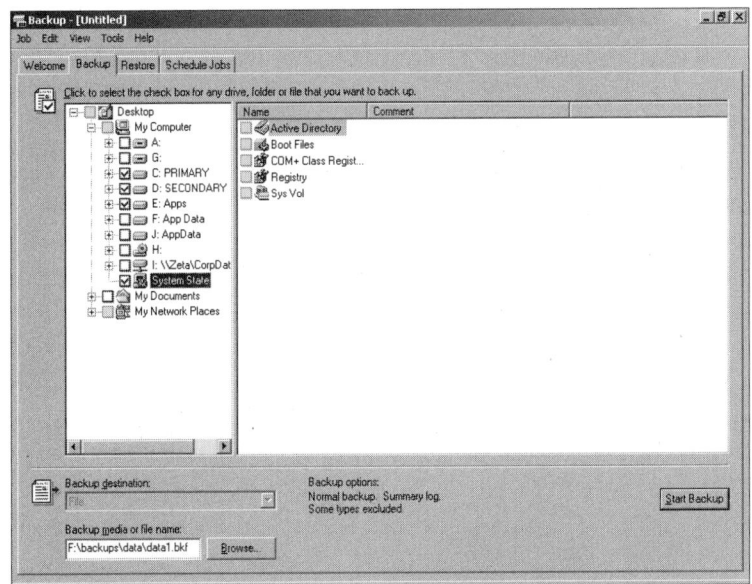

Figure 14-5. *Use the Backup tab to configure backups by hand, and then click Start Backup.*

- If you want to back up system state data, select System State below the My Computer node. For Windows 2000 Professional and servers that aren't domain controllers, system state data includes essential boot and system files, the Windows registry, and the COM+ class registration database. For domain controllers, system state data includes Active Directory data and Sysvol files as well.

- If you're backing up Microsoft Exchange server, be sure to select the Microsoft Exchange icon below the My Computer node. When you do this, you'll be prompted to type the Universal Naming Convention (UNC) name of the Microsoft Exchange server you want to backup, such as **CorpMail.**

4. Use the Backup Destination selection list to choose the media type for the backup. Choose File if you want to back up to a file. Choose a storage device if you want to back up files and folders to a tape or removable disk.

Tip When you write backups to a file, the backup file normally has the .BKF file extension. However, you can use another file extension if you want. Also, keep in mind that Removable Storage is used to manage tapes and removable disks. If no media are available, you'll be prompted to allocate media to the Backup media pool. Follow the instructions given in the section of this chapter entitled "Managing Media Pools."

5. In Backup Media Or File Name, select the backup file or media you want to use. If you're backing up to a file, type a path and file name for the backup file, or click Browse to find a file. If you're backing up to a tape or removable disk, choose the tape or disk you want to use.

6. In the Backup tab, click Start Backup. This displays the Backup Job Information dialog box shown in Figure 14-6. The options in this dialog box are used as follows:

   - **Backup Description**   Sets the backup label, which applies to the current backup only.

   - **Append This Backup To The Media**   Adds the backup after existing data.

   - **Replace The Data On The Media With This Backup**   Over-writes existing data.

   - **If The Media Is Overwritten, Use This Label To Identify The Media**   Sets the media label, which is only changed when you're writing to a blank tape or overwriting existing data.

7. Click Advanced if you want to override the default options. The advanced options are

   - **Back Up Data That Is In Remote Storage**   Archives placeholder files for Remote Storage with the backup. This ensures that you can recover an entire file system with necessary Remote Storage references intact.

   - **Verify Data After Backup**   Instructs Backup to verify data after the backup procedure is completed. If selected, every file on the backup tape is compared to the original file. Verifying data can protect against write errors or failures.

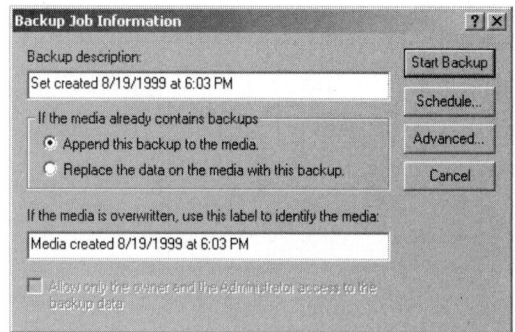

Figure 14-6. *Use the Backup Job Information dialog box to configure backup options and information, as necessary, and then click Start Backup.*

Caution Backing up system protected files can substantially increase the size of the backup. With Windows 2000 Professional, this can add 200+ MB to the size of the backup. With Windows 2000 Server, this can add 700–1000 MB to the size of the backup.

- **If Possible, Compress Backup Data To Save Space** Allows Backup to compress data as it's written to the storage device. This option is available only if the device supports hardware compression, and only compatible drives can read the compressed information, which may mean that only a drive from the same manufacturer can recover the data.

- **Automatically Back Up System Protected Files With The System State** Backs up all the system files in the %SystemRoot% folder, in addition to the boot files that are included with the system state data.

- **Backup Type** Indicates the type of backup to perform. The available types are Normal, Copy, Differential, Incremental, and Daily.

8. Click Schedule if you want to schedule the backup for a later date. When prompted to save the backup settings, click Yes. Next, type a name for the backup selection script, and then click Save. In the Scheduled Job Options dialog box, type a job name, click Properties, and then set a run schedule as explained in the section of Chapter 4 entitled "Scheduling Tasks." Skip the remaining steps.

Note Backup selection scripts and backup logs are stored in %USERPROFILE%\Local Settings\Microsoft\WindowsNT\NTBackup\ Data. Backup selection scripts are saved with the .BKS extension. Backup logs are saved with the .LOG extension. You can view these files with any standard text editor.

9. Click Finish to start the backup using the default backup options. This starts the backup operation. You can cancel the backup by clicking Cancel in the Set Information and Backup Progress dialog boxes.

10. When the backup is completed, click Close to complete the process or click Report to view the backup log.

Recovering Data Using the Restore Wizard

You can restore files with the Windows 2000 Backup utility using the Restore Wizard or the Restore tab. To recover data with the Restore Wizard, follow these steps:

1. Make sure that the backup set you want to work with is loaded into the library system, if possible.

2. Start Backup. In the Welcome tab, click Restore Wizard, and then click Next.

Note You can select files in the Restore tab and then start the Restore Wizard. If you do this, you'll be given the opportunity to restore the selected files only. Clicking Yes takes you directly to the dialog box shown in Figure 14-8. Clicking No clears the selected files and starts the wizard as usual.

3. As shown in Figure 14-7, you can now choose the data you want to restore. The left view displays files organized by volume. The right view displays media sets.

- Select the check box next to any drive, folder, or file that you want to restore. If the media set you want to work with isn't shown, click Import File, and then type the path to the catalog for the backup.

- To restore system state data, select the check box for System State as well as other data you want to restore. If you're restoring to the original location, the current system state will be replaced by the system state data you're restoring. If you restore to an alternate location, only the registry, Sysvol, and system boot files are restored. You can only restore system state data on a local system.

 Tip By default, Active Directory and other replicated data, such as Sysvol, aren't restored on domain controllers. This information is instead replicated to the domain controller after you restart it, which prevents accidental overwriting of essential domain information. To learn how to restore Active Directory, see the "Restoring Active Directory" section of this chapter.

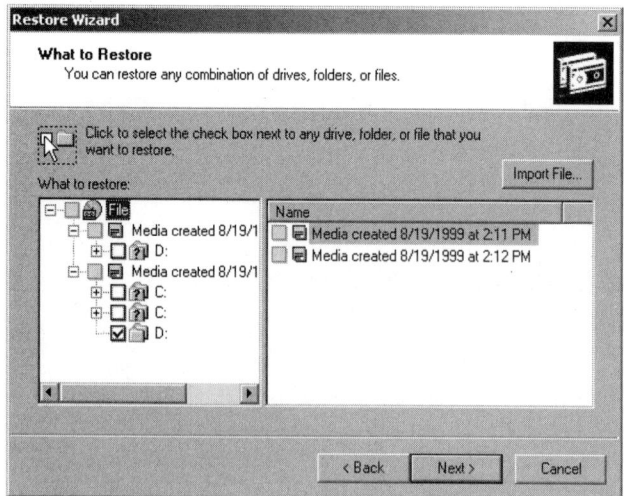

Figure 14-7. *Select the files and folders to restore.*

* If you're restoring Microsoft Exchange, select the Microsoft Exchange data to restore. Before the restore starts, you'll see the Restoring Microsoft Exchange dialog box. If you're restoring the Information Store, type the UNC name of the Microsoft Exchange server you want to restore, such as **CorpMail.** If you're restoring to a different server, select Erase All Existing Data. This destroys all existing data and creates a new Information Store.

4. Click Next. Click Advanced if you want to override default options, and then follow steps 5–7. Otherwise, skip to step 8.

5. Select the restore location using one of the following options:

   * **Original Location**   Restores data to the folder or files it was in when it was backed up.

   * **Alternate Location**   Restores data to a folder that you designate, preserving the directory structure. After selecting this option, enter the folder path to use or click Browse to select the folder path.

   * **Single Folder**   Restores all files to a single folder without preserving the directory structure. After selecting this option, enter the folder path to use or click Browse to select the folder path.

Tip   If you aren't entirely sure that you want to overwrite the files in the original location, select Alternate Path, and then specify a new location for the files, such as **C:\temp.** Once the files are in the temp directory, you can compare them to the existing files and determine if you want to recover them. Keep in mind that you should always restore files backed up from Windows NT file system (NTFS) drives to NTFS drives. This ensures that the security permissions can be restored and that NTFS compression and encryption can be retained.

6. Specify how you want to restore files. The available options are

   * **Do Not Replace The Files On My Computer (Recommended)**   Select this option if you don't want to copy over existing files.

   * **Replace The File On Disk Only If the File On Disk Is Older**   Select this option to replace older files on disk with newer files from the backup.

   * **Always Replace The File On My Computer**   Select this option to replace all the files on disk with files from the backup.

7. If they're available, you can choose to restore security and system files using the following options:

   * **Restore Security**   Restores security settings for files and folders on NTFS volumes.

   * **Restore Removable Storage Database**   Restores the Removable Storage configuration if you archived SystemRoot%\System32\

Ntmsdata. Choosing this option will delete existing Removable Storage information.

- **Restore Junction Points, Not The Folder And File Data They Reference**   Restores network drive mappings but doesn't restore the actual data to the mapped network drive. Essentially, you're restoring the folder that references the network drive.

8. Click Next, and then click Finish. If prompted, type the path and name of the backup set to use. You can cancel the backup by clicking Cancel in the Operation Status and Restore Progress dialog boxes.

9. When the restore is completed, click Close to complete the process or click Report to view a backup log containing information about the restore operation.

Recovering Data Without the Wizard

You don't have to use the Restore Wizard to recover data. You can recover archives manually by completing the following steps:

1. As necessary, load the backup set you want to work with in the library system.

2. Start Backup, and then click the Restore tab, shown in Figure 14-8.

3. Choose the data you want to restore. The left view displays files organized by volume. The right view displays media sets.

   - Select the check box next to any drive, folder, or file that you want to restore. If the media set you want to work with isn't shown, right-click File in the left view, select Catalog, then type the name and path of the catalog you want to use.

   - To restore system state data, select the check box for System State as well as other data you want to restore. If you're restoring to the original location, the current system state will be replaced by the system state data you're restoring. If you restore to an alternate location, only the registry, Sysvol, and system boot files are restored. You can only restore system state data on a local system.

 Tip   By default, Active Directory and other replicated data, such as Sysvol, aren't restored on domain controllers. Instead, this information is replicated to the domain controller after you restart it, which prevents accidental overwriting of essential domain information. To learn how to restore Active Directory, see the section of this chapter entitled "Restoring Active Directory."

   - If you're restoring Microsoft Exchange, select the Microsoft Exchange data to restore. Before the restore starts, you'll see the Restoring Microsoft Exchange dialog box. If you're restoring the Information Store, type the UNC name of the Microsoft Exchange server you want to restore, such as **CorpMail.** If you're restoring to a different server, select Erase All Existing Data. This destroys all existing data and creates a new Information Store.

Note On the Exchange server, the Information Store and Directory services are stopped prior to running the restore. After the restore is finished, you may need to restart these services.

4. Use the Restore Files To selection list to choose the restore location. The options are

- **Original Location** Restores data to the folder or files it was in when it was backed up.

- **Alternate Location** Restores data to a folder that you designate, preserving the directory structure. After you select this option, enter the folder path to use or click Browse to select the folder path.

- **Single Folder** Restores all files to a single folder without preserving the directory structure. After you select this option, enter the folder path to use or click Browse to select the folder path.

5. Specify how you want to restore files. Click Tools, and then select Options. This displays the Options dialog box with the Restore folder selected. The available options are

- **Do Not Replace The Files On My Computer (Recommended)** Select this option if you don't want to copy over existing files.

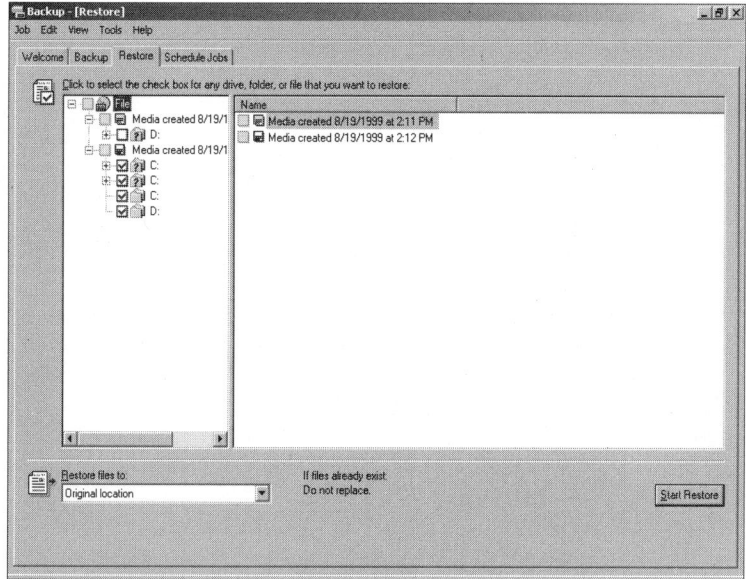

Figure 14-8. *Specify the files and folders to restore.*

- **Replace The File On Disk Only If The File On Disk Is Older** Select this option to replace older files on disk with newer files from the backup.

- **Always Replace The File On My Computer** Select this option to replace all files on disk with files from the backup.

6. In the Restore tab, click Start Restore. This displays the Confirm Restore dialog box.

7. If you want to set advanced restore options, click Advanced, and then set any of the following options:

   - **Restore Security** Select this option to restore security settings for files and folders on NTFS volumes.

   - **Restore Removable Storage Database** Select this option if you archived %SystemRoot%\System32\Ntmsdata and want to restore the Removable Storage configuration. Choosing this option will delete existing Removable Storage information.

   - **Restore Junction Points, And Restore File And Folder Data Under Junction Points To The Original Location** Select this option to restore network drive mappings and the actual data to mapped network drives. Choose this option only if you're trying to recover a drive on a remote system. Otherwise, clear this option to restore folder references to network drives only.

   - **When Restoring Replicated Data Sets, Mark The Restored Data As The Primary Data For All Replicas** Select this option if you're restoring replicated data and want the restored data to be published to subscribers. If you don't choose this option, the data may not be replicated because it will appear older than existing data on the subscribers.

   - **Preserve Existing Volume Mount Points** Select this option if you're restoring an entire file system (which includes the volume mount points) and want to retain the current mount points rather than those in the archive. This option is useful if you've remapped a drive and created additional volumes and want to keep the current volume mappings.

8. In the Confirm Restore dialog box, click OK to start the restore operation. If prompted, enter the path and name of the backup set to use. You can cancel the backup by clicking Cancel in the Operation Status and Restore Progress dialog boxes.

9. When the restore is completed, you can click Close to complete the process or click Report to view a backup log containing information about the restore operation.

Restoring Active Directory

When restoring system state data to a domain controller, you must choose whether you want to perform an authoritative or nonauthoritative restore. The default is nonauthoritative. In this mode, Active Directory and other replicated data is restored using the information from other domain controllers. Thus, you can safely restore a failed domain controller without overwriting the latest Active Directory information. On the other hand, if you're trying to restore Active Directory throughout the network using archived data, you must use authoritative restore. With authoritative restore, the restored data is restored on the current domain controller and then replicated to other domain controllers.

To restore Active Directory on a domain controller and enable the restored data to be replicated throughout the network, follow these steps:

1. Make sure the domain controller server is shut down.
2. Restart the domain controller server. When you see the prompt Please Select The Operating System To Start, press F8 to enter ~~Safe Mode~~. *Boot Loader Menu*
3. Select Directory Services Restore Mode.
4. When the system starts, use the Backup utility to restore the system state data and other essential files. *2) Command Prompt help*
5. After restoring the data, but before restarting the server, use the Ntdsutil tool to mark objects as authoritative. Be sure to check the Active Directory data thoroughly. *Type Authoritating Restore Type Restore Database*
6. Restart the server. When the system finishes startup, the Active Directory data should begin to replicate throughout the domain.

Backing Up and Restoring Data on Remote Systems

You can use the Windows 2000 Backup utility to back up data on remote systems. To do this, you must create network drives for the remote file systems before you begin the backup procedure. When backing up data on network drives, be sure to select the General option Back Up The Contents Of Mounted Drives. If you don't, only folder references are backed up and not the actual data.

You can also use Backup to restore data on Remote Systems. When you do this, you can select restore locations in My Network Places. If you're restoring to a mapped network drive instead of to a specific system, be sure to select the advanced restore option Restore Junction Points, And Restore File And Folder Data Under Junction Points To The Original Location.

Disaster Recovery and Preparation

Backups are only one part of a comprehensive disaster recovery plan. You also need to have Emergency Repair disks and Boot disks on hand to ensure that you can recover systems in a wide variety of situations. You may also need to install the Recovery Console.

When you set out to recover a system, you should follow these steps:

1. Try to start the system in Safe Mode, as described in the section of this chapter entitled "Starting a System in Safe Mode."

2. Try to recover the system using the Emergency Repair disk (if available). See the section of this chapter entitled "Using the Emergency Repair Disk to Recover a System."

3. Try to recover the system using the Recovery Console. See the section of this chapter entitled "Working with the Recovery Console."

4. Restore the system from backup. Be sure to restore the system state data as well as any essential files.

Creating an Emergency Repair Disk

The Emergency Repair disk can often help you recover a system that won't boot. This disk stores the essential system files, partition boot sector, and startup environment for a particular system. You should create a repair disk for each computer on the network, starting with Windows 2000 servers. Normally, you'll want to update this disk when you install service packs, manipulate the boot drive, or modify the startup environment.

 Tip When you completed the installation of the operating system, basic recovery information was saved in the %SystemRoot%\Repair folder on the system partition. The Repair folder contains a copy of the local Security Account Manager (SAM) data and other essential system files. It doesn't contain a backup of the Windows registry. You should create a registry backup when you create the Emergency Repair disk.

You can create an Emergency Repair disk by completing the following steps:

1. Start Backup. In the Welcome tab, click Emergency Repair Disk.

2. When prompted as shown in Figure 14-9, insert a blank 3.5-inch, 1.44-MB disk into the floppy drive.

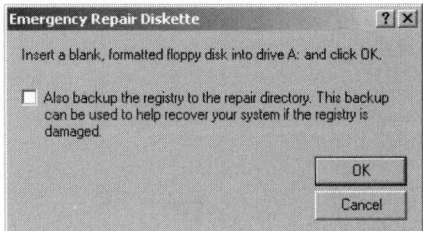

Figure 14-9. *Insert a blank disk at prompt. You can also back up the registry.*

3. If you want to back up the registry as well, select Also Backup The Registry To The Repair Directory. A backup of the Windows registry will then be made

in the %SystemRoot%\Repair folder. If you need to restore the registry, you must use the Recovery Console.

4. Click OK. When prompted, remove the disk and label it as an emergency repair disk for the system.

Creating Setup Boot Disks

You should create boot disks for each version of Windows 2000 running on the network. For example, if you're running Windows 2000 Professional and Windows 2000 Server, you should create boot disks for both of these versions. You use the boot disks to start a system that won't boot so that you can use the Emergency Repair disk or the Recovery Console to fix the system.

Note If all of your computers can boot from CD-ROM, you don't need the setup boot disks. Just insert the Windows 2000 CD-ROM when starting the system.

To create boot disks, follow these steps:

1. Insert the Windows 2000 CD into the CD-ROM drive.

2. Click the Start menu, and then click Run.

3. In the Run dialog box, type **h:\bootdisk\makeboot a:** where h is the CD-ROM drive letter and a is the floppy drive letter. Click OK.

4. You'll need four blank disks. When prompted, insert a blank 3.5-inch, 1.44-MB disk. Then press any key.

5. When prompted, remove the disk and label it as 1 of 4. Repeat this procedure for the remaining disks.

Starting a System in Safe Mode

If a system won't boot normally, you can use Safe Mode to recover or troubleshoot system problems. In Safe Mode, Windows 2000 loads only basic files, services, and drivers. The drivers loaded include the mouse, monitor, keyboard, mass storage, and base video. No networking services or drivers are started—unless you choose the Safe Mode With Networking option. Because Safe Mode loads a limited set of configuration information, it can help you troubleshoot problems. In most cases, you'll want to use Safe Mode before trying to use the Emergency Repair disk or the Recovery Console.

You start a system in Safe Mode by completing the following steps:

1. Start (or restart) the problem system.

2. During startup you should see a prompt labeled Please Select The Operating System To Start. Press F8.

3. Use the arrow keys to select the Safe Mode you want to use, and then press ENTER. The Safe Mode option you use depends on the type of problem you're experiencing. The key options you may see are

- **Safe Mode**   Loads only basic files, services, and drivers during the initialization sequence. The drivers loaded include the mouse, monitor, keyboard, mass storage, and base video. No networking services or drivers are started.

- **Safe Mode With Command Prompt**   Loads basic files, services, and drivers, and then starts a command prompt instead of the Windows 2000 graphical interface. No networking services or drivers are started.

- **Safe Mode With Networking**   Loads basic files, services, and drivers, as well as services and drivers needed to start networking.

- **Enable Boot Logging**   Allows you to create a record of all startup events in a boot log.

- **Enable VGA Mode**   Allows you to start the system in Video Graphics Adapter (VGA) mode, which is useful if the system display is set to a mode that can't be used with the current monitor.

- **Last Known Good Configuration**   Starts the computer in Safe Mode using registry information that Windows 2000 saved at the last shutdown.

- **Directory Services Recovery Mode**   Starts the system in Safe Mode and allows you to restore the directory service. Option available on Windows 2000 domain controllers.

- **Debugging Mode**   Starts the system in debugging mode, which is only useful for troubleshooting operating system bugs.

4. If a problem doesn't reappear when you start in Safe Mode, you can eliminate the default settings and basic device drivers as possible causes. If a newly added device or updated driver is causing problems, you can use Safe Mode to remove the device or reverse the update.

Using the Emergency Repair Disk to Recover a System

When you can't start or recover a system in Safe Mode, your next step is to try to recover the system using the Emergency Repair disk. This disk comes in handy in two situations. If the boot sector or essential system files are damaged, you may be able to use the repair disk to recover the system. If the startup environment is causing problems on a dual or multi-boot system, you may be able to recover the system as well. You can't recover a damaged registry, however. To do that, you must use the Recovery Console.

You can repair a system using the Emergency Repair disk by completing the following steps:

1. Insert the Windows 2000 CD or the first setup boot disk into the appropriate drive, and then restart the computer. When booting from a floppy disk, you'll need to remove and insert disks when prompted.

2. When the Setup program begins, follow the prompts, and then choose the Repair Or Recover option by pressing R.

3. If you haven't already done so, insert the Windows 2000 CD in the appropriate drive when prompted.

4. Choose emergency repair by pressing R, and then do one of the following:

   - **Press M For Manual Repair**   Select this option to choose whether you want to repair system files, the partition boot sector, or the startup environment. Only advanced users or administrators should use this option.

   - **Press F For Fast Repair**   Select this option to have Windows 2000 attempt to repair problems related to system files, the partition boot sector, and the startup environment.

5. Insert the Emergency Repair disk when prompted. Damaged or missing files are replaced with files from the Windows 2000 CD or from the %SystemRoot%\ Repair folder on the system partition. These replacement files will not reflect any configuration changes made after setup, and you may need to reinstall service packs and other updates.

6. If the repair is successful, the system is restarted and should boot normally. If you still have problems, you may need to use the Recovery Console.

Working with the Recovery Console

The Recovery Console is one of your last lines of defense in recovering a system. The Recovery Console operates much like the command prompt and is ideally suited to resolving problems with files, drivers, and services. Using the Recovery Console, you can fix the boot sector and master boot record; enable and disable device drivers and services; change the attributes of files on FAT (file allocation table), FAT32, and NTFS volumes; read and write files on FAT, FAT32, and NTFS volumes; copy files from floppy or CD to hard disk drives; and run check disk and format drives.

The sections that follow discuss techniques you can use to work with the Recovery Console. As you'll learn, you can start the Recovery Console from the setup boot disks or you can install the Recovery Console as a startup option.

Installing the Recovery Console as a Startup Option

On a system with frequent or recurring problems, you may want to install the Recovery Console as a startup option. In this way, you don't have to go through the setup boot disks to access the Recovery Console. You can only use this option if the system is running. If you can't start the system, see the section of this chapter entitled "Starting the Recovery Console."

You install the Recovery Console as a startup option by completing the following steps:

1. Insert the Windows 2000 CD into the CD-ROM drive.

2. Click the Start menu, and then click Run. This displays the Run dialog box.

3. Type **h:\i386\winnt32.exe /cmdcons** in the Open field, where h is the CD-ROM drive letter.

4. Click OK, and then when prompted, click Yes. The Recovery Console is then installed as a startup option.

 Note Normally, only administrators can install and run the Recovery Console. If you want normal users to be able to run the Recovery Console, you must enable the Auto Admin Logon policy for the local computer policy (Computer Configuration/Windows Settings/Security Settings/Local Policies/Security Options/Auto Admin Logon).

Starting the Recovery Console

If a computer won't start and you haven't installed the Recovery Console as a startup option, you can start the computer and the Recovery Console by completing the following steps:

1. Insert the Windows 2000 CD or the first setup boot disk into the appropriate drive, and then restart the computer. When booting from a floppy disk, you'll need to remove and insert disks when prompted.

2. When the Setup program begins, follow the prompts, and then choose the Repair Or Recover option by pressing R.

3. If you haven't already done so, insert the Windows 2000 CD into the appropriate drive when prompted.

4. Choose Recovery Console by pressing C. When prompted, type the local administrator password.

5. When the system starts, you'll see a command prompt into which you can type Recovery Console commands. Exit the console and restart the computer by typing **exit.**

Recovery Console Commands

The Recovery Console is run in a special command prompt. At this command prompt, you can use any of the commands summarized in Table 14-5.

Table 14-5. Recovery Console Commands

Command	Description
ATTRIB	Changes the attributes of a file or directory.
BATCH	Executes a series of commands set in a text file.
CD	Changes the current directory.
CHKDSK	Runs the Chkdsk utility to check the integrity of a disk.
CLS	Clears the screen.
COPY	Copies a single file to another location.
DEL	Deletes one or more files.

(continued)

Table 14-5. *(continued)*

Command	Description
DIR	Displays a directory listing.
DISABLE	Disables a system service or a device driver.
DISKPART	Manages partitions on hard disk drives.
ENABLE	Starts or enables a system service or a device driver.
EXIT	Exits the Recovery Console and restarts your computer.
EXPAND	Expands a compressed file.
FIXBOOT	Writes a new partition boot sector.
FIXMBR	Repairs the master boot record.
FORMAT	Formats a disk.
HELP	Displays a list of Recovery Console commands.
LISTSVC	Lists the services and drivers available on the computer.
LOGON	Logs on to a Windows 2000 installation.
MAP	Displays drive letter mappings.
MD	Creates a directory.
MORE	Displays a text file one page at a time.
REN	Renames a single file.
RD	Removes a directory.
SET	Displays and sets environment variables.
SYSTEMROOT	Changes to the systemroot directory.
TYPE	Displays a text file.

Deleting the Recovery Console

If you installed Recovery Console as a startup option and no longer want this option to be available, you can delete the Recovery Console. To do that, follow these steps:

1. Start Windows Explorer, and then select the hard disk drive on which you installed the Recovery Console. This is normally the boot drive.
2. From the Tools menu, select Folder Options.
3. In the View tab, select Show Hidden Files And Folders, and then clear the Hide Protected Operating System Files check box. Click OK.
4. The right pane should show the root directory for the boot drive. Delete the Cmdcons folder and the Cmldr file.
5. Right-click the Boot.ini file, and then click Properties.
6. In the Properties dialog box, clear the Read-Only check box. Then click OK.
7. Open Boot.ini in Notepad. Then remove the startup entry for the Recovery Console. The entry looks like this:

```
C:\CMDCONS\BOOTSECT.DAT="Microsoft   Windows   2000   Recovery
Console"  /cmdcons
```

8. Save the Boot.ini file, and then change its property settings back to read-only.

Once deleted, the Recovery Console is no longer listed as a startup option. You can reinstall the console if you need to at a later date or run the console as described in the "Starting the Recovery Console" section of this chapter.

Managing Media Pools

Collections of tapes are organized into media pools. The tasks you use to work with media pools are explained in the following sections.

Understanding Media Pools

You manage media pools through the Removable Storage node in Computer Management. With Removable Storage all media belongs to a pool of a specific media type. The concept of a media pool is very dynamic. Libraries can have multiple media pools, and some media pools can span multiple libraries.

You can also use media pools to establish a hierarchy in which top-level media pools contain lower-level media pools and these media pools in turn contain collections of tapes or discs.

Removable Storage categorizes media pools into types. The different types of media pools are

- **Unrecognized** Media pools containing media that Removable Storage doesn't recognize, as well as new media that hasn't been written to yet. To make Unrecognized media available for use, move the media to the Free media pool. If you eject the media before doing this, the media are automatically deleted from the Removable Storage database and no longer tracked.

- **Free** Media pools containing media that aren't currently in use and don't contain useful data. These media are available for use by applications.

- **Import** Media pools containing media that Removable Storage recognizes but that haven't been used before in a particular Removable Storage system. For example, if you're transferring media from one office to another, the media may be listed as Import. To reuse the media at the new location, move the media to Free media or Application media pools.

- **Application** Media pools containing media that are allocated to and controlled by an application, such as Windows 2000 Backup. Members of the Administrators and the Backup Operators groups can control Application media pools as well. You can configure Application media pools to automatically draw media from Free media pools, as necessary. Once they're allocated, you can't move Application media between media pools.

Free, Unrecognized, and Import media pools are referred to as *system media* pools. Unlike Application media pools that you can delete, you can't delete system media pools.

Preparing Media for Use in the Free Media Pool

If media have information that you don't need anymore, you can initialize the media and prepare them for use in the Free media pool. When you do this, you destroy the information on the media and move the media to the Free media pool.

To prepare media for the Free media pool, follow these steps:

1. In Computer Management, access Removable Storage, and then double-click Physical Locations.
2. Expand the library and the library's Media folder by double-clicking them.
3. Right-click the media you want to prepare, and then click Prepare.
4. Confirm the action by clicking Yes.

Moving Media to a Different Media Pool

You can move media to a different media pool to make it available for use or to allocate it to an application. To do that, follow these steps:

1. In Computer Management, access Removable Storage, and then double-click Physical Locations.
2. Expand the library and the library's Media folder by double-clicking them.
3. In the Details pane, drag the media you want to move to the applicable media pool in the console tree.

Caution Moving media to the Free media pool destroys the data on the media. Additionally, you can't move read-only media to the Free media pool.

Creating Application Media Pools

The only type of media pool you can create is an Application media pool. To do this, follow these steps:

1. In Removable Storage, right-click Media Pools, and then click Create Media Pool. Or right-click an existing Application media pool and then click Create Media Pool.
2. In the Create New Media Pool Properties dialog box, type a name and description of the media pool.
3. If the media pool will contain other media pools, select Contains Other Media Pools. Otherwise, click Contains Media Of Type, and select an appropriate media type from the list.
4. Complete the process by clicking OK. As necessary, allocate media and configure security. These procedures are described in the "Setting Allocation and Deallocation Policies" and "Setting Access Permissions for Removable Storage" sections of this chapter.

Changing the Media Type in a Media Pool

Each media pool can only contain one type of media. The media type is normally assigned when you create the media pool, but you can change the media type, provided no media is currently assigned to the media pool.

To change the media type, follow these steps:

1. In Removable Storage, double-click Media Pools.
2. Right-click the media pool you want to work with, and then select Properties.
3. In the General tab, select Contains Media Of Type, and then select an appropriate media type from the list. Click OK.

Setting Allocation and Deallocation Policies

You can configure Application media pools to automatically allocate and deallocate Free media. By enabling this process, you ensure that when an application needs media, the application can obtain it. Then, when the media is no longer needed, it can be returned to the Free media pool.

You configure allocation and deallocation of media by completing the following steps:

1. In Removable Storage, double-click Media Pools.
2. Right-click the media pool you want to work with, and then select Properties. This media pool must contain media of a specific type and can't be a container for other media pools.
3. In the General tab, use the following check boxes under Allocation/Deallocation Policy to control media allocation:

   * **Draw Media From Free Media Pool**   Select this option to automatically draw unused media from a Free media pool when needed.

   * **Return Media To Free Media Pool**   Select this option to automatically return media to a Free media pool when no longer needed.

   * **Limit Reallocations**   Select this option if you want to limit the number of times that tapes or discs can be reused. Then use the Reallocations field to set a specific limit.

4. Click OK.

Deleting Application Media Pools

In Removable Storage, you delete Application media pools by right-clicking them and selecting Delete. Do this only if you no longer need the media pool.

 Note   You shouldn't delete Application media pools created by Windows 2000, such as Backup and Remote Storage. These are used by the operating system.

Part IV

Microsoft Windows 2000 Network Administration

In Part IV of this book, "Microsoft Windows 2000 Network Administration," we'll discuss advanced network administration tasks. Chapter 15 provides the essentials for installing, configuring, and testing TCP/IP networking on Microsoft Windows 2000 systems. Chapter 16 begins with a troubleshooting guide for common printer problems, and then goes on to explain procedures for installing and configuring local printers and network print servers. Chapter 17 provides details on managing DHCP clients and servers. Chapter 18 explores tasks for configuring WINS clients and servers. Finally, Chapter 19 covers tasks for setting up DNS on Windows 2000 networks.

Chapter 15
Managing TCP/IP Networking

As an administrator, you enable networked computers to communicate by using the basic networking protocols built into Microsoft Windows 2000. The key protocol you'll use is Transmission Control Protocol/Internet Protocol (TCP/IP). TCP/IP is actually a collection of protocols and services used for communicating over a network. It's the primary protocol used for internetwork communications. Compared to configuring other networking protocols, configuring TCP/IP communications is fairly complicated, but TCP/IP is the most versatile protocol available.

In this chapter you'll learn about configuring and managing TCP/IP networking. Whenever you work with TCP/IP networking, you must tell the computer about the network. You do this by telling the computer how to route information on the network and how to access other computers. Once you configure TCP/IP, you also need to make the computer a member of the network so it can access network resources.

More Info   Group policy can affect your ability to install and manage
TCP/IP networking. Key policies you'll want to examine are those in User
Configuration\Network\Network And Dial-Up Connections and Computer
Configuration\System\Group Policy. Group policy is discussed in Chapter
4.

Installing TCP/IP Networking

TCP/IP networking relies on network adapters and the TCP/IP protocol. To access the network using TCP/IP, you'll need to install one or more network adapters on the computer and then set up the TCP/IP protocol.

Installing Network Adapters

Network adapter cards are hardware devices that are used to communicate on networks. You can install and configure network adapters by completing the following steps:

1. Configure the network adapter card following the manufacturer's instructions. For example, you may need to modify the Interrupt setting or the Port setting of the card by using the software provided by the manufacturer.

2. Disconnect the computer, unplug it, and install the adapter card in the appropriate slot on the computer. When you're finished, boot the system.

3. As Figure 15-1 shows, Windows 2000 should detect the new adapter during startup. If you have a separate driver disk for the adapter, you should insert it now. Otherwise, you may be prompted to insert a driver disk.

4. If Windows 2000 doesn't detect the adapter automatically, follow the installation instructions in the section of Chapter 2 entitled "Managing Hardware Devices and Drivers."

5. If networking services aren't installed on the system, install them as described in the next section.

Installing the TCP/IP Protocol

TCP/IP networking is normally installed during Windows 2000 installation. You can also install TCP/IP networking through Network And Dial-Up Connections. If you're installing TCP/IP after installing Windows 2000, log on to the computer using an account with Administrator privileges and then follow these steps:

1. Network And Dial-Up Connections is shown in Figure 15-2. Access this dialog box by clicking Start, then Settings, and then selecting Network And Dial-Up Connections.

2. Local area network (LAN) connections are created automatically if the computer has a network adapter and is connected to a network. If a computer has multiple adapter cards and is connected to a network, you'll see one LAN connection for each adapter card. If no network connection is available, you should connect the computer to the network or create a different type of connection, as explained in the section of this chapter entitled "Managing Network Connections."

3. Each network connection is configured separately. Right-click the network connection you want to work with, and then click Properties. This opens the Local Area Network Connection Properties dialog box.

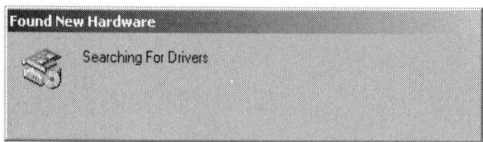

Figure 15-1. *Windows 2000 automatically detects plug and play devices.*

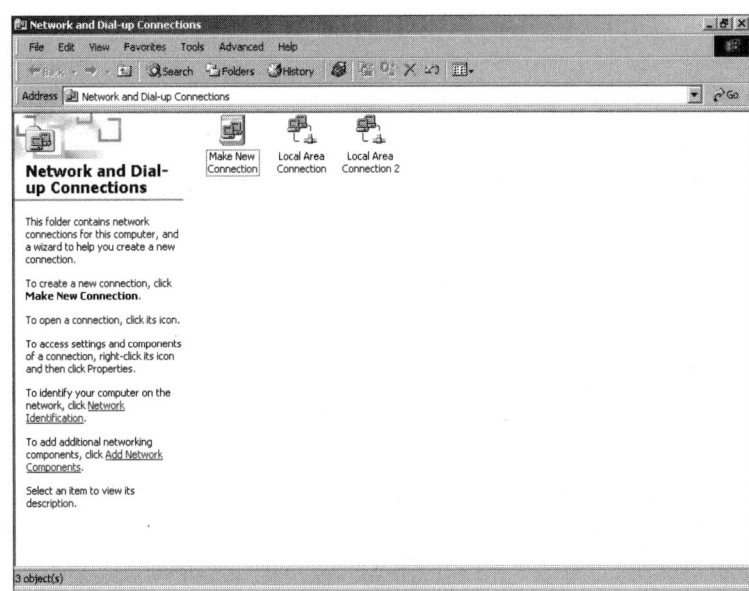

Figure 15-2. *Network connections can be managed in Network And Dial-Up Connections. You'll find one local area network connection for each adapter card.*

4. If Internet Protocol (TCP/IP) isn't shown in the list of installed components, you'll need to install it. Click Install. Click Protocol, and then click Add. In the Select Network Protocol dialog box, click Internet Protocol (TCP/IP), and then click OK.

5. Make sure that the Internet Protocol (TCP/IP) check box is selected, and then click OK.

6. As necessary, follow the instructions in the next section for configuring TCP/IP for the computer.

Configuring TCP/IP Networking

Computers use IP addresses to communicate over TCP/IP. Windows 2000 provides two ways to configure IP addressing:

- **Dynamically** A Dynamic Host Configuration Protocol (DHCP) server (if one is installed on the network) assigns dynamic IP addresses at startup, and the addresses may change over time. Dynamic IP addressing is the default configuration and is set up automatically in most cases on Windows 2000 Professional.

- **Manually** IP addresses that are assigned manually are called *static* IP addresses. Static IP addresses are fixed and don't change unless you change them. You'll usually assign static IP addresses to Windows 2000 servers, and when you do this, you'll need to configure additional information to help the server navigate the network.

Configuring Static IP Addresses

When you assign a static IP address, you need to tell the computer the IP address you want to use, the subnet mask for this IP address, and, if necessary, the default gateway to use for internetwork communications. The IP address is a numeric identifier for the computer. IP addressing schemes vary according to how your network is configured, but they're normally assigned from a range of addresses for a particular network segment. For example, if you're working with a computer on the network segment 192.168.10.0, the address range you have available for computers is usually from 192.168.10.1 to 192.168.10.254. The address 192.168.10.255 normally is reserved for network broadcasts.

If the network is connected directly to the Internet and you've reserved a range of IP addresses, you can use the IP addresses you've been assigned. If you're on a private network that is indirectly connected to the Internet, you should use private IP addresses. Private network addresses are summarized in Table 15-1.

Table 15-1. Private Network Addresses

Private Network ID	Subnet Mask	IP Address Range
10.0.0.0	255.0.0.0	10.0.0.1 – 10.255.255.254
172.16.0.0	255.240.0.0	172.16.0.1 – 172.31.255.254
192.168.0.0	255.255.0.0	192.168.0.1 – 192.168.255.254

All other network addresses are public and must be leased or purchased.

Using "Ping" to Check an Address

Before you assign an IP address, you should make sure that the address isn't already in use or reserved for use with DHCP. You can check to see if an address is in use with the Ping utility. Open a command prompt and type **ping,** followed by the IP address you want to check. To test the IP address 192.168.10.12, you would use the following command:

```
ping 192.168.10.12
```

Assigning a Static IP Address

You assign a static IP address by doing the following:

1. Access Network And Dial-Up Connections by clicking Start, then Settings, and then selecting Network And Dial-Up Connections.

2. Right-click the network connection you want to work with, and then select Properties. This opens the dialog box shown in Figure 15-3. The dialog box may look slightly different if you aren't using Internet Connection Sharing.

3. Open the Internet Protocol (TCP/IP) Properties dialog box shown in Figure 15-4 by double-clicking Internet Protocol (TCP/IP). Or you could select Internet Protocol (TCP/IP) and then click Properties.

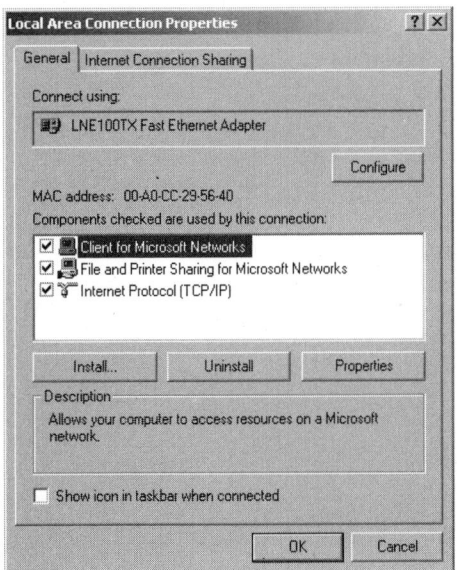

Figure 15-3. *The Local Area Connection Properties dialog box lists the currently installed networking components.*

Note LAN connections are created automatically when you start a computer that's attached to a network; you don't need to create a connection. One LAN connection is shown for each network adapter installed. If you use a dial-up or other type of connection, you must create the connection as described in the "Managing Network Connections" section of this chapter.

4. Select the Use The Following IP Address button, then type the IP address in the IP Address field. The IP address you assign to the computer must not be used anywhere else on the network.

5. The Subnet Mask field ensures that the computer communicates over the network properly. Windows 2000 should insert a default value for the subnet mask into the Subnet Mask field. If the network doesn't use subnets, the default value should suffice. But if it does use subnets, you'll need to change this value as appropriate for your network.

6. If the computer needs to access other TCP/IP networks, the Internet, or other subnets, you must specify a default gateway. Type the IP address of the network's default router in the Default Gateway field.

7. When you're finished, click OK. Repeat this process for other network adapters you want to configure. Keep in mind that each network adapter must have a unique IP address.

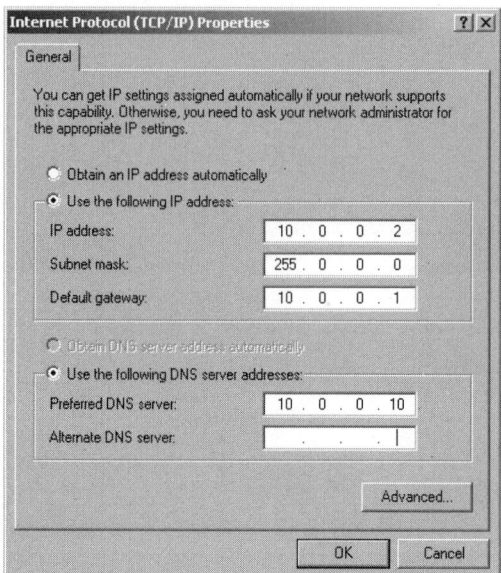

Figure 15-4. *Use the Internet Protocol (TCP/IP) Properties dialog box to configure dynamic and static IP addressing.*

8. Configure Domain Name Service (DNS) and Windows Internet Naming Service (WINS) as necessary.

Configuring Dynamic IP Addresses

DHCP gives you centralized control over IP addressing and TCP/IP default settings. If the network has a DHCP server, you can assign a dynamic IP address to any of the network adapter cards on a computer. Afterward, you rely on the DHCP server to supply the basic information necessary for TCP/IP networking. Because the dynamic IP address can change, you shouldn't use a dynamic IP address for Windows 2000 servers. You configure dynamic IP addressing by completing the following steps:

1. Access Network And Dial-Up Connections by clicking Start, then Settings, and then selecting Network And Dial-Up Connections.

2. Right-click the network connection you want to work with, and then select Properties. If a connection isn't available, see the section of this chapter entitled "Managing Network Connections."

3. Open the Internet Protocol (TCP/IP) Properties dialog box by double-clicking Internet Protocol (TCP/IP). Or you could select Internet Protocol (TCP/IP) and then click Properties.

4. Select Obtain An IP Address Automatically.

Note One local area network connection is shown for each network adapter installed. These connections are created automatically.

5. If desired, select Obtain DNS Server Address Automatically.

6. When you're finished, click OK.

Configuring Multiple IP Addresses and Gateways

Windows 2000 computers can have multiple IP addresses—even if the computers only have a single network adapter card. Multiple IP addresses are useful in several situations:

- You want a single computer to appear to be several different computers. For example, if you're installing an intranet server, you may also want the server to provide Web, File Transfer Protocol (FTP), and Simple Mail Transfer Protocol (SMTP) services. You can use a different IP address for each service, and you can use different IP addresses for the intranet and the FTP services.

- If your network is divided into multiple logical IP networks (subnets), and the computer needs access to these subnets to route information or provide other internetworking services, you may want a single network adapter card to have multiple IP addresses. For example, the address 192.168.10.8 could be used for workstations accessing a server from the 192.168.10.0 subnet, and the address 192.168.11.8 could be used for workstations accessing a server from the 192.168.11.0 subnet.

Caution When you use a single network adapter, IP addresses must be assigned to the same network segment or segments that are part of a single logical network. If your network is divided into multiple physical networks, you must use multiple network adapters, with each network adapter being assigned an IP address in a different physical network segment.

Assigning Addresses and Gateways

Each network adapter installed on a computer can have one or more IP addresses. These addresses can also be associated with one or more default gateways. You assign multiple IP addresses and gateways to a single network adapter card by doing the following:

1. Access Network And Dial-Up Connections by clicking Start, then Settings, and then selecting Network And Dial-Up Connections.

2. Right-click the network connection you want to work with, and then select Properties. If a connection isn't available, see the "Managing Network Connections" section of this chapter.

3. Open the Internet Protocol (TCP/IP) Properties dialog box by double-clicking Internet Protocol (TCP/IP). Or you could select Internet Protocol (TCP/IP) and then click Properties.

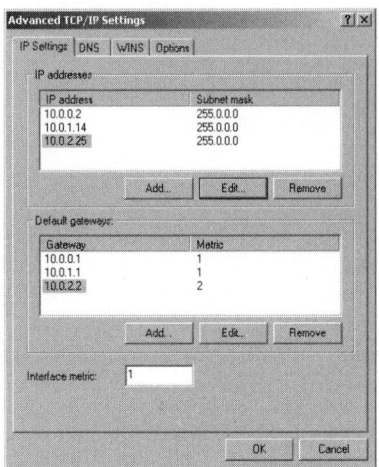

Figure 15-5. *Use the Advanced TCP/IP Settings dialog box to configure multiple IP addresses and gateways.*

4. Click Advanced to open the dialog box shown in Figure 15-5.

5. In the IP Settings tab, click Add in the IP Addresses area, and then type the IP address in the IP Address field and the subnet mask in the Subnet Mask field. Repeat this step for each IP address you want to add to the network adapter card.

6. You can enter additional default gateways, as necessary. Click Add, and then type the gateway address in the Gateway field and a metric in the Metric field. Repeat this step for each gateway you want to add.

 Tip The metric indicates the relative cost of using a gateway. If there are multiple default routes available for a particular IP address, the gateway with the lowest cost is used first. If the computer can't communicate with the initial gateway, Windows 2000 tries to use the gateway with the next lowest metric.

Configuring DNS Resolution

DNS is a host name resolution service. You use DNS to determine the IP address of a computer from its host name. This allows users to work with host names, such as *http://www.msn.com* or *http://www.microsoft.com*, rather than an IP address, such as 192.168.5.102 or 192.168.12.68. DNS is the primary name service for Windows 2000 and the Internet.

 Tip A DNS server must be installed on the network (or be available to the network) for DNS to function properly. Managing DNS servers is covered in Chapter 19.

Basic DNS Settings

You can configure basic DNS settings by completing the following steps:

1. Access Network And Dial-Up Connections by clicking Start, then Settings, and then selecting Network And Dial-Up Connections.

2. Right-click the network connection you want to work with, and then select Properties. If a connection isn't available, see the "Managing Network Connections" section of this chapter.

3. Open the Internet Protocol (TCP/IP) Properties dialog box by double-clicking Internet Protocol (TCP/IP). Or you could select Internet Protocol (TCP/IP) and then click Properties.

4. If the computer is using DHCP and you want DHCP to specify the DNS server address, select Obtain DNS Server Address Automatically. Otherwise, select Use The Following DNS Server Addresses and then type a primary and alternate DNS server address in the fields provided.

Advanced DNS Settings

You configure advanced DNS settings by using the DNS tab of the Advanced TCP/IP Settings dialog box shown in Figure 15-6. You use the fields of the DNS tab as follows:

- **DNS Server Addresses, In Order Of Use**   Use this area to specify the IP address of the DNS servers that are used for domain name resolution. Use the Add button to add a server IP address to the list. Use the Remove button to remove a server from the list. Use the Edit button to edit the selected entry. You can specify multiple servers to use for DNS resolution. These servers are used in priority order. If the first server isn't available to respond to a host name resolution request, the next DNS server on the list is accessed, and so on. It's important to note that TCP/IP doesn't go to the next server if the first server can't resolve the name, only if the first server doesn't respond. To change the position of a server in the list box, click it and then use the Up or Down arrow button.

- **Append Primary And Connection Specific DNS Suffixes**   Select this option to resolve unqualified computer names in the primary domain. For example, if the computer name "Rage" is used and the parent domain is microsoft.com, the computer name would resolve to rage.microsoft.com. If the fully qualified computer name doesn't exist in the parent domain, the query fails. The parent domain used is the one set in the Network Identification tab of the System Properties dialog box. Normally, this option is selected by default.

- **Append Parent Suffixes Of The Primary DNS Suffix**   Select this option to resolve unqualified computer names using the parent-child domain hierarchy. If a query fails in the immediate parent domain, the suffix for the parent of the parent domain is used to try to resolve the query. This process continues until the top of the DNS domain hierarchy is reached. For example, if the computer name "Rage" is used in the dev.microsoft.com domain, DNS would attempt to resolve the computer name to rage.dev.microsoft.com. If

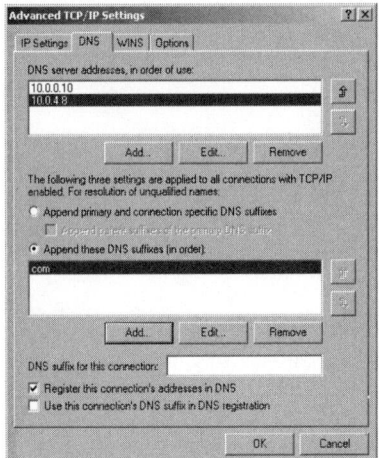

Figure 15-6. *Use the DNS tab of the Advanced TCP/IP Settings dialog box to configure advanced DNS settings.*

this didn't work, DNS would attempt to resolve the computer name to rage.microsoft.com. Normally, this option is selected by default.

- **Append These DNS Suffixes (In Order)** Select this option to set specific DNS suffixes to use rather than resolving through the parent domain. Use the Add button to add a domain suffix to the list. Use the Remove button to remove a domain suffix from the list. Use the Edit button to edit the selected entry. You can specify multiple domain suffixes. These suffixes are used in priority order. If the first suffix doesn't resolve properly, DNS attempts to use the next suffix in the list. If this fails, the next suffix is used, and so on. To change the order of the domain suffixes, select the suffix, and then use the Up or Down arrow buttons to change its position.

- **DNS Suffix For This Connection** Sets a specific DNS suffix for the connection that overrides DNS names already configured for use on this connection. You'll usually want to set the DNS domain name through the Network Identification tab of the System Properties dialog box instead.

- **Register This Connection's Addresses In DNS** Select this option if you want all IP addresses for this connection to be registered in DNS under the computer's fully qualified domain name. This option is selected by default.

- **Use This Connection's DNS Suffix In DNS Registration** Select this option if you want all IP addresses for this connection to be registered in DNS under the parent domain.

Configuring WINS Resolution

You use WINS to resolve NetBIOS computer names to IP addresses. You can use WINS to help computers on a network determine the address of other computers on the network. If a WINS server is installed on the network, you can use the server to resolve computer names. While WINS is supported on all versions of Windows, Windows 2000 primarily uses WINS for backward compatibility.

You can also configure Windows 2000 computers to use the local file LMHOSTS to resolve NetBIOS computer names. However, LMHOSTS is consulted only if normal name resolution methods fail. In a properly configured network these files are rarely used. Thus, the preferred method of NetBIOS computer name resolution is WINS in conjunction with a WINS server.

You can configure WINS by completing the following steps:

1. Access the Advanced Internet Protocol (TCP/IP) Properties dialog box, and then click the WINS tab. This displays the window shown in Figure 15-7.

2. The box named WINS Addresses, In Order Of Use allows you to specify the IP address of the WINS servers that are used for NetBIOS name resolution. Use the Add button to add a server IP address to the list. Use the Remove button to remove a server from the list. Use the Edit button to edit the selected entry.

3. You can specify multiple servers to use for WINS resolution. These servers are used in priority order. If the first server isn't available to respond to a NetBIOS name resolution request, the next WINS server on the list is accessed, and so on. It's important to note that TCP/IP doesn't go to the next server if the first server can't resolve the name, only if the first server doesn't respond. To change the position of a server in the list box, click it and then use the Up or Down arrow button.

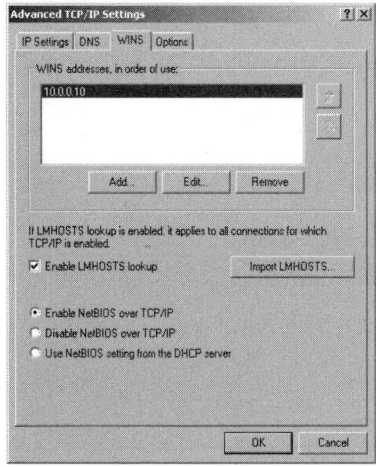

Figure 15-7. *Use the WINS tab of the Advanced TCP/IP Settings dialog box to configure WINS resolution for NetBIOS computer names.*

4. To enable LMHOSTS lookups, select the Enable LMHOSTS Lookup check box. If you want the computer to use an existing LMHOSTS file defined somewhere on the network, retrieve this file with the Import LMHOSTS button. You generally use LMHOSTS only when other name resolution methods fail.

 Best Practice LMHOSTS files are maintained locally on a computer-by-computer basis, which can eventually make them unreliable. Rather than relying on LMHOSTS, ensure that your DNS and WINS servers are configured properly and are accessible to the network. This way, you can ensure centralized administration of name resolution services.

5. NetBIOS Over TCP/IP services are required for WINS name resolution. If you use DHCP and dynamic addressing, you can get the NetBIOS setting from the DHCP server. Select Use NetBIOS Setting From The DHCP Server. Otherwise, enable or disable NetBIOS by selecting Enable NetBIOS Over TCP/IP or Disable NetBIOS Over TCP/IP.

6. Repeat this process for other network adapters, as necessary.

Configuring Additional Networking Components

You can configure Windows 2000 systems to use additional networking clients, services, and protocols. You install these networking components through the Network Connection Properties dialog box or through the Windows Optional Networking Components Wizard. Each one offers different components.

Installing and Uninstalling Networking Components

You use the Network Connection Properties dialog box to install networking clients, services, and protocols. Table 15-2 provides a brief overview of the various network components you can install using this dialog box. Some components are only available on Windows 2000 servers.

Table 15-2. Network Components Available on Windows 2000

Component	Description
Client for Microsoft Networks	Allows the computer to access resources on Windows networks.
Gateway (and Client) Services for NetWare	Allows the computer to access NetWare networks.
File and Printer Sharing for Microsoft Networks	Allows other computers to access resources on the computer.
AppleTalk Protocol	Allows other computers to communicate with the computer through the AppleTalk protocol. Allows Windows 2000 servers to be AppleTalk routers.

(continued)

Table 15-2. *(continued)*

Component	Description
NWLink NetBIOS	Enables the computer to communicate with NetWare servers running NetBIOS.
NWLink IPX/SPX/ NetBIOS Compatible Transport Protocol	Enables the computer to communicate with NetWare servers running IPX/SPX.
Network Monitor Driver	Driver that allows Netmon to capture network packets. Netmon is the network monitor utility.
QoS Packet Scheduler	Quality of Service packet scheduler, which provides network traffic control services.
SAP Agent	Installs Service Advertising Protocol Agent, which advertises servers and addresses on the network.
DLC Protocol	Installs Data Link Control, which enables the computer to connect to an IBM mainframe.
NetBEUI Protocol	NetBIOS Enhanced User Interface is the standard Microsoft protocol for network communications on Windows NT.

You install and uninstall these network components by completing the following steps:

1. Access Network And Dial-Up Connections by clicking Start, then Settings, and then selecting Network And Dial-Up Connections.

2. Right-click the network connection you want to work with, and then select Properties. If a connection isn't available, see the "Managing Network Connections" section of this chapter.

3. The Network Connection Properties dialog box shows a list of components currently installed.

4. To disable a component, clear its related check box.

5. To uninstall a component, select it, and then click Uninstall. Confirm the action by clicking Yes when prompted.

6. To install additional components, click Install. This displays the Select Network Component Type dialog box. Select the type of network component by choosing Client, Protocol, or Service and then clicking Add. Select the component to add.

Installing Optional Networking Components

You can install additional networking components through the Windows Optional Networking Components Wizard. When you install these components, Windows 2000 may also install utilities that the components need in order to operate. These utilities are installed in the Administrative Tools (Common) folder.

Table 15-3 provides a brief overview of optional network components you can install. The component package is the name of the component shown in the

Windows Components dialog box. The individual component names are the components you can select individually through the Details button. Some components are only available on Windows 2000 servers.

Table 15-3. Optional Network Components Available on Windows 2000

Component Package	Individual Component Name	Description
Management and Monitoring Tools	Connection Manager Components	Installs the Connection Manager Administration Kit and the Phone Book Service.
	Network Monitor Tools	Installs network monitoring tools for analyzing network traffic.
	Simple Network Management Protocol (SNMP)	Installs SNMP and SNMP agents.
Networking Services	COM Internet Services Proxy	Allows distributed Component Object Model (COM) objects to travel over Hypertext Transfer Protocol (HTTP).
	Domain Name System (DNS)	Allows the computer to be configured as a DNS server.
	Dynamic Host Configuration Protocol (DHCP)	Allows the computer to be configured as a DHCP server.
	Internet Authentication Service	Allows authentication, authorization, and accounting of dial-up and Virtual Private Network (VPN) users.
	QoS Admission Control Service	Allows you to control the quality of network connections.
	Simple TCP/IP Services	Installs the basic TCP/IP services Character Generator, Daytime, Discard, Echo, and Quote of the Day.
	Site Server ILS Services	Allows site server to update directory information.
	Windows Internet Naming Service (WINS)	Allows the computer to be configured as a WINS server.
Other Network File and Print Services *(continued)*	File Services for Macintosh	Enables Macintosh users to work with files on a Windows 2000 server.

Table 15-3. *(continued)*

Component Package	Individual Component Name	Description
	Print Services for Macintosh	Enables Macintosh users to send print jobs to a print spooler on a Windows 2000 server.
	Print Services for Unix	Enables Unix users to send print jobs to a print spooler on a Windows 2000 server.

Install optional networking components by completing the following steps:

1. Access Network And Dial-Up Connections by clicking Start, then Settings, and then selecting Network And Dial-Up Connections.

2. Click Add Network Components. This starts the Windows Optional Networking Components Wizard. Click Next.

3. As shown in Figure 15-8, you can now select component packages to install by selecting any of the following: Management And Monitoring Tools, Networking Services, or Other Network File And Print Services.

4. To select or cancel individual components, select a component category and then click Details.

5. Click OK, and then click Next. The selected components are then installed.

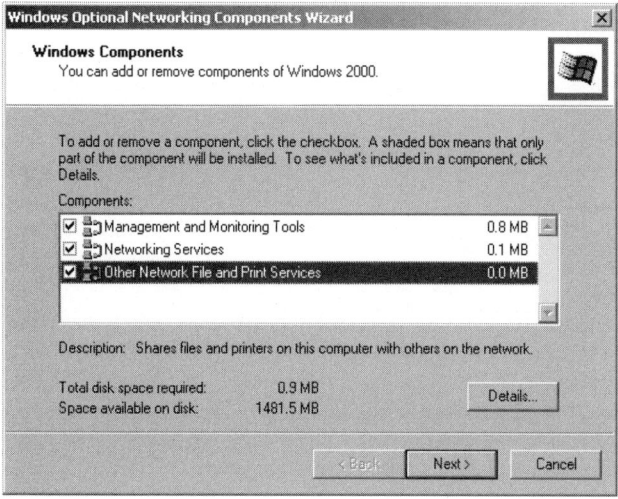

Figure 15-8. *Select the components to add. Click Details to select individual components.*

Managing Network Connections

Dial-up and network connections make it possible for computers to access remote resources. This section examines techniques you can use to create and manage network connections. Keep in mind that local area connections are created automatically when you start a computer that's attached to a network; you don't need to create this type of connection.

Creating Network Connections

You can configure many different types of dial-up and network connections. You create connections by completing the following steps:

1. Access Network And Dial-Up Connections by clicking Start, then Settings, and then selecting Network And Dial-Up Connections.

2. Double-click Make New Connection. This starts the Network Connection Wizard. Click Next. If prompted, enter your telephone area code and dialing information.

3. Select the type of connection you want to make (see Figure 15-9). The available options are

   - **Dial-Up To Private Network**   Enables a computer to connect to a corporate network using remote access. Dial-up connections use modems or Integrated Services Digital Network (ISDN) lines.

   - **Dial-Up To The Internet**   Enables a computer to connect to the Internet using remote access. Dial-up connections use modems or ISDN lines. Once you set up a connection to an Internet service provider, you can share the connection, which allows one computer to provide access for other computers.

   - **Connect To A Private Network Through The Internet**   Enables a computer to connect securely to a corporate network over the Internet. A secure VPN connection is established using Point To Point Tunneling Protocol (PPTP) or Layer 2 Tunneling Protocol (L2TP).

   - **Accept Incoming Connections**   Enables a computer to access incoming calls through remote access services. If a computer accepts VPN, direct, or dial-up connections, you need to configure incoming connections as well.

   - **Connect Directly To Another Computer**   Enables a computer to connect directly to another computer through a serial, parallel, or infrared port. This type of link is commonly used to synchronize a handheld computer with a PC.

4. The dialog boxes you see depend on the type of connection. Follow the onscreen prompts. When you're done, click Finish and the connection is created.

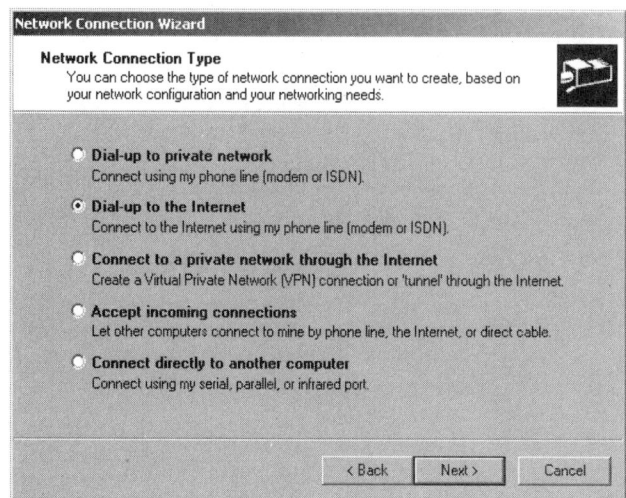

Figure 15-9. *Select the type of connection and then create it.*

Enabling and Disabling Network Connections

Local area network connections are created and connected automatically. If you want to disconnect from the network or start another connection, you can complete the following steps:

1. Access Network And Dial-Up Connections by clicking Start, then Settings, and then selecting Network And Dial-Up Connections.

2. Right-click the connection, and then select Disconnect to deactivate the connection.

3. Later, if you want to activate the connection, you can right-click it and then select Connect.

Deleting Network Connections

If they aren't needed anymore, you can delete network connections that you created. To do that, follow these steps:

1. Access Network And Dial-Up Connections by clicking Start, then Settings, and then selecting Network And Dial-Up Connections.

2. Right-click the connection, and then select Delete. When prompted, confirm the action by clicking Yes.

Note You can't delete a local area network connection. This connection is managed by Windows 2000.

Modifying and Duplicating Connections

You can modify the properties of a connection by right-clicking the connection and then selecting Properties. But before you make changes that may invalidate the connection, you may want to create a copy of the existing connection. Right-click the connection, and then select Create Copy. You can only create copies of connections you create and not local area network connections.

Testing the TCP/IP Configuration

Whenever you install a new computer or make configuration changes to the computer's network settings, you should test the configuration. The most basic TCP/IP test is to use the PING command to test the computer's connection to the network. Ping is a command-line utility and is used as follows:

```
ping host
```

where host is the host computer you're trying to reach.

On Windows 2000, there are several ways to test the configuration using Ping:

- **Try to Ping IP addresses**   If the computer is configured correctly and the host you're trying to reach is accessible to the network, Ping should receive a reply. If Ping can't reach the host, Ping will time out.

- **On domains that use WINS, try to Ping NetBIOS computer names**   If NetBIOS computer names are resolved correctly, the NetBIOS facilities, such as WINS, are correctly configured for the computer.

- **On domains that use DNS, try to Ping DNS host names**   If fully qualified DNS host names are resolved correctly, DNS name resolution is configured properly.

You may also want to test network browsing for the computer. If the computer is a member of a Windows 2000 domain and computer browsing is enabled throughout the domain, log on to the computer and then use the Windows Explorer or My Network Places to browse other computers in the domain. Afterward, log on to a different computer in the domain and try to browse the computer you just configured. These tests tell you if the DNS resolution is being handled properly in the local environment. If you can't browse, check the configuration of the DNS services and protocols.

Chapter 16

Administering Network Printers and Print Services

As an administrator, you need to do two main things so users throughout a network can access print devices connected to a Microsoft Windows 2000 workstation or server: you need to set up a workstation or server as a print server, and you need to use the print server to share print devices on the network.

This chapter covers the basics of setting up shared printing and accessing it from the network. You'll also find advice on administering printers and troubleshooting printer problems, which is where we'll begin. The chapter doesn't examine Internet printing.

Note In Windows 2000 the terms used for printers and print devices are slightly different than the conventional ones. In Windows 2000 a *print device* is the actual hardware device that produces printed output. Print devices attached locally to print servers are known as *local* print devices. Print devices attached directly to a network are referred to as *network interface* print devices. A *printer*, on the other hand, is the software interface between the operating system and the print device. Printers are installed on print servers. Further, it's important to note that in documentation and dialog windows, these terms are sometimes used as if they're interchangeable. If this happens, focus on whether the developers are referring to a physical device (a print device) or a software interface (a printer).

Troubleshooting Printer Problems

An understanding of how printing works can go a long way when you're trying to troubleshoot printer problems. When you print documents, many processes, drivers, and devices work together so that the documents are printed. If you use a printer connected to a printer server, the key operations are as follows:

- **Printer driver** When you print a document in an application, your computer loads a printer driver. If the print device is attached to your computer physically, the printer driver is loaded from a local disk drive. If the print device is located on a remote computer, the printer driver may be downloaded from the remote computer.

The availability of printer drivers on the remote computer is configurable by operating system and chip architecture. If the computer can't obtain the latest printer driver, it's probably because an administrator hasn't enabled the driver for the computer's operating system. For more information, see the section of this chapter entitled "Managing Printer Drivers."

- **Local print spool and print processor** The application you're printing from uses the printer driver to translate the document into a file format understandable by the selected print device. Then your computer passes the document off to the local print spooler. The local spooler in turn passes the document to a print processor, which creates the raw print data necessary for printing on the print device.

- **Print router and print spooler on the print server** The raw data is passed back to the local print spooler. If you're printing to a remote printer, the raw data is then routed to the print spooler on the print server. On Windows 2000 systems, the printer router, WINSPOOL.EXE, handles the tasks of locating the remote printer, routing print jobs, and downloading printer drivers to the local system, if necessary. If any one of these tasks fails, the print router is usually the culprit. See the sections of this chapter entitled "Solving Spooling Problems" and "Setting Printer Access Permissions" to learn possible fixes for this problem. If these procedures don't work, you may want to replace or restore WINSPOOL.EXE.

  The main reason for downloading printer drivers to clients is to provide a single location for installing driver updates. This way, instead of having to install a new driver on all the client systems, you install the driver on the print server and allow clients to download the new driver. For more information on working with printer drivers, see the section of this chapter entitled "Managing Printer Drivers."

- **Printer (print queue)** The document goes from the print spooler into the printer stack—which in some operating systems is called the print queue—for the selected print device. Once in the queue, the document is referred to as a *print job*—a task for the print spooler to handle. The length of time the document waits in the printer stack is based on its priority and position within the printer stack. For more information, see the section of this chapter entitled "Scheduling and Prioritizing Print Jobs."

- **Print monitor** When the document reaches the top of the printer stack, the print monitor sends the document to the print device, where it's actually printed. If the printer is configured to notify users that the document has been printed, you see a message confirming this.

  The specific print monitor used by Windows 2000 depends on the print device configuration and type. The default monitor is LOCALMON.DLL. You may also see monitors from the print device manufacturer, such as HPMON.DLL, which is used with most Hewlett-Packard print devices. This DLL (dynamic link-library) is required to print to the print device. If it's corrupted or missing, you may need to reinstall it.

- **Print device** The print device is the physical device that prints documents on paper. Common print device problems and display errors include
  - **Insert Paper Into Tray X** Print device is looking for paper in a specific tray. Add paper to it.
  - **Low Toner** When a laser print device gets low on toner, you may need to remove the toner cartridge, shake it several times, and put it back into the print device. Shaking the cartridge moves the toner around and sometimes allows you to print additional documents.
  - **Out Of Paper** Print device is out of paper (or thinks it is). Add paper.
  - **Out Of Toner; Out Of Ink** Print device is out of toner or ink. Replace the toner cartridge or ink cartridge.
  - **Paper Jam** Paper is stuck in the print device. Open the print device, remove the jammed paper, and then put the print device back on line.
  - **Printer Off-Line** Print device may be warming up or initializing. If so, the print device should come online when finished. Otherwise, you'll need to put the print device back online using the print device control buttons.

Group policy can affect your ability to install and manage printers. If you're having problems and believe they are related to group policy, the key policies you'll want to examine are those in

- Computer Configuration\Printers
- User Configuration\Control Panel\Printers
- User Configuration\Start Menu & Taskbar

Installing Printers

The following sections examine techniques you can use to install printers. Windows 2000 allows you to install and manage printers anywhere on the network. You install and manage printers through the Printers folder. On a local system, you access this folder by clicking Start, choosing Settings, and then selecting Printers. On a remote system, you can access this folder through My Network Places. In My Network Places, access a domain, select a computer whose printer settings you want to manage, and then double-click Printers.

Using Local and Network Printers

Two types of print devices are used on a network:

- **Local print device** A print device that's physically attached to the user's computer and employed only by the user who's logged on to that computer.
- **Network print device** A print device that is set up for remote access over the network. This can be a print device attached directly to a print server or a print device attached directly to the network through a network adapter card.

You install new network printers on print servers or as separate print devices attached to the network. A *print server* is a Windows 2000 workstation or server that is configured to share one or more printers. These printers can be physically attached to the computer or the network.

Any Windows 2000 workstation or server can be configured as a print server. The primary job of the print server is to share the print device out to the network and to handle print spooling. The main advantages of print servers are that the printer will have a centrally managed print queue and you don't have to install printer drivers on client systems.

 Note Print servers on Windows 2000 Professional are limited to 10 concurrent connections from other computers and don't support printing from Macintosh or NetWare clients.

You don't have to use a print server, however. You can connect users directly to a network-attached printer. When you do this, the network printer is handled much like a local printer attached directly to the user's computer. The key differences are that multiple users can connect to the printer and that each user will have a different print queue. Each individual print queue is managed separately, which can make administration and problem resolution difficult.

To install or configure a new printer, you must be a member of one of the privileged groups shown in Table 16-1.

Table 16-1. Groups Who Can Configure Printers, According to System Type

Group	Windows 2000 Professional	Windows 2000 Server
Administrators	X	X
Power Users	X	
Print Operators		X
Server Operators		X

To connect to and print documents to the printer, you must have the appropriate access permissions. See the section of this chapter entitled "Setting Printer Access Permissions" for details.

Installing Print Devices on a Local or Remote Print Server

You install a print device on a print server by completing the following steps:

1. Access the Printers folder on the computer you want to configure as a print server. On a local system, you access this folder by clicking Start, choosing Settings, and then selecting Printers. On a remote system, you can access this folder through My Network Places. In My Network Places, access a domain, select a computer whose printer settings you want to manage, and then double-click Printers.

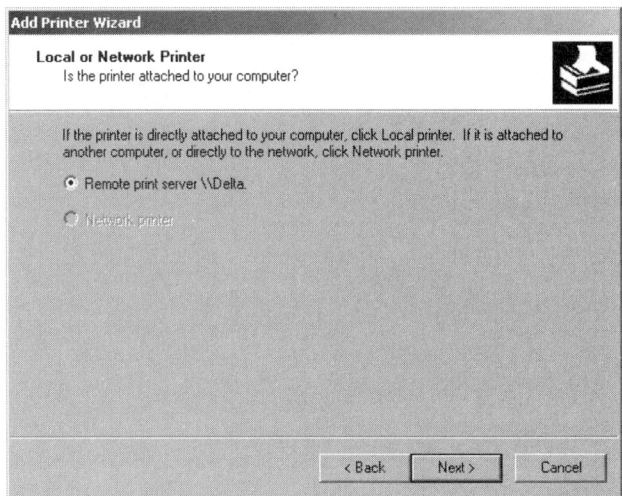

Figure 16-1. *You can configure network print servers remotely, but you'll have to go through a few extra steps.*

2. Double-click the Add Printer icon to open the Add Printer Wizard. Click Next.

3. If you're accessing the computer remotely, you'll see a dialog box similar to the one shown in Figure 16-1. The Remote Print Server option is selected automatically and can't be changed. Click Next.

4. If you're accessing the computer through a local logon, you'll see a dialog box similar to the one shown in Figure 16-2. Select Local Printer, and then specify that you want Windows 2000 to try to automatically detect a plug and play printer. Click Next.

5. During installation of a new network printer, Windows 2000 can automatically detect a new print device that is physically attached to a local or remote print server. But the print device must be plug and play compatible. The way you continue depends on whether the print device is found.

Print Device Found

If Windows 2000 finds the new print device, you see a dialog box similar to the one shown in Figure 16-3. Windows 2000 will begin installing the device and the necessary drivers. If the necessary drivers aren't found, you may need to insert the Windows 2000 CD into the CD-ROM drive or a driver disk into the floppy disk drive. Complete the installation by following these steps:

1. After configuring the print device, the Add Printer Wizard will give you the opportunity to print a test. Select Yes to print a test page. Otherwise select No.

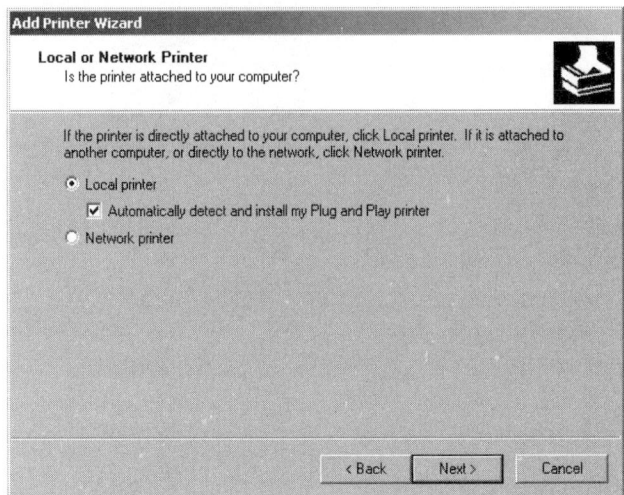

Figure 16-2. *You can also configure network print servers through a local logon.*

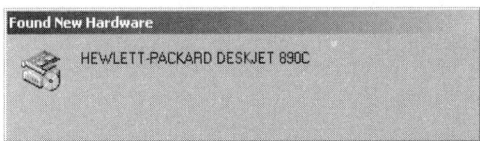

Figure 16-3. *If you see the Found New Hardware dialog box, a new print device has been detected and Windows 2000 is installing it.*

2. Click Next , and then click Finish to complete the printer installation. The Add Printer Wizard sets the printer name and sharing automatically. By default, the printer name is set to the printer model. For example, if you install an HP DeskJet 890 C printer, the printer name would be set to HP DeskJet 890 C.

3. If you configured the printer on a Windows 2000 workstation, the printer is now available for local access but isn't available for network access. You'll need to share the printer. Right-click the printer icon in the Printers folder, and then select Sharing. In the Properties dialog box, select Shared As, and then type a name for the printer share. In a large organization, you'll want the share name to be logical and helpful in locating the printer. For example, you may want to name the printer that points to the print device in the northeast corner of the twelfth floor TwelveNE.

4. If you configured the printer on a Windows 2000 server, the printer is shared automatically. The share name is set to the first eight characters of the printer name—not including spaces. Any spaces in the printer name are omitted. Thus, the printer name HP DeskJet 890C is set to the printer share HPDeskJet.

You may want to rename the printer share. If you do, follow the procedure outlined in step 3.

Print Device Not Found

If Windows 2000 doesn't find the new print device, you see a dialog box similar to the one shown in Figure 16-4. Click Next. You'll then need to manually install the print device by completing the following steps:

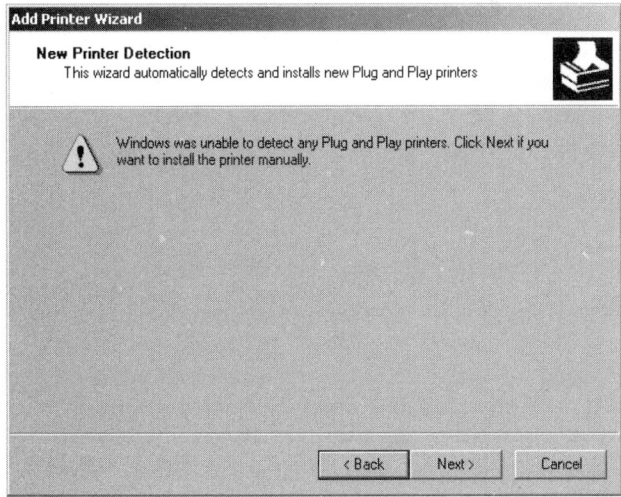

Figure 16-4. *If you see the Add Printer Wizard dialog box, Windows 2000 didn't find the new print device. You'll need to manually install the print device.*

1. You need to configure the port used by the printer (see Figure 16-5).

   * For a print device physically connected to the print server, select the appropriate LPT or COM port. You can also print to a file. If you do, Windows 2000 prompts users for a file name each time they print. Click Next, and then skip steps 2–8.

   * For a print device physically connected to the network, click Create A New Port, and then select Standard TCP/IP Port. Click Next to start the Add Standard TCP/IP Printer Port Wizard.

2. In the Standard TCP/IP Printer Port Wizard, type the printer name or IP address for the printer device. A port name is filled in for you automatically. For example, if you type the IP address 192.168.12.8, the port name is entered as IP_192.168.12.8.

Tip The port name doesn't matter as long as it's unique on the system. If you're configuring multiple printers on the print server, be sure to write down the port to printer mapping.

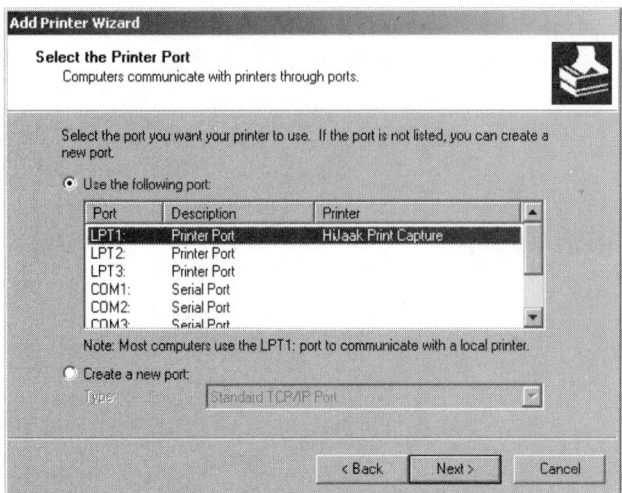

Figure 16-5. *In the Add Printer Wizard window, select a printer port for a local printer or select the Create A New Port option button for a network-attached printer.*

3. Click Next and the wizard will attempt to automatically detect the print device. If the wizard is unable to detect the print device, make sure that

   - The print device is turned on and connected to the network.
   - The printer is configured properly.
   - You typed the correct IP address or printer name in the previous dialog box.

4. Click Back if the IP address or printer name is incorrect and then retype this information.

5. If the information is correct, you may need to identify the device further. In the Device Type area, click Standard, and then select the printer. Or click Custom, and then click Settings to define custom settings for the printer, such as protocol and Simple Network Management Protocol (SNMP) status.

6. Click Next, and then click Finish. This completes the configuration of the new port. You now need to continue with the printer installation in the Add Printer Wizard.

7. As shown in Figure 16-6, you must now specify the print device manufacturer and model. This allows Windows 2000 to assign a printer driver to the print device. After you choose a print device manufacturer, choose a printer model. If the print device manufacturer and model you're using isn't displayed in the list, choose Have Disk to install a new driver.

8. Click Next. If a printer driver is already installed, you can choose to keep the existing driver or replace it. Click Next.

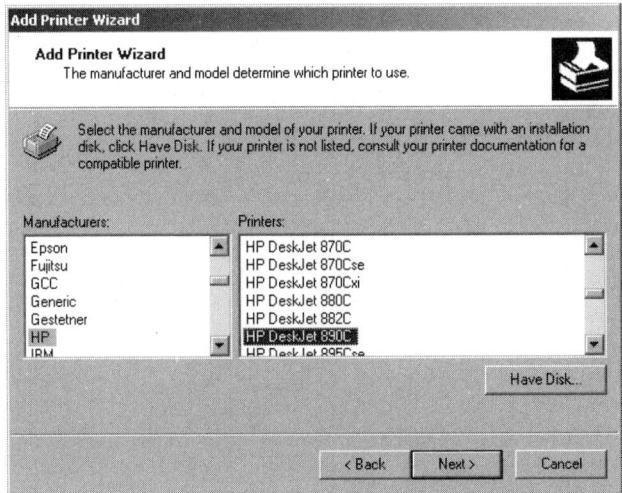

Figure 16-6. *Select a print device manufacturer and printer model with the Add Printer Wizard.*

Note   If a driver for the specific printer model you're using isn't available, you can usually select a generic driver or a driver for a similar print device. Consult the print device documentation for pointers.

9. Assign a name to the printer. This is the name you'll see in the Printers folder of Control Panel. On a local system you can also set the printer as the local default, if you like.

10. Specify whether the printer is available to remote users (see Figure 16-7). To create a network printer that's accessible to remote users, select the Share As option button and enter a name for the shared resource. In a large organization, you'll want the share name to be logical and helpful in locating the printer. For example, you may want to name the printer that points to the print device in the northeast corner of the twelfth floor TwelveNE.

Note   If Windows 3.1 or MS-DOS systems will access the printer, be sure the printer name conforms to the standard MS-DOS naming rule. For example, use the name NORTH12.PRT rather than NORTH_PRINTER_ FLOOR12. For more information on MS-DOS naming, see the section of Chapter 12 entitled "Accessing Long File Names Under MS-DOS."

11. Next, if you want, you can enter a location description and comment. This information can help users find a printer and determine its capabilities.

12. The final window lets you test the installation by printing a test page to the print device. If you want to do this, select Yes. Otherwise select No. When you're ready to complete the installation, click Finish.

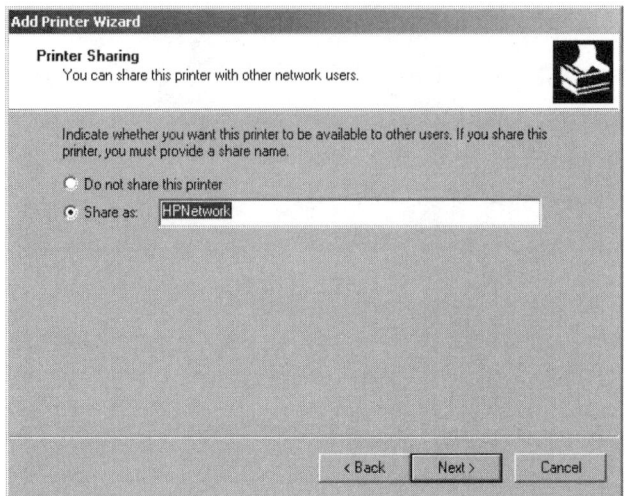

Figure 16-7. *Share the network printer and assign it a name in the Add Printer Wizard.*

When the Add Printer Wizard finishes installing the new printer, the Printers folder in the Control Panel will have an additional icon with the name set the way you specified. You can change the printer properties and status at any time. For more information, see the section of this chapter entitled "Configuring Printer Properties."

 Tip If you repeat this process, you can create additional printers for the same print device. All you need to do is change the printer name and share name. Having additional printers for a single print device allows you to set different properties to serve different needs. For example, you could have a high priority printer for print jobs that need to be printed immediately and a low priority printer for print jobs that aren't as urgent.

Installing Local Print Devices

A local print device is physically connected to a user's computer and accessible only on that computer. Installing printing on a local system is much like installing a print device on a print server. The key difference is that the printer isn't shared. Accordingly, follow the steps for creating a printer specified in the section of this chapter entitled "Installing Print Devices on a Local or Remote Print Server." Specify that the printer is *not* shared.

 Note A local printer can easily be made a network printer. To learn how to do this, see the section of this chapter entitled "Starting and Stopping Printer Sharing."

Connecting to Printers Created on the Network

Once you create a network printer, remote users can connect to it and use it much like any other printer. You'll need to set up a connection on a user-by-user basis or have users do this themselves. To create the connection to the printer on a Windows 2000 system, follow these steps:

1. With the user logged on, double-click the Printers icon in the Control Panel or in the Start menu, select Settings, and then choose the Printers option. This opens the Printers folder.

2. Double-click the Add Printer icon to start the Add Printer Wizard shown.

3. Select the Network Printer option button, and then click Next.

4. In the Locate Your Printer dialog box, shown in Figure 16-8, choose a method for finding the network printer. The available options are

   • **Find A Printer In The Directory**   Choose this option if you want to search Active Directory directory service for the printer. All printers configured for sharing on Windows 2000 systems are automatically listed in Active Directory. Printers can be removed from the directory, however.

   • **Type The Printer Name, Or Click Next To Browse For A Printer** Choose this option if you want to browse the network for shared printers just as you would browse in My Network Places.

   • **Connect To A Printer On The Internet Or On Your Intranet** Choose this option if you want to enter the Uniform Resource Locator (URL) of an Internet printer.

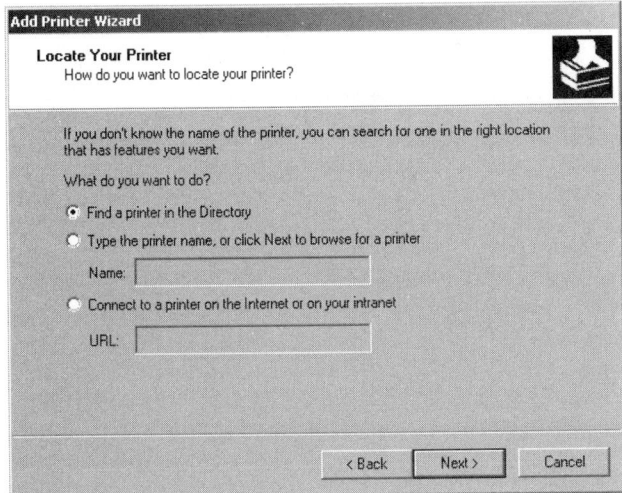

Figure 16-8. *Find the printer on the network or in Active Directory.*

5. When the printer is selected, click OK.

6. Determine whether the printer is the default used by Windows applications. Choose Yes or No, and then click Next.

7. Choose Finish to complete the operation.

The user can now print to the network printer by selecting the printer in an application. The Printers folder on the user's computer shows the new network printer. You can configure local property settings using this icon. By default, the printer name is set to Printer on Computer, such as HP DeskJet on Zeta.

Solving Spooling Problems

Windows 2000 uses a service to control the spooling of print jobs. If this service isn't running, print jobs can't be spooled. You can check the status of the Print Spooler using the Services utility in Control Panel. Follow these steps to check and restart the Print Spooler service:

1. Choose Start, then Programs, then Administrative Tools, and then click Computer Management. Or select Computer Management in the Administrative Tools folder.

2. Right-click the Computer Management entry in the console tree and select Connect To Another Computer on the shortcut menu. You can now choose the system whose services you want to manage.

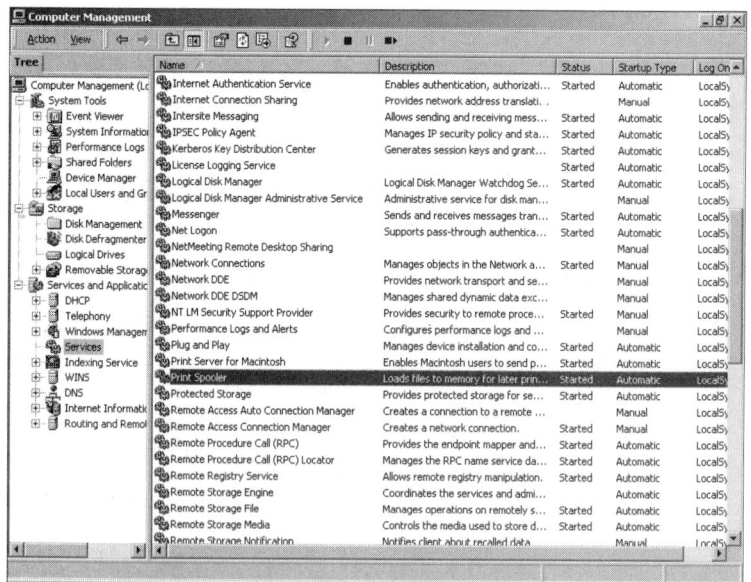

Figure 16-9. *The Print Spooler service handles print spooling.*

3. Expand the Services And Applications node by clicking the plus sign (+) next to it, and then choose Services.

4. Select the Print Spooler service, as shown in Figure 16-9. The Status should be "Started." If it isn't, right-click Print Spooler, and then select Start. The Startup Type should be "Automatic." If it isn't, double-click Print Spooler, and then set Startup Type to Automatic.

5. If this doesn't resolve the problem, you may want to check other related services, including

- TCP/IP Print Server
- Print Server for Macintosh
- Print Server for Unix

Tip   Spoolers can become corrupted. Symptoms include a frozen printer or one that doesn't send jobs to the print device. Sometimes the print device may print pages of garbled data. In most of these cases, stopping and starting the Print Spooler service will resolve the problem.

Other spooling problems may be related to permissions. See the section of this chapter entitled "Setting Printer Access Permissions" for details.

Configuring Printer Properties

Once you install network printing, you can use the Properties dialog box to set its properties. You access the Properties dialog box by doing the following:

1. Access the Printers folder on the computer you want to configure as a print server. On a local system, you access this folder by clicking Start, choosing Settings, and then selecting Printers. On a remote system, you can access this folder through My Network Places. In My Network Places, access a domain, select a computer whose printer settings you want to manage, and then double-click Printers.

2. Right-click the icon of the printer you want to configure and then from the pop-up menu, select Properties.

3. This opens the dialog box shown in Figure 16-10. You can now set the printer properties.

The sections that follow explain how to set commonly used printer properties.

Adding Comments and Location Information

To make it easier to determine which printer to use when, you can add comments and location information to printers. Comments provide general information about the printer, such as the type of print device and who is responsible for it. Location describes the actual site of the print device. Once set, applications can display these fields. For example, Microsoft Word displays this information when you select Print from the File menu in the Comment and Where fields, respectively.

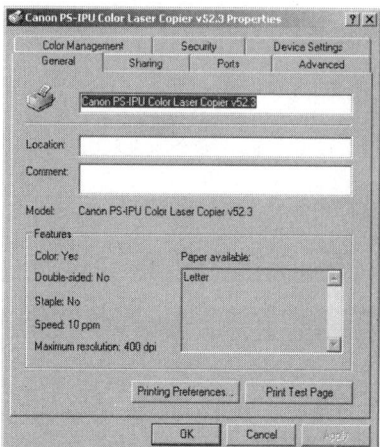

Figure 16-10. *Set printer properties with the dialog box for the printer you want to configure.*

You can add comments and location information to a printer by using the fields in the General tab of the printer's Properties dialog box. Type your comments in the Comment field. Type the printer location in the Location field.

Managing Printer Drivers

In a Windows 2000 domain, you should configure and update printer drivers only on your print servers. You don't need to update printer drivers on Windows clients. Instead, you configure the network printer to provide the drivers to client systems, as necessary.

Updating a Printer Driver

You can update a printer's driver by doing the following:

1. Open the printer's Properties dialog box and select the Advanced tab.

2. The Driver field lets you select the driver from a list of currently installed drivers. Use the Driver drop-down list to select a new driver from a list of known drivers.

3. If the driver you need isn't listed or if you obtained a new driver, click New Driver. This starts the Add Printer Driver Wizard. Click Next. Choose Have Disk to install the new driver from a file or disk.

4. Click Next, and then click Finish.

Configuring Drivers for Network Clients

After you install a printer or change drivers, you may want to select the operating systems that should download the driver from the print server. By allowing clients to download the printer driver, you provide a single location for installing driver updates. This way, instead of having to install a new driver on all the client systems, you install the driver on the print server and allow clients to download the new driver.

You can allow clients to download the new driver by doing the following:

1. Right-click the icon of the printer you want to configure, and then select Properties.

2. Click the Sharing tab, and then click Additional Drivers.

3. Use the Additional Drivers dialog box to select operating systems that can download the printer driver. As necessary, insert the Windows 2000 distribution CD or printer driver disks, or both, for the selected operating systems. The Windows 2000 distribution CD-ROM has drivers for most Windows operating systems and chip architectures.

Setting a Separator Page and Changing Print Device Mode

Separator pages have two uses on Windows 2000 systems:

- They can be used at the beginning of a print job to make it easier to find a document on a busy print device.

- They can be used to change the print device mode, such as whether the print device uses PostScript or Printer Control Language (PCL).

To set a separator page for a print device, follow these steps:

1. Access the Advanced tab of the printer's Properties dialog box, and then click Separator Page.

2. In the Separator Page dialog box, click Browse, and then select one of the available separator pages, including:

   - **PCL.SEP** Switches the print device to PCL mode and prints a separator page before each document.

   - **PSCRIPT.SEP** Sets the print device to PostScript mode but doesn't print a separator page.

   - **SYSPRINT.SEP** Sets the print device to PostScript mode and prints a separator page before each document.

To stop using the separator page, access the Separator Page dialog box and remove the file name.

Changing the Printer Port

You can change the port used by a print device at any time by using the Properties dialog box for the printer you're configuring. Open the Properties dialog box, and then click the Ports tab. You can now either add a port for printing by selecting its check box or remove a port by clearing its check box. To add a new port type, click Add Port and then follow the instructions on what to do when a print device isn't found, given in the "Installing Print Devices on a Local or

Remote Print Server" section of this chapter. To remove a port permanently, select it and then click Delete Port.

Scheduling and Prioritizing Print Jobs

You use the Properties dialog box for the printer you're configuring to set default settings for print job priority and scheduling. Open the dialog box, and then click the Advanced tab. You can now set the default schedule and priority settings using the fields shown in Figure 16-11. Each of these fields is discussed in the sections that follow.

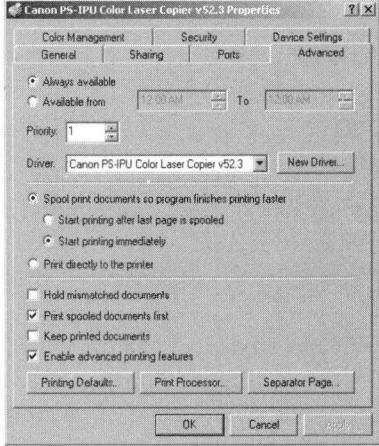

Figure 16-11. *Configure print job scheduling and priority using the Advanced tab.*

Scheduling Printer Availability

Printers are either always available or available only during the hours specified. You set printer availability using the Advanced tab. Access the Advanced tab, and then select Always Available to make the printer available at all times or select Available From to set specific hours of operation.

Setting Printer Priority

Use the Priority box of the Advanced tab to set the default priority for print jobs. Print jobs always print in order of priority. Jobs with higher priority print before jobs with lower priority.

Configuring Print Spooling

For print devices attached to the network, you'll usually want the printer to spool files rather than print files directly. Print spooling makes it possible to use a printer to manage print jobs.

Enabling spooling   To enable spooling, use one of the following options:

- **Spool Print Documents So Program Finishes Printing Faster**   Select this option to spool print jobs.

- **Start Printing After Last Page Is Spooled** Select this option if you want the entire document to be spooled before printing begins. This option ensures that the entire document makes it into the print queue before printing. If for some reason printing is canceled or not completed, the job won't be printed.

- **Start Printing Immediately** Select this option if you want printing to begin immediately when the print device isn't already in use. This option is preferable when you want print jobs to be completed faster or when you want to ensure that the application returns control to users as soon as possible.

Other spooling options You can disable spooling by selecting the Print Directly To The Printer option button. Additional check boxes let you configure other spooling options. These check boxes are used as follows:

- **Hold Mismatched Documents** If selected, the spooler holds print jobs that don't match the setup for the print device. Selecting this option is a good idea if you frequently have to change printer form or tray assignments.

- **Print Spooled Documents First** If selected, jobs that have completed spooling will print before jobs in the process of spooling—regardless of whether the spooling jobs have higher priority.

- **Keep Printed Documents** Normally documents are deleted from the queue after they're printed. To keep a copy of documents in the printer, select this option. Use this option if you're printing files that can't easily be recreated. In this way you can reprint the document without having to recreate it. For details, see the section of this chapter entitled "Pausing, Resuming, and Restarting Individual Document Printing."

- **Enable Advanced Printing Features** When this option is enabled, you can use advanced printing options (if available), such as Page Order and Pages Per Sheet. If you note compatibility problems when using advanced options, you should disable the advanced printing features by clearing this checkbox.

Starting and Stopping Printer Sharing

You use the Properties dialog box of the printer you're configuring to set printer sharing. Right-click the icon of the printer you want to configure, and then select Sharing. You can use this tab to change the name of a network printer as well as to start sharing or stop sharing a printer. Printer sharing tasks that you can perform include

- **Sharing a local printer (thus making it a network printer)** To share a printer, select Share As and specify a name for the shared resource. If Windows 3.1 or MS-DOS systems will access the printer, be sure the printer name conforms to the standard 8.3 naming rule, such as SOUTHEAS.PRT rather than SOUTHEAST_PRINTER. Click OK when you're finished.

- **Changing the shared name of a printer** To change the shared name, simply type a new name in the Share As field and click OK.

- **Stopping the sharing of a printer** To quit sharing a printer, select the Not Shared option button. Click OK when you're finished.

Setting Printer Access Permissions

Network printers are a shared resource, and as such, you can set access permissions for them. You use the Properties dialog box of the printer you're configuring to set access permissions. Open the dialog box, and then click the Security tab. Next, open the Printer Permissions dialog box by clicking Permissions.

Permissions that can be granted or denied for printers are Print, Manage Documents, and Manage Printers. Table 16-2 summarizes the capabilities of these permissions.

Table 16-2. Printer Permissions Used by Windows 2000

Permission	Print	Manage Documents	Manage Printers
Print documents	X	X	X
Pause, restart, resume, and cancel own documents	X	X	X
Connect to printers	X	X	X
Control settings for print jobs		X	X
Pause, restart, and delete print jobs		X	X
Share printers			X
Change printer properties			X
Change printer permissions			X
Delete printers			X

The default settings of the Printer Permissions dialog box are used for any new network printer you create. These settings are as follows:

- Administrators, Print Operators, and Server Operators have full control over printers by default. This allows you to administer a printer and its print jobs.

- Creator or Owner of the document can manage his or her own document. This allows the person who printed a document to change its settings and to delete it.

- Everyone can print to the printer. This makes the printer accessible to all users on the network.

As with other permission sets, you create the basic permissions for printers by combining special permissions into logical groups. Table 16-3 shows special permissions used to create the basic permissions for printers. Using Advanced permission settings, you can assign these special permissions individually, if necessary.

Table 16-3. Special Permissions for Printers

Permission	Print	Manage Documents	Manage Printers
Print	X		X
Manage Documents		X	
Manage Printers			X
Read Permissions	X	X	X
Change Permissions		X	X
Take Ownership		X	X

Auditing Print Jobs

Windows 2000 lets you audit common printer tasks. To do this, follow these steps:

1. Open the printer's Properties dialog box, then click the Security tab. Open the Access Control Settings dialog box by clicking Advanced.

Note Actions aren't audited by default. You must first enable auditing by establishing a group policy to audit the printer.

2. In the Auditing tab, add the names of users or groups you want to audit with the Add button and remove names of users or groups with the Remove button.
3. Select the events you want to audit by selecting the check boxes under the Successful and Failed headings, as appropriate.
4. Click OK when you're finished.

Setting Document Defaults

Document default settings are only used when you print from non-Windows applications, such as when you print from the MS-DOS prompt. You can set document defaults by doing the following:

1. In the Printers folder, double-click the printer's icon.
2. In the Printer Management window, from the Printer menu, select Printing Preferences.
3. Use the fields in the Layout tab and the Paper/Quality tab to configure the default settings.

Configuring Print Server Properties

Windows 2000 allows you to control global settings for print servers by using the Print Server Properties dialog box. Access this dialog box by doing the following:

1. Access the Printers folder on the print server you want to configure. On a local system, you access this folder by clicking Start, choosing Settings, and then selecting Printers. On a remote system, you can access this folder through My Network Places. In My Network Places, access a domain, select a computer whose printer settings you want to manage, and then double-click Printers.
2. In the Printers window, select Server Properties from the File menu or right-click in an empty area and select Server Properties from the shortcut menu.

Viewing and Creating Printer Forms

The print server uses forms to define the standard sizes for paper, envelopes, and transparencies. To view the current settings for a printer form, follow these steps:

1. Open the Print Server Properties dialog box, and then click the Forms tab, shown in Figure 16-12.

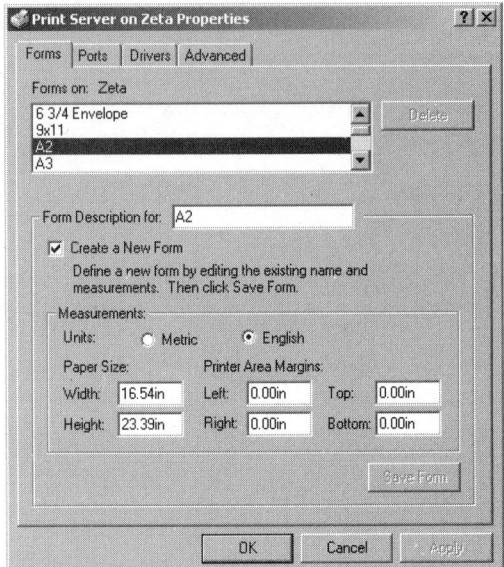

Figure 16-12. *Use the Forms tab of the Print Server Properties dialog box to view printer forms.*

2. Use the Forms On list box to select the form you want to view.

3. The form settings are shown in the Measurements area. You can't change or delete the default system forms.

To create a new form, follow these steps:

1. Access the Forms tab of the Print Server Properties dialog box.

2. Use the Forms On list box to select the existing form on which you want to base the new form.

3. Select the Create A New Form check box.

4. Type a new name for the form in the Form Description For field.

5. Use the fields in the Measurements area to set the paper size and margins.

6. Click Save Form to save the form.

Locating the Spool Folder and Enabling Printing on NTFS

The Spool folder holds a copy of all documents in the printer spool. By default, this folder is located at *%SystemRoot%*\system32\spool\PRINTERS. On Windows NT file system (NTFS), all users who access the printer must have Change permission on this directory. If they don't, they won't be able to print documents. To check the permission on this directory if you're experiencing problems, follow these steps:

1. Access the Printers folder on the print server you want to configure. On a local system, you access this folder by clicking Start, choosing Settings, and then selecting Printers. On a remote system, you can access this folder through My Network Places. In My Network Places, access a domain, select a computer whose printer settings you want to manage, and then double-click Printers.

2. In the Printers window, from the File menu, select Server Properties.

3. Select the Advanced tab. The location of the Spool folder is shown in the Spool Folder field. Note this location.

4. Right-click the Spool folder in Microsoft Windows 2000 Explorer, and then from the pop-up menu, select Properties.

5. Select the Security tab. Now you can verify that the permissions are set appropriately.

Managing High Volume Printing

Printers used in corporate environments can print hundreds or thousands of documents daily. This heavy load puts a high burden on print servers, which can cause printing delays, document corruption, and other problems. To alleviate some of this burden, you should

- Use network-attached printers rather than printers attached through serial, parallel, or infrared ports. Network-attached printers use less system resources (namely CPU time) than other printers do.

- Dedicate the print server to handle print services only. If the print server is handling other network duties, it may not be very responsive to print requests and management. To increase responsiveness, you can move other network duties to other servers.

- Move the Spool folder to a drive dedicated to printing. By default, the Spool folder is on the same file system as the operating system. To further improve disk input/output (I/O), use a drive that has a separate controller.

Logging Printer Events

You can use the Print Server Properties dialog box to configure the logging of printer events. Access this dialog box, and then click the Advanced tab. Use the check boxes provided to determine which spooler events are logged.

Removing Print Job Completion and Notification

Print servers can notify users when a document has finished printing. By default, this feature is turned off, since it can become annoying. If you want to activate or remove notification, access the Advanced tab of the Print Server Properties dialog box. Then select or clear the check box labeled Notify When Remote Documents Are Printed. You may also want to select or clear the check box labeled Notify Computer, Not User, When Remote Documents Are Printed.

Managing Print Jobs on Local and Remote Printers

You manage print jobs and printers using the print management window.

If the printer is configured on your system, you can access the print management window by completing the following steps:

1. Double-click the Printers icon in the Control Panel or in the Start menu, select Settings, and then choose the Printers option.

2. Double-click the icon of the printer you want to work with.

If the printer isn't configured on your system, you can manage the printer remotely by doing the following:

1. Start Windows 2000 Explorer, and then use My Network Places to access the print server.

2. Access the Printers folder on the print server and then double-click the icon of the printer you want to work with.

Using the Print Management Window

You can now manage print jobs and printers using the print management window shown in Figure 16-13. The print management window shows information about documents in the printers. This information tells you

- **Document Name**   The document file name, which can include the name of the application that printed it.

- **Status**   The status of the print job, which can include the status of the document as well as the status of the printer. Document status entries you'll see include Printing, Spooling, Paused, Deleting, and Restarting. Document status can be preceded by the printer status, such as Printer Off-Line.

- **Owner**   The document's owner.

- **Pages**   The number of pages in the document.

- **Size**   The document size in kilobytes or megabytes.

- **Submitted**   The time and date the print job was submitted.

- **Port**   The port used for printing, such as LPT1, COM3, or File (if applicable).

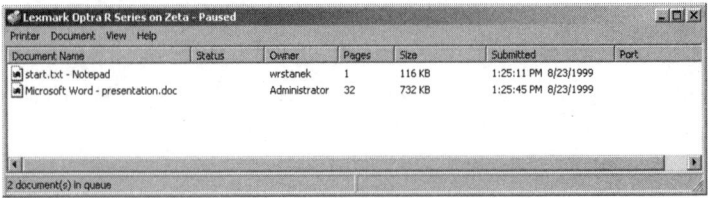

Figure 16-13. *Manage print jobs and printers using the print management window.*

Pausing the Printer and Resuming Printing

Sometimes you need to pause a printer. Using the print management window, you do this by selecting the Pause Printing option on the Printer menu (a check mark indicates that the option is selected). When you pause printing, the printer completes the current job and then puts all other jobs on hold.

To resume printing, select the Pause Printing option a second time. This should remove the check mark next to the option.

Emptying the Print Queue

You can use the print management window to empty the print queue and delete all of its contents. To do this, on the Printer menu select the Cancel All Documents option.

Pausing, Resuming, and Restarting Individual Document Printing

You set the status of individual documents using the Document menu in the print management window. To change the status of a document, follow these steps:

1. Select the document in the print management window.

2. Use the Pause, Resume, and Restart options on the Document menu to change the status of the print job.

   - **Pause**   Puts the document on hold and lets other documents print.
   - **Resume**   Tells the printer to resume printing the document from where it left off.
   - **Restart**   Tells the printer to start printing the document again from the beginning.

Removing a Document and Canceling a Print Job

To remove a document from the printer or cancel a print job, follow these steps:

1. Select the document in the print management window.

2. Select Cancel from the Document menu or press DEL.

Note   When you cancel a print job that's currently printing, the print device may continue to print part or all of the document. This is because most print devices cache documents in an internal buffer, and the print device may continue to print the contents of this cache.

Checking the Properties of Documents in the Printer

Document properties can tell you many things about documents that are in the printer, such as the page source, orientation, and size. You can check the properties of a document in the printer by doing either of the following:

- Select the document in the print management window and then, from the Document menu, select Properties.
- Double-click the document name in the print management window.

Setting the Priority of Individual Documents

Scheduling priority determines when documents print. Documents with higher priority print before documents with lower priority. You can set the priority of individual documents in the printer by doing the following:

1. Select the document in the print management window and then, from the Document menu, select Properties.
2. In the General tab, use the Priority slider to change the priority of the document. The lowest priority is 1 and the highest is 99.

Scheduling the Printing of Individual Documents

In a busy printing environment, you may need to schedule the printing of documents in the printer. For example, you may want large print jobs of low priority to print at night. To set the printing schedule, follow these steps:

1. Select the document in the print management window and then, from the Document menu, select Properties.
2. In the General tab, select the Only From option button and then specify a time interval. The time interval you set determines when the job is allowed to print. For example, you can specify that the job can print only between the hours of 12:00 midnight and 5:00 A.M.

Chapter 17

Running DHCP Clients and Servers

Dynamic Host Configuration Protocol (DHCP) is designed to simplify administration of Active Directory directory service domains, and in this chapter you'll learn how to manage it. You use DHCP to dynamically assign Transmission Control Protocol/Internet Protocol (TCP/IP) configuration information to network clients. This not only saves time during system configuration but also provides a centralized mechanism for updating the configuration. To enable DHCP on the network, you need to install and configure a DHCP server. This server is responsible for assigning the necessary network information.

Understanding DHCP

DHCP gives you centralized control over Internet Protocol (IP) addressing and more. If the network has a DHCP server, you can assign a dynamic IP address to any of the network adapter cards on a computer. Once DHCP is installed, you rely on the DHCP server to supply the basic information necessary for TCP/IP networking, which can include the following: IP address, subnet mask, and default router; primary and secondary Domain Name System (DNS) servers; primary and secondary Windows Internet Naming Service (WINS) servers; and the DNS domain name.

The DHCP Client and the IP Address

A computer that uses dynamic addressing is called a *DHCP client*. When you boot a DHCP client, an IP address is retrieved from a pool of IP addresses defined for the network's DHCP server and assigned for a specified time period known as a *lease*. When the lease is approximately 50 percent expired, the client tries to renew it. If the client can't renew the lease, it'll try again before the lease expires. If this attempt fails, the client will try to contact a new DHCP server. IP addresses that aren't renewed are returned to the address pool. If the client is able to contact the DHCP server but the current IP address can't be reassigned, the DHCP server assigns a new IP address to the client.

The availability of a DHCP server doesn't effect startup or logon (in most cases). DHCP clients can start and users can log on even if a DHCP server isn't available. During startup, the client looks for a DHCP server. If a DHCP server is available, the client gets its configuration information from the server. If a DHCP server isn't available and the client's previous lease is still valid, the client pings the default gateway listed in the lease. A successful ping tells the client that it's probably on the same network it was on when it was issued the lease, and the client will continue to use the lease as described previously. A failed ping tells the client that it may be on a different network. In this case, the client uses IP autoconfiguration. The client also uses IP autoconfiguration if a DHCP server isn't available and the previous lease has expired.

IP autoconfiguration works like this:

1. The client computer selects an IP address from the Microsoft-reserved class B subnet 169.254.0.0 and uses the subnet mask 255.255.0.0. Before using the IP address, the client performs an Address Resolution Protocol (ARP) test to make sure that no other client is using this IP address.

2. If the IP address is in use, the client repeats step 1, testing up to 10 IP addresses before reporting failure.

 Note When a client is disconnected from the network, the ARP test will always succeed. As a result, the client uses the first IP address it selects.

3. If the IP address is available, the client configures the network interface with this address. The client then attempts to contact a DHCP server, sending out a broadcast every five minutes to the network. When the client successfully contacts a server, the client obtains a lease and reconfigures the network interface.

Checking IP Address Assignment

You can use IPCONFIG to check the currently assigned IP address and other configuration information. To obtain information for all network adapters on the computer, type the command **IPCONFIG /ALL** at the command prompt. If the IP address has been assigned automatically, you'll see an entry for Autoconfiguration IP Address. In this example, the autoconfiguration IP address is 169.254.98.59:

```
Windows 2000 IP Configuration

        Host Name . . . . . . . . . . . . . : DELTA

        Primary DNS Suffix  . . . . . . . . : microsoft.com

        Node Type . . . . . . . . . . . . . : Hybrid

        IP Routing Enabled. . . . . . . . . : No
```

```
WINS Proxy Enabled. . . . . . . . . : No
DNS Suffix Search List. . . . . . . : microsoft.com
Ethernet adapter Local Area Connection:
    Connection-specific DNS Suffix. . . :
    Description . . . . . . . . . . . . : NDC ND5300 PnP
                                          Ethernet Adapter
    Physical Address. . . . . . . . . : 03-82-C6-F8-EA-69
    DHCP Enabled. . . . . . . . . . . : Yes
    Autoconfiguration Enabled . . . . . : Yes
    Autoconfiguration IP Address. . . . : 169.254.98.59
    Subnet Mask . . . . . . . . . . . : 255.255.0.0
    Default Gateway . . . . . . . . . :
    DNS Servers . . . . . . . . . . . :
```

Understanding Scopes

Scopes are pools of IP addresses that you can assign to clients through leases and reservations. A reservation differs from a lease in that an IP address is assigned to a particular computer until you remove the reservation. This allows you to set semipermanent addresses for a limited number of DHCP clients.

You'll create scopes to specify IP address ranges that are available for DHCP clients. For example, you could assign the IP address range 192.168.12.2 – 192.168.12.250 to a scope called Enterprise Primary. Scopes can use public or private IP addresses on

- **Class A networks**   IP addresses from 1.0.0.0 to 126.255.255.255
- **Class B networks**   IP addresses from 128.0.0.0 to 191.255.255.255
- **Class C networks**   IP addresses from 192.0.0.0 to 223.255.255.255
- **Class D networks**   IP addresses from 224.0.0.0 to 239.255.255.255

Note   The IP address 127.0.0.1 is used for local loopback.

A single DHCP server can manage multiple scopes. Three types of scopes are available:

- **Normal scopes**   Used to assign IP address pools for class A, B, and C networks.
- **Multicast scopes**   Used to assign IP address pools for class D networks. Computers use multicast IP addresses as secondary IP addresses in addition to a standard IP address assigned from a class A, B, or C network.

- **Superscopes** These are containers for other scopes and are used to simplify management of multiple scopes.

 Tip Although you can create scopes on multiple network segments, you'll usually want these segments to be in the same network class, such as all class C IP addresses. Don't forget that you must configure DHCP relays to relay DHCP broadcast requests between network segments. You can configure relay agents with the Microsoft Windows 2000 Routing and Remote Access Service (RRAS) and the DHCP Relay Agent Service provided in Microsoft Windows NT Server 4.0. You can also configure some routers as relay agents.

Installing a DHCP Server

Dynamic IP addressing is only available if a DHCP server is installed on the network. You install the DHCP components through the Windows Components Wizard, and then you use the DHCP console to start and authorize the server in the domain. Only authorized DHCP servers can provide dynamic IP addresses to clients.

Installing DHCP Components

On a Windows 2000 server, you complete the following steps to allow it to function as a DHCP server:

1. Click Start, choose Settings, and then click Control Panel.
2. In Control Panel, double-click Add/Remove Programs, and then click Add/Remove Windows Components. This changes the view in the Add/Remove Programs dialog box.
3. Click Components to start the Windows Components Wizard, and then click Next.
4. Under Components, click Networking Services, and then click Details.
5. Under Subcomponents Of Networking Services, select the Dynamic Host Configuration Protocol (DHCP) check box.
6. Click OK, and then click Next. If prompted, type the full path to the Windows 2000 distribution files and click Continue.

From now on, the Microsoft DHCP service should start automatically each time you reboot the server. If it doesn't start, you'll need to start it manually. See the section of this chapter entitled "Starting and Stopping a DHCP Server."

Starting and Using the DHCP Console

Once you've installed a DHCP server, you use the DHCP console to configure and manage dynamic IP addressing. To start the DHCP console, choose Start, choose Programs, choose Administrative Tools, and then click DHCP. The main window for the DHCP console is shown in Figure 17-1. As you see, the main window is divided into two panes. The left pane lists the DHCP servers in the domain by IP address as well as the local machine (if it's a DHCP server). By double-clicking an entry, you can expand the listing to show the scopes and options defined for each DHCP server. The right pane shows the expanded view of the current selection.

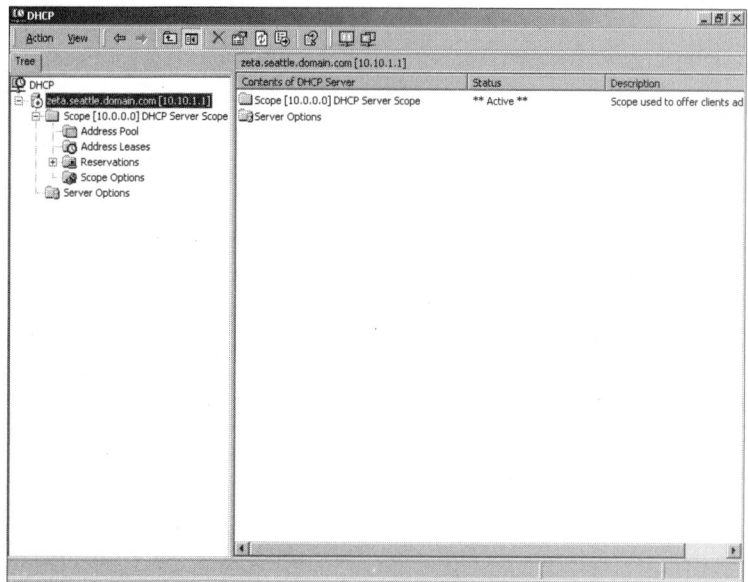

Figure 17-1. *Use the DHCP console to create and manage DHCP server configurations.*

Icons on the server and scope nodes show their current status. For servers, icons you may see are as follows:

- A green Up arrow indicates that the DHCP service is running and the server is active.

- A red X indicates that the console can't connect to the server. The DHCP service has been stopped or the server is inaccessible.

- A red Down arrow indicates that the DHCP server hasn't been authorized.

- A blue warning icon indicates that the state of the server has changed or a warning has been issued.

For scopes, icons you may see are as follows:

- A red Down arrow indicates that the scope hasn't been activated.

- A blue warning icon indicates that the state of the scope has changed or a warning has been issued.

Connecting to Remote DHCP Servers

When you start the DHCP console, you'll be connected directly to a local DHCP server, but you won't see entries for remote DHCP servers. You can connect to remote servers by completing the following steps:

1. Right-click DHCP in the console tree, and then select Add Server. This opens the dialog box shown in Figure 17-2.

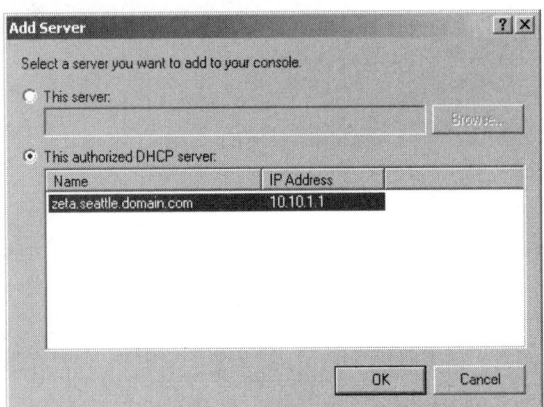

Figure 17-2. *If your DHCP server isn't listed, you'll need to add it to the DHCP console.*

2. Select This Server, and then type the IP address or computer name of the DHCP server you want to manage. If you want to manage authorized DHCP servers only, select This Authorized DHCP Server, and then click the server you want to add. Keep in mind that you can only manage DHCP servers in trusted domains.

3. Click OK. An entry for the DHCP server is added to the console tree.

 Note You can also manage local and remote DHCP servers through Computer Management. Start Computer Management, then connect to the server you want to manage. Afterward, expand Services And Applications, and then select DHCP.

Starting and Stopping a DHCP Server

You manage DHCP servers through the DHCP Server service. Like any other service, you can start, stop, pause, and resume the DHCP Server service in the Services node of Computer Management or from the command line. You can also manage the DHCP service in the DHCP console. Right-click the server you want to manage in the DHCP console, choose All Tasks, and then select Start, Stop, Pause, Resume, or Restart, as appropriate.

Note In Computer Management, right-click DHCP, choose All Tasks, and then select Start, Stop, Pause, Resume, or Restart, as appropriate.

Authorizing a DHCP Server in Active Directory

Before you can use a DHCP server in the domain, you must authorize it in Active Directory directory service. By authorizing the server, you specify that the server is authorized to provide dynamic IP addressing in the domain. Windows 2000 requires authorization to prevent unauthorized DHCP servers from serving domain clients. This in turn ensures that network operations can run smoothly.

In the DHCP console, you authorize a DHCP server by right-clicking the server entry in the tree view and then selecting Authorize. To remove the authorization, right-click the server, and then select Unauthorize.

Note In Computer Management, right-click DHCP and then select Authorize. To remove the authorization, right-click DHCP and then select Unauthorize.

Configuring DHCP Servers

When you install a new DHCP server, configuration options are optimized for the network environment automatically. You don't normally need to change these settings unless you have performance problems that you need to resolve or you have options that you'd like to add or remove. With DHCP server, you change configuration options through the Properties dialog box shown in Figure 17-3. In the DHCP console, you access this dialog box by right-clicking the server in the console tree and then selecting Properties. In Computer Management, right-click DHCP and then select Properties.

Binding a Multihomed DHCP Server to a Specific IP Address

A server with multiple network adapter cards has multiple local area network connections and can provide DHCP services on any of these network connections. Unfortunately, you may not want DHCP to be served over all available connections. For example, if the server has a 10 megabit per second connection and a 100 megabit per second connection, you may want all DHCP traffic to go over the 100 megabit connection.

To bind DHCP to a specific network connection, follow these steps:

1. Start the DHCP console. Click Start, choose Programs, choose Administrative Tools, and then click DHCP.

2. In the DHCP console, right-click the server you want to work with, and then select Properties.

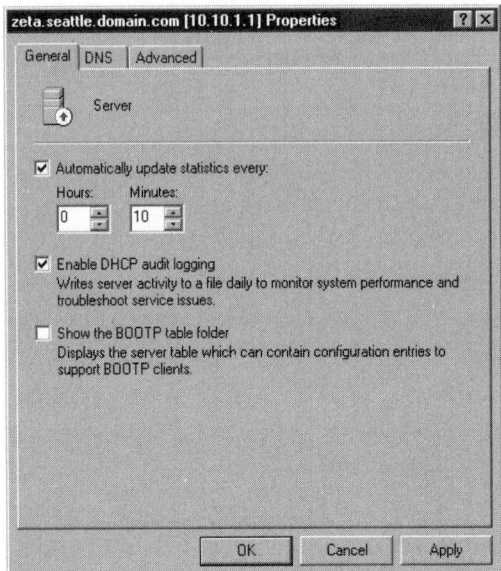

Figure 17-3. *You can control statistics, auditing, DNS integration, and other options through the DHCP Server Properties dialog box.*

3. On the Advanced tab of the Properties dialog box, click Bindings.

4. The Bindings dialog box displays a list of available network connections for the DHCP server. If you want the DHCP Server service to use a connection to service clients, select the check box for the connection. If you don't want the service to use a connection, clear the related check box.

Updating DHCP Statistics

The DHCP console provides statistics concerning IP address availability and usage. By default, these statistics are updated only when you start the DHCP console or when you click the Refresh button on the toolbar. If you monitor DHCP routinely, you may want these statistics to update automatically. To do that, follow these steps:

1. In the DHCP console, right-click the server you want to work with, and then select Properties.

2. In the General tab, select Automatically Update Statistics Every, and then enter an update interval in hours and minutes. Click OK.

DHCP Auditing and Troubleshooting

Windows 2000 is configured to audit DHCP processes by default. Auditing tracks DHCP processes and requests in log files.

Understanding DHCP Auditing

You can use audit logs to help you troubleshoot problems with a DHCP server. The default location for DHCP logs is *%SystemRoot%*\system32\DHCP. In this directory you'll find a different log file for each day of the week. The log file for Monday is named DhcpSrvLog.Mon. The log file for Tuesday is named DhcpSrvLog.Tue, and so on.

When you start the DHCP server or a new day arrives, a header message is written to the log file. This header provides a summary of DHCP events and their meaning. Stopping and starting the DHCP Server service doesn't necessarily clear out a log file. Log data is only cleared when a log hasn't been written to in the last 24 hours. You don't have to monitor space usage by DHCP server. DHCP server is configured to monitor disk space usage by default.

Enabling or Disabling DHCP Auditing

You can enable or disable DHCP auditing by completing the following steps:

1. In the DHCP console, right-click the server you want to work with, and then select Properties.

2. In the General tab, select or clear Enable DHCP Audit Logging. Click OK.

Changing the Location of DHCP Logs

By default, DHCP logs are stored in *%SystemRoot%*\system32\DHCP. You can change the location of DHCP logs by completing the following steps:

1. In the DHCP console, right-click the server you want to work with, and then select Properties.

2. Click the Advanced tab. The Audit Log File Path field shows the current folder location for log files. Enter a new folder location or click Browse to find a new location.

3. Click OK. Windows 2000 will need to restart the DHCP Server service. When prompted to confirm that this is OK, click Yes. The service will be stopped and then started.

Changing the Log Usage

DHCP server has a self-monitoring system that checks disk space usage. By default, the maximum size of all DHCP server logs is 7 MB, with each individual log being limited to one-seventh of this space. If the server reaches the 7 MB limit or an individual log grows beyond the allocated space, logging of DHCP activity stops until log files are cleared out or space is otherwise made available. Normally, this happens when a new day is reached and the server clears out the previous week's log file.

Registry keys that control the log usage and other DHCP settings are located in the folder

```
HKEY_LOCAL_MACHINE\SYSTEM\CurrentControlSet\Services
\DHCPServer\Parameters
```

The following keys control the logging:

- **DhcpLogFilesMaxSize** Sets the maximum file size for all logs. The default is 7 MB.

- **DhcpLogDiskSpaceCheckInterval** Determines how often DHCP checks disk space usage. The default interval is 50 minutes.

- **DhcpLogMinSpaceOnDisk** Sets the free space threshold for writing to the log. If the disk has less free space than the value specified, logging is temporarily disabled. The default value is 20 MB.

Integrating DHCP and DNS

DNS is used to resolve computer names in Active Directory domains and on the Internet. Thanks to the DNS update protocol, you don't need to register DHCP clients in DNS manually. The protocol allows either the client or the DHCP server to register the necessary forward lookup and reverse lookup records in DNS, as necessary. When configured using the default setup for DHCP, Windows 2000 DCHP clients automatically update their own DNS records after receiving an IP address lease, and DHCP server updates records for pre-Windows 2000 clients after issuing a lease.

 Tip Windows NT 4.0 DNS servers don't support the dynamic update protocol, and records aren't updated automatically. One workaround is to enable WINS lookup for DHCP clients that use NetBIOS. This allows the client to find other computers through WINS. A better long-term solution is to upgrade older DNS servers to Windows 2000.

You can view and change the DNS integration settings by completing the following steps:

1. In the DHCP console, right-click the server you want to work with, and then select Properties.

2. Click the DNS tab. Figure 17-4 shows the default DNS integration settings for DHCP. Because these settings are configured by default, you don't need to modify the configuration in most cases.

Avoiding IP Address Conflicts

IP address conflicts are a common cause of problems with DHCP. No two computers on the network can have the same unicast IP address. If a computer is assigned the same unicast IP address as another, one or both of the computers may become disconnected from the network. To better detect and avoid potential conflicts, you may want to enable IP address conflict detection by completing the following steps:

1. In the DHCP console, right-click the server you want to work with, and then select Properties.

2. On the Advanced tab, set Conflict Detection Attempts to a value other than zero. The value you enter determines the number of times DHCP server checks an IP address before leasing it to a client. DHCP server checks IP addresses by sending a ping request over the network.

Real World   A unicast IP address is a standard IP address for class A, B, and C networks. When a DHCP client requests a lease, a DHCP server checks its pool of available addresses and assigns the client a lease on an available IP address. By default, the server only checks the list of current leases to determine if an address is available. It doesn't actually query the network to see if an address is in use. Unfortunately, in a busy network environment, another computer may have been assigned this IP address by an administrator, or an offline computer may have been brought online with a lease that it believes hasn't expired, even though the DHCP server believes the lease has expired. Either way, you have an address conflict that will cause problems on the network. To reduce these types of conflicts, set conflict detection to a value greater than zero.

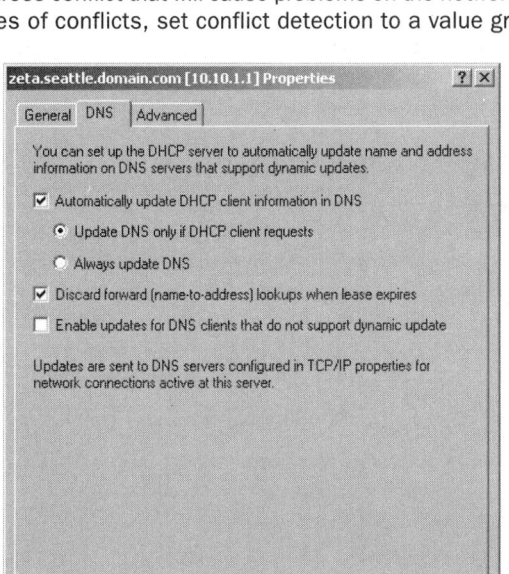

Figure 17-4. *The DNS tab shows the default settings for DNS integration with DHCP.*

Saving and Restoring the DHCP Configuration

Once you configure all the necessary DHCP settings, you may want to save the DHCP configuration so that you can restore it on the DHCP server. To save the configuration, enter the following command at the command prompt:

```
netsh dhcp dump >> dhcpconfig.dmp
```

In this example, dhcpconfig.dmp is the name of the configuration script you want to create. Once you create this script, you can restore the configuration by entering the following command at the command prompt:

```
netsh exec dhcpconfig.dmp
```

 Tip You can also use this technique to set up another DHCP server with the same configuration. Simply copy the configuration script to a folder on the destination computer and then execute it.

Managing DHCP Scopes

Once you install a DHCP server, you need to configure the scopes that the DHCP server will use. Scopes are pools of IP addresses that you can lease to clients. As explained in the section of this chapter entitled "Understanding Scopes," you can create three types of scopes: superscopes, normal scopes, and multicast scopes.

Creating and Managing Superscopes

A superscope is a container for scopes in much the same way that an organizational unit is a container for Active Directory objects. Superscopes help you manage scopes available on the network. With a superscope you can activate or deactivate multiple scopes through a single action. You can also view statistics for all scopes in the superscope rather than having to check statistics for each scope.

Creating Superscopes

You create a superscope by completing the following steps:

1. In the DHCP console, right-click the server you want to work with, and then select New Superscope. This starts the New Superscope Wizard.
2. Click Next, and then type a name for the superscope.
3. Select scopes to add to the superscope. Select individual scopes by clicking their entry in the Available Scopes list box. Select multiple scopes by clicking while holding down SHIFT or CTRL.
4. Click Next, and then click Finish.

Adding Scopes to a Superscope

You can add scopes to a superscope when you create it or you can do it later. To add a scope to an existing superscope, follow these steps:

1. Right-click the scope you want to add to an existing superscope, and then select Add To Superscope.

2. In the Add Scope ... To Superscope dialog box, select a superscope.

3. Click OK. The scope is then added to the superscope.

Removing Scopes from a Superscope

To remove a scope from a superscope, follow these steps:

1. Right-click the scope you want to remove from a superscope, and then select Remove From Superscope.

2. Confirm the action by clicking Yes when prompted. If this is the last scope in the superscope, the superscope is deleted automatically.

Activating and Deactivating a Superscope

When you activate or deactivate a superscope, you make all the scopes within the superscope active or inactive. To activate a superscope, right-click the superscope, and then select Activate. To deactivate a superscope, right-click the superscope, and then select Deactivate.

Deleting a Superscope

Deleting a superscope removes the superscope container and all the scopes it contains. If you don't want to delete the member scopes, remove them from the superscope before you delete it.

To delete a superscope, right-click the superscope, and then select Delete. When prompted, click Yes to confirm the action.

Creating and Managing Scopes

Scopes provide a pool of IP addresses for DHCP clients. A normal scope is a scope with class A, B, or C network addresses. A multicast scope is a scope with class D network addresses. Although you create normal scopes and multicast scopes differently, you manage them in much the same way. The key differences are that multicast scopes can't use reservations and you can't set additional options for WINS, DNS, routing, and so forth.

Creating Normal Scopes

You can create a normal scope by completing the following steps:

1. In the DHCP console, right-click the server on which you want to create the scope. If you want to add the new scope to an existing superscope automatically, right-click the superscope instead.

2. From the shortcut menu, choose New Scope. This starts the New Scope Wizard. Click Next.

3. Type a name and description for the scope, and then click Next.

4. The Start Address and End Address fields define the valid IP address range for the scope. Enter a start address and an end address in these fields.

Note Generally, the scope doesn't include the x.x.x.0 and x.x.x.255 addresses, which are usually reserved for network addresses and broadcast messages, respectively. Accordingly, you would use a range of 192.168.10.1 to 192.168.10.254 rather than 192.168.10.0 to 192.168.10.255.

5. When you enter an IP address range, the bit length and subnet mask are filled in for you automatically (see Figure 17-5). Unless you use subnets, you should use the default values.

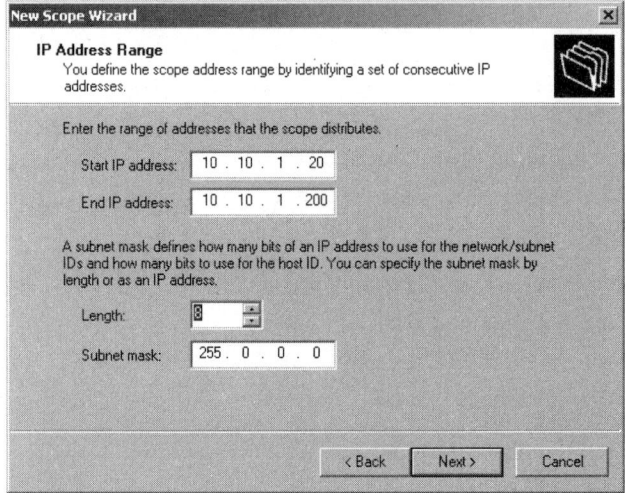

Figure 17-5. *In the New Scope Wizard, enter the IP address range for the scope.*

6. Click Next. If the IP address range you entered is on multiple networks, you'll have the opportunity to create a superscope that contains separate scopes for each network. Select the Yes option button to continue, and then click Next. If you made a mistake, click Back and modify the IP address range you entered.

7. Use the Exclusion Range fields to define IP address ranges that are to be excluded from the scope. You can exclude multiple address ranges as follows:

    ● To define an exclusion range, type a start address and an end address in the Exclusion Range's Start Address and End Address fields, respectively, and then click Add. To exclude a single IP address, use that address as both the start IP address and the end IP address.

    ● To track which address ranges are excluded, use the Excluded Addresses list box.

- To delete an exclusion range, select the range in the Excluded Addresses list box and click Remove.

8. Specify the duration of leases for the scope using the Day(s), Hour(s), and Minutes fields. The default duration is eight days.

Best Practice Take a few minutes to plan the lease duration you want to use. A lease duration that's set too long can reduce the effectiveness of DHCP and may eventually cause you to run out of available IP addresses, especially on networks with mobile users or other types of computers that aren't fixed members of the network. A good lease duration for most networks is from one to three days.

9. Next, you have the opportunity to set common DHCP options for DNS, WINS, gateways, and more. If you want to set these options now, click Yes. Otherwise, click No and skip steps 10–16.

10. Click Next. The first option you can configure is the default gateway. In the IP Address field enter the IP address of the primary default gateway. Click Add. Repeat this process for other default gateways.

11. The first gateway listed is the one clients will try to use first. If the gateway isn't available, clients will try to use the next gateway, and so on. Use the Up and Down buttons to change the order of the gateways, as necessary.

12. Click Next, and then, as shown in Figure 17-6, configure default DNS settings for DHCP clients. Enter the name of the parent domain to use for DNS resolution of computer names that aren't fully qualified.

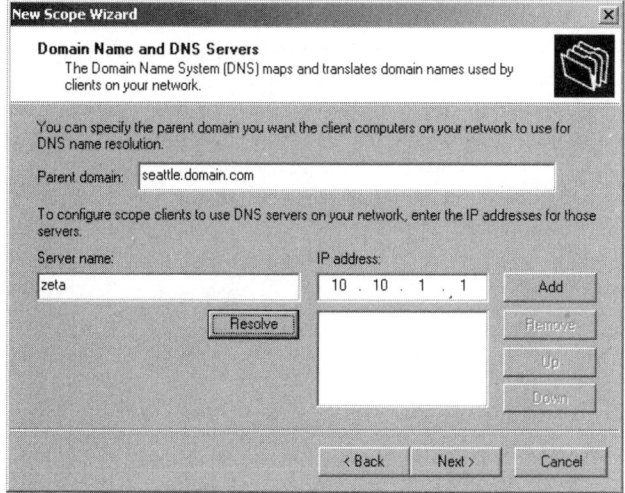

Figure 17-6. *Configure default DNS settings for DHCP clients.*

13. In the IP Address field enter the IP address of the primary DNS. Click Add. Repeat this process to specify additional DNS servers. Again, the order of the entries determines which IP address is used first. Change the order as necessary using the Up and Down buttons.

 Tip If you know the name of a server instead of its IP address, enter the name in the Server Name field and then click Resolve. The IP address is then entered in the IP Address field, if possible. Add the server by clicking Add.

14. Configure default WINS settings for the DHCP clients. The techniques you use are the same as those previously described.

15. If you want to activate the scope, click Yes, I Will Activate This Scope Now and then click Next. Otherwise, just click Next.

16. Complete the process by clicking Finish.

Creating Multicast Scopes

To create a multicast scope, follow these steps:

1. In the DHCP console, right-click the server on which you want to create the scope. If you want to add the new scope to an existing superscope, right-click the superscope instead.

2. From the shortcut menu, choose New Multicast Scope. This starts the New Multicast Scope Wizard. Click Next.

3. Enter a name and description for the scope, and then click Next.

4. The Start Address and End Address fields define the valid IP address range for the scope. Enter a start address and an end address in these fields.

5. Messages sent by computers using multicast IP addresses have a specific time-to-live value. The time-to-live value specifies the maximum number of routers the message can go through. The default value is 32, which is sufficient on most networks. If you have a large network, you may need to increase this value to reflect the actual number of routers that may be used.

6. Click Next. If you made a mistake, click Back and modify the IP address range you entered.

7. Use the Exclusion Range fields to define IP address ranges that are to be excluded from the scope. You can exclude multiple address ranges.

   - To define an exclusion range, enter a start address and an end address in the Exclusion Range's Start Address and End Address fields, respectively, and then click Add.

   - To track which address ranges are excluded, use the Excluded Addresses list box.

   - To delete an exclusion range, select the range in the Excluded Addresses list box and then click Remove.

8. Specify the duration of leases for the scope using the Day(s), Hour(s), and Minutes fields. The default duration is 30 days.

Tip If you haven't worked a lot with multicast, you shouldn't change the default value. Multicast leases aren't used in the same way as normal leases. A multicast IP address can be used by multiple computers, and all of these computers can have a lease on the IP address. A good multicast lease duration for most networks is from 30 to 60 days.

9. If you want to activate the scope, click Yes. Otherwise, just click Next.

10. Complete the process by clicking Finish.

Setting Scope Options

Scope options allow you to precisely control the functioning of a scope and to set default TCP/IP settings for clients that use the scope. For example, you can use scope options to enable clients to automatically find DNS servers on the network. You can also define settings for default gateways, WINS, and more. Scope options only apply to normal scopes, not to multicast scopes.

You can set scope options in any of the following ways:

- Globally, for all scopes, by setting default server options
- On a per scope basis, by setting scope options
- On a per client basis, by setting reservation options
- On a client class basis, by configuring user or vendor-specific classes

Scope options use a hierarchy to determine when certain options apply. The order of this hierarchy is as shown in the previous list. Basically, this means that

- Per scope options override global options.
- Per client options override per scope and global options.
- Client class options override all other options.

Viewing and assigning server options Server options are applied to all scopes configured on a particular DHCP server. You can view and assign server options by completing the following steps:

1. Start the DHCP console, and then double-click the server you want to work with to expand its folder in the tree view.

2. To view current settings, click Server Options. Currently configured options are displayed in the right pane.

3. To assign new settings, right-click Server Options and then select Configure Options. This opens the Server Options dialog box. Under Available Options, select the check box for the first option you want to configure. Then, with the option selected, enter any required information in the fields of the Data Entry panel. Repeat this step to configure other options.

Viewing and assigning scope options   Scope options are specific to an individual scope and override the default server options. You can view and assign scope options by completing the following steps:

1. Expand the entry for the scope you want to work with in the DHCP console.

2. To view current settings, click Scope Options. Currently configured options are displayed in the right pane.

3. To assign new settings, right-click Scope Options and then select Configure Options. This opens the Scope Options dialog box. Under Available Options, select the check box for the first option you want to configure. Then, with the option selected, enter any required information in the fields of the Data Entry panel. Repeat this step to configure other options.

Viewing and assigning reservation options   Reservation options can be assigned to a client that has a reserved IP address. These options are specific to an individual client and override server-specific and scope-specific options. You can view and assign reservation options by completing the following steps:

1. Expand the entry for the scope you want to work with in the DHCP console.

2. Double-click the Reservations folder for the scope.

3. To view current settings, click the reservation you want to examine. Currently configured options are displayed in the right pane.

4. To assign new settings, right-click the reservation and then select Configure Options. This opens the Reservation Options dialog box. Under Available Options, select the check box for the first option you want to configure. Then, with the option selected, enter any required information in the fields of the Data Entry panel. Repeat this step to configure other options.

Modifying Scopes

You can modify an existing scope by doing the following:

1. Start the DHCP console and then double-click the entry for the DHCP server you want to configure. This should display the currently configured scopes for the server.

2. Right-click the scope you want to modify, and then choose Properties.

3. When you modify normal scopes, you have the option of setting an unlimited lease expiration time. If you do, you create permanent leases that reduce the effectiveness of pooling IP addresses with DHCP. Permanent leases aren't released unless you physically release them or deactivate the scope. As a result, you may eventually run out of addresses, especially as your network grows. A better alternative to unlimited leases is to use address reservations—and then only for specific clients that need fixed IP addresses.

4. When you modify multicast scopes, you have the option of setting a lifetime for the scope. The scope lifetime determines the amount of time the scope is valid. By default, multicast scopes are valid as long as they are activated. To change this setting, click the Advanced tab, select Multicast Scope Expires On, and then set an expiration date.

5. Finish modifying the scope, as necessary, and then close the Scope Properties dialog box by clicking OK. The changes are saved in the DHCP console.

Activating and Deactivating Scopes

In the DHCP console, inactive scopes are displayed with an icon showing a red arrow pointing down. Active scopes display a normal folder icon.

Activating a scope   You can activate an inactive scope by right-clicking it in the DHCP console and then selecting Active.

Deactivating a scope   You can deactivate an active scope by right-clicking it in the DHCP console and then selecting Deactive.

Tip   Deactivating turns off a scope but doesn't terminate current client leases. If you want to terminate leases, follow the instructions in the section of this chapter entitled "Releasing Addresses and Leases."

Enabling the BOOTP Protocol

BOOTP is a dynamic IP addressing protocol that predates DHCP. Normal scopes don't support the BOOTP protocol. To enable a scope to support bootstrap protocol (BOOTP), follow these steps:

1. Right-click the scope you want to modify, and then choose Properties.

2. In the Advanced tab, click Both to support DHCP and BOOTP clients.

3. As necessary, set a lease duration for BOOTP clients, and then click OK.

Removing a Scope

Removing a scope permanently deletes the scope from the DHCP server. To remove a scope, follow these steps:

1. Right-click the scope you want to remove in the DHCP console, and then choose Delete.

2. When prompted to confirm that you want to delete the scope, click Yes.

Configuring Multiple Scopes on a Network

You can configure multiple scopes on a single network. A single DHCP server or multiple DHCP servers can serve these scopes. However, anytime you work with multiple scopes, it's extremely important that the address ranges used by different scopes don't overlap. Each scope must have its own unique address range. If it doesn't, the same IP address may be assigned to different DHCP clients, which can cause severe problems on the network.

To understand how you can use multiple scopes, consider the following scenario. On server A, you create a DHCP scope with an IP address range of 192.168.10.1 to 192.168.10.99. On server B, you create a DHCP scope with an IP address range of 192.168.10.100 to 192.168.10.199. On server C, you create a DHCP scope with an IP address range of 192.168.10.100 to 192.168.10.199. All of these servers will respond to DHCP discovery messages, and any of them can assign IP addresses to clients. If one of the servers fails, the other servers can continue to provide DHCP services to the network.

Managing the Address Pool, Leases, and Reservations

Scopes have separate folders for address pools, leases, and reservations. By accessing these folders, you can view current statistics for the related data and manage existing entries.

Viewing Scope Statistics

Scope statistics provide summary information on the address pool for the current scope or superscope. To view statistics, right-click the scope or superscope and then select Display Statistics. This displays a dialog box similar to the one shown in Figure 17-7.

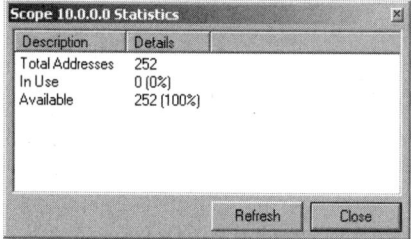

Figure 17-7. *The Statistics dialog box provides summary information on the address pool for the current scope or superscope.*

The primary fields of this dialog box are used as follows:

- **Total Addresses** Shows the total number of IP addresses assigned to the scope.

- **In Use** Shows the total number of addresses being used, as a numerical value and as a percentage of the total available addresses. If the total reaches 85 percent or more, you may want to consider assigning additional addresses or freeing up addresses for use.

- **Available** Shows the total number of addresses available for use, as a numerical value and as a percentage of the total available addresses.

Setting a New Exclusion Range

You can exclude IP addresses from a scope by defining an exclusion range. Scopes can have multiple exclusion ranges. To define an exclusion range, follow these steps:

1. In the DHCP console, expand the scope you want to work with, and then right-click the Address Pool folder. On the shortcut menu, choose New Exclusion Range.

2. Enter a start address and an end address in the Exclusion Range's Start Address and End Address fields, respectively, and then click Add. The range specified must be a subset of the range set for the current scope and must not be currently in use. Repeat this step to add other exclusion ranges.

3. Click Close when you're finished.

Deleting an Exclusion Range

If you don't need exclusion any more, you can delete it. Right-click the exclusion and then select Delete.

Reconciling Leases and Reservations

To reconcile leases and reservations, right-click the scope you want to work with, and then select Reconcile. Reconciling checks the client leases and reservations against the DHCP database on the server. This is useful if you want to make sure that the list of leases shown is actually in use.

Reserving DHCP Addresses

DHCP provides several ways to assign permanent addresses to clients. One way is to use the Unlimited setting in the Scope dialog box to assign permanent addresses to all clients that use the scope. Another way is to reserve DHCP addresses on a per client basis. When you reserve a DHCP address, the client is always assigned the same IP address by the DHCP server, and you can do so without sacrificing the centralized management features that make DHCP so attractive.

To reserve a DHCP address for a client, follow these steps:

1. In the DHCP console, expand the scope you want to work with, and then right-click the Reservations folder. On the shortcut menu, choose New Reservation. This opens the dialog box shown in Figure 17-8.

2. In the Reservation Name field, type a short but descriptive name for the reservation. This field is used only for identification purposes.

3. In the IP Address field, enter the IP address you want to reserve for the client. Note that this IP address must be within the valid range of addresses for the currently selected scope.

4. The MAC Address field specifies the Media Access Control (MAC) address for the client computer's network adapter card. You can obtain the MAC address by typing the command **IPCONFIG /ALL** at the Command prompt on the client computer. The Physical Address entry shows the client's MAC address. You must type this value *exactly* for the address reservation to work.

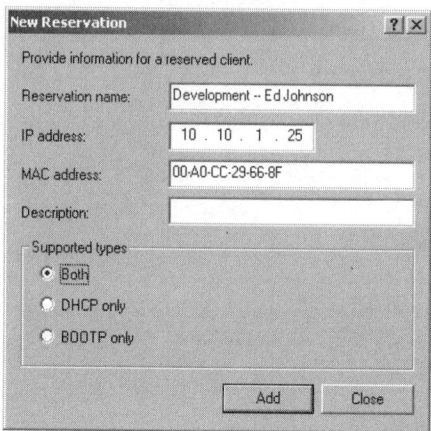

Figure 17-8. *Use the New Reservation dialog box to reserve an IP address for a client.*

5. Enter an optional comment in the Description field if you like.

6. By default, both DHCP and BOOTP clients are supported. This option is fine and only needs to be changed if you want to exclude a particular type of client.

7. Click Add to create the address reservation.

Releasing Addresses and Leases

When you work with reserved addresses, there are a couple of caveats you should know about:

- Reserved addresses aren't automatically reassigned. So if the address is already in use, you'll need to release the address to ensure that the appropriate client can obtain it. You can force a client to release an address by terminating the client's lease or by logging on to the client and typing the command **IPCONFIG /RELEASE** at the Command prompt.

- Clients don't automatically switch to the reserved address. So if the client is already using a different IP address, you'll need to force the client to release the current lease and request a new one. You can do this by terminating the client's lease or by logging on to the client and typing the command **IPCONFIG /RENEW** at the Command prompt.

Modifying Reservation Properties

You can modify the properties of reservations by doing the following:

1. In the DHCP console, expand the scope you want to work with, and then click the Reservations folder.

2. Right-click a reservation, and then select Properties. You can now modify the reservation properties. Fields that are shaded can't be modified. Other fields

can be modified. These fields are the same fields described in the previous section.

Deleting Leases and Reservations

You can delete active leases and reservations by completing the following steps:

1. In the DHCP console, expand the scope you want to work with, and then click the Address Leases or Reservations folder, as appropriate.

2. Right-click the lease or reservation you want to delete, and then choose Delete.

3. Confirm the deletion by clicking Yes.

4. The lease or reservation is now removed from DHCP. However, the client isn't forced to release the IP address. To force the client to release the IP address, log on to the client that holds the lease or reservation and type the command **IPCONFIG /RELEASE** at the Command prompt.

Backing Up
and Restoring the DHCP Database

DHCP servers store DHCP lease and reservation information in database files. By default, these files are stored in the *%SystemRoot%*\System32\dhcp directory. The key files in this directory are used as follows:

- **DHCP.MDB**   The primary database file for the DHCP server

- **DHCP.TMP**   A temporary working file for the DHCP server

- **J50.LOG**   A transaction log file used to recover incomplete transactions in case of a server malfunction

- **J50.CHK**   A checkpoint file used in truncating the transaction log for the DHCP server

The Backup Directory

The backup directory in the *%SystemRoot%*\System32\dhcp folder contains backup information for the DHCP configuration and the DHCP database. By default, the DHCP database is backed up every 60 minutes. Registry keys that control the location and timing of DHCP backups as well as other DHCP settings are located in the folder

```
HKEY_LOCAL_MACHINE
            \SYSTEM
                    \CurrentControlSet
                            \Services
                                    \DHCPServer
                                            \Parameters
```

Restoring the Database from Backup

If you want to force DHCP to restore the database from backup, follow these steps:

1. Stop the DHCP Server service. You can do this either by using the Services And Applications icon on the Computer Management console or by double-clicking the DHCP icon in the Administrative Tools shortcut. Next, right-click the DHCP server, choose All Tasks, and select Stop.

2. Restore a good copy of the *%SystemRoot%*\System32\dhcp\backup directory from a tape or other archive source.

3. Use the Registry Editor to edit the key HKEY_LOCAL_MACHINE\SYSTEM\ CurrentControlSet\Services\DHCPServer\Parameters. Set the key's RestoreFlag value to 1.

4. Start the DHCP Server service. Note that you may have to reauthorize the DHCP. If the arrow next to the DHCP icon is pointing down and is red, select the DHCP server, right-click the server, and then select Authorize.

Chapter 18

Maintaining WINS

Microsoft Windows Internet Naming Service (WINS) is a name resolution service that resolves computer names to Internet Protocol (IP) addresses. Using WINS, the computer name OMEGA, for example, could be resolved to an IP address that enables computers on a Microsoft network to find one another and transfer information. WINS is needed to support pre-Windows 2000 systems and older applications that use Network Basic Input/Output System (NetBIOS) over Transmission Control Protocol/Internet Protocol (TCP/IP), such as the NET command-line utilities. If you don't have pre-Windows 2000 systems or applications on the network, you don't need to use WINS.

The underlying application programming interface (API) that enables WINS name resolution and information transfers between computers is NetBIOS. The NetBIOS API contains a set of commands that applications can use to access session-layer services. Commonly used extensions for NetBIOS are NetBEUI (NetBIOS Enhanced User Interface) and NBT (NetBIOS over TCP/IP). This chapter focuses on WINS and NBT.

In Microsoft Windows 2000, WINS isn't automatically installed. To install WINS, you'll need to perform the following tasks:

1. Click Start, choose Settings, and then click Control Panel.
2. Double-click the Add/Remove Programs icon.
3. Click Add/Remove Windows Components, and then click Next.
4. Under Components, scroll to and click Networking Services.
5. Click Details.
6. Under Subcomponents of Networking Services, click Windows Internet Naming Service (WINS), and then click OK.
7. If prompted, type the full path to the Windows 2000 distribution files, and then click Continue.

Note The WINS server should have a static address.

Understanding WINS and NetBIOS Over TCP/IP

WINS works best in client-server environments where WINS clients send queries to WINS servers for name resolution and WINS servers resolve the query and respond. To transmit WINS queries and other information, computers use NetBIOS. NetBIOS provides an API that allows computers on a network to communicate. When you install TCP/IP networking on a Microsoft client or server, NetBIOS over TCP/IP is also installed. NetBIOS over TCP/IP is a session-layer service that enables NetBIOS applications to run over the TCP/IP protocol stack. NetBIOS applications rely on WINS or the local LMHOSTS file to resolve computer names to IP addresses.

On pre-Windows 2000 networks, WINS is the primary name resolution service available. On Windows 2000 networks, Domain Name System (DNS) is the primary name resolution service and WINS has a different role. This new role is to allow pre-Windows 2000 systems to browse lists of resources on the network and to allow Windows 2000 systems to locate NetBIOS resources.

Configuring WINS Clients and Servers

To enable WINS name resolution on a network, you need to configure WINS clients and servers. When you configure WINS clients, you tell the clients the IP addresses of WINS servers on the network. Using the IP address, clients can communicate with WINS servers anywhere on the network, even if the servers are on different subnets. WINS clients can also communicate using a broadcast method in which clients broadcast messages to other computers on the local network segment requesting their IP addresses. Because messages are broadcast, the WINS server isn't used. Any non-WINS clients that support this type of message broadcasting can also use this method to resolve computer names to IP addresses.

When clients communicate with WINS servers, they establish sessions that have three key parts:

- **Name registration** During name registration, the client gives the server its computer name and its IP address and asks to be added to the WINS database. If the specified computer name and IP address aren't already in use on the network, the WINS server accepts the request and registers the client in the WINS database.

- **Name renewal** Name registration isn't permanent. Instead, the client has use of the name for a specified period, which is known as a *lease*. The client is also given a time period within which the lease must be renewed, which is known as the *renewal interval*. The client must reregister with the WINS server during the renewal interval.

- **Name release** If the client can't renew the lease, the name registration is released, allowing the computer name or IP address, or both, to be used by another system on the network. The names are also released when you shut down a WINS client.

Note Configuring a WINS client is described in the section of Chapter 15 entitled "Configuring WINS Resolution." Configuring a WINS server is described in the section of this chapter entitled "Configuring WINS Servers."

Name Resolution Methods

Once a client establishes a session with a WINS server, the client can request name resolution services. What method is used to resolve computer names to IP addresses depends on how the network is configured. Four name resolution methods are available:

- **B-node (broadcast node)** Uses broadcast messages to resolve computer names to IP addresses. Computers that need to resolve a name broadcast a message to every host on the local network, requesting the IP address for a computer name.

- **P-node (point-to-point node)** Uses WINS servers to resolve computer names to IP addresses. As explained earlier, client sessions have three parts: name registration, name renewal, and name release. When a client needs to resolve a computer name to an IP address, the client sends a query message to the server and the server responds with an answer.

- **M-node (modified node)** Combines b-node and p-node. With it, a WINS client first tries to use b-node for name resolution. If the attempt fails, the client then tries to use p-node. Because b-node is used first, this method has the same problems with network bandwidth usage as b-node.

- **H-node (hybrid node)** Also combines b-node and p-node. With it, a WINS client first tries to use p-node for point-to-point name resolution. If the attempt fails, the client then tries to use broadcast messages with b-node. Because point-to-point is the primary method, h-node offers the best performance on most networks. H-node is also the default method for WINS name resolution.

If WINS servers are available on the network, Windows clients use the p-node method for name resolution. If no WINS servers are available on the network, Windows 2000 clients use the b-node method for name resolution. Windows computers can also use DNS and the local files LMHOSTS and HOSTS to resolve network names. Working with DNS is covered in the next chapter.

Tip When you use Dynamic Host Configuration Protocol (DHCP) to dynamically assign IP addresses, you should set the name resolution method for DHCP clients. To do this, you need to set DHCP scope options for the 046 WINS/NBT Node Type as specified in the section of Chapter 17 entitled "Setting Scope Options." The best method to use is h-node. You'll get the best performance and have reduced traffic on the network.

Using the WINS Console

When you install a new server, it's configured with default settings. You can view and change these settings at any time using the WINS console.

Getting to Know the WINS Console

To manage WINS servers on a network, you'll use the WINS console. This console is found in the Administrative Tools (Common) folder. The main window for the WINS console is shown in Figure 18-1. As you see, the main window is divided into two panes. The left pane lists the WINS servers in the domain by IP address, as well as the local machine, if it's a WINS server.

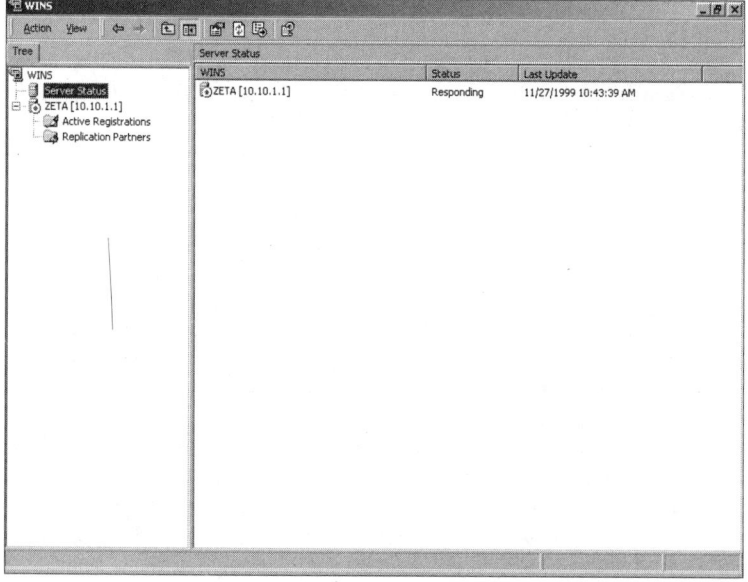

Figure 18-1. *Use the WINS console to manage WINS server configurations.*

By double-clicking an entry in the left pane, you can expand the listing to display the Active Registrations and Replication Partners folders. The Active Registrations folder displays information on the status of registered computer names. The Replication Partners folder shows summary information for WINS servers with which the server replicates registration information.

Adding a WINS Server to the WINS Console

If the WINS console doesn't list the WINS server you want to configure, you can add the server by completing the following steps:

1. Right-click WINS in the console tree, and then select Add Server.

2. Enter the IP address or computer name of the WINS server you want to manage.

3. Click OK. An entry for the WINS server is added to the console tree.

Note You can also manage local and remote WINS servers through Computer Management. Start Computer Management, and then connect to the server you want to manage. Afterward, expand Services And Applications and then select WINS.

Starting and Stopping a WINS Server

You manage WINS servers through the Windows Internet Naming Service. Like any other service, you can start, stop, pause, and resume WINS in the Services node of Computer Management or from the command line. To manage WINS servers using the Computer Management node, right-click WINS, choose All Tasks, and then select Start, Stop, Pause, Resume, or Restart, as appropriate. You can also manage WINS in the WINS console. Right-click the server you want to manage in the WINS console, choose All Tasks, and then select Start, Stop, Pause, Resume, or Restart, as appropriate.

Viewing Server Statistics

Server statistics provide summary information for WINS that can be helpful in monitoring and troubleshooting WINS. To view server statistics, right-click the server in the WINS console and then select Display Server Statistics. As Figure 18-2 shows, the statistics are displayed in a summary format.

The statistics provide the following information:

- **Server Start Time** The time that WINS started on the server.
- **Database Initialized** The time the server's WINS database was initialized.
- **Statistics Last Cleared** The time the server's statistics were last cleared.
- **Last Periodic Replication** The time the WINS database was last replicated based on the replication interval set in the Pull Partner Properties dialog box.
- **Last Manual Replication** The time the WINS database was last replicated by an administrator.
- **Last Net Update Replication** The time the WINS database was last replicated based on a push notification message that requested propagation.
- **Last Address Change Replication** The time the WINS database was last replicated based on an address change message.
- **Total Queries** The total number of queries received by the server since it was last started. Records Found indicates the number of queries successfully resolved. Records Not Found indicates the number of queries that failed.
- **Total Releases** The total number of messages received that indicate a NetBIOS application has released its name registration and shut itself down.

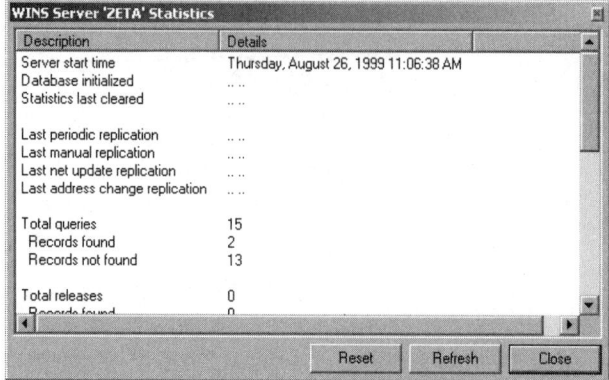

Figure 18-2. *WINS statistics provide information that's useful in monitoring and troubleshooting the service.*

Records Found indicates the number of successful releases. Records Not Found indicates the number of failed releases.

- **Unique Registrations** The total number of name registration messages received and accepted from WINS clients. Conflicts indicate the number of name conflicts encountered for each unique computer name. Renewals indicate the number of renewals received for each unique computer name.

- **Group Registrations** The total number of name registration messages received and accepted from groups. Conflicts indicate the number of name conflicts encountered for group names. Renewals indicate the number of renewals received for group names.

- **Total Registrations** The total number of name registration messages received from WINS clients.

- **Last Periodic Scavenging** The last time a cleaning took place because of the renewal interval set in the WINS Server Configuration dialog box.

- **Last Manual Scavenging** The last time a cleaning was initiated by an administrator.

- **Last Extinction Scavenging** The last time a cleaning took place because of the extinction interval set in the WINS Server Configuration dialog box.

- **Last Verification Scavenging** The last time a cleaning took place because of the verification interval set in the WINS Server Configuration dialog box.

Configuring WINS Servers

When you install a WINS server, the server is configured with default settings. You can change these settings by completing the following steps:

1. Right-click the server you want to work with in the WINS console, and then select Properties. This displays the dialog box shown in Figure 18-3.

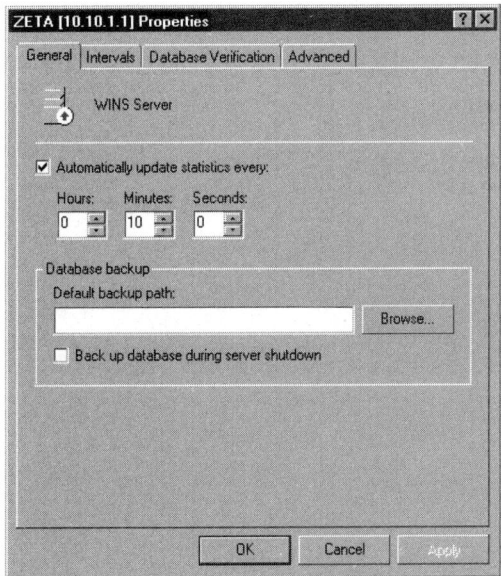

Figure 18-3. *Use the Properties dialog box to configure settings for the WINS server.*

2. Change property values on the General, Interval, Database Verification, and Advanced tabs as explained in the sections that follow.

3. Click OK when you're finished making changes.

Updating WINS Statistics

The WINS console provides statistics on address registrations and replication. By default, these statistics are updated every 10 minutes. If you want, you can change the update interval or stop automatic updates altogether. To do this, follow these steps:

1. In the WINS console, right-click the server you want to work with, and then select Properties.

2. Click the General tab.

3. To set an update interval, select Automatically Update Statistics Every and then type an update interval in hours, minutes, and seconds.

4. To stop automatic updates, clear the Automatically Update Statistics Every check box. Click OK.

Managing Name Registration, Renewal, and Release

Computer names are registered in the WINS database for a specified amount of time known as a *lease*. By setting renewal, extinction, and verification intervals, you can control many aspects of the lease.

1. In the WINS console, right-click the server you want to work with, and then select Properties.

2. Access the Interval tab, shown in Figure 18-4, and then use the following fields to configure the WINS server:

   - **Renewal Interval** Sets the interval during which a WINS client must renew its computer name. It's also known as the *lease period*. Generally, clients attempt to renew when they reach 50 percent of the lease. The minimum value is 40 minutes. The default value is six days, meaning clients attempt to renew their lease every three days. A computer name that isn't renewed is marked as released.

   - **Extinction Interval** Sets the interval during which a computer name can be marked as extinct. Once a computer name has been released, the next step is to mark it as extinct. This value must be greater than or equal to the renewal interval or four days, whichever is smaller.

   - **Extinction Timeout** Sets the interval during which a computer name can be purged from the WINS database. Once a computer name has been marked as extinct, the next step is to purge it from the database. The default value is four days.

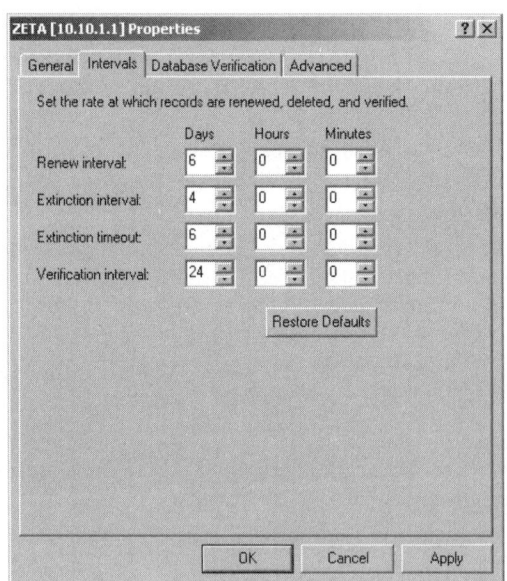

Figure 18-4. *Configure intervals to customize server operation for your network needs.*

⚬ **Verification Interval** Sets the interval after which a WINS server must verify old names it doesn't own. If the names aren't active, they can be removed. The minimum value is 24 days. Generally, computer names registered in a different WINS server have a different owner, and thus they fall into this category.

Tip Think of these intervals as giving you a timeline for names listed in the WINS database. Renewal Interval affects when leases are renewed. Extinction Interval affects when names that aren't renewed are marked as extinct. Extinction Timeout affects when extinct names are purged from the database. If you set Renewal Interval to 24 hours, Extinction Interval to 48 hours, and Extinction Timeout to 24 hours, it could take as long as 96 hours for a record to clear out of the WINS database.

Logging WINS Events in the Windows Event Logs

WINS events are logged in the System event log automatically. While you can't turn this feature off, you can turn on detailed logging temporarily to help troubleshoot WINS problems. To turn on detailed logging, follow these steps:

1. In the WINS console, right-click the server you want to work with, and then select Properties.

2. Access the Advanced tab, and then select Log Detailed Events To The Windows Event Logs.

Note Detailed logging on a busy network can cause a heavy load on the WINS server. Because of this, you should only use detailed logging during testing, troubleshooting, or optimizing.

Setting the Version ID for the WINS Database

The version ID for the WINS database is updated automatically when changes are made to the database. If the WINS database becomes corrupt and you need to restore the database throughout the network, you'll need to access the primary WINS server and then set the version ID to a value higher than the version number counter on all remote partners. Setting a higher version number ensures that the latest information is replicated to replication partners.

You can view and change the current version ID number by completing the following steps:

1. In the WINS console, right-click Active Registrations, and then select Find By Owner. This displays the Find By Owner dialog box.

2. On the Owners tab, the Highest ID column shows the highest version ID number being used on each server. The value is set in hexadecimal format and the maximum value is 2^31.

3. Note the highest version ID value, and then click Cancel.

4. Right-click the entry for the primary WINS server in the console tree, and then select Properties.

5. In the Advanced tab, type a new value in the Starting Version ID field. This value must be entered in hexadecimal format, such as E8B, and should be higher than the value you noted previously. Click OK.

Configuring Burst Handling of Name Registrations

Multiple WINS clients often try to register with a WINS server at the same time. Sometimes this can overload a WINS server, especially if hundreds of computers are all trying to register at the same time. Rather than being unresponsive to new requests, the WINS server can switch to a burst-handling mode. In this mode, the server sends a positive response to client requests before the server processes and enters the requests in the WINS database.

You can modify the threshold for when burst handling occurs to fit the size of your network and the capacity of the server. The default threshold occurs when there are more than 500 registration and name requests in the burst queue. You can set this threshold to a different value by completing the following steps:

1. In the WINS console, right-click the server you want to work with, and then select Properties.

2. In the Advanced tab, make sure that Enable Burst Handling is selected, and then use the following fields to set a new threshold:

   * **Low** Sets the threshold to 300 registration and name requests.
   * **Medium** Sets the threshold to 500 registration and name requests. This is the default value.
   * **High** Sets the threshold to 1000 registration and name requests.
   * **Custom** Allows you to set a threshold value between 50 and 5000.

3. Click OK when you're finished.

 Note The maximum number of registration and name requests that WINS can handle at any one time is 25,000. The WINS server will drop requests if this limit is exceeded.

Saving and Restoring the WINS Configuration

Once you configure all the necessary WINS settings, you may want to save the WINS configuration so that you can restore it on the WINS server. To save the configuration, type **netsh WINS dump >> winsconfig.dmp** at the command prompt.

In this example, winsconfig.dmp is the name of the configuration script you want to create. Once you create this script, you can restore the configuration by typing **netsh exec winsconfig.dmp** at the command prompt.

Tip You can also use this technique to set up another WINS server with the same configuration. Simply copy the configuration script to a folder on the destination computer and then execute it.

Configuring WINS Database Replication

You can configure WINS servers to replicate their databases with each other. This ensures that each server's database is current and reflects changes on the network. As an administrator, you have many options for controlling when replication occurs. You can also force replication at any time.

Replication is handled with push partners and pull partners. A *push partner* is a WINS server that notifies other WINS servers of changes on the network. A *pull partner* is a WINS server that requests replicas from a push partner. You can configure any WINS server as a push partner or pull partner, or both.

To increase the reliability of replication, you can configure persistent connections between replication partners. With persistent connections, replication partners keep connections open even when they're idle. This allows the WINS servers to replicate changes throughout the network quickly and efficiently.

Setting Default Replication Parameters

Before you create replication partners, you'll want to set default parameters. These parameters are used to configure new push and pull partners.

Assigning General Parameters

General parameters control replication and migration. You can set general parameters by completing the following steps:

1. Expand the view for the server you want to work with in the WINS console.
2. Right-click Replication Partners in the tree view, and then choose Properties.
3. In the General tab, select or clear Replicate Only With Partners. If it's selected, this option ensures that WINS information is only replicated with designated replication partners. If it's cleared, you can manually replicate WINS information with any WINS server on the network.
4. Static mappings are created for non-WINS clients on the network, which allows their computer names to be registered in WINS. If multiple computers may use the same IP addresses, you may want WINS to overwrite existing entries with information from new registrations. To do this, select Overwrite Unique Static Mappings At This Server. Click OK.

Assigning Default Push Replication Parameters

By default, replication partners are configured to use both push and pull replication. In this scenario, you usually don't want push replication to occur automatically and instead rely primarily on pull replication for automatic updates. Additionally, because partners are configured for both push and pull replication, you can still initiate push replication manually if need be.

If you want push replication to occur automatically or you want to change the default settings, follow these steps:

1. Expand the view for the server you want to work with in the WINS console.

2. Right-click Replication Partners in the tree view, and then choose Properties.

3. Click the Push Replication tab, shown in Figure 18-5.

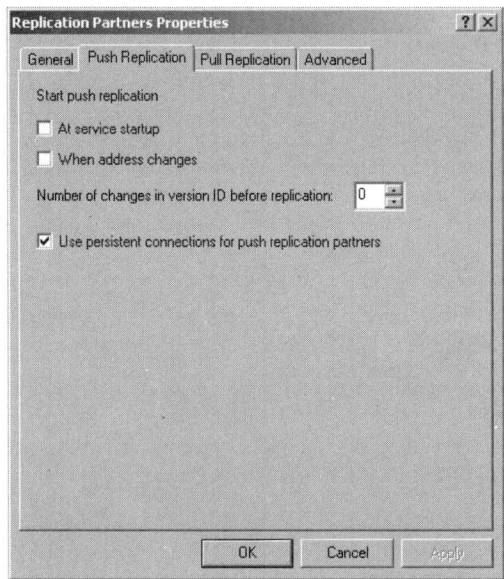

Figure 18-5. *Assign default parameters to manage push replication in the enterprise.*

4. Push replication can be initiated when WINS starts and when address changes occur. By default, these options aren't selected. To change this behavior, select At Service Startup or When Address Changes or both.

5. Number Of Changes In Version ID Before Replication specifies the number of registrations and changes that must take place before pull partners are notified, which triggers database replication. This counter is for local changes only and doesn't tally changes pulled from other partners. If the field is set to zero, no push replication takes place.

6. By default, push replication partners use persistent connections. If you don't want to use persistent connections, clear the Use Persistent Connections For Push Replication Partners check box. Click OK.

Assigning Default Pull Replication Parameters

Pull replication is the default replication technique for replication partners. Because of this, most of the default pull replication parameters are enabled automatically. If you'd rather use push replication as the primary replication technique, you should enable automatic push replication using the options of the Push Replication tab and then disable pull replication defaults using the Pull Replication tab.

To change pull replication settings, follow these steps:

1. Expand the view for the server you want to work with in the WINS console.

2. Right-click Replication Partners in the tree view, and then choose Properties.

3. Click the Pull Replication tab, shown in Figure 18-6.

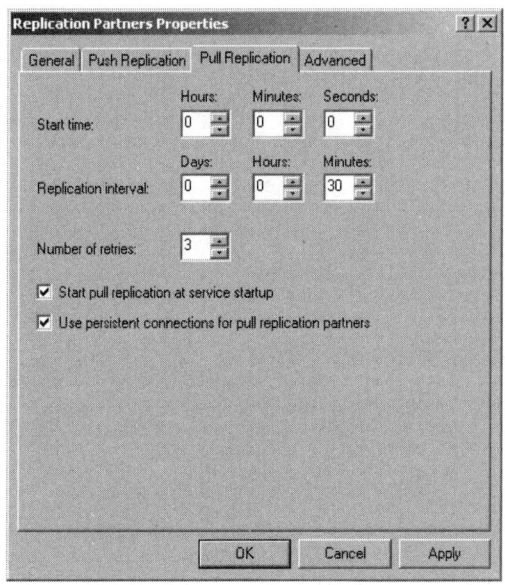

Figure 18-6. *Pull replication is the primary replication technique you should use.*

4. Start Time sets the hour in the day when replication should begin. The time is set using a 24-hour clock.

5. Replication Interval sets the intervals at which scheduled replication should occur, such as every 30 minutes.

6. Number Of Retries sets the number of times the WINS server will retry a connection to a pull partner in the event of a failed connection.

7. By default, pull replication starts when the WINS server starts. To change this behavior, clear the Start Pull Replication At Service Startup check box. When it's cleared, pull replication starts only at the specified Start Time.

8. By default, push replication partners use persistent connections. If you don't want to use persistent connections, clear the Use Persistent Connections For Pull Replication Partners check box. Click OK.

Creating Push and Pull Partners

Push and pull partners are needed to replicate WINS databases whenever there are multiple WINS servers on a network. Replication partners get their initial settings from the default replication parameters you've configured for a server. You must configure replication separately for each WINS server on the network.

To designate WINS servers as push and pull partners, follow these steps:

1. Expand the entry for the server you want to work with in the WINS console. This server is the one for which you'll configure replication partners.

2. Right-click Replication Partners in the console tree, and then select New Replication Partner.

3. Type the name or IP address of the replication partner. Or click Browse to search for a computer to work with in the Select Computer dialog box.

4. Click OK. If the server can be contacted, the replication entry is created automatically using the default settings. The server is configured as a push and pull replication partner.

Changing Replication Type and Settings for Partners

Default settings are used to initialize the parameters for replication partners. You can change these parameters on a per partner basis at any time by completing the following steps:

1. Expand the entry for the server you want to work with in the WINS console. This server is the one for which you'll configure replication partners.

2. In the console tree, select Replication Partners. This displays current replication partners for the server in the right pane.

3. Right-click the replication partner you want to work with, and then select Properties.

4. Click the Advanced tab, shown in Figure 18-7.

5. The Replication Partner Type selection list shows what type of replication is configured for the partner. By default, most clients are set to use both push and pull replication. You can change this behavior by selecting the Push option or the Pull option.

6. The remaining settings are the same as those discussed previously in the sections of this chapter entitled "Assigning Default Push Replication Parameters" and "Assigning Default Pull Replication Parameters." Note that you can only configure some of the options through the Replication Partners Properties dialog box.

7. Click OK when you're finished.

Triggering Database Replication

Sometimes you may want to immediately update the WINS databases on replication partners. You can do this by forcing immediate database replication with partners or by triggering replication among partners. You can also specify the type of replication to initiate.

- **Forcing replication with all partners**   To force replication with all partners, right-click the Replication Partners folder for the server whose database you want to replicate, and then select Replicate Now.

- **Triggering push replication with all partners**   To start push replication with all partners, right-click the server whose database you want to replicate, and then select Start Push Replication.

- **Triggering pull replication with all partners**   To start pull replication with all partners, right-click the server whose database you want to replicate, and then select Start Pull Replication.

- **Triggering push or pull replication with an individual partner**   To start push or pull replication with an individual partner, follow these steps:

1. In the WINS console, click the Replication Partners folder for the server whose database you want to replicate. Currently configured partners are displayed in the right pane.

2. Right-click the partner with which you want to replicate the database, and then select Start Push Replication or Start Pull Replication, as appropriate.

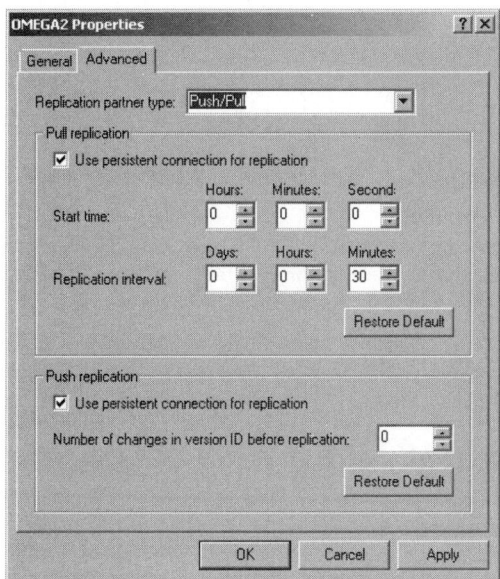

Figure 18-7. *You can change the default replication settings for each replication partner, if necessary.*

Managing the WINS Database

You should actively manage the WINS database to maintain the health of WINS name resolution on the network. The sections that follow examine common management tasks.

Examining WINS Database Mappings

When the Active Registrations folder is selected in the console tree, the right pane of the WINS console displays the records that you've selected for viewing. Each entry represents a record in the WINS databases. At the left side of the entry, you'll see one of two icons. An icon of a single computer shows that the mapping is for a unique name. An icon with multiple computers shows that the mapping is for a group, domain, Internet group, or multihomed entry. Mappings also show the following:

- **Record Name** The complete NetBIOS name of the computer, group, or service registered in the database.
- **Type** The record type associated with this mapping, such as 00h WorkStation.
- **IP Address** The IP address associated with the mapping.
- **State** The state of the record, such as active or released.
- **Static** An X in this column indicates a static mapping.
- **Owner** The IP address of the WINS server that owns the record.
- **Version** The database version ID from which the record originates.
- **Expiration** The time and date the mapping expires. Static mappings have an expiration date of Infinite, which means they don't expire (unless they are overwritten or deleted).

Cleaning and Scavenging the WINS Database

You should periodically clean the WINS database to ensure that old computer names are removed. The process of cleaning the database, called *scavenging*, is initiated automatically according to the relationship between the Extinction Interval and the Extinction Timeout set in the Server Properties dialog box.

You can also initiate scavenging manually. To do this, select the server you want to work with in the WINS console, and then, from the Action menu, choose Scavenge Database.

Verifying the Consistency of the WINS Database

On a large network with multiple WINS servers, the databases on different servers can sometimes get out of sync with each other. To help maintain the integrity of the databases, you may want to verify their consistency periodically. You can perform two types of consistency checking: database consistency and version ID consistency.

When you verify database consistency, WINS checks the integrity of database records on WINS servers. To verify database consistency, select the server you want to work with in the WINS console and then, from the Action menu, choose Verify Database Consistency.

When you verify version ID consistency, WINS checks the local records with records on other WINS servers to ensure that the correct record versions are being maintained. To verify version ID consistency, select the server you want to work with in the WINS console and then, from the Action menu, choose Verify Version ID Consistency.

To configure automatic database consistency checks, complete the following steps:

1. Right-click the server you want to work with in the WINS console, and then select Properties.

2. On the Database Verification tab, select Verify Database Consistency Every ..., as shown in Figure 18-8. Then in the field provided, type a time interval for the checks, such as every 24 hours or every 48 hours.

3. In the Begin Verifying At field, enter the time when you want verification to start. You set the time with a 24-hour clock.

4. As necessary, set the Maximum Number Of Records Verified Each Period. The default value is 30,000.

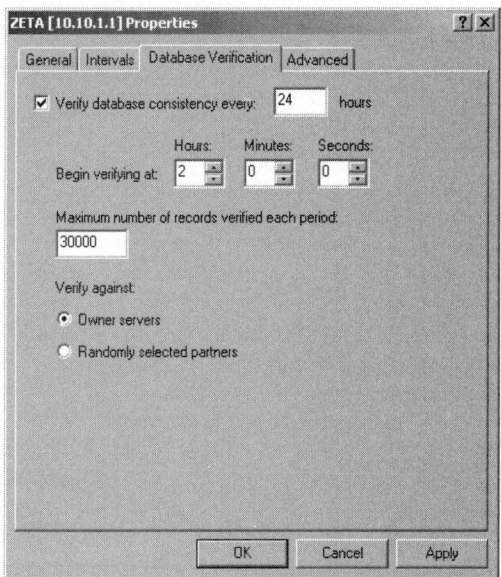

Figure 18-8. *Rather than manually verifying data, you can configure automatic consistency checks.*

Best Practice Don't forget that consistency checks can use considerable system and network resources. To gain better control over when checks occur, you'll usually want to check the WINS database in 24-hour increments, and then use the Begin Verifying At fields to set a time that occurs after hours. For example, if you set the database checks on a 24-hour cycle, then enter a begin time of 2 hours, 0 minutes, and 0 seconds, WINS will verify the database at 2 A.M. every 24 hours.

5. You can verify records against servers designated as owners or against randomly selected partners. Random selection works best if you have a very large network and can't check all the records at any one time. Otherwise, select Owner Servers to verify records on the servers designated as record owners.

6. Click OK when you're finished.

Backing Up and Restoring the WINS Database

Two WINS server tasks that administrators often overlook are backup and restore.

Configuring WINS for Automatic Backups

The WINS database isn't backed up by default. If you have problems with the database you won't be able to recover it. To protect against database failure, you should configure automatic backups or run manual backups periodically. To prepare WINS to perform automatic backups, follow these steps:

1. Right-click the server you want to work with in the WINS console, and then select Properties.

2. In the General tab, enter the folder path that you want to use for backups in Default Backup Path. Click Browse if you want to search for a folder.

3. To ensure that backups are created whenever the WINS server is stopped, select Backup Database During Server Shutdown.

4. Click OK. Automatic backups will then be performed every three hours.

Restoring the Database

If you have a good backup of the WINS database, you can restore it by completing the following steps:

1. Select the server you want to work with in the WINS console.

2. Click the Action menu, choose All Tasks, and then select Stop.

3. Click the Action menu, and then select Restore Database.

4. In the Browse For Folder dialog box, select the wins_bak subdirectory containing the most recent backup and then click OK.

5. If the restore is successful, the WINS database is restored to its state at the time of the backup. Click the Action menu, choose All Tasks, and then select Start.

6. If the restore is unsuccessful, you may need to clear out all WINS files and then start with a fresh database.

Clearing Out WINS
and Starting with a Fresh Database

If WINS won't restore using a backup or won't start normally, you may need to clear out all WINS records and logs and then start with a fresh database. To do this, follow steps:

1. Right-click the server you want to work with in the WINS console, and then select Properties.

2. On the Advanced tab, note the folder path set in Database Path, and then click OK to close the Properties dialog box.

3. Stop the server by clicking the Action menu, choosing All Tasks, and then selecting Stop.

4. Using Microsoft Windows Explorer, delete all files in the WINS database folder.

5. In the WINS console, right-click the server you're recovering, choose All Tasks, and then select Start. This starts the WINS servers.

Chapter 19

Optimizing DNS

This chapter discusses the techniques you'll use to set up and manage DNS (Domain Name System) on a network. DNS is a name resolution service that resolves computer names to IP addresses. Using DNS, the fully qualified host name omega.microsoft.com, for example, could be resolved to an IP address, which enables computers to find one another. DNS operates over the Transmission Control Protocol/Internet Protocol (TCP/IP) protocol stack and can be integrated with Windows Internet Naming Service (WINS), Dynamic Host Configuration Protocol (DHCP), and Active Directory directory service. Full integration with these Microsoft Windows networking features allows you to optimize DNS for Windows 2000 domains.

Understanding DNS

DNS organizes groups of computers into *domains*. These domains are organized into a hierarchical structure, which can be defined on an Internet-wide basis for public networks or on an enterprise-wide basis for private networks (also known as intranets and extranets). The various levels within the hierarchy identify individual computers, organizational domains, and top-level domains. For the fully qualified host name omega.microsoft.com, *omega* represents the host name for an individual computer, *Microsoft* is the organizational domain, and *com* is the top-level domain.

Top-level domains are at the root of the DNS hierarchy and are therefore also called *root domains*. These domains are organized geographically, by organization type and by function. Normal domains, such as microsoft.com, are also referred to as *parent domains*. They are called parent domains because they're the parents of an organizational structure. Parent domains can be divided into subdomains, which can be used for groups or departments within an organization. Subdomains are often referred to as *child domains*. For example, the fully qualified domain name for a computer within a human resources group could be designated as jacob.hr.microsoft.com. Here, *jacob* is the host name, *hr* is the child domain, and *microsoft.com* is the parent domain.

Integrating Active Directory and DNS

As stated in Chapter 5, Active Directory domains use DNS to implement their naming structure and hierarchy. Active Directory directory service and DNS are tightly integrated, so much so that you must install DNS on the network before you can install Active Directory.

During installation of the first domain controller on an Active Directory network, you'll have the opportunity to automatically install DNS if a DNS server can't be found on the network. You'll also be able to specify whether DNS and Active Directory should be integrated fully. In most cases, you should respond affirmatively to both requests. With full integration, DNS information is stored directly in Active Directory. This allows you to take advantage of the capabilities of Active Directory. The difference between partial integration and full integration is very important:

- **Partial integration**   With partial integration, the domain uses standard file storage. DNS information is stored in text-based files that end with the .DNS extension, and the default location of these files is %SystemRoot%\System32\ Dns. Updates to DNS are handled through a single authoritative DNS server. This server is designated as the primary DNS server for the particular domain or area within a domain called a *zone*. Clients that use dynamic DNS updates through DHCP must be configured to use the primary DNS server in the zone. If they aren't, their DNS information won't be updated. Likewise, dynamic updates through DHCP can't be made if the primary DNS server is offline.

- **Full integration**   With full integration, the domain uses directory-integrated storage. DNS information is stored directly in Active Directory and is available through the container for the dnsZone object. Because the information is part of Active Directory, any domain controller can access the data and a multimaster approach can be used for dynamic updates through DHCP. This allows any domain controller running the DNS Server service to handle dynamic updates. Further clients that use dynamic DNS updates through DHCP can use any DNS server within the zone. An added benefit of directory integration is the ability to use directory security to control access to DNS information.

When you look at the way DNS information is replicated throughout the network, you also see advantages to full integration with Active Directory. With partial integration, DNS information is stored and replicated separately from Active Directory. By having two separate structures, you reduce the effectiveness of both DNS and Active Directory and make administration more complex. Because DNS is less efficient than Active Directory at replicating changes, you may also increase network traffic and the amount of time it takes to replicate DNS changes throughout the network.

Enabling DNS on the Network

To enable DNS on the network, you need to configure DNS clients and servers. When you configure DNS clients, you tell the clients the IP addresses of DNS servers on the network. Using these addresses, clients can communicate with DNS servers anywhere on the network, even if the servers are on different subnets. When the network uses DHCP, you should configure DHCP to work with DNS. To do this, you need to set the DHCP scope options 006 DNS Servers and 015 DNS Domain Name as specified in the section of Chapter 17 entitled "Setting Scope Options."

Additionally, if computers on the network need to be accessible from other Active Directory domains, you need to create records for them in DNS. DNS records are organized into zones, where a zone is simply an area within a domain.

Note   Configuring a DNS client is explained in the section of Chapter 15 entitled "Configuring DNS Resolution." Configuring a DNS server is explained in the following section of this chapter.

Installing DNS Servers

You can configure any Microsoft Windows 2000 server as a DNS server. Four types of DNS servers are available:

- **Active Directory-integrated primary**   A DNS server that is fully integrated with Active Directory. All DNS data is stored directly in the Directory.

- **Primary server**   The main DNS server for a domain that uses partial integration with Active Directory. This server stores a master copy of DNS records and the domain's configuration files. These files are stored as text with the .DNS extension.

- **Secondary server**   A DNS server that provides backup services for the domain. This server stores a copy of DNS records obtained from a primary server and relies on zone transfers for updates. Secondary servers obtain their DNS information from a primary server when they're started, and they maintain this information until the information is refreshed or expired.

- **Forwarding-only server**   A server that caches DNS information after lookups and that always passes requests to other servers. These servers maintain DNS information until it's refreshed or expired or until the server is restarted. Unlike secondary servers, forwarding-only servers don't request full copies of a zone's database files. This means that when you start a forwarding-only server, its database contains no information.

Before you configure a DNS server, you must install the DNS Server service. Afterward, you can configure the server to provide integrated, primary, secondary, or forwarding-only DNS services.

Installing the DNS Server Service

All domain controllers can act as DNS servers, and you may be prompted to install and configure DNS during installation of the domain controller. If you responded affirmatively to the prompts, DNS is already installed and the default configuration is set automatically. You don't need to reinstall.

If you're working with a member server instead of a domain controller or if you haven't installed DNS, complete the following steps to install DNS:

1. Click Start, choose Settings, and then click Control Panel.

2. In Control Panel, double-click Add/Remove Programs, and then click Add/Remove Windows Components. This changes the view in the Add/Remove Programs dialog box.

3. Click Components to start the Windows Components Wizard, and then click Next.

4. Under Components, click Networking Services, and then click Details.

5. Under Subcomponents Of Networking Services, select the Domain Name System (DNS) check box.

6. Click OK, and then click Next. If prompted, type the full path to the Windows 2000 distribution files and click Continue.

From now on, Windows Internet Name Service (WINS) should start automatically each time you reboot the server. If it doesn't start, you'll need to start it manually. See the section of this chapter entitled "Starting and Stopping a DNS Server."

Configuring a Primary DNS Server

Every domain should have a primary DNS server. This server can be integrated with Active Directory or it can act as a standard primary server. Primary servers should have forward lookup zones and reverse lookup zones. Forward lookups are used to resolve domain names to IP addresses. Reverse lookups are needed to authenticate DNS requests by resolving IP addresses to domain names or hosts.

Once you install the DNS Server service on the server, you can configure a primary server by completing the following steps:

1. Start the DNS console. Click the Start menu, choose Programs, choose Administrative Tools (Common), and then select DNS. This displays the DNS console shown in Figure 19-1.

2. If the server you want to configure isn't listed in the tree view, you'll need to connect to the server. Right-click DNS in the tree view and then choose Connect To Computer. Now do one of the following:

   * If you're trying to connect to a local server, select This Computer and then click OK.

   * If you're trying to connect to a remote server, select The Following Computer and then type the server's name or IP address. Then click OK.

3. An entry for the DNS server should be listed in the tree view window of the DNS console. Right-click the server entry and then from the pop-up menu, choose New Zone. This starts the New Zone Wizard. Click Next.

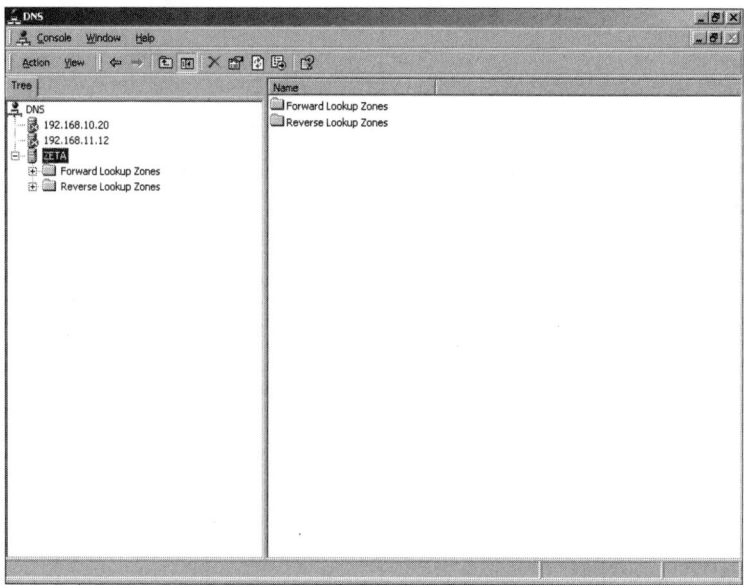

Figure 19-1. *You use the DNS console to manage DNS servers on the network. An alternative to the DNS console is to use the Services And Applications node in Computer Management. Access the node and then click DNS.*

4. As Figure 19-2 shows, you can now select the zone type. If you're configuring a primary server integrated with Active Directory, select Active Directory-Integrated and then click Next. Otherwise, choose Standard Primary and then click Next.

5. Select Forward Lookup Zone, and then click Next.

6. Enter the full DNS name for the zone. The zone name should help determine how the server or zone fits into the DNS domain hierarchy. For example, if you're creating the primary server for the microsoft.com domain, you should type **microsoft.com** as the zone name.

7. If you're configuring a standard primary zone, you need to set the zone file name. A default name for the zone's DNS database file should be filled in for you. You can use this name or type a new file name.

8. Click Next, and then click Finish to complete the process. The new zone is added to the server and basic DNS records are created automatically.

9. A single DNS server can provide services for multiple domains. If you have multiple parent domains, such as microsoft.com and msn.com, you can repeat this process to configure other forward lookup zones. You also need to configure reverse lookup zones. Follow the steps listed in the section of this chapter entitled "Configuring Reverse Lookups."

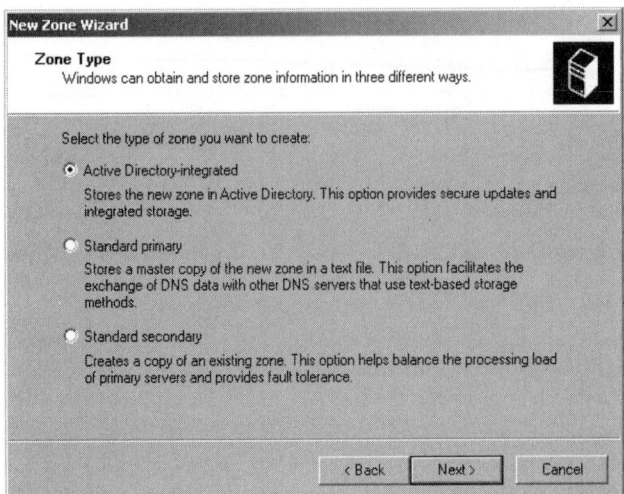

Figure 19-2. *In the New Zone Wizard, select Active Directory-Integrated or Standard Primary for the zone type.*

10. You need to create additional records for any computers that should be accessible to other DNS domains. Follow the steps listed in the section of this chapter entitled "Managing DNS Records."

Configuring a Secondary DNS Server

Secondary servers provide backup DNS services on the network. If you're using full Active Directory integration, you don't really need to configure secondaries. Instead, you should configure multiple domain controllers to handle DNS services. On the other hand, if you're using partial integration, you may want to configure secondaries to lessen the load on the primary server. On a small-sized or medium-sized network, you may be able to use your Internet service provider's (ISP) name servers as secondaries, and in this case you should contact your Internet service provider to configure secondary DNS services for you.

Since secondary servers use forward lookup zones for most types of queries, reverse lookup zones may not be needed. But reverse lookup zone files are essential for primary servers, and they must be configured for proper domain name resolution.

If you want to set up your own secondaries for backup services and load balancing, follow these steps:

1. Start the DNS console and connect to the server you want to configure as described previously.

2. Right-click the server entry, and then from the pop-up menu, choose New Zone. This starts the New Zone Wizard. Click Next.

3. In the Zone Type dialog box, select Standard Secondary. Click Next.

4. Secondary servers can use both forward and reverse lookup zone files. You'll create the forward lookup zone first, so select Forward Lookup Zone and then click Next.

5. Enter a name for the zone file and then click Next.

6. Secondary servers should copy zone files from primary servers. Type the IP address for the primary server for the zone, and then click Add. If you want to copy data from other zones, type the IP address of additional servers.

7. Click Next and then click Finish.

8. On a busy or large network, you may need to configure reverse lookup zones on secondaries. If so, follow the steps listed in the following section of this chapter, "Configuring Reverse Lookups."

Configuring Reverse Lookups

Forward lookups are used to resolve domain names to IP addresses. Reverse lookups are used to resolve IP addresses to domain names. Each segment on your network should have a reverse lookup zone. For example, if you have the subnets 192.168.10.0, 192.168.11.0, and 192.168.12.0, you should have three reverse lookup zones.

The standard naming convention for reverse lookup zones is to type the network ID in reverse order and then use the suffix in-addr.arpa. With the previous example, you'd have reverse lookup zones named 10.168.192.in-addr.arpa, 11.168.192.in-addr.arpa, and 12.168.192.in-addr.arpa. Records in the reverse lookup zone must be in sync with the forward lookup zone. If the zones get out of sync, authentication may fail for the domain.

You create reverse lookup zones by doing the following:

1. Start the DNS console and connect to the server you want to configure as described previously.

2. Right-click the server entry, and then from the pop-up menu, choose New Zone. This starts the New Zone Wizard. Click Next.

3. Select Active Directory-Integrated, Standard Primary, or Standard Secondary based on the type of server you're working with.

4. Select Reverse Lookup Zone. Click Next.

5. Type the network ID and subnet mask for the reverse lookup zone. The values you enter set the default name for the reverse lookup zone.

Tip If you have multiple subnets on the same network, such as 192.168.10 and 192.168.11, enter only the network portion for the zone name. That is, you would use 168.192.in-addr.arpa and allow the DNS console to create the necessary subnet zones when needed.

6. If you're configuring a standard primary or secondary server, you need to set the zone file name. A default name for the zone's DNS database file should be filled in for you. You can use this name or type a new file name.

7. If you're configuring a secondary server, type the IP address for the primary server for the zone and then click Add. If you want to copy data from other zones, type the IP address of additional servers.

8. Click Next, and then click Finish.

Once you set up the reverse lookup zones, you need to ensure that delegation for the zone is handled properly. Contact the Information Services department or your Internet service provider to ensure that the zones are registered with the parent domain.

Managing DNS Servers

The DNS console is the tool you'll use to manage local and remote DNS servers. As shown in Figure 19-3, the main window of the DNS console is divided into two panes. The left pane allows you to access DNS servers and their zones. The right pane shows the details for the currently selected item. You can work with the DNS console in several ways:

- Double-click an entry in the left pane to expand the list of files for the entry.

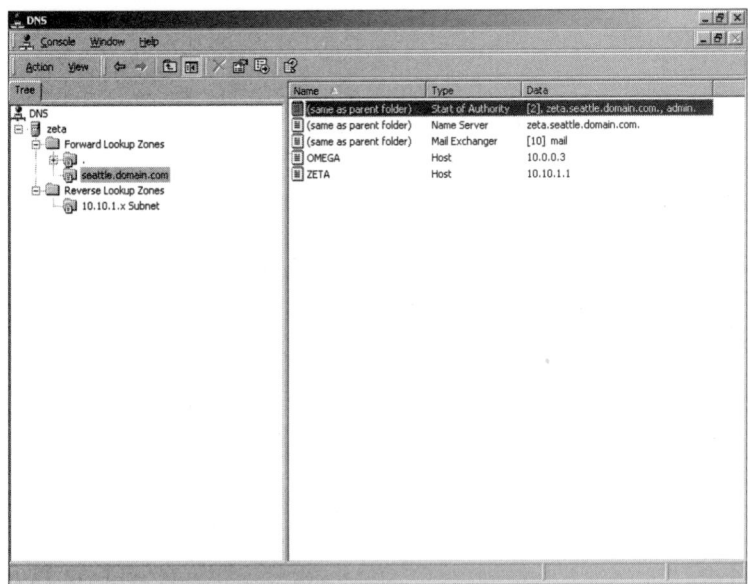

Figure 19-3. *You manage domains and subnets through the Forward Lookup Zones and Reverse Lookup Zones folders.*

- Select an entry in the left pane to display details such as zone status and domain records in the right pane.
- Right-click an entry to display a context menu with available options.

The Forward Lookup Zones and Reverse Lookup Zones folders provide access to the domains and subnets configured for use on this server. When you select domain or subnet folders in the left pane, you can manage DNS records for the domain or subnet.

Adding Remote Servers to the DNS Console

You can manage servers running DNS from the DNS console by doing the following steps:

1. Right-click DNS in the console tree, and then select Connect To Computer. This opens the dialog box shown in Figure 19-4.
2. If you're trying to connect to the local computer, select This Computer. Otherwise, select The Following Computer and then type the IP address or fully qualified host name of the remote computer to which you want to connect.
3. Click OK. Windows 2000 attempts to contact the server, and if it does, it adds the server to the console.

Note If a server is offline or otherwise inaccessible due to security restrictions or problems with the remote procedure call (RPC) service, the connection will fail. You can still add the server to the console by clicking Yes when prompted.

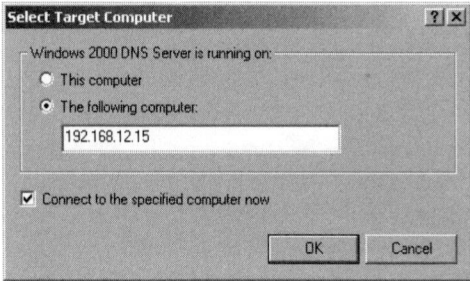

Figure 19-4. *Connect to a local or remote server through the Select Target Computer dialog box.*

Removing a Server from the DNS Console

In the DNS console, you can delete a server by selecting its entry and then pressing DEL. When prompted, click OK to confirm the deletion. Deleting a server only removes it from the Server List. It doesn't actually delete the server.

Starting and Stopping a DNS Server

To manage DNS servers, you use the DNS Server service. You can start, stop, pause, and resume the DNS Server service in the Services node of Computer Management or from the command line. You can also manage the DNS Server service in the DNS console. Right-click the server you want to manage in the DNS console, choose All Tasks and then select Start, Stop, Pause, Resume, or Restart, as appropriate.

 Note In Computer Management, right-click DNS, choose All Tasks, and then select Start, Stop, Pause, Resume, or Restart, as appropriate.

Creating Child Domains Within Zones

Using the DNS console, you can create child domains within a zone. For example, if you created the primary zone microsoft.com, you could create hr.microsoft.com and mis.microsoft.com subdomains for the zone. You create child domains by completing the following steps:

1. In the DNS console, expand the Forward Lookup Zones folder for the server you want to work with.
2. Right-click the parent domain entry, and then from the pop-up menu, select New Domain.
3. Enter the name of the new domain, and then click OK. For hr.microsoft.com, you would enter **hr.** For mis.microsoft.com, you would enter **mis.**

Creating Child Domains in Separate Zones

As your organization grows, you may want to organize the DNS name space into separate zones. At the corporate headquarters you could have a zone for the parent domain microsoft.com. At branch offices you could have zones for each office, such as memphis.microsoft.com, newyork.microsoft.com, and la.microsoft.com.

You create child domains in separate zones by completing the following steps:

1. Install a DNS server in each child domain, and then create the necessary forward and reverse lookup zones for the child domain as described in the section of this chapter entitled "Installing DNS Servers."
2. On the authoritative DNS server for the parent domain, you delegate authority to each child domain. Delegating authority allows the child domain to resolve and respond to DNS queries from computers inside and outside the local subnet.

You delegate authority to a child domain by completing the following steps:

1. In the DNS console, expand the Forward Lookup Zones folder for the server you want to work with.

2. Right-click the parent domain entry, and then from the pop-up menu, select New Delegation. This starts the New Delegation Wizard.

3. As shown in Figure 19-5, type the name of the child domain and then click Next. The name you enter updates the value in the Fully Qualified Domain Name field.

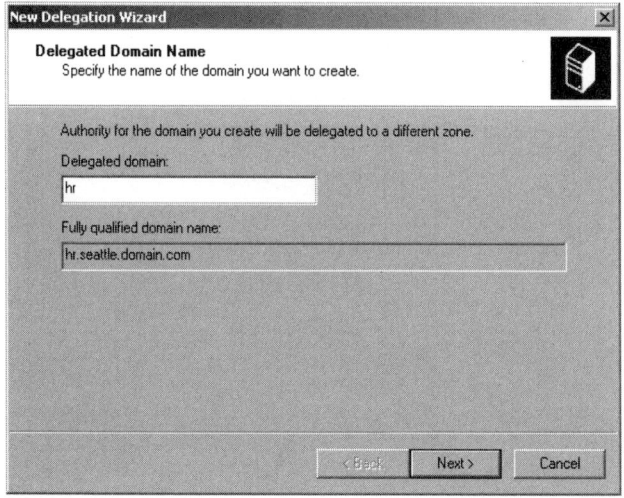

Figure 19-5. *Entering the name of the child domain sets the fully qualified domain name.*

4. Click Add. This displays the dialog box shown in Figure 19-6.

5. In the Server Name field, type the fully qualified host name of a DNS server for the child domain.

6. In the IP Address field, type the primary IP address for the server. Click Add. Repeat this process to specify additional IP addresses for the server. The order of the entries determines which IP address is used first. Change the order as necessary using the Up and Down buttons.

Tip If you know the name of a server rather than its IP address, type the name in the Server Name field, and then click Resolve. The IP address is then entered in the IP Address field, if possible. Add the server by clicking Add.

7. Click OK, and then repeat steps 3–5 to specify other authoritative DNS servers for the child domain.

8. Click Next, and then click Finish to complete the process.

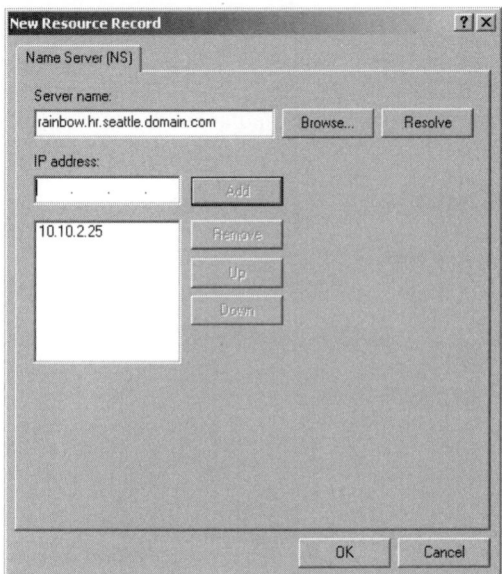

Figure 19-6. *Type the fully qualified name of a DNS server for the child domain and then type the IP address(es) for the server.*

Deleting a Domain or Subnet

Deleting a domain or subnet permanently removes it from the DNS server. To delete a domain or subnet, follow these steps:

1. In the DNS console, right-click the domain or subnet entry.

2. From the pop-up menu, select Delete, and then confirm the action by clicking OK.

 Note Deleting a domain or subnet deletes all DNS records in a zone file but doesn't actually delete the zone file on a standard primary or standard secondary server. You'll find that the actual zone file remains in the %SystemRoot%/System32/Dns directory. You can delete this file if you like.

Managing DNS Records

After you create the necessary zone files, you can add records to the zones. Computers that need to be accessed from Active Directory and DNS domains must have DNS records. Although there are many different types of DNS records, most of these record types aren't commonly used. So rather than focus on record types you probably *won't* use, let's focus on the ones you *will* use:

- **A (address)** Maps a host name to an IP address. When a computer has multiple adapter cards or IP addresses, or both, it should have multiple address records.

- **CNAME (canonical name)** Sets an alias for a host name. For example, using this record, zeta.microsoft.com can have an alias as www.microsoft.com.

- **MX (mail exchange)** Specifies a mail exchange server for the domain, which allows mail to be delivered to the correct mail servers in the domain.

- **NS (name server)** Specifies a name server for the domain, which allows DNS lookups within various zones. Each primary and secondary name server should be declared through this record.

- **PTR (pointer)** Creates a pointer that maps an IP address to a host name for reverse lookups.

- **SOA (start of authority)** Declares the host that's the most authoritative for the zone and, as such, is the best source of DNS information for the zone. Each zone file must have an SOA record (which is created automatically when you add a zone).

Adding Address and Pointer Records

The A record maps a host name to an IP address and the PTR record creates a pointer to the host for reverse lookups. You can create address and pointer records at the same time or separately.

You create a new host entry with A and PTR records by doing the following:

1. In the DNS console, expand the Forward Lookup Zones folder for the server you want to work with.

2. Right-click the domain you want to update, and then from the pop-up menu, choose New Host. This opens the dialog box shown in Figure 19-7.

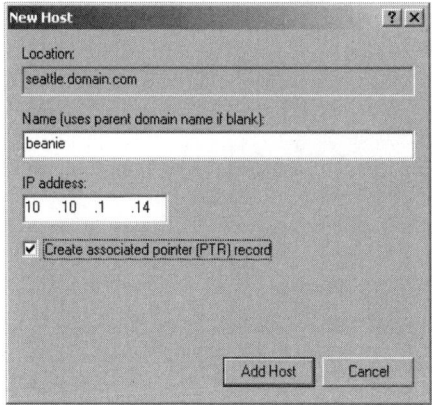

Figure 19-7. *Create A records and PTR records simultaneously with the New Host option.*

3. Type the single-part computer name and IP address.

4. Select the Create Associated Pointer (PTR) Record check box.

5. Click OK.

 Note You can only create PTR records if the corresponding reverse lookup zone is available. You can create this file by following the steps listed in the section of this chapter entitled "Configuring Reverse Lookups."

6. Click Add Host. Repeat as necessary to add other hosts.

7. Click Done when you're finished.

Adding a PTR Record Later

If you need to add a PTR record later, you can do so by completing the following steps:

1. In the DNS console, expand the Reverse Lookup Zones folder for the server you want to work with.

2. Right-click the subnet you want to update, and then from the pop-up menu, choose New Pointer. This opens the dialog box shown in Figure 19-8.

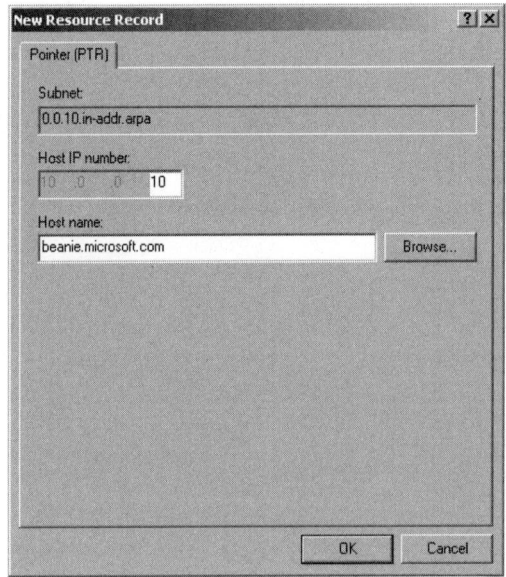

Figure 19-8. *You can add PTR records later, if necessary, with the New Resource Record dialog box.*

3. Type the host IP number, and then type the fully qualified domain name of the computer, such as 10.10.1.14 and beanie.microsoft.com. Click OK.

Adding DNS Aliases with CNAME

You specify host aliases using CNAME records. Aliases allow a single host computer to appear to be multiple host computers. For example, the host gamma.microsoft.com can be made to appear as www.microsoft.com and ftp.microsoft.com.

To create a CNAME record, follow these steps:

1. In the DNS console, expand the Forward Lookup Zones folder for the server you want to work with.

2. Right-click the domain you want to update and then from the pop-up menu, choose New Alias. This opens the dialog box shown in Figure 19-9.

3. Type the alias in the Alias Name field. The alias is a single-part host name, such as www or ftp.

4. In the Fully Qualified Name For Target Host Field, type the full host name of the computer for which the alias is to be used.

5. Click OK.

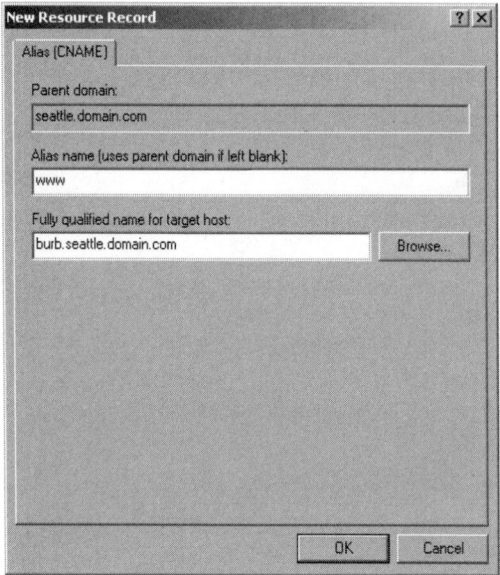

Figure 19-9. *When you create the CNAME record, be sure to use the single-part host name and then the fully qualified host name.*

Adding Mail Exchange Servers

MX records identify mail exchange servers for the domain. These servers are responsible for processing or forwarding mail within the domain. When you create an MX record, you must specify a preference number for the mail server. A preference number is a value from 0 to 65,535 that denotes the mail server's priority within the domain. The mail server with the lowest preference number has the highest priority and is the first to receive mail. If mail delivery fails, the mail server with the next lowest preference number is tried.

You create a MX record by doing the following:

1. In the DNS console, expand the Forward Lookup Zones folder for the server you want to work with.

2. Right-click the domain you want to update, and then from the pop-up menu, choose New Mail Exchanger. This opens the dialog box shown in Figure 19-10.

3. You can now create a record for the mail server by filling in these fields:

   - **Host Or Domain**   Enter the optional host name.

   - **Mail Server**   Enter the fully qualified host name.

   - **Mail Server Priority**   Enter a preference number for the host from 0 to 65,535.

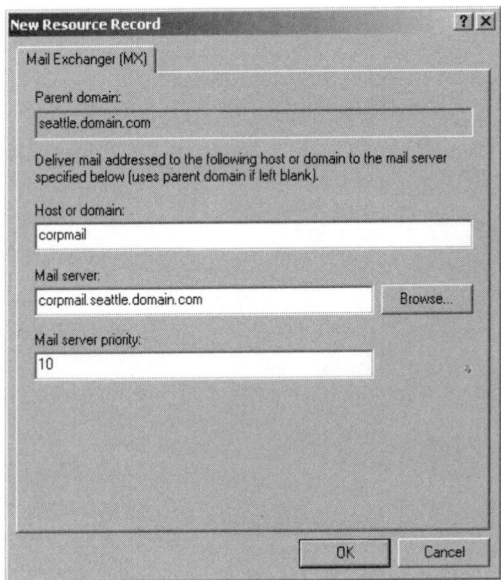

Figure 19-10. *Mail servers with the lowest preference number have the highest priority.*

Tip   Assign preference numbers that leave room for growth. For example, use 10 for your highest priority mail server, 20 for the next, and 30 for the one after that.

4. Click OK.

Adding Name Servers

Name Server records specify the name servers for the domain. Each primary and secondary name server should be declared through this record. If you obtain secondary name services from an Internet service provider, be sure to insert the appropriate Name Server records.

You create a Name Server record by doing the following:

1. In the DNS console, expand the Forward Lookup Zones folder for the server you want to work with.

2. Display the DNS records for the domain by selecting the domain folder in the tree view.

3. Right-click an existing Name Server record in the view pane, and then select Properties. This opens the Properties dialog box for the domain with the Name Servers tab selected, as shown in Figure 19-11.

4. Click Add.

5. In the Server Name field, type the fully qualified host name of the DNS server you're adding.

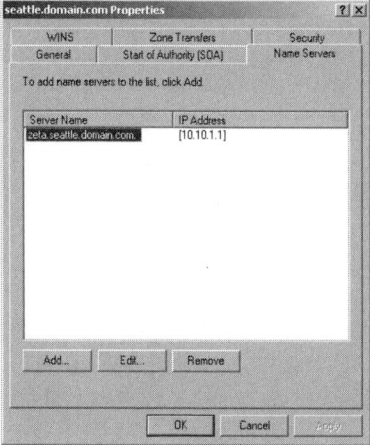

Figure 19-11.   *Configure name servers for the domain through the domain's Properties dialog box.*

6. In the IP Address field, type the primary IP address for the server. Click Add. Repeat this process to specify additional IP addresses for the server. The order of the entries determines which IP address is used first. Change the order as necessary using the Up and Down buttons.

7. Click OK. Repeat steps 5–7 to specify other DNS servers for the domain.

Viewing and Updating DNS Records

To view or update DNS records, follow these steps:

1. Double-click the zone you want to work with. Records for the zone should be displayed in the right pane.

2. Double-click the DNS record you want to view or update. This opens the record's Properties dialog box. Make the necessary changes and click OK.

Updating Zone Properties and the SOA Record

Each zone has separate properties that you can configure. These properties set general zone parameters by using the start of authority (SOA) record, change notification, and WINS integration. In the DNS console, you set zone properties by doing the following:

1. Right-click the zone you want to update, and then from the pop-up menu, choose Properties.

2. Select the zone, and then from the Action menu, choose Properties.

Properties dialog boxes for forward and reverse lookup zones are identical except for the WINS and WINS-R tabs. In forward lookup zones, you use the WINS tab to configure lookups for NetBIOS computer names. In reverse lookup zones, you use the WINS-R tab to configure reverse lookups for NetBIOS computer names.

Modifying the Start Of Authority Record

A start of authority (SOA) record designates the authoritative name server for a zone and sets general zone properties, such as retry and refresh intervals. You can modify this information by doing the following:

1. In the DNS console, right-click the zone you want to update and then from the pop-up menu, choose Properties.

2. Click the Start Of Authority (SOA) tab, and then update the fields shown in Figure 19-12.

You use the fields of the Start Of Authority (SOA) tab as follows:

- **Serial Number** A serial number that indicates the version of the DNS database files. The number is updated automatically whenever you make changes to zone files. You can also update the number manually. Secondary servers use this number to determine if the zone's DNS records have changed. If the primary server's serial number is larger than the secondary server's serial number, the records have changed and the secondary server can request the DNS records have changed and the secondary server can request the DNS records for the zone. You can also configure DNS to notify secondary servers of changes (which may speed up the update process).

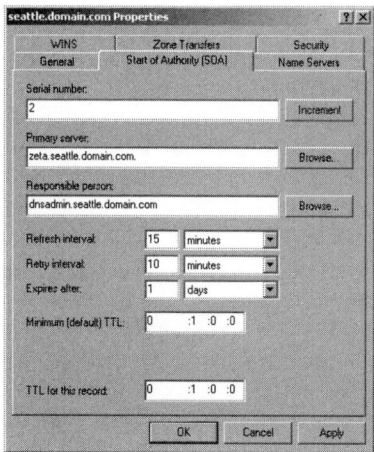

Figure 19-12. *Use the zone's Properties dialog box to set general properties for the zone and to update the SOA record.*

- **Primary Server**   The fully qualified domain name for the name server, followed by a period. The period is used to terminate the name and ensure that the domain information isn't appended to the entry.

- **Responsible Person**   The e-mail address of the person in charge of the domain. The default entry is *administrator* followed by a period, meaning administrator@your_domain. If you change this entry, substitute a period in place of the at (@) symbol in the e-mail address and terminate the address with a period.

- **Refresh Interval**   The interval at which a secondary server checks for zone updates. If it's set to 60 minutes, NS record changes may not get propagated to a secondary server for up to an hour. You reduce network traffic by increasing this value.

- **Retry Interval**   The time the secondary server waits after a failure to download the zone database. If it's set to 10 minutes and a zone database transfer fails, the secondary server will wait 10 minutes before requesting the zone database once more.

- **Expires After**   The period of time for which zone information is valid on the secondary server. If the secondary server can't download data from a primary server within this period, the secondary server lets the data in its cache expire and stops responding to DNS queries. Setting Expires After to seven days allows the data on a secondary server to be valid for seven days.

- **Minimum (Default) TTL** The minimum time-to-live value for cached records on a secondary server. The value is set in the format Days : Hours : Minutes : Seconds. When this value is reached, the secondary server expires the associated record and discards it. The next request for the record will need to be sent to the primary server for resolution. Set the minimum TTL to a relatively high value, such as 24 hours, to reduce traffic on the network and increase efficiency. However, keep in mind that a higher value slows down the propagation of updates through the Internet.

- **TTL For This Record** The time-to-live value for this SOA record itself. The value is set in the format Days : Hours : Minutes : Seconds and generally should be the same as the minimum TTL for all records.

Notifying Secondaries of Changes

You set properties for a zone with its start of authority record. These properties control how DNS information is propagated on the network. You can also specify that the primary server should notify secondary name servers when changes are made to the zone database. To do this, follow these steps:

1. In the DNS console, right-click the domain or subnet you want to update and then from the pop-up menu, choose Properties.

2. On the Zone Transfers tab, click Notify. This displays the dialog box shown in Figure 19-13.

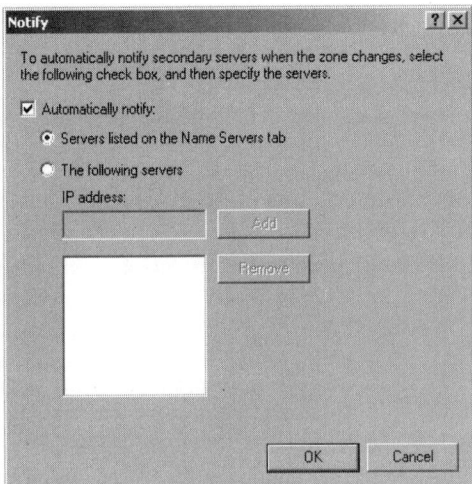

Figure 19-13. *You can notify all secondaries listed on the Name Servers tab or specific servers that you designate.*

3. By default, all secondary servers listed on the Name Servers tab are notified of changes. If you want to designate specific servers to notify, select The Following Servers, and then type the IP addresses of secondary servers to notify. Click OK.

Restricting Zone Transfers

Restricting access to zone information is a security precaution you may want to consider using on your network. When you restrict access to zone information, only servers that you've identified can request updates from the zone's primary server. This allows you to funnel requests through a select group of secondary servers, such as your Internet service provider's secondary name servers, and to hide the details of your internal network from the outside world.

To restrict access to the primary zone database, follow these steps:

1. In the DNS console, right-click the domain or subnet you want to update and then from the pop-up menu, choose Properties.

2. Click the Zone Transfers tab. Zone transfers send a copy of zone information to other DNS servers. These servers can be in the same domain or in other domains. By default, zone information is transferred to any server that requests it.

3. To restrict transfers to name servers listed on the Name Servers tab, select Allow Zone Transfers and then click Only To Servers Listed On The Name Servers Tab.

4. To restrict transfers to designated servers, select Allow Zone Transfers and then click Only To The Following Servers. Afterward, type the IP addresses for the servers that should receive zone transfers. Click OK.

Setting the Zone Type

When you create zones, they are designated as Active Directory-integrated, standard primary, or standard secondary. You can change the type at any time by completing the following steps:

1. In the DNS console, right-click the domain or subnet you want to update and then from the pop-up menu, choose Properties.

2. On the General tab, click Change. In the Change Zone Type dialog box, select the new type for the zone.

Enabling and Disabling Dynamic Updates

Dynamic updates allow DNS clients to register and maintain their own address and pointer records. This is useful for computers dynamically configured through DHCP. By enabling dynamic updates, you make it easier for dynamically configured computers to locate each other on the network. When a zone is integrated with Active Directory, you have the option of requiring secure updates. With secure updates, you use access control lists to control which computers and users can dynamically update DNS.

You can enable and disable dynamic updates by completing the following steps:

1. In the DNS console, right-click the domain or subnet you want to update and then from the pop-up menu, choose Properties.

2. Use the following options of the Allow Dynamic Updates selection list to enable or disable dynamic updates:

   - **No**   Disable dynamic updates.
   - **Yes**   Enable dynamic updates.
   - **Only Secure Updates**   Enable dynamic updates with Active Directory security. This is available only with Active Directory integration.

3. Click OK.

 Note   DNS integration settings must also be configured for DHCP. See the section of Chapter 17 entitled "Integrating DHCP and DNS."

Managing DNS Server Configuration and Security

You use the Server Properties dialog box to manage the general configuration of DNS servers. Through it, you can enable and disable IP addresses for the server and control access to DNS servers outside the organization. You can also configure monitoring, logging, and advanced options.

Enabling and Disabling IP Addresses for a DNS Server

By default, multihomed DNS servers respond to DNS requests on all available network adapters and the IP addresses they're configured to use.

Through the DNS console, you can specify that the server can only answer requests on specific IP addresses. To do this, follow these steps:

1. In the DNS console, right-click the server you want to configure and then from the pop-up menu, choose Properties.

2. In the Interfaces tab, shown in Figure 19-14, select Only The Following IP Addresses and then type the IP addresses that should respond to DNS requests. Only these IP addresses will be used for DNS. All other IP addresses on the server will be disabled for DNS.

Controlling Access to DNS Servers Outside the Organization

Restricting access to zone information allows you to specify which internal and external servers can access the primary server. For external servers, this controls which servers can get in from the outside world. You can also control which DNS

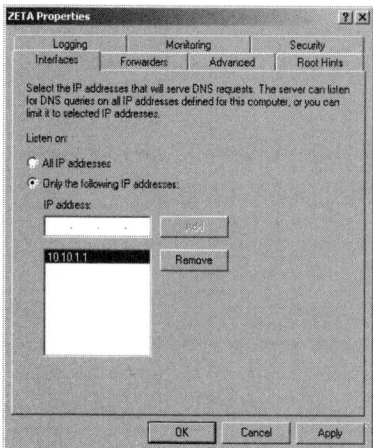

Figure 19-14. *Use the Interfaces tab to set the IP addresses that should handle DNS requests and responses.*

servers within your organization can access servers outside it. To do this, you need to set up DNS forwarding within the domain.

With DNS forwarding, you configure DNS servers within the domain as

- **Nonforwarders**   Servers that must pass DNS queries they can't resolve on to designated forwarding servers. These servers essentially act like DNS clients to their forwarding servers.

- **Forwarding-only**   Servers that can only cache responses and pass requests on to forwarders. This is also known as a *caching-only* DNS server.

- **Forwarders**   Servers that receive requests from nonforwarders and forwarding-only servers. Forwarders use normal DNS communication methods to resolve queries and to send responses back to other DNS servers.

Note   The root server for a domain can't be configured for forwarding. But all other servers can be configured for forwarding.

Creating Nonforwarding DNS Servers.

To create a nonforwarding DNS server, follow these steps:

1. In the DNS console, right-click the server you want to configure and then from the pop-up menu, choose Properties.

2. In the Forwarders tab, select Enable Forwarders.

3. Enter the IP addresses of the network's forwarders.

4. Set the Forward Time Out. This value controls how long the server tries to query the server if it gets no response. When the Forward Time Out interval passes, the server tries the next forwarder on the list. The default is 0 seconds. Click OK.

Creating Forwarding-Only Servers

To create a forwarding-only server, follow these steps:

1. In the DNS console, right-click the server you want to configure and then from the pop-up menu, choose Properties.

2. In the Forwarders tab, select Enable Forwarders and then select Operate As Slave Server.

3. Enter the IP addresses of the network's forwarders.

4. Set the Forward Time Out. This value controls how long the server tries to query the server if it gets no response. When the Forward Time Out interval passes, the server tries the next forwarder on the list. The default is 0 seconds. Click OK.

Creating Forwarders Servers

Any DNS server that isn't designated as a nonforwarder or a forwarding-only server will act as a forwarder. Thus, on the network's designated forwarders, you should make sure that Enable Forwarders and Operate As Slave Server are *not* selected.

Logging DNS Activity

You normally use the DNS Server event log to track DNS activity on a server. This log records all applicable DNS events and is accessible through the Event View node in Computer Management. If you're trying to troubleshoot DNS problems, it's sometimes useful to configure a temporary debug log to track certain types of DNS events. To do this, follow these steps:

1. In the DNS console, right-click the server you want to configure and then from the pop-up menu, choose Properties.

2. In the Logging tab, shown in Figure 19-15, select the events you want to track temporarily. These events are logged in %SystemRoot%\System32\Dns\ Dns.log by default.

3. Click OK. When you're finished debugging, turn off logging by clearing any of the selected check boxes in the Logging tab.

Monitoring DNS Server

Windows 2000 has built-in functionality for monitoring DNS server. You can configure monitoring to occur manually or automatically by completing the following steps:

1. In the DNS console, right-click the server you want to configure and then from the pop-up menu, choose Properties.

2. Select the Monitoring tab, shown in Figure 19-16. You can perform two types of tests. To test DNS resolution on the current server, select A Simple Query Against This DNS Server. To test DNS resolution in the domain, select A Recursive Query To Other DNS Servers.

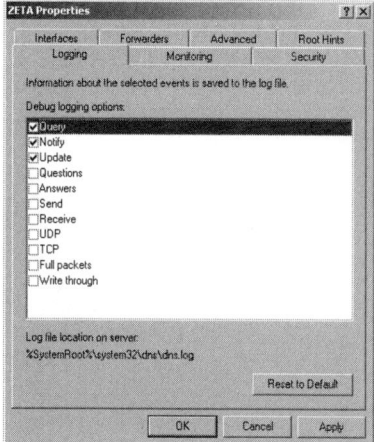

Figure 19-15. *Select the events you want to log, and then click OK. Don't forget to clear these events after you've finished debugging.*

3. You can perform a manual test by clicking Test Now or schedule the server for automatic monitoring by selecting Perform Automatic Testing At The Following Interval and then setting a time interval in seconds, minutes, or hours.

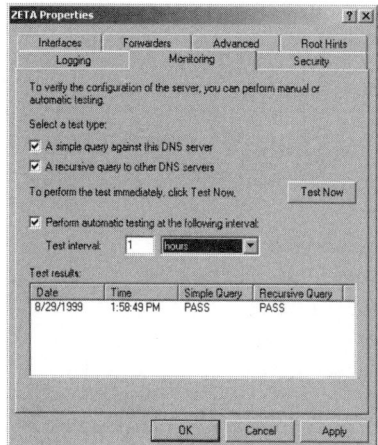

Figure 19-16. *You can configure a DNS server for manual or automatic monitoring. Monitoring is useful to ensure that DNS resolution is configured properly.*

Real World If you're actively troubleshooting a DNS problem, you may want to configure testing to occur every 10–15 seconds. This will provide a rapid succession of test results. If you're monitoring DNS for problems as part of your daily administrative duties, you'll want a longer time interval, such as two or three hours.

4. The results of testing are shown in the Test Results area. You'll see a date and time stamp indicating when the test was performed and a result, such as Pass or Fail. While a single failure may be the result of a temporary outage, multiple failures normally indicate a DNS resolution problem.

Integrating WINS with DNS

You can integrate DNS with WINS. WINS integration allows the server to act as a WINS server or to forward WINS requests to specific WINS servers. When you configure WINS and DNS to work together, you can configure forward lookups using NetBIOS computer names, reverse lookups using NetBIOS computer names, caching and time-out values for WINS resolution, and full integration with NetBIOS scopes.

Configuring WINS Lookups in DNS

When you configure WINS lookups in DNS, the leftmost portion of the fully qualified domain name can be resolved using WINS. The procedure works like this: The DNS server looks for an address record for the fully qualified domain name. If a record is found, the server uses the record to resolve the name using only DNS. If a record isn't found, the server extracts the leftmost portion of the name and uses WINS to try to resolve the name (as a NetBIOS computer name). You configure WINS lookups in DNS by doing the following:

1. In the DNS console, right-click the domain you want to update and then from the pop-up menu, choose Properties.
2. Click the WINS tab, shown in Figure 19-17.
3. Select Use WINS Forward Lookup and then type the IP addresses of the network's WINS servers. You must specify at least one WINS server.
4. If you want to ensure that the WINS record on this server isn't replicated to other DNS servers in zone transfers, select Do Not Replicate This Record. Selecting this option is useful to prevent errors and transfer failures to non-Microsoft DNS servers. Click OK.

Configuring Reverse WINS Lookups in DNS

When you configure reverse WINS lookups in DNS, the IP address of the host can be resolved to a NetBIOS computer name. The procedure works like this: The DNS server looks for a pointer record for the specified IP address. If a record is found, the server uses the record to resolve the fully qualified domain name.

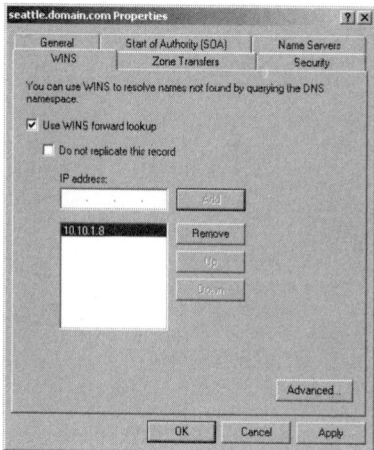

Figure 19-17. *Use the WINS tab to configure WINS lookups in DNS.*

If a record isn't found, the server sends a request to WINS, and, if possible, WINS returns the NetBIOS computer name for the IP address and the host domain is appended to this computer name.

You configure reverse WINS lookups in DNS by doing the following:

1. In the DNS console, right-click the subnet you want to update and then from the pop-up menu, choose Properties.

2. Click the WINS-R tab, shown in Figure 19-18.

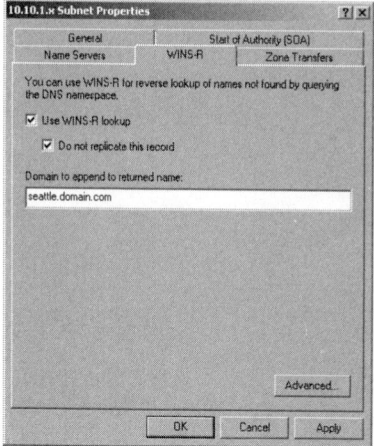

Figure 19-18. *Use the WINS-R tab to configure WINS reverse lookups in DNS.*

3. Select Use WINS-R Lookup, and then, if you wish, select Do Not Replicate This Record. As with forward lookups, you usually don't want to replicate the WINS-R record to non-Microsoft DNS servers.

4. In the Domain To Append To Returned Name field, type the host domain information. The domain is appended to the computer name returned by WINS. For example, if you type **seattle.domain.com** and WINS returns the NetBIOS computer name gamma, the DNS server will combine the two values and return gamma.seattle.domain.com.

5. Click OK.

Setting Caching and Time-Out Values for WINS in DNS

When you integrate WINS and DNS, you should also set WINS caching and time-out values. The caching value determines how long records returned from WINS are valid. The time-out value determines how long DNS should wait for a response from WINS before timing out and returning an error. These values are set for both forward and reverse WINS lookups.

You set caching and time-out values for WINS in DNS by doing the following:

1. In the DNS console, right-click the domain or subnet you want to update and then from the pop-up menu, choose Properties.

2. Select the WINS or WINS-R tab, as appropriate, and then click Advanced. This opens the dialog box shown in Figure 19-19.

3. Set the caching and time-out values using the Cache Time-Out field and the Lookup Time-Out field. By default, DNS caches WINS records for 15 minutes and times out after 2 seconds. For most networks, you should increase these values. Sixty minutes for caching and three seconds for time-outs may be better choices.

4. Click OK. Repeat this process for other domains and subnets, as necessary.

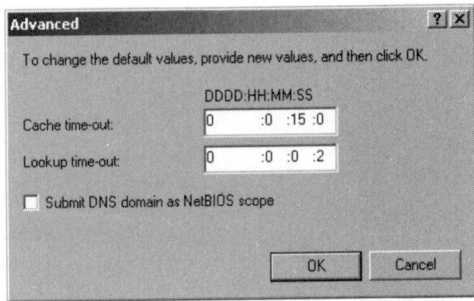

Figure 19-19. *In the Advanced dialog box, set caching and time-out values for DNS.*

Configuring Full Integration with NetBIOS Scopes

When you configure full integration, lookups can be resolved using NetBIOS computer names and NetBIOS scopes. Here, a forward lookup works like this: The DNS server looks for an address record for the fully qualified domain name. If it finds a record, the server uses the record to resolve the name using only DNS. If it doesn't find a record, the server extracts the leftmost portion of the name as the NetBIOS computer name and the remainder of the name as the NetBIOS scope. These values are then passed to WINS for resolution.

You configure full integration of WINS and DNS by doing the following:

1. In the DNS console, right-click the domain or subnet you want to update, and then from the pop-up menu, choose Properties.

2. Select the WINS or WINS-R tab, as appropriate, and then click Advanced.

3. In the Advanced dialog box, select Submit DNS Domain As NetBIOS Scope.

4. Click OK. Repeat this process for other domains and subnets, as necessary.

Before you use this technique, make sure that the NetBIOS scope is properly configured on the network. You should also make sure that a consistent naming scheme is used for all network computers. Because NetBIOS is case-sensitive, queries resolve only if the case matches exactly. Note also that if the domain has subdomains, the subdomains must be delegated the authority for name services in order for WINS and DNS integration to work properly.

Index

About the Author

William R. Stanek (win2000-consulting@tvpress.com) has a master of science degree in information systems received with distinction, a bachelor of science degree in computer science magna cum laude, and 15 years of hands-on experience with advanced programming and development. He is a leading network technology expert and an award-winning author. Over the years, his practical advice has helped programmers, developers and network engineers all over the world. He is also a regular contributor to leading publications like *PC Magazine*, where you'll often find his work in the "Solutions" section. He has written, co-authored or contributed to over 20 computer books. Current or forthcoming books include *Microsoft Windows NT Server 4.0 Administrator's Pocket Consultant, Microsoft SQL Server 7.0 Administrator's Pocket Consultant,* and *Windows 2000 Scripting Administrator's Guide.*

Mr. Stanek has been involved in the commercial Internet community since 1991. His core business and technology experience comes from over 11 years of military service. He has experience in developing server technology, encryption, Internet development, and a strong understanding of e-Commerce technology and its deployment. During 1998 and 1999, Mr. Stanek worked as a senior member of the technical staff at Intel Corporation's IDS new business division at iCat.

Mr. Stanek is proud to have served in the Persian Gulf War as a combat crewmember on an electronic warfare aircraft. He flew on numerous combat missions into Iraq and was awarded nine medals for his wartime service, including one of the United States of America's highest flying honors, the Air Force Distinguished Flying Cross. Currently, he resides in the Pacific Northwest with his wife and four children. His goal for 2000 is to find a high-level technical management position.

The manuscript for this book was prepared and submitted to Microsoft Press in electronic form. Text files were prepared using Microsoft Word 98 for Windows. Pages were composed by nSight, Inc., using Adobe PageMaker 6.5 for Windows, with text in Garamond Light and display type in ITC Franklin Gothic. Composed pages were delivered to the printer as electronic prepress files.

Cover Designer
Tim Girvin Design

Cover Illustrator
Tom Draper

Interior Illustrator
Angela M. Montoya

Layout Artist
Angela M. Montoya

Project Manager
Lisa A. Wehrle

Tech Editors
Eben Werber, Richard Taha, and Darian Taha

Copy Editor
Joseph Gustaitis

Proofreaders
Joanne Crerand, Rebecca Merz, and Denise Sadler

Indexer
Jack Lewis